DIGITAL ART ITS ART AND SCIENCE

activeBook
Access Card

Thank you for purchasing *Digital Art Its Art and Science*, by Yue-Ling Wong. The information below provides instruction on how to access the activeBook site which brings the world of digital media alive.

This textbook is delivered as an *integrated learning system*. Students can learn from the printed text and/or by using the *first-time free* access code to access the **activeBook** and associated **online learning aids**.

The *Digital Art Its Art and Science* activeBook is embedded with numerous active examples, programming exercises, problem-solving and concept-testing worksheets, interactive tutorials, and video tutorials that makes learning about digital media fun and interactive.

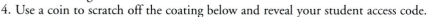 – Margin icons in your textbook let you know that an online learning aid is available for a particular concept or technique.

To access the activeBook for Digital Art Its Art and Science:

1. Go to www.prenhall.com/digitalmedia
2. Click on the title *Digital Art Its Art and Science* by Yue-Ling Wong.
3. Click on the link to Digital Art activeBook. There you can register as a F. and Returning User.
4. Use a coin to scratch off the coating below and reveal your student access code.
   ****Do not use a knife or other sharp object as it may damage the code.*

5. On the registration page, enter your student access code. Do not type the dashes. You can use lower or uppercase letters.
6. Follow the on-screen instructions. If you need help during the online registration process, simply click on Need Help?
7. Once your personal Login Name and Password are confirmed, you can begin viewing using the integrated digital content.

To login to the Digital Art activeBook for the first time <u>after</u> you've registered:
Follow steps 1 and 2 to return to the Digital Art activeBook link. Then, follow the prompts for "Returning Users" to enter your Login Name and Password.

IMPORTANT: The access code on this page can only be used once to establish a subscription to the *Digital Art Its Art and Science*, by Yue-Ling Wong activeBook site. If this access code has already been scratched off, it may no longer be valid. If this is the case, you can purchase a subscription by going to the *www.prenhall.com/digitalmedia* website and selecting "Purchase."

PEARSON
Prentice Hall

Upper Saddle River, NJ 07458
www.prenhall.com
To get help with registration, visit http://247.prenhall.com

D0138987

Digital Art

ITS ART AND SCIENCE

Yue-Ling Wong

Wake Forest University

Prentice Hall

Upper Saddle River London Singapore Toronto
Tokyo Sydney Hong Kong Mexico City

Vice President and Editorial Director, ECS: *Marcia J. Horton*
Executive Editor: *Tracy Dunkelberger*
Assistant Editor: *Melinda Haggerty*
Senior Managing Editor: *Scott Disanno*
Production Editor: *Rose Kernan*
Cover Designer: *Kristine Carney*
Art Editor: *Gregory Dulles*
Director, Image Resource Center: *Melinda Reo*

Manager, Rights and Permissions: *Zina Arabia*
Manager, Visual Research: *Beth Brenzel*
Manager, Cover Visual Research and Permissions: *Karen Sanatar*
Media Editor: *Daniel Sandin*
Manufacturing Buyer: *Lisa McDowell*
Marketing Manager: *Erin Davis*
Marketing Coordinator: *Mack Patterson*

Library of Congress Cataloging-in-Publication Data on File

Printed in the United States of America
10 9 8 7 6 5 4 3 2 1

Prentice Hall
is an imprint of

PEARSON
www.pearsonhighered.com

ISBN: 0-13-175703-2
978-0-13-175703-5

Brief Table of Contents

Table of Contents

Preface

Welcome to the *Digital Art: Its Art and Science*, a book for students who are interested in learning digital media from the art perspective. This book is the **Art Module** in a 3-book digital media series. It is written to use in combination with the *Digital Media Primer*—a book of this digital media series that provides the foundational concepts of digital media. There is no specific prerequisite to use this book. However, this book refers to the *Digital Media Primer* for the foundational science concepts and techniques in digital media. The courses for which you will find this textbook useful include:

- introductory digital art courses that hope to integrate the general art and design organizational principles with the digital media tools
- introductory media production courses that introduce students to a solid foundation of digital video and audio from the art perspective and expose them to other media such as digital images and the Web
- non-major introductory computer science courses that adopt a digital media theme, integrating the art-making in the curriculum

After completing this book, students will be able to make the connection of general art and design organizational principles with the tools and techniques of digital media application programs. This connection will help students make decisions based on their aesthetic intents. After completing Chapters 1–7, students will be able to create, edit, and critique digital images, audio, and video from the art perspective. Students will also learn basic Web authoring through HTML, Cascading Style Sheets (CSS), and dynamic HTML (Chapters 8–10).

Text Organization

The digital media curriculum of this book is organized around the organizational principles of art and design and visual perception. These include unity and harmony, balance, repetition and rhythm, emphasis and focus, perspective, and several of Gestalt's principles of visual perception.

One Chapter on Concepts and One on Applications

Each of the image, audio, and video topics are covered in two chapters: one on **concepts** and the second one on **applications**.

Chapter 1: Background

Chapter 2: Digital Image (concepts)

Chapter 3: Digital Image (applications)

Chapter 4: Digital Audio (concepts)

Chapter 5: Digital Audio (applications)

Chapter 6: Digital Video (concepts)

Chapter 7: Digital Video (applications)

Chapter 8–10: Web Authoring

Aesthetic and scientific concepts are discussed in the concepts chapters (Chapters 2, 4, 6). How the application programs work, and the tools and techniques in general, are discussed in the application chapters (Chapters 3, 5, and 7). For example, Chapter 2 explains the art and design elements and the organizational principles. Correspondingly, Chapter 3 discusses how to apply digital imaging tools to these elements based on these principles.

For the Web authoring chapters, Chapter 8 provides the fundamentals of Web design and HTML coding. Chapter 9 introduces Cascading Style Sheets (CSS) and their applications. Chapter 10 gives an introduction on JavaScript programming, followed by discussions of examples that combine HTML, CSS, and JavaScript to add interactivity.

Approach to Teaching Software Tools

Media creation and production is an important component in digital media education. It is important to recognize the fluency in software application tools in order to improve the student's performance in digital media. However, one of the greatest challenges in teaching digital media is keeping up with rapidly evolving technology and software application tools.

This book introduces students to these tools by focusing on the underlying ideas and concepts (both aesthetic and scientific). The concepts chapters provide the foundations of art and design principles as well as the scientific principles required to understand the tools. The applications chapters discuss the tools from a task-based perspective first, followed by a demonstration of the corresponding command in a software program. These tasks are organized around the organizational principles of art and design and human perception for all media. The goal is to instill in the students the ability to teach themselves new software and use the tools from the art and design perspective.

Features in the Textbook

There are several elements used in the text.

- **Key terms:** Key terms are boldfaced. When a key term appears at several places in the text, the term is usually boldfaced at where its definition is given.

- **Learning aids:** There are several types of learning aids accompanying this text (see the sub-section below). They are integral to the text and noted in the text in blue boxes. A title and a brief description are given for each learning aid. The learning aids can be found on the accompanying Web site of this book.

- **Boxed materials:** These boxes intend to provide more in-depth discussions or an explanation of the concept or terminology relevant to the current part of the text. The materials may be branched off from the main flow of the text. Thus, they are designed to separate from the main text to avoid diversion from the flow of thoughts.

- **Side notes:** These notes are generally used for a quick reminder of terminology or for referring to the chapter that covers the basics that are needed for the current part of the text.

- **Self-test questions:** These questions are found in the text of some chapters. The answers are provided at the bottom of the page. These questions, unlike the end-of-chapter review questions, intend to provide the students an instant review of the topics. These topics are self-contained.

- **End-of-chapter review questions:** These questions are multiple-choice and short-answer type questions designed to help students review the foundational knowledge introduced in the chapter. They are designed to ensure that every student reaches the same level of competence and foundational knowledge.

- **Exercises and activities:** These are relatively short activities designed to help students explore ideas or prepare them for assignments and projects, such as making sketches for projects. Most of the activities do not require using digital media software, but require thinking conceptually.

- **Assignments:** Assignments require producing digital media files. They are shorter than projects and deal with one task or one concept at a time. The assignment descriptions are also more structured and specific than the projects.

- **Projects:** These are open-ended projects to encourage the students' creativity. They are more extensive in substance than assignments. The concept behind the work requires more depth. The completed work involves a combination of tools and techniques, or even multiple media.

Learning Aids and Supplementary Materials

There are several types of learning aids accompanying this text. Their descriptions appear in blue boxes with a small icon (a computer mouse or a film strip) followed by a title. The computer mouse icon indicates that the learning aid is interactive or has a hands-on component. These include interactive tutorials and demonstrations, labs, and worksheets. The film strip icon means that the learning aid is a movie, for example, screen-captured movies that show how to use a tool in an application program.

- **Tutorials:** All the tutorials can be used as outside class review by students. Some of the tutorials can be used by the instructor in class as interactive animated aids to explain a concept or a term that may be hard to explain on chalkboard. See for example Chapter 2's *Human Visual Perception: Psychological Depth Cues*, Chapter 3's *Understanding and Applying Curves For Color Adjustments*, and Chapter 6's *Camera Location, Sightline, and Screen Direction*.

  The tutorials are used for various purposes:

  - Conceptual: To explain concepts
  - Software tool how-to's: Short screen-captured movies showing how-to's of application programs
  - Example files: Files, such as HTML and CSS documents, that you can download to open and see how they work
  - Explanation of terms

- **Demonstrations:** For example, audio files that let you hear sounds of different timbre and contrasting sounds.

- **Worksheets:** Worksheets are question-based PDF files that can be downloaded and printed out. They require more thinking than the end-of-chapter review questions. Some may require exploration or experimentation to discover the answers.

- **Labs:** There are lab manuals for the Web-authoring chapters. These labs emphasize the tasks rather than giving step-by-step recipe-type of instructions.

Worksheets, labs, assignments, and projects are designed to help students apply various learned concepts and techniques and put them into practice. They have different pedagogic purposes:

- Worksheets are question-based homework assignments intended to help students review the textbook material.
- Labs are hands-on instruction-based activities that will help students create or modify media files.
- Each assignment deals with one task at a time. Unlike the labs, they do not have detailed instructions. They allow some freedom in exploring ideas and tools.
- Projects are open-ended and require the most creativity. They also require a combination of tools and media.

Integrated Learning System

This textbook is delivered as an *integrated learning system*. Students can learn from the printed text and/or by using the *first-time free* access code to gain access to the activeBook. The activeBook is a rich, dynamic, online version of the printed text with **learning aids** embedded right in the text. The digital assets and activeBook can be accessed at www.prenhall .com/digitalmedia.

The activeBook touches students on multiple levels. It is embedded with numerous active examples, programming exercises, problem-solving and concept-testing worksheets, interactive tutorials, mathematical modeling exercises, and video tutorials. The online text stimulates student learning by making them active participants in the learning process. Because activeBook marries the printed book with dynamic digital assets, content is brought to life and available anytime, from anywhere.

The activeBook experience is customizable by faculty and students. Students can annotate their activeBook and customize their view of the book's dynamic resources. The diagnostic tools within activeBook can create custom study plans tailored to the student's or the class's weaknesses and strengths in the subject matter. An activeBook can contain course management tools, exist only as a linked resource from an external course management system, or it can be used as a help link with no navigation between online pages.

Digital Media Community Website

The ability to exchange ideas and experiences make every learning experience more meaningful. Access to the Digital Media Community site is free with the activeBook subscription. Instructors are encouraged to share ideas and learning materials, digital media projects, labs, assignment ideas, showcase student projects, make contributions, participate in discussion forums, and connect with other faculty teaching digital media. Please visit the Digital Media Community Website at www.prenhall.com/digitalmedia.

Accessing the Learning Aids and Supplementary Materials

The learning aids and supplementary materials that are noted in the book can be accessed through the publisher's Web site and the author's Web site for this book at www. prenhall.com/digitalmedia.

Some learning aids require Shockwave plug-in, some require Flash player, some require QuickTime player, and some require JavaScript enabled. The file format and requirements of each of these learning aids are noted with its link on the Web site.

Instructor Resources

Protected instructor resources are available on the Prentice Hall Instructor Resource Center (IRC). Please contact your local Prentice Hall Sales Representative to gain access to this site. Instructors will find the following support material on the IRC:

- Answers to the end-of-chapter questions
- Answers to the worksheets
- Completed lab files

Software Tools for Practice and Labs

Although our approach to teaching media production application tools emphasizes tasks, it is advisable to select some representative application programs to illustrate the tools and techniques in the text and in the practice exercises, such as labs and worksheets. Table 1 lists the different application programs used as examples in this text.

TABLE I	Application Programs Used as Examples in the Text
Media Topic	
Digital Image	**Adobe Photoshop,** Adobe Illustrator
Digital Audio	**Adobe Audition,** Apple Garage Band
Digital Video	**Adobe Premier Pro,** Apple Final Cut Pro
Multimedia Authoring	**Adobe Dreamweaver**

This Book is a Part of a 3-Book Digital Media Series

This book is the **Art Module** in a 3-book digital media series. The purpose of this series is to connect the digital media tools and techniques with the underlying scientific concepts. This book (the Art Module of the series) introduces these concepts and techniques from the **art perspective** for students who are majoring in art (with concentration in digital art) or taking computer science courses that adopt a digital media theme.

Digital media encompasses a broad range of academic disciplines—from art to computer science. This 3-book series intends to pull interdisciplinary elements together in a coherent and organized manner. The three books (sometimes referred to as modules in the text) include a primer and two advanced modules—one on art (this book) and one on computer science.

- **Primer:** *Digital Media Primer*[1] ISBN: 0132239442
- **Art Module:** *Digital Art: Its Art and Science* (this book) ISBN: 0131757032
- **Computer Science Module:** *The Science of Digital Media*[2] ISBN: 0132435802

---

[1]By this author.
[2]By Jennifer Burg.

All three books cover the following digital media topics:

- **Digital images**
- **Digital audio**
- **Digital video**
- **Multimedia authoring** (Primer and Computer Science Module) and **Web authoring** (Art Module)

Primer

Despite the different disciplinary perspectives of digital media, there is a common ground of all perspectives; for example, resolution, bit depth, and file size optimization. This common ground is grouped into the Primer. It presents the central concepts of digital media necessary for all students, regardless of their later area of specialization. The Primer is designed to serve as the **core module for all students** interested in digital media.

The Primer also intends to explain concepts using analogies from everyday life and everyday reasoning. For example, in Chapter 1, eye signals are used to illustrate the concept of bits in the binary system.

Advanced Modules

The two **advanced modules** (Art and Computer Science) allow further specialization at the advanced, discipline-specific level.

- **Art Module:** *Digital Art: Its Art and Science* (this book)
  The Art Module follows the topics of the Primer but elaborates further from the perspective of art making.
- **CS Module:** *The Science of Digital Media*
  The CS Module includes more in-depth explanations of the underlying mathematical principles, computer algorithms, and elementary physics and electronics.

Parallel Chapters Across the Three Books

All three books maintain the same number of parallel chapters—one on background, two on each of the image, audio, and video, and one (or more) on multimedia/Web authoring. Parallel chapters allow students to easily look up relevant information across perspectives.

Coordinating Coursework with This Text

For Non-Computer Science Courses

Because the in-depth foundational scientific concepts of digital media are covered in the Primer, this book often makes references to the explanations of scientific concepts covered in the Primer. The Primer is highly recommended as an accompanying text of this book.

Table 2 below shows several suggested treatments employing this book and the series of three books. The three books' parallel chapters help students look up information across different perspectives.

TABLE 2	Suggested Chapter Coverage
A course that covers all three media: images, audio, and video	• Chapters 1–7 (this book) • Chapters 1–7 (Primer)
A course that covers any one medium	• Chapter 1 (this book) • Two chapters of the medium (this book) • Chapter 1 (Primer) • Two chapters of the medium (Primer) For example, for a course that focuses on digital images, you could cover Chapters 1, 2, 3 of this book, and Primer Chapters 1, 2, 3.
A course that covers Web authoring	• Chapters 1–3 (this book) • Chapters 8–10 (this book) • Chapters 1–3 (Primer) • Chapters 8–11 (Primer, if the course also covers multimedia authoring using Adobe Flash)
A course that focuses on concepts with minimal hands-on	• Chapters 1, 2, 4, 6 (this book) • Chapters 1, 2, 4, 6 (Primer)
A course that focuses on hands-on practice	• Chapters 1, 3, 5, 7 (this book) • Chapters 1, 3, 5, 7 (Primer) • The concepts chapters (Chapters 2, 4, and 6) are highly recommended. If it is not possible to go over the concepts in class, refer students to self-study these concepts chapters. You may want to assign the end-of-chapter review questions to ensure they understand the concepts.

For digital art courses, it seems to work best if you start using the Art Module chapters before assigning the Primer chapters. Although the Primer contains the foundational scientific concepts that are needed to understand the terminology and how and why a tool works that way, students tend to learn better after they have hands-on experience with the creation and production of the media first. The foundational concepts and terminology in the Primer text will then make more sense to the students. They see the application of concepts through using the software applications.

For Computer Science Courses That Adopt a Digital Media Theme

The Primer is more suitable for computer science courses, but this book can be used as an accompanying text to give students an art perspective on digital media.

- Lower-level courses for non-CS majors can use all the chapters of this book and the Primer although the Primer is more suitable as the main text.
- For the upper-level courses for CS-majors, *The Science of Digital Media* is most suitable as the main text. For more suggestions, please see the Preface of *The Science of Digital Media*. The Primer can be used as outside class background reading.

Acknowledgments

The materials have been class-tested and I would like to thank our students who provided us feedbacks to help us improve the text and its organization for the three books.

I am very grateful for the artists, graphic designers, Web designers, and my former students who let me include their works in my book. I would like to thank Heather Childress for her help in acquiring permission for works from John. P. Anderson Collection of Student Art, Wake Forest University.

My thanks also go to the professors who participated in pilot-testing of these modules: Julie Carrington of Rollins College, Kristian Damkjer of University of Florida, Ian Douglas of Florida State University, Edward A. Fox of Virginia Polytechnic Institute and State University, Martha Garrett of Bishop McGuinness High School (North Carolina), Kim Nelson of University of Windsor (Ontario, Canada), Naomi Spellman of The University of California San Diego and San Diego State University, Christopher Stein of Borough of Manhattan Community College, and Mark Watanabe of Keaau High School (Hawaii).

I would also like to thank the reviewers of this text for their comments and suggestions: David R. Burns, Sarah Kanouse, Andy Curran of University of Cincinnati, Simone Paterson of Virginia Tech, Ann Bell of University of Wisconsin-Stout, and James Morgan.

Support

This material is based on work supported by the National Science Foundation under Grant No. DUE-0127280 and DUE-0340969. Any opinions, findings and conclusions or recommendations expressed in this material are those of the author(s) and do not necessarily reflect the views of the National Science Foundation. The PI and co-PI of the two grants are Yue-Ling Wong and Jennifer J. Burg, respectively. Professor Leah McCoy is the assessment expert in the second grant.

Trademarks

Adobe Flash, Adobe Photoshop, Adobe Illustrator, Adobe Premier Pro, Adobe Encore DVD are trademarks of Adobe Systems, Incorporated.

Audacity is a trademark of Dominic Mazzoni.

Apple Garage Band and Apple DVD Studio Pro are trademarks of Apple, Inc.

Sony Sound Forge, Sony ACID Pro, Sony Vegas, and Sony DVD Architect are trademarks of Sony Electronics, Inc.

SONAR is a trademark of Twelve Tone Systems, Inc.

Prentice Hall's
◉ Digital Media
Series
AN INTEGRATED LEARNING SYSTEM

Textbook, *activeBook*, dynamic multimedia learning aids, collaborative online community portal

At the section level, the textbook contains margin icons that indicate the availability of online learning aids.

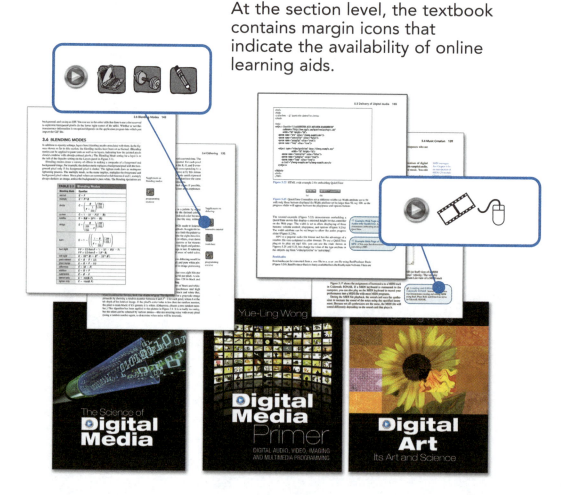

The Science of **Digital Media**

Yue-Ling Wong

Digital Media Primer
DIGITAL AUDIO, VIDEO, IMAGING AND MULTIMEDIA PROGRAMMING

Digital Art
Its Art and Science

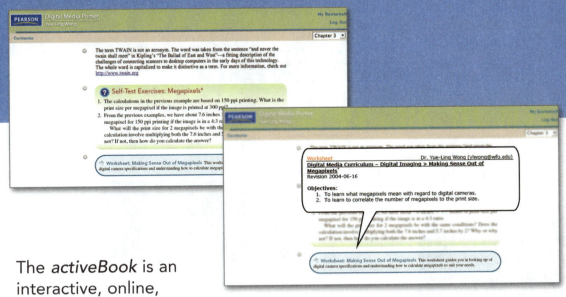

The *activeBook* is an
interactive, online,
digital book that integrates robust multimedia resources
with the textbook to enhance the learning experience.
activeBooks are embedded with:

- active examples
- programming exercises
- problem-solving and concept-testing worksheets
- interactive tutorials and demos
- mathematical modeling exercises
- video tutorials

The authors and Prentice Hall
have worked together to
integrate the textbook, the
activeBook and the dynamic
multimedia learning aids to
make teaching and learning
easier!

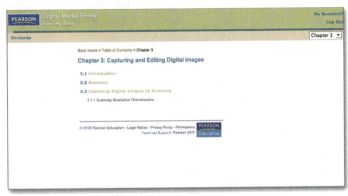

Everything works together for a unified teaching
and learning experience!

STUDENTS BECOME PARTICIPANTS IN THE LEARNING PROCESS!

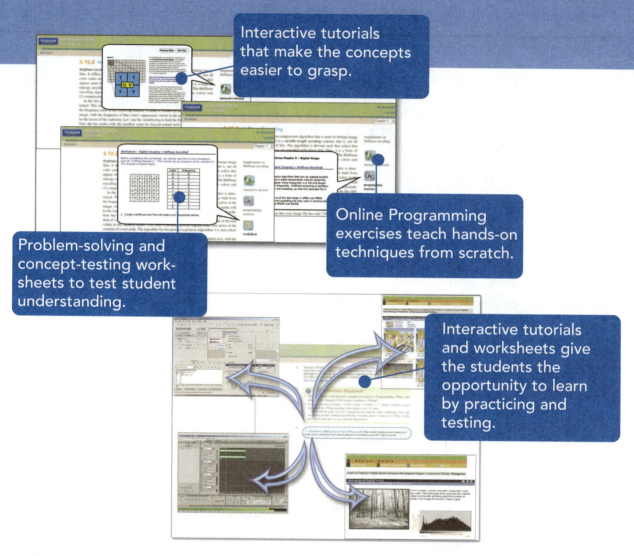

Interactive tutorials that make the concepts easier to grasp.

Problem-solving and concept-testing worksheets to test student understanding.

Online Programming exercises teach hands-on techniques from scratch.

Interactive tutorials and worksheets give the students the opportunity to learn by practicing and testing.

To gain access to the *activeBook*, the community portal and the dynamic and interactive media that accompanies this product, visit

www.prenhall.com/digitalmedia

and enter the access code printed on the card in the front of this book. If your book does not include an access card, you can purchase access at www.prenhall.com/digitalmedia.

Digital Media Series

We heard the cry! In response to the need for new interdisciplinary curriculum material, Prentice Hall is publishing a three-book set of interactive digital media products:

- *Digital Media Primer*, by Yue-Ling Wong, fundamentals of digital media that are relevant to both artists and scientists

- *The Science of Digital Media*, by Jennifer Burg, the mathematics, science, and algorithms that underlie digital media applications

- *Digital Art: Its Arts and Science*, by Yue-Ling Wong, digital media from the perspective of making art

Digital Art

ITS ART AND SCIENCE

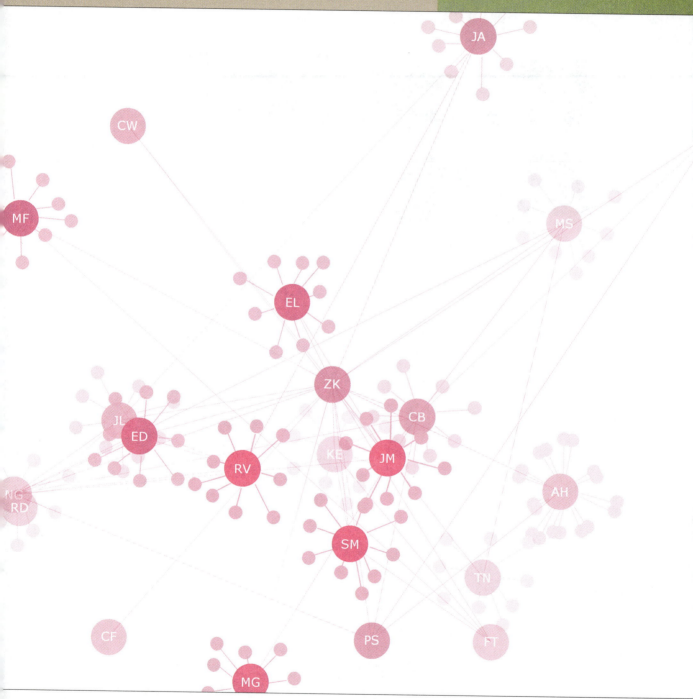

Zach Klein, *Digital Life,* Interactive media, created with Adobe Flash

Art in Digital and Digital in Art

GENERAL LEARNING OBJECTIVES

In this chapter, you will learn:

- The role of digital in digital art.
- The role of art in digital art.
- How technology is used as a tool in digital art.
- How technology is used as a medium in digital art.
- How the digital art process, from creation to display, differs from that of traditional media.
- Technological properties that distinguish digital media from traditional media.
- Other characteristics that distinguish digital art from traditional art.
- To critique digital art in the studio art course environment.
- Effects of memory size, storage size, and CPU speed on digital media production processes.
- The distinction between the need for computer memory (RAM) and hard disk space.
- To assess memory and storage needs.
- To use folders to organize digital art files.
- The distinction between opening and importing files.
- To determine the proper media for file storage and backup.

See *Digital Media Primer*, Chapter 1, on analog vs. digital, continuous vs. discrete, and infinite vs. finite concepts. These pertain to the important role of the terms discrete and numbers in digital technology. You will see their significance in later chapters in this module.

Two other important terms for digital media are sampling and quantizing. These explain resolution and bit depth across different media, including digital images, audio, and video. See *Digital Media Primer*, Chapter 1.

1.1 WHAT IS DIGITAL ART?

Nowadays, we associate the word *digital* with computers in general. Computers rely on digital technology (a discrete system that uses numbers to represent information). The words *discrete* and *numbers* are crucial to understanding the science behind digital art: its capabilities and limitations. It's true that you will not encounter these terms directly when using digital-media software application programs. However, keeping these two words in mind is important, because their characteristics help form many other terms you will encounter in working with digital art.

Unlike *digital,* which has a clear scientific definition, defining *art* is more problematic. In its simplest and broadest definition, art is a product of human creativity. It may be governed by commonly held principles and aesthetics across different media, but each medium has properties that set it apart from the others. The properties that make the digital medium unique, however, are *interactivity*, wide *accessibility*, *manipulability*, and *volatility.* The display of the electronic versions of digital art relies on a computer environment. Being digital does not eliminate or invalidate any of its underlying principles and aesthetics.

Interactivity

Interactivity loosely refers to the relationship between the viewer and the art. It plays a role in the communication between the viewer and the artwork. Generally speaking, any medium has this kind of interaction. A painting or a sculpture can provoke thought and influence the viewer's visual, emotional, or intellectual path within the work. Because different thoughts can be evoked for different viewers, each viewer's experience can be unique. Because different viewers follow different paths while looking at the painting or sculpture, their experience also can be nonlinear. However, in traditional media, the visual and physical content of the art remain unchanged during this interaction.

For digital media, interactivity has a more specific meaning. It allows a direct input from viewers, which may change their communication with the art. The direct input is usually a physical action, like mouse clicking, pressing a key on a keyboard, or even body movement captured by an electronic sensor. The action results in changes to the visual or auditory content of the work. Interactivity can provide nonlinearity when the viewer input changes the order of the experience. In some digital artwork, viewers' input becomes part of the work's content; the content evolves with the viewers' input.

Wide Accessibility

With the exception of site-specific installations, most digital-media works can be reproduced and distributed to a larger audience than traditional media. The Web is a popular outlet for displaying digital art due to its wide accessibility. Web technologies also support the use of multimedia and the kind of interactivity particularly appropriate to digital art.

Manipulability

Digital technologies make extensive manipulation and alteration of file content possible. Digital media also allow the artist to mix many different components—image, video, and audio—into a single work. The layering, transparency, and blending controls of digital-imaging tools present artists with new possibilities in composing and collage. The artist can adjust the level of seamlessness or juxtaposition in combining different visual components to create the intended reality. Some digital artworks exhibit distinctive digital qualities. However, digital content can be created to have the same visual qualities as traditional media, so that the digital manipulation is not apparent to the viewer.

Volatility of Digital Art

The volatility of digital technologies makes the preservation of digital art different from that of traditional art. In the traditional model, rarity increases economic value, and the archival quality of the materials determines the

> **Selected URLs of Digital Art**
> A selected list of URLs of digital artworks.

work's preservation for generations. Because of the mass reproduction capability of digital media, most digital art can reach a broader audience with greater ease, and in this sense, it is of less economic value. However, the presentation of the electronic format of digital art relies on many rapidly changing environments, such as computer hardware, software, and operating systems. Such digital art may be short-lived if the required technological environment is not preserved. One initiative aimed at preserving digital art is developing emulators that can run works created on older computer systems.

Interactivity of digital media is achieved by computer programming. Many of the digital artworks on the Web are programmed using Java or Flash ActionScript. *Digital Media Primer* in this book series covers fundamentals of Flash ActionScript programming. JavaScript is also a common programming language for the Web. Chapter 10 of this book covers the fundamentals and examples for adding interactivity to Web documents using JavaScript.

Emulators are not a new concept in the computer world. Software emulators have been used to simulate a virtual computer environment; for example, to run software written for one platform on a totally different operating system, like running Linux under Windows or Windows under Mac OS.

1.1.1 Digital Art as Fine Art and as Design

Fine art often refers to the visual arts which include painting, drawing, printmaking, sculpture, and some performance art—not including art forms such as music, dance, literature, and poetry.* *Graphic design* is an area where digital technologies are frequently used. They are also valuable for three dimensional (3-D) design. In the AIGA's graphic design career guide, it explains that graphic design is "a creative process that combines art and technology to communicate ideas." In addition, graphic designers work with a variety of media, such as "drawn, painted, photographed, or computer-generated images (pictures), but they also design the letterforms that make up various typefaces found in movie credits and TV ads; in books, magazines, and menus; and even on computer screens. Designers create, choose, and organize these elements—typography, images, and the so-called 'white space' around them—to communicate a message."[†] Works of graphic design include logos, posters, medical illustrations, print layout, packages, signs, and web design. Figures 1.1 through 1.9 show examples of different types of graphic-design works.

AIGA (American Institute of Graphic Arts) is the professional association for design. Visit their Web site at http://www.aiga.org/

Figure 1.1 Logo design for *Stories From the Field* (Courtesy of Stella Priscilla Poco— http://www.xstellax.com)

Figure 1.2 Logo design for *Paint Your Heart Out Tampa* (Courtesy of Stella Priscilla Poco—http://www.xstellax. com)

---

*http://www.bbc.co.uk/dna/h2g2/classic/A779448

[†]http://www.aiga.org/content.cfm/guide-whatisgraphicdesign

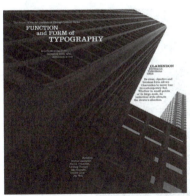

Figure 1.3 *Function and Form Typography Series* poster design (Courtesy of Barry Harmon—http://aigadesignjobs. org/bharmon)

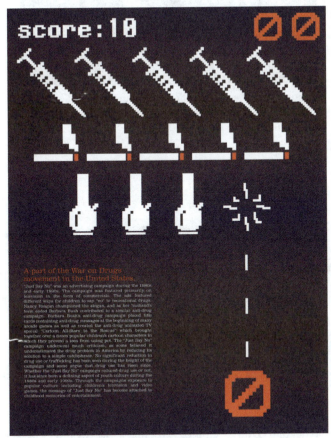

Figure 1.4 *Just Say No* poster design (Courtesy of Barry Harmon—http://aigadesignjobs.org/bharmon)

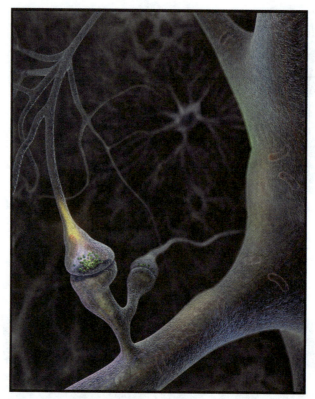

Figure 1.5 *The Synapse Revealed*, created by Graham Johnson of www.fivth.com for the Howard Hughes Medical Institute Bulletin ©2004

Figure 1.6 Layout and cover design for *Bark* magazine (Courtesy of Stella Priscilla Poco—http://www.xstellax.com)

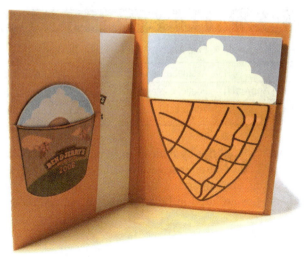

Figure 1.7 Annual report layout and package design for Ben & Jerry's Ice Cream Company (Courtesy of Stella Priscilla Poco—http://www.xstellax.com)

Figure 1.8 Postcard promotional campaign design for new Pantone colors (Courtesy of Stella Priscilla Poco—http://www.xstellax.com)

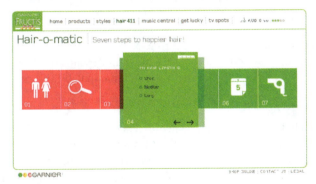

Figure 1.9 *Garnier Fructis* Web design (Courtesy of Liza Pagano—http://www.thegraphicdetail.com)

TABLE 1.1	Different Aspects of Fine Art and Design	
	Fine Art	**Design**
Intention	Aesthetic, self-expression	Functional, utility
Communication Approach	Poetic, contemplative	Clear, effective, immediate
Origin of Idea	The artist	Clients, employers

Fine art and graphic design differ by their intentions, communication approaches, and the origin of their ideas. Table 1.1 summarizes the different aspects of fine art and graphic design. These distinctions are important, because they determine how the works are judged. Digital technologies are used in both art and design, and these distinctions also apply to digital art.

Intention

The main difference between fine art and design is the primary intention of the products. Fine art is created for its own aesthetic purpose and self-expression. Design, on the other hand, is created for a practical function. Graphic designers still use artistic skills—fundamental art elements and organizational principles—in their works. For example, Graham Johnson's medical illustration (Figure 1.5) was built on a pencil composition based on the scientific information. Sketches were worked up before the image was modeled on the computer. The rendered image of the 3-D model then was touched up in Adobe Photoshop (for aesthetics); for example, to increase depth by enhancing highlights and shadows.

Communication Approach

Because of their different intentions, fine art and design differ in the ways they communicate their ideas to the audience. Fine art often has a poetic quality, provokes thoughts, and prompts contemplation. Graphic design usually strives for clear, immediate, and effective communication of the idea to the audience.

Origin of the Idea

The ideas and purposes of a designer's projects often come from clients or employers. In contrast, the fine artist generates the work's idea and intention.

1.1.2 Digital Technologies as a Tool and as a Medium in Digital Art

The digital component plays two different roles in digital art: as a tool and as a medium. Whether the technology is used as a tool or a medium depends on the extent to which its different properties—interactivity, accessibility, and manipulability—are exploited.

Digital Technology as a Tool

The ease with which digital media can be manipulated makes their technology a very good tool for creativity. In particular, the capability to "undo" enhances the artist's creative freedom to experiment. When used as a tool, strong motives are often the manipulability, wide accessibility, and rapid reproduction capability of digital technology. Sometimes, digital technology is used to aid art creation in traditional media; that is, the final product is not in digital format, and the use of the technology is not apparent. For example, the composition for an oil painting can be experimented using digital images before transferring to the canvas. Digital imaging and digital video are the common media that are used as a tool for this purpose.

Digital Technology as a Medium

When digital technology is used as a medium, its intrinsic characteristics (especially interactivity) are exploited to a greater extent. Such artworks exhibit some common distinctive aspects, although not all characteristics must exist within a single work.

1. Physical interaction.

Viewers often have to perform some kind of action (especially to interact with the computer) either through the mouse, keyboard, or other devices to experience the entire piece. Just being a spectator will not initiate much communication with this type of artwork.

For example, in Camille Utterback's *Untitled 6* (Figure 1.10), the viewer makes marks through the bodily movement. The following is an excerpt about this piece.[‡]

> "*Untitled 6* is the sixth piece in Utterback's *External Measures Series*. The series began with Utterback's attempts to create interactive paintings and has evolved as she

Figure 1.10 An installation still of Camille Utterback's *Untitled 6*, 2005 (Photographed by Peter Harris © 2007) (Courtesy of Camille Utterback—http://www.camilleutterback.com)

[‡]http://www.camilleutterback.com

(a)   **(b)**

Figure 1.11 Installation stills of Camille Utterback's *Potent Objects*, 2003 (a) *Shaken* (b) *Balance* (Courtesy of Camille Utterback—http://www.camilleutterback.com)

continues to experiment with the possibilities for hinging digital aesthetic systems to human movement. . . . While Utterback's work is computer generated and detects movement in the space via a video camera, it shares a lineage with analog works like mobiles and kinetic sculptures, where artists create a framework for various possibilities to occur through the physical relationships between parts of the sculpture."

In Camille Utterback's *Potent Objects* (Figure 1.11), the viewer can hold and move a physical device. The live-action character displayed on the device reacts to the viewer's interaction with the device. Figure 1.11 shows installation stills of two objects: *Shaken* and *Balance'*. Here is an excerpt describing the work.[§]

"Through the use of double entendres and plays on words, *Potent Objects* examines the tropes of interactivity as metaphors for human emotion. Each object is based on a word that refers to both a physical gesture and an emotional state. Some objects will try to 'learn' about certain emotions or interactive behaviors by capturing and incorporating users' actions into the object's own repertoire of 'emotion'."

2. Use of multimedia.

See Chapter 4 for detailed description about *Spacequatica* and *Drum Machine*.

Image, video, audio, and even text may be used to make up a whole piece, and they can be shown asynchronously. For example, The Sancho Plan's audiovisual works, *Spacequatica* (Figure 1.12) and *Drum Machine*, combine sound, music, and animation.

[§]http://www.camilleutterback.com/potentobjects.html

Figure 1.12 The Sancho Plan's *Spacequatica* (Courtesy of The Sancho Plan—
www.thesanchoplan.com)

3. Nonsequential experience.

Digital technology allows navigation of the work based on the choice of the viewer. This creates new possibilities for nonlinear experience of the work. Directing the viewer's eye around the canvas is not a new concept in visual art composition, but digital technology can direct viewers' experience by moving their attention *across* and *within* components or "pages". For example, hypertext documents allow nonlinear navigation. The viewer does not need to follow a specific order to view the documents. The order of viewing depends on the viewer's choices.

With digital technology, an originally linear sequence can be reconstructed into new sequences. The viewer can make choices to control how the different elements are recombined into a new sequence. For example, in the author's *Mannequin*, the body movement of a motion-captured dance sequence is segregated into two parts: upper and lower body. This severs the timing relationships between the upper and lower body (Figure 1.13). The motion of the two body parts then can be recombined by allowing each part to have different speeds and direction of playback, which also can be reversed. The new sequence depends on the viewer's choices. The work was created for a dance performance in which two such mannequins were controlled by two dancers behind a projection screen (Figure 1.14a). Two dancers in front of the screen were trying to mimic the movement of the mannequins (Figure 1.14b). Despite the rehearsal, the new motion was different and unpredictable in each show. The piece explores the idea of control in addition to the experimentation of non-linear recombination of body movement.

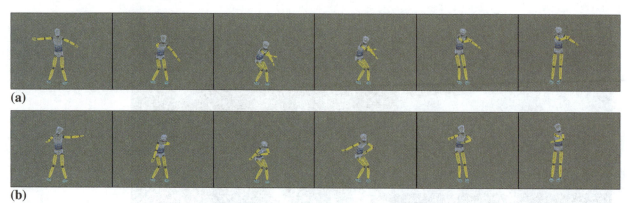

(a)

(b)

Figure 1.13 (a) Frames of the original dance applied onto a 3-D mannequin character (b) The movements of the upper body and the lower body are recombined with different timing (controlled by the user) to create new movement

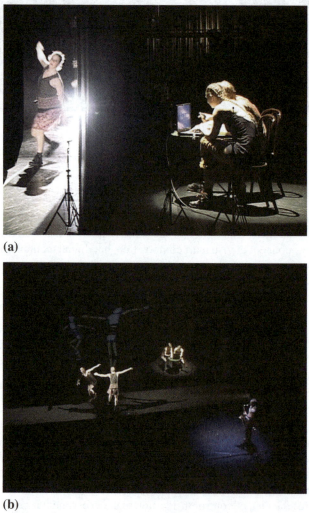

(a)

(b)

Figure 1.14 Stills of *Mannequin* in the dance performance *Fibonacci and Phi*, Alban Elved Dance Company, 2003

4. Viewer involvement.

Viewer involvement is not limited to the moment of the viewer's physical presence. The involvement also can be captured and becomes part of the content of the work. The viewers can leave marks that influence how the piece will communicate with future viewers. For instance, viewers can input words, and images or videos can capture their actions in time.

In Marek Walczak and Martin Wattenberg's *Apartment* found at http://turbulence.org/Works/apartment/, viewers can enter a sentence to create rooms. The apartments are grouped visually based on their linguistic relationships. Here is an excerpt from the artists' Web site about the work.

> "Viewers are confronted with a blinking cursor. As they type, rooms begin to take shape in the form of a two-dimensional plan, similar to a blueprint. The architecture is based on a semantic analysis of the viewer's words, reorganizing them to reflect the underlying themes they express. The apartments are then clustered into buildings and cities according to their linguistic relationships.

> Each apartment is translated into a navigable three-dimensional dwelling, so contrasting between abstract plans/texts and experiential images/sounds.

> … establishing an equivalence between language and space, *Apartment* connects the written word with different forms of spatial configurations."

In *Life SpaciesII* (Figure 1.15) of Christa Sommerer and Laurent Mignonneau, new creatures are created through e-mails from people all over the world. The characteristics of the creature and the food (text characters) it seeks to eat are based on the e-mail content that creates it. Here is an excerpt from the artists about the concept of this project.**

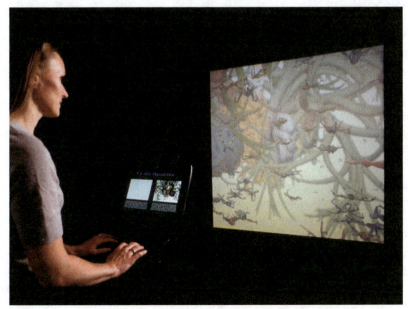

Figure 1.15 An installation still of *Life SpaciesII* (© 1999, by Christa Sommerer and Laurent Mignonneau, developed at ATR MIC Labs Japan, collection of the NTT-ICC Japan)

**http://www.interface.ufg.ac.at/christa-laurent/WORKS/CONCEPTS/LifeIIConcept.html

"Through the 'Life SpaciesII' web page, people all over the world interact with the system; by simply typing and sending an email message to the 'Life SpaciesII' web site at http://www.ntticc.co.jp/~lifespacies, one can create one's own artificial creature.

We developed a special text-to-form coding system that enables us to use written text as genetic code and translate it into visual creatures. In a way similar to the genetic code in nature, letters, syntax and sequencing of the text is used to code certain parameters in the creature's design functions. Form, shape, color, texture and the number of bodies and limbs are influenced by the text parameters. As there is a great variation in the texts sent by different people, the creatures themselves also vary greatly in their appearance.

As soon as a message is sent, the produced creature starts to live and move around in the 'Life SpaciesII' environment. Depending on the complexity of the written text message the creatures body design and its ability to move is determined. Some creatures might move very fast whereas others might be slower. Creatures also look for food and aim to eat text characters that can be interactively released by the visitors: creatures always eat the same characters as contained in their genetic code. For example 'John' creature will only eat 'J', 'o', 'h' and 'n.' Since other creatures might want to eat the same characters as well, competition among creatures for certain types of food will occur. Creatures also might starve and die if they do not succeed to catch enough text characters. On the other hand if a creature has eaten enough food (=text characters) it will look for a mating partner and bear a child. Offspring creatures will then carry the genetic code of the parent creatures and live and interact with the other creatures in 'Life SpaciesII.'"

INFORMATION VISUALIZATION AND DIGITAL ART

Information visualization deals with transforming large amounts of data into a visual form that enables the viewer to understand and make sense of the data. With computer technology, the visualization process often allows dynamic updates of the data and user interaction with the visual display of the data. Like the art creation, the process of transforming information into a visual form requires communicating information to the viewer and an understanding of human perception.

In addition, it is a thoughtful process for choosing or creating symbols or metaphors for the data. Information visualization has its aesthetic and utility purposes. To quote Edward R. Tufte:[††]

"To envision information—and what bright and splendid visions can result—is to work at the intersection of image, word, number, art, . . . and the standards of quality are those derived from visual principles that tell us how to put the right mark in the right place."

Information visualization has served as an inspiration, a basis, and premise for many digital art projects.[‡‡] Carolin Horn's *Anymails* at http://carohorn.de/anymails/ (Figure 1.16a) was developed during the artist's MFA thesis entitled "Natural Metaphor For Information Visualization." It uses microorganism-like creatures (Figure 1.16b) to represent different types of e-mails (Figure 1.16c) in her e-mail inbox. The size and

---

[††]Edward R. Tufte, *Envisioning Information*, Graphic Press, 1990.

[‡‡]More examples of information visualization works can be found at: http://rhizome.org/art/?tag=informationvisualization

(a)

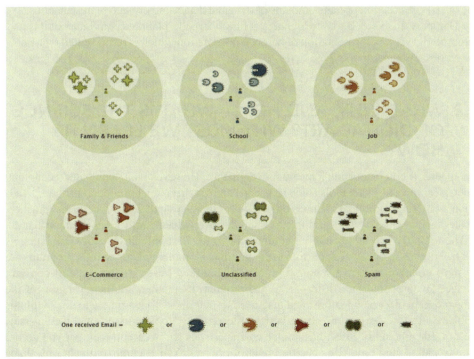

(b)

Figure 1.16 Screenshots of Carolin Horn's *Anymails*—http://carohorn.de/anymails/
(Courtesy of Carolin Horn)

Figure 1.17 A screenshot of Ben Fry's Genome Valence project—
http://benfry.com/genomevalence/

opacity of the microbe represent its age. The amount of hair and the speed of the microbe's motion are used to represent the status of an e-mail (read, replied, and unread).

Ben Fry's *Genome Valence* project at http://benfry.com/genomevalence/ is a visual representation for genome searches that deal with large amounts of data. The information is represented as points, arcs and a ribbon of text (of nucleic acid symbols, A, C, G, and T) in space (Figure 1.17). The project evolved from the artist's Masters thesis which focused on visual construction of large amounts of dynamic data using organic representations.

Daniel A. Becker's Barcode Plantage at http://barcode-plantage.com/index.htm is an algorithmic visual representation of barcode information which is rerpresented by a network of lines and curves.

1.2 WHAT, WHY, AND HOW—WHAT IS THE SCIENCE OF DIGITAL ART? WHY MUST WE LEARN IT? HOW?

Your skill level is reflected in the craftsmanship and professionalism of your art. Skills can be acquired by studying artworks, continuous experimentation, and practice on your own.

A computer is both a tool and a medium in digital art. However, using computer technology is not as intuitive as using tools (such as pencils and brushes) in a traditional medium. In addition, mastering traditional methods often requires more systematic instruction and practice. It takes time to get past the learning curve and discover what a software application can do.

The tools for digital art can be commercial software application programs (such as Adobe Photoshop), as well as custom programming. Commercial application programs are the most common choice for nonprogrammers, but they pose the challenge of constant change. The user-interface differs from one program to another, and new versions of the same program offer new features and disguise familiar ones. To learn how to deal with this problem, let's draw experience from how you learn to use tools in traditional media—say, brushes. Each brand of brush has unique characteristics and a certain feel, but you do not learn to paint using only one specific brand of brushes. You generalize brushes by shape and material to associate their qualities with functions and visual effects—that is, the tasks.

Digital art cannot be separated from the fundamental elements and aesthetics of art and design. This textbook approaches the teaching and learning of digital art using both art and science perspectives. Both are integrated. A good understanding of art principles and skills helps you to make digital art *art*. Understanding the underlying scientific concepts of the digital tools and human perception helps you make educated decisions to create the intended effects—your artistic vision will not be compromised by the tools' default settings or arbitrary choices.

Art Perspective

This book approaches digital media from the fundamentals of art and design that can be applied across different types of media. An overview of the basic art elements and art and design organizational principles will appear in Chapter 2 and will be referred to over and over in chapters on each different medium—image, video, audio, and Web. They serve as the foundation for discussion and extrapolation to digital art.

Science Perspective

In integrating the science component, this book aims to help students (1) acquire skills that are transferable to new situations and (2) adapt to changing software applications. It is not the intention of this book to provide software training. This book is not intended to be a user reference, going over what each menu item does in an application program. Instead, it emphasizes concepts and tasks which can serve as guides to search for procedural information.

Application programs of the same media type have very much the same functionalities. They usually have an online Help index and let you perform keyword searches to navigate their content. Of course, you need a general idea of how an application program works in order for the content of the Help menu to make sense. You have to know the keywords it uses for the functionalities you seek. For each imaging, audio, and video topic, there are two chapters—one on the conceptual level and the other on the practical. The practicum chapters use a task-oriented approach and discuss the general functionalities and common user-interface of application programs for that media.

1.2.1 Common Mistakes in Learning Digital Art

There two common misunderstandings about digital art: one related to the art component and the other to the digital tools. Be conscious of these traps so you do not fall into them when you work on your projects.

1. Ignoring the art component.

Be careful not to get so involved in learning to use the software itself that you lose sight of the intent and direction of your art projects. Without a solid integration of art components, the piece will appear incoherent or empty in emotion and substance.

2. Misconception about digital technology.

The common belief that computers make things easier often leads to a fatal assumption that digital technology makes digital art much easier to produce than traditional art. In fact, digital tools are not as intuitive as traditional tools and often require more systematic instruction in addition to basic computer skills.

1.3 ART AND DESIGN ELEMENTS

Line, **shape**, **value**, **color**, **texture**, and **space** are the basic visual elements for art and design across media. It cannot be emphasized enough that using digital technologies is by no means divorced from traditional aesthetics.

Because visual concepts are so interrelated and their visual results somewhat overlap, trying to break down the subject of composition into individual principles is problematic. Different artists and authors may have slightly different lists and groupings of these principles.

The basic elements often are integrated to create more complex visual statements in art and design according to their fundamental principles. The term *composition* is used to describe the structure of a work or arrangement of these elements according to certain organizing principles, which include *variety and harmony*, *balance*, *repetition and rhythm*, *emphasis and focus*, and *perspective*. Chapter 2 will present an overview of both basic elements and organizational principles for art and design.

1.4 CRITIQUING DIGITAL ART

Class critique is an important component of studio art courses in which every student should participate. Critique is a sharing and learning experience. If peers do not understand the subject matter or emotion the work intends to communicate, their responses may provide clues to identify the weaknesses and the possible solution.

The way to critique digital art (especially digital images) does not differ very much from the methods used to critique traditional media, because many of the visual, aesthetic, and organizational principles still hold. Time-based media (such as video and animation) and interactive media add extra dimensions that become additional aspects for the critique. For example, images can change with time, and more than one medium (sound and images) can be used to convey the whole experience. In interactive works, the navigation structure introduces a design principle foreign to traditional media.

Here are some general suggestions for stepwise critique in studio art courses. Later chapters on specific media will discuss more specific criteria.

1. Describe what you see and/or hear.

The first step in critique is a straightforward, factual description of the sight and sound. Do not jump to make any interpretation or association yet. Watch for any adjectives in your description of what you see and/or hear.

You may be reluctant to stick with simple factual description (because it seems trivial and silly) when everyone can see the image or hear the sound. But what is obvious to you may not be picked up by others. An image theoretically contains an infinite amount of information—not every bit is the artist's intention, and not every bit makes sense to the viewer. It is not uncommon to identify an unintentional emphasis while the intentional aspects are ignored. Going through this step of describing what you see helps other students to see too.

2. Describe what you see in terms of the art and design elements and principles.

In the next step of critique, refer to the basic elements and art and design principles as a guideline for discussion. As objectively as you can, discuss the visual components in terms of line, shape, value, color, texture, and space. Also, discuss the composition in terms of variety and harmony, balance, repetition and rhythm, emphasis and focus, and perspective.

Referring to the basic elements and principles keeps you conscious of them. Think of it as training. The discussion will not be limited to them, but they will establish a model and starting point from which the discussion can be expanded.

3. Discuss the subject matter.

Based on what you see, what do you think the work is about? What does it mean? What do you think it is trying to communicate? Does everyone agree? Do other students' responses change your initial thoughts about the piece?

Note that the subject matter that is being discussed so far is the viewer's interpretation only. In the studio art class environment, the student artist may keep silent until the critique of the piece is over. This way, other students will not be influenced by the original intent, and the artist can get more direct and unbiased responses. The work ultimately stands on its own.

4. Discuss the execution of techniques.

How is the piece executed? How skillful is the technical craftsmanship? Craftsmanship includes the care in execution and neatness. Neatness is not a requirement for a good art. However, if it is unintentional, it may divert attention, and the work also may look sloppy, amateurish, and accidental.

5. Student artist responses.

At the end of the critique, student artists can respond to their peers' reactions and talk about the original intent, intended subject matter, and any unsolved problems in the piece. Other students are encouraged to respond, initiating a communal discussion, because the class now has new information about the piece.

1.5 DIGITAL CANVAS

In traditional visual art, the work you are creating is truly WYSIWYG (what you see is what you get) throughout the process. An oil painting, for example, has the same dimension in the exhibition as when it is being developed in your studio. The pigment stays on the canvas. The color may look a little different under different lighting or at different times of day. But you still have a pretty good idea of how the color will look in a show.

On the other hand, digital art is created or prepared on computers. It is probably seen on only one computer display during the creation process, but the finished work will probably be shown on another display system—for example, a projector or a different monitor—or output to another medium—for example, an inkjet print or video. If the finished digital artwork is going to be shown in a controlled environment (such as a gallery) where a specific computer monitor is set up to display your work, you need only to set up that one system to match your vision for your work. If your work is intended for the audience to install and view on their own computers, then you will have little control over how your work is displayed. You will be uncertain whether it will look exactly the way you intended.

When a digital artwork is transferred from your computer to another medium or even another computer display, physical dimension and color may change. These elements are important to the work's essence. To make the exhibiting artwork match what you see on your computer, you have to understand what may cause changes, how you can preserve the color from your computer to another display medium, and how to predict the destined physical dimension of the artwork.

The discussion on color management can be found in Chapter 2.

The skills needed to control and predict these changes require understanding of technical concepts—one of the most important of which is *resolution*. Resolution has been explained and discussed in the *Digital Media Primer*. Later, in Chapter 2 on digital imaging, we will revisit this topic using pegboards as an analogy to explain resolution from the creative-process point of view—from capturing to displaying on screen to printing—and to clarify ppi and different uses of dpi.

Digital technologies influence the art process from creation to exhibition, and different technologies present different considerations. The types of consideration that influence the *creation* process can be divided into two areas: *delivery* and *display*. As with traditional media, you have to determine the delivery and intended display method before you begin creation.

Creation

During the creation process, the computer monitor is your working canvas. However, unlike traditional media, its dimension does not necessarily reflect the displaying dimension and the actual colors of the final product. The monitor display is measured in pixels, while a physical artwork is measured in inches or centimeters. In addition, color may differ slightly from one display medium—computer monitor or print—to another.

Delivery

Delivery in the digital realm refers to how viewers receive the files. Examples of delivery methods include CD-ROM, DVD, print, and the Web. The delivery method influences the file format. While creating digital media, you often work with a file format that is not the same as the final delivery format. For example, you composite and layer images of higher resolution in Photoshop in its native format—the Photoshop file or PSD. To make the image available on a Web page, you would have to resize it and save it as a Web-image format, such as JPEG, GIF, or PNG.

Display

The intended display method is another important factor in the creation process. It influences such file settings as image resolution. Therefore, you should determine the method by which you intend to display your digital artwork before you start creating it. Display methods include print, computer monitor, projector, and television set. The computer-monitor display can be a specific monitor in a controlled situation (like a gallery). It can be on anyone's monitor if the work is going to be accessed on the Web. In the first case, you have a certain control by adjusting display settings like color and resolution before the exhibition. If possible, try to find out the resolution of the exhibiting computer monitor before you finish your project. In the second case, you have no control over the viewer's monitor settings. It may be adjusted too brightly or dimly. It may have a resolution different from the one you intended; your work may be sized too large or too small. When you cannot control the viewer's monitor settings, you should use the most common, current monitor resolution, which at the time of this writing is 1024×768 pixels. Many existing laptops and desktops support higher resolution, such as 1280×800 pixels.

1.6 MEMORY AND STORAGE

Digital art files often are large. Compared to word-processing tasks, handling these files—image, video, and audio—demands much more memory and processor speed. The files also require more disk space for storage, especially because (like traditional art) their creation commonly involves a long process of experimentation and the evolution of ideas. Computers offer the advantage of keeping an archive of the process. Many different versions of a digital artwork can be produced before reaching the finished work, which will probably be large in itself. You must consider the capacity of different media—whether CDs, DVDs, or online.

The high requirements for both memory and disk space commonly are expressed in megabyte units, although currently, personal computer disk space is in gigabytes, and many servers are installed with gigabytes of memory. Because the units are the same, the terms *memory* (RAM) and *disk space* often are mixed up. However, they serve different functions. To be able to assess your equipment needs, you must be able to distinguish these terms and the problems caused when they are insufficient.

1.6.1 Memory

What is RAM, and does increasing RAM always make a computer faster? Before answering these questions, you need to understand what RAM does. A processor consists of a main memory device and a ***central processing unit (CPU)***. ***Random access memory (RAM)*** is one of the most important and best-known forms of main memory. Both data and instructions are stored in a main memory unit. For example, when you open your image file (data) with the image-editing program (instructions), they are stored in the RAM.

You may have been told that insufficient memory causes slow processing of a file, but why? Does adding more RAM *always* boost the speed? Not always. With a very large image file and several different programs running simultaneously, your computer may run out of memory. The operating system then creates extra virtual memory by using its hard disk space to create a *swap file*—moving the data and instructions back and forth between the RAM and the swap file on the hard disk. Because the hard disk is slower than the RAM, such swapping can cause noticeable delay. In this situation, adding more RAM can boost the speed by eliminating the need for swapping. However, if the slowness is not caused by the swapping, increasing the RAM will not help the computer performance.

The speed of the CPU also determines the performance of a computer. For example, the CPUs in older computers are slower. Increasing the RAM will not make an older and slower computer perform like a newer faster computer.

1.6.2 Storage Media

The most common categories of storage media today are magnetic disks (such as hard disks) and optical disks (such as CDs and DVDs.) Recently, removable hard disks and memory keys have become more popular as portable media for transferring files.

New computers come installed with DVD/CD writers and DVD-authoring software. CD-R (compact disc-recordable) and CD-RW (compact disc-rewritable) devices are very common storage and backup media. The storage capacity ranges from 650 to 700 MB. The disk space of files erased from a rewritable disk can be recovered and rewritten. Depending on the recording option set in the CD-recording software, a CD-R can be recorded multiple times (multi-session). In this case, you still can add files to the CD-R. However, the disk space of previously recorded files on a CD-R cannot be recovered.

DVDs offer higher storage capacity. Currently, there are DVD-R, DVD-RW, DVD+R, DVD+RW discs. Writing to any of them requires the appropriate hardware and software. Check the user guide of your DVD writer to see which types of disc it supports. Many CD-recording software applications also can record files on DVD discs, but producing DVD movies with menu navigation requires DVD-authoring software, such as Adobe EncoreDVD, Apple DVD Studio Pro, Sony DVD Architect, and Ulead DVD Workshop. At the time of this writing, the capacity of most DVD-R, DVD-RW, DVD+R, and DVD+RW discs you see in the store is 4.7 GB—the equivalent of almost seven 700-MB CDs. The single-sided, double-layered, or dual-layered DVD disc available in stores has an 8.5-GB capacity.

If you are distributing your work on CDs or DVDs to a larger audience, CD-ROMs (compact disc-read-only memory) and DVD-ROMs (digital versatile disc-read-only memory) offer a cheaper solution per disc. However, you must send them to a company that has the equipment for mastering and pressing. While these companies also may offer silk screening and packaging services which give the product a more professional look and feel, disc mastering is costly. Therefore, the CD-ROM or DVD-ROM is an economical choice only if your work is, produced in large quantities. Moreover, since CD-ROM and DVD-ROM storage is permanent (read-only memory), it cannot be updated without replacing the entire disc. If the presentation of your digital artwork relies on specific versions of certain applications on the audience's computers, then you should consider the following options.

- Press a small number of CD-ROMs or DVD-ROMs, just enough for your immediate needs, because the computers of future audiences—say, after a year—no longer may support the required player.
- Include the installer of the specific player on your disc, which usually requires obtaining a license agreement with the company who owns the application.
- Consider other media. For example, websites are very good for showing work that is updated frequently.

Writing data to CD-R, CD-RW, DVD-R, DVD-RW, DVD+R, and DVD+RW requires a continuous flow. The computer system must be fast enough to sustain the continuous data transfer to the CD-R, DVD-R, or DVD+R drive, otherwise errors may occur. The data to be transferred must be on the local hard drive not on a remote network drive. Any network slowdown during the writing will disrupt the continuous flow of data and cause failure, ruining the disc. Before writing, copy all of the data to be transferred to the disc onto the local hard drive. Close all other applications to minimize the possibility of slowing down your computer system during the actual writing.

Choosing storage media

Price and speed are important factors in choosing storage media. Table 1.2 indicates the relative speeds of some different storage media.

TABLE 1.2	**Relative Speeds of Different Storage Media**		
Relative Speed	**Media**		**Capacity**

↑	Hard Drive	• Fixed
		• Removable
			• Most common:
			  100 MB to 500 GB
			• Also, in Tera bytes (TB),
			  where 1 TB = 1000 GB

	Removable Flash Memory	• Compact Flash • Memory Key	• 16 MB to 64 GB
	Optical Disc	• DVD-R • DVD+R • DVD-RW • DVD+RW	• 4.7 GB • 8.5 GB
		• CD-R • CD-RW	• 650 MB • 700 MB

When distributing your artwork, your media's compatibility with your target audience's computer system is crucial. Most CD-ROM drives can play CD-R discs, but not all can play CD-RWs. Some DVD-ROM drives on computers only can play DVD-R discs, some only DVD+R, and some both. Older generations of set-top DVD players do not support any of these DVD discs. The newer ones can play them, and some can play movies on DVD-R discs but not DVD+R.

1.7 COMPUTER SKILLS FOR WORKING WITH FILES

This section discusses two basic computer skills that commonly are overlooked: (1) **file and folder organization**, and (2) **file opening and importing**. They do not seem to have any direct relation with digital art creation. However, poor file handling can cause many frustrations later on and waste time.

1.7.1 Organizing Files and Folders

Whether you are creating digital art or writing a term paper on a computer, you have to open files. Knowing where you saved them so that you can find and reopen them easily for future editing or backing them up to a CD will spare you a lot of time and frustration.

Files can be organized using folders. Think of your computer hard drive as a filing cabinet. A *folder*, also called a directory, can contain files and other folders. A path designates the location of each file and folder.

For digital-art projects, you often have to create many files. Organize them logically, and do not save them all in one folder or on your computer desktop. There are many ways to organize your files, depending on the nature of your project and (sometimes) personal preferences.

One way to categorize your digital art project files is by their intended use—for example, raw working files and final products. Let's look at a Web project. You may have images that you edited in Photoshop and saved as Photoshop files. However, when you complete the editing and want to place them on a Web page, you must save them in a Web format, such as a .jpg file. The Photoshop files (which are working files) cannot be used directly on the Web page. The .jpg file (which is not suitable for further editing but is suitable for the Web) is a final product. You only have to upload the files of the final product to the Web site. Thus, separating the raw working files from the final product helps you to easily locate the files that suit your intention—for example, to upload final files or to rework originals.

If your project uses more than one type of media, you can categorize your files further by type—image, audio, video, or text. You can organize by intended use and by media types at the same time.

For Windows systems, the hard drive, by default is assigned a letter C. It is found under My Computer. More drives can be assigned letters higher than C. Say you create a folder called artproject directly in the C drive. Then you create another folder called images inside this artproject folder. When you save a file—say, a .jpg image called background.jpg—in this images folder, its path is

C:\artproject\images\background.jpg

For Mac OS X, the hard drive by default is represented by the Macintosh HD icon on the desktop (Figure 1.18).

Saving file on the desktop is often a personal preference. Putting too many files on the desktop will clutter the desktop, making it hard to locate a file or folder. In addition, the desktop is a special folder. The file path is not a simple, obvious path. You need to be able to identify the file path for a Web project.

Figure 1.18 Macintosh HD icon on the desktop

Figure 1.19 The content in Macintosh HD is listed when you open Macintosh HD

Say you create a folder called `artproject` inside Machintosh HD (Figure 1.19). You also create another folder called `images` inside this `artproject` folder. Suppose you have saved a .jpg file called `background.jpg` in this `images` folder. To find this .jpg file later, you will go to Macintosh HD, open the `artproject` folder, and open the `images` folder. Although you may not see the file path by default, the file actually has a file path. When you use the Terminal (in Macintosh HD > Applications > Utilities) to navigate the files and folders on the computer, file paths are used. The file path for this `background.jpg` is

`/artproject/images/background.jpg`

Shortcuts and Aliases

Shortcuts in Windows and *aliases* on the Macintosh are types of files that behave like pointers to a document, folder, or application program. Double-clicking on a shortcut or alias opens the original application, folder, or document wherever it is located. These shortcuts and aliases provide a convenient way for you to open a document, folder, or application program immediately, without having to navigate to its actual folder location. However, if you do not understand how shortcuts and aliases work, they may cause confusion in some situations. For example, when you open or import files in an application program, you will have to navigate in the open-file window to the folder where the file is located; selecting the shortcut or alias may not work. In addition, deleting a shortcut or alias does *not* delete the file or folder to which it is linked—nor does backing up a shortcut or alias back up the linked file or folder.

No matter the medium—traditional or digital—you have to be familiar with the basic working of your tools to realize the art you envision. The more knowledge you have about them, the less frustration you will experience during the creative process. You must become very familiar with creating, organizing, and navigating the folders and files on your computer as well as develop basic computer skills such copying, deleting, and renaming files and folders. Mastering these very basic computer skills will help you learn to use digital tools to create digital art.

1.7.2 Opening Files versus Importing Files

Some digital media application programs, such as digital video-editing programs and multimedia authoring programs, use a model of a **project**, which embeds or links to the media files (**imported files**) that are used to create the work. A project is not a folder but a file saved in the application program's native format. When you save your work, you save the *project file*, and the next time you want to continue you have to *open* the *project file*. Some programs, such as Adobe Premiere Pro and Encore DVD, call its file a project file. For example, there are Open Project and New Project commands under the File menu in these programs. Other programs, such as Adobe Flash and Adobe Director, use the project model but do not use the term *project* to describe the file. In working with these files, you import (instead of open) other media files to include them.

If you want to use other media files in your digital work, you often must *import* them first into the *project*. Some application programs let you open non-project files to view the media file in the view-only mode. Some will not let you open non-project files. In either case, if you do not understand the difference between importing and opening files, you will have hard time working on your piece—thinking that the program does not let you open your *project* files or not let you use other media files.

Figures 1.20 through 1.22 use Adobe Premiere Pro as an example application to illustrate the difference between importing a file and opening a *project* file. Figure 1.20 shows the Open Project and Import commands found under the File menu. When the Open Project command is selected, the Open Project window (Figure 1.21a) comes up. As shown in Figure 1.21a, only the Premiere Pro Project file is listed in the window, and there is only one choice in the dropdown list of file type. This means only the Premiere Pro Project file is accepted.

The *project* model often is found in digital video and multimedia authoring programs where many other media files are used to produce the final product. The project model is not common in digital image applications, such as Adobe Photoshop and Illustrator. The file Import command in these programs is not the same as in those applications that use the *project* model.

Video-editing applications are discussed in *Digital Media Primer*, Chapter 7. The purpose of discussing the Adobe Premiere Pro workspace here is to demonstrate the distinction between *importing* a file and *opening* a *project* file.

(a)

(b)

Figure 1.20 Screenshots of the File menu of Adobe Premiere Pro (a) The Open Project command (highlighted) (b) The Import command (highlighted)

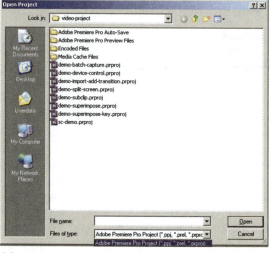

(a)

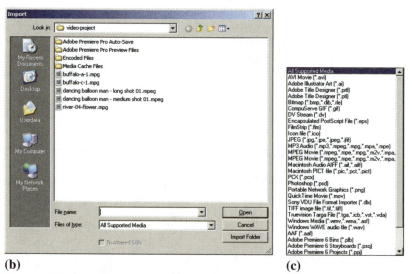

(b)   **(c)**

Figure 1.21 (a) The Open Project window (b) The Import file window (c) The dropdown list of supported media file types for import

When the Import command is selected, the Import window (Figure 1.21b) comes up. All of the supported media files listed in the window can be selected to import. The dropdown list of file type (Figure 1.21c) has many choices of accepted file type. Figure 1.22 shows the Adobe Premiere Pro workspace, and the red rectangle points out the list of imported media files. The imported files can be placed on the timeline for sequencing. In this example, the project is a single Adobe Premiere Pro file that contains references to the imported media files and video sequences. It also stores information about sequences and media, such as transitions and audio mixing. The list of imported files is only part of the project file.

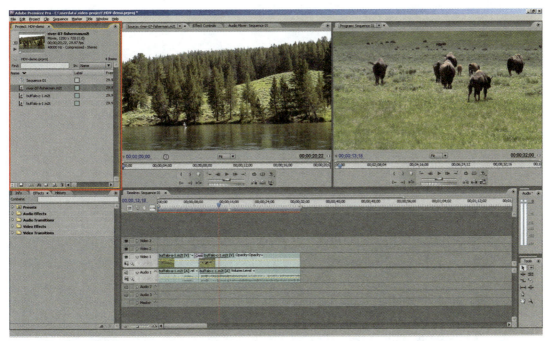

Figure 1.22 A screen capture of Adobe Premiere Pro CS3 workspace; the red rectangle marks the window where lists the imported media assets; these imported media files are ready to place on the timeline for sequencing

TERMS

LEARNING AIDS

The following learning aid can be found at the book's companion Web site.

⌐ **Selected URLs of Digital Art**
A selected list of URLs of digital artworks.

REVIEW QUESTIONS

When applicable, please choose all correct answers.

1. As suggested in this chapter, what is the first step in a classroom critique?

2. When you try to save a file, your computer gives you a warning that you do not have enough disk space. Which of the following upgrades target the warning?

    A. adding more memory or RAM
    B. adding more disk space
    C. all of the above

3. **True/False:** Adding more RAM *always* will make the computer run faster.

4. **True/False:** Adding more disk space *always* will make the computer run faster.

5. **True/False:** Deleting a shortcut or alias will delete the file or folder to which it links.

6. **True/False:** Backing up a shortcut or alias will back up the file or folder to which it links.

7. In most digital-media application programs that use a *project* model, you should select the menu File > Open in such programs when you want to

    A. open a project file
    B. import other media files
    C. open other media files
    D. all of the above

EXERCISES AND ACTIVITIES

1. Discuss the following.

    i. Do you think software training should be integrated in digital art courses? Why or why not?
    ii. Is a photograph of an oil painting digital art? If a documentary film is digitized onto a DVD, does it make the film digital video? Why or why not?
    iii. Is a work digital art when its entire purpose is to imitate the analog media? Why or why not?

2. Search online for digital artworks. Discuss the following.

    i. Whether the works are fine art or graphic design works.
    ii. Whether they use digital technology as a tool or a medium.

    (The list of URLs of digital artworks provided as a learning aid for this chapter can serve as a starting point to look up digital artworks online.)

3. Check the memory of your computer.

    i. How much memory (RAM) is installed on your computer?

        • *Windows users:* Right-click on My Computer and choose Properties. Look up the RAM in the General tab.
        • *Mac OSX users:* Click on the Apple Menu and choose About This Mac.

ii. While you are running an application—for example, opening an image file with Photoshop—check out how much RAM you use and how much is free.

- *Windows XP users:* Open Windows Task Manager by pressing Control-Alt-Delete, and click the Task Manager button. Click the Performance tab. Check out Total and Available under Physical Memory.
- *Mac OSX users:* Run the CPU Monitor and Process Viewer found in the Utilities folder inside Applications.

4. Check out the approximate pricing for each medium in the table below, and calculate the price per MB for each. Complete the table. There is a wide range of hard-drive capacity. Choose the one most suitable for your needs.

Relative Speed	Media		Storage Capacity (MB)	Price per Unit (Disk or Disc)	Price per MB Storage
↑	Hard Drive	Fixed, Removable			
	Removable Flash Memory	Compact Flash, Memory Key			
	Optical Disc	DVD-R, DVD+R			
		DVD-RW, DVD+RW			
		CD-R			
		CD-RW			

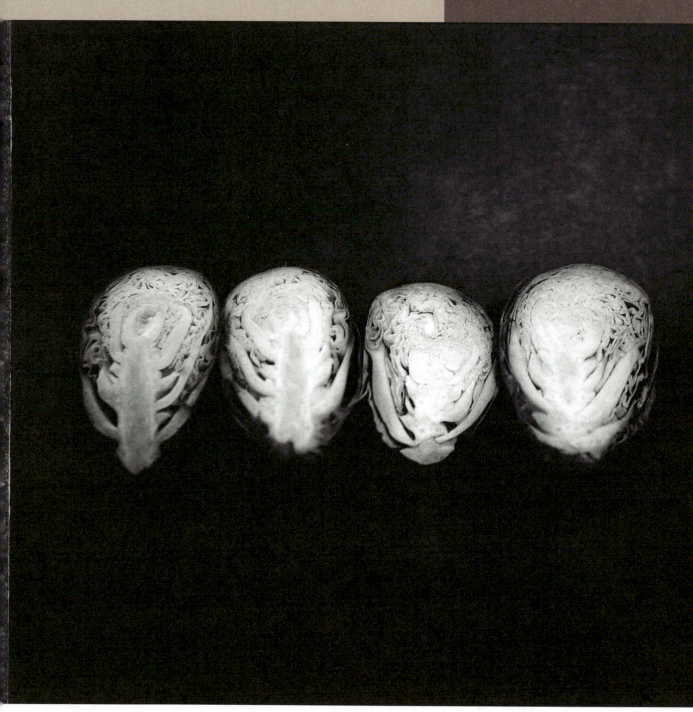

Yue-Ling Wong, *Sprouts*

GENERAL LEARNING OBJECTIVES

In this chapter, you will learn:

- Common terms related to the resolution of digital imaging.
- About dpi, ppi, pixel dimensions, and physical dimensions and their interrelationships.
- How to determine resolution for scanning, printing, and on-screen display.
- Resolution factors that affect the level of image detail.
- The purpose of color profiles and how they work.
- The steps for desktop color management workflow.
- To choose a rendering intent for printing a digital image.
- To apply basic art and design elements.
- To apply basic art and design organization principles.
- To critique of digital images in a classroom setting.

2.1 WHAT ARE DIGITAL IMAGES?

This section serves as a review of bitmap and vector graphics. A detailed explanation of these topics is covered in *Digital Media Primer*, Chapter 2.

In its simplest definition, a digital image is a visual representation stored in digital format. To help you understand how an image is described in digital format, let's draw a parallel from the traditional media. A painting can be thought of as an image in two-dimensional space built up with different color pigments. Thus, the image content can be described according to two properties: (1) spatial location on the surface and (2) color.

When applied to digital images, these properties can be described using two different methods: **bitmap images** use pixels to describe the image content and **vector graphics** uses mathematical description—for example, equations.

Bitmap Images

How they are described:

- *Spatial location*: The x and y coordinates of the pixel
- *Color*: Pixel by pixel using numeric values; for instance, an RGB value of (255, 0, 0) represents a red color

The different ways to create them:

- *Digital photography*
- *Scanning* hard copy or an object
- *From scratch*, such as drawing and painting digitally using application programs for bitmap images

Editing methods:

- *Manipulating pixels*—for example, changing colors, erasing, and distorting the image content

Advantages over vector graphics:

- *Editing* is more intuitive pixel by pixel

Examples of applications:

- Digital photographs, scanned images, Web images

Examples of software application programs:

- Adobe Photoshop, Corel Paint Shop Pro

Vector Graphics

How they are described:

- *Spatial location*: Vector graphics do not use pixels but equations. The images of vector graphics are produced for output or display by calculating the points according to the equations that make up of the graphics. The coordinate system for the equations is arbitrary. That is, its scale can be set to any level, and hence, it is resolution independent.
- *Color*: Stored using numeric values but associated with the objects or elements instead of pixels

The different ways to create them:

- *Using application programs* for vector graphics
- *Defining paths* and fills in the vector graphic application programs

Editing methods:

- *Altering anchor point locations* and the tangent of a vector shape's path
- *Altering properties of the paths and fills*—for example, their color or width

Advantages over bitmap images:

- *Smaller file size*
- *Resolution independent*: i.e., it can be scaled to any size and printed on any output device at any resolution, without losing detail or clarity in the picture.

Examples of applications:

- Illustrations, logo designs, business schematics

Examples of software application programs:

- Adobe Illustrator, Adobe Flash

2.2 MEASURING THE DIGITAL CANVAS— RESOLUTION, RESOLUTION, RESOLUTION!

For digital images, your computer screen serves as your *working* canvas. The finished artwork probably will be displayed on another display system (that is, a different monitor or projector) or output in another medium—for example, an inkjet print or video. Thus, the physical dimensions of a digital image in the creation stage may differ from what the viewer will see. In traditional media, an artwork's dimensions are its physical dimensions—height, width, and possibly depth measured in, for example, inches or centimeters. In the digital realm, an image is measured in pixel dimensions—that is, the number of pixels. A digital image does not have physical dimensions until it is printed.

In the following sections, we are going to use the pegboard as a metaphor to explain image resolution for capturing (scanning), displaying (on monitors), and printing. A

You do not need to write equations to create vector graphics. Vector-graphic application programs allow you to manipulate the anchor-point location and the tangent of a path to define an equation.

Erasing Image Content: Unlike bitmap application programs, vector-graphics application programs generally do not have an eraser tool. Image content can be erased by altering the path of a shape—for example, moving an anchor point inward. It also can be done by applying an intersection or subtraction operation between two shapes.

> ⬆ **Pegboard and Resolution** An interactive tutorial using the pegboard as an analogy to explain resolution in capturing and displaying digital images.

picture can be composed on a pegboard by placing individual pegs in the grid of holes. Each peg has one solid color. A digital image is made up of a matrix of pixels and is similar to a pegboard. An interactive tutorial that complements the following discussion is available online. Here, we will elaborate in detail and expand the discussion to include printing resolution.

- How are *dpi* (*dots per inch*) or *ppi* (*pixels per inch*), pixel dimensions, and the physical dimensions of a picture related to one another?
- Which dimension factor(s) can affect the level of image detail that can be captured?
- Why does higher scanning dpi give more image detail?
- What do higher-resolution monitors mean to you? Does the image *gain* more detail when displayed on a higher-resolution monitor? What are the advantages or disadvantages of higher screen resolution? Should we always choose the highest possible monitor resolution?

The following discussion about resolution will help answer these questions.

2.2.1 Scanning Resolution

Before we discuss scanning resolution, imagine you are going to reproduce a picture using a pegboard. Given pegboards with different numbers of holes per inch, as shown in Figure 2.1, which will give the most image detail? Figure 2.2 illustrates the reproduction of an image of musical notes on these different pegboards. The pegboard with the highest peg-holes per inch (Figure 2.2c) reproduces the most details of the musical notes.

A CCD (charge-coupled device) is the most common technology for image capturing in scanners and digital cameras. It consists of a matrix or array of many tiny, light-sensitive photosites.

What does the pegboard analogy tell us about scanner resolution? Let's look first at how a scanner works. The scan head has a **CCD array** across the flatbed. Each photosite in the CCD array samples the light intensity reflected from the image during scanning. The scan head is moved slowly across the document. Its speed is controlled by a stepper motor. The vertical resolution of a flatbed scanner is determined by the precision of the stepper motor of the scanner. The number of the photosites determines a scanner's horizontal resolution in dots per inch (dpi).

Each hole on the pegboard in this analogy is a photosite. These tiny sensors are referred to as *dots* in the dots-per-inch unit used to describe the scanner's resolution. The color information captured by each *dot* will be stored as the color information of a *pixel* in the resulting digital image at the corresponding location on the image plane.

The inch in the "per inch" unit is a linear inch not a square inch.

Thus, the unit *peg-holes per inch* on the pegboard is analogous to the unit dots per inch (dpi) in scanning. Scanning a picture at a higher dpi gives more image detail in the similar way that more peg-holes per inch yields a more detailed image (Figure 2.2c). The resulting digital image will be made up of more pixels—that is, it will have larger **pixel dimensions**, which leads to a larger file size.

In Figure 2.2, pegboards (b) and (d) have the same pixel dimensions. However, (d) can fit in two musical notes, although sacrificing image detail. So, for example, scanning a 1-inch × 1-inch area at 300 dpi will give an image of the same pixel dimensions and, thus, the same file size as scanning a 2-inch × 2-inch area at 150 dpi. Of course, scanning at 150 dpi will yield less image detail than 300 dpi.

In summary, the unit dots per inch (dpi) in *scanning* describes the **scanning resolution**. It determines the level of image detail you can *capture*. The resulting pixel dimensions

Scale |—————1"—————|—————2

	Pegboard	Physical Dimension	Dimension in Peg Holes	Peg-Holes Per Inch
(a)	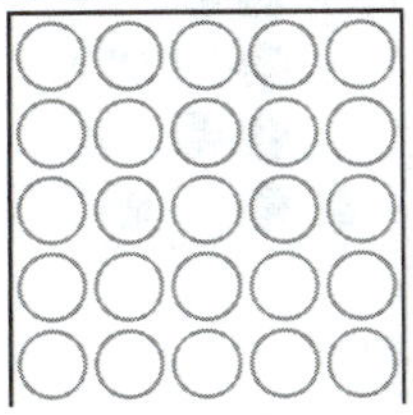	1" × 1"	5 × 5 peg holes = 25 peg holes	5
(b)	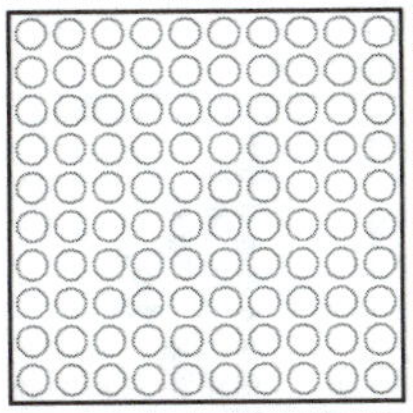	1" × 1"	10 × 10 peg holes = 100 peg holes	10
(c)	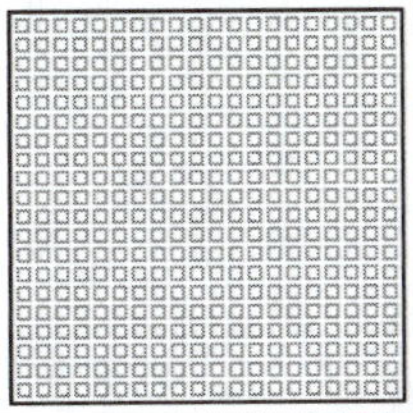	1" × 1"	20 × 20 peg holes = 400 peg holes	20
(d)	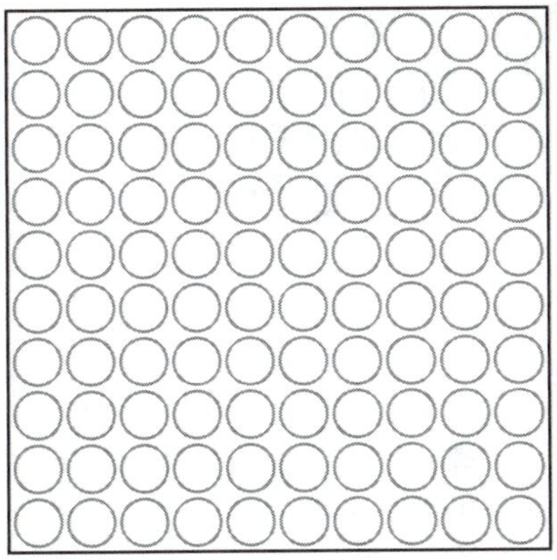	2" × 2"	10 × 10 peg holes = 100 peg holes	5

Figure 2.1 Pegboards of different "resolutions"

of the scanned image can be calculated as follows:

Pixel dimension of the scanned image = **Physical dimension** of the picture to
be scanned × **Scanning dpi**

The parameter, pixel dimension, in the equation is expressed as singular because each of the width and height dimension is multiplied with the scanning dpi separately.

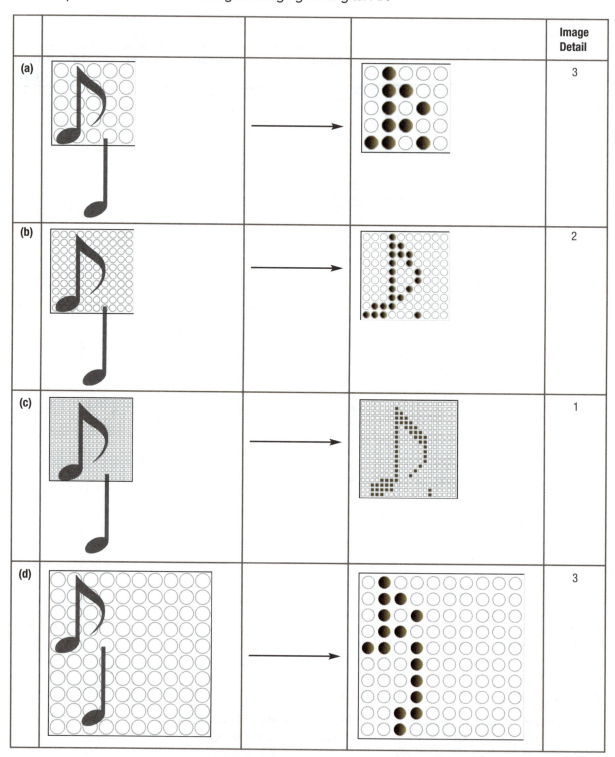

Figure 2.2 A sample image of musical notes reproduced on pegboards with different "resolutions" where the number in the last column indicate the relative image detail (1 = best; 3 = worst)

For example, to calculate the pixel dimensions of an image (such as 3-inch wide and 2-inch high) scanned at 300 dpi:

Pixel width of the scanned image = **3 inches** $\times$ **300 dpi** = **900 dpi**

Pixel height of the scanned image = **2 inches** $\times$ **300 dpi** = **600 dpi**

Total number of pixels of the scanned image: **900** $\times$ **600 pixels** = **540,000 pixels**

Note that the total number of pixels is NOT 3 inches $\times$ 2 inches $\times$ 300 dpi (or 1800 pixels)!

Therefore, when you scan a picture, you must make two decisions.

1. Physical Dimensions of the Source.
   You must first decide what part of the image or object you want to scan.
2. Scanning dpi.
   You must determine how the image will be used. Is it for online viewing or printing? If it is for print, then you must know the pixel dimensions of the resulting scan so that you can calculate the scanning dpi by arranging the above equation as:

Scanning dpi = **Pixel dimension** of the scanned image/

Physical dimension of the picture to be scanned

To determine the **pixel dimensions** of the scanned image, you need to know how the image will be printed, which entails two other decisions: (1) the image's output ppi and (2) the physical dimensions of the final print.

Pixel dimension of an image = Image's output ppi $\times$ Physical dimension of the final print

If an image is intended for on-screen viewing, such as embedded in a Web page, then you do not have to consider the output ppi or the image's physical dimensions. For Web images, the physical dimensions of an image are not a useful reference. Different monitors have different resolutions. A 4-inch $\times$ 3-inch image on your monitor will not necessarily be displayed as 4-inches $\times$ 3-inches on others. You should estimate the pixel dimensions. Try to picture the size of the image relative to the resolution of the intended monitor. For instance, if you want an image to take up one-half of the width and height of a computer screen with a resolution of 1024 $\times$ 768 pixels, then the image's pixel dimensions should be 512 $\times$ 384 pixels.

See also *Digital Media Primer* Chapter 3 for a detailed discussion of printing resolution.

2.2.2 Screen Resolution

What does monitor resolution mean to you? Should you always choose the monitor with the highest resolution? Does a higher resolution monitor increase the detail or resolution of your artwork?

Let's draw on the pegboard analogy again. Copying an image from one pegboard to another is like displaying the same image on different monitors. The peg holes are analogous to the dots on the monitor. The *physical dimensions* of the pegboard are analogous to the *physical dimensions of the monitor's display*. The *total number of holes* on the pegboard is analogous to the *monitor's screen resolution*.

Unlike scanning dpi and output ppi, the dpi of a monitor display is not an important measure in creating digital images. Besides price, the two factors you must consider in selecting a monitor are (1) the physical dimensions of the viewable area and (2) the screen resolution in pixel dimensions. For monitor displays, resolution refers to the number of individual dots of color (known as **screen pixels**), contained in a display. A monitor's resolution typically is expressed by the pixel dimensions in width by height. For examples, the common screen resolution settings are 800×600, 1024×768, 1280×960, and 1600×1200 pixels. Depending on the video memory of the graphic card in your computer, you may be able to change the screen resolution to the highest resolution that the monitor supports.

High-Resolution Display—Does It Matter?

Figure 2.3a shows an image of 10×10 pixels displayed on a small monitor with a hypothetical screen resolution of 10×10 pixels. The same 10×10 pixel image would appear to be smaller when displayed on the same-sized monitor with a screen resolution set to 20×20 pixels (Figure 2.3b). Does the higher resolution increase the image detail? No, the image has the same detail—same number of pixels. But you now have more screen space, which gives you at least the following advantages.

- You can see more of a large image on the higher-resolution display. The same image may not fit on one screen with the lower-resolution display.
- Most image editing programs let you zoom in or out on an image. You do not have to zoom out as much when you are working on a higher resolution display.

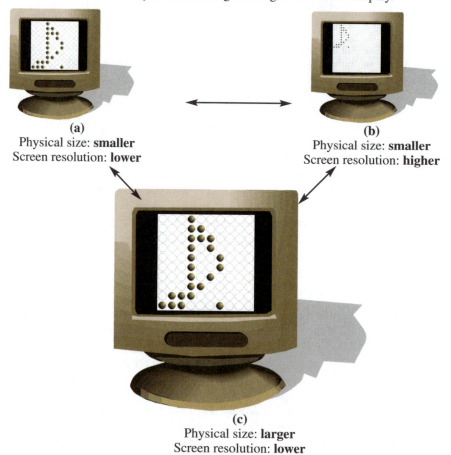

(a)
Physical size: **smaller**
Screen resolution: **lower**

(b)
Physical size: **smaller**
Screen resolution: **higher**

(c)
Physical size: **larger**
Screen resolution: **lower**

Figure 2.3 The same image displayed on monitors of different viewable dimensions and screen resolutions illustrated using the pegboard metaphor (a) A smaller monitor with a lower resolution (b) A smaller monitor with a higher resolution (c) A larger monitor with lower resolution

MAGNIFICATION OF DIGITAL IMAGES

Image-editing programs let you zoom in and out on an image. An image viewed at 100% magnification is displayed with actual pixels—each image pixel is translated directly into a screen pixel.

A large image viewed at 100% magnification in an image-editing program may not fit on one screen with a lower-resolution display. You may have to zoom out to see more or to fit the whole image on the screen.

When you zoom out to less than 100%, fewer monitor pixels than image pixels are used to display the image, and the image displayed has less than its actual detail.

With a higher screen resolution, you may be able to view the whole image on screen at 100% magnification or a magnification level closer to the actual pixels.

Notice that, without increasing the monitor's viewable dimensions, a higher screen resolution can make an image look smaller on screen. Sometimes, the screen content may become too small to read on a high-resolution monitor—compare Figure 2.3a with Figure 2.3b. It is not uncommon for users to set their display at lower than its highest resolution for which they have paid extra. Understanding how resolution works helps you to choose the equipment that suits your needs without paying for features that you do not need.

Monitor Size—Does It Matter?

Another common misunderstanding or overgeneralization about a computer display is that the larger the monitor, the better. Does a bigger monitor necessarily mean higher resolution? Nowadays, this premise usually holds true, but the highest resolution that the monitor can display also depends on the memory of the graphic card in the computer. Figure 2.3c shows a larger monitor with a viewable area four times those in Figure 2.3a and b, but it has the same screen resolution as the one in Figure 2.3a—10 × 10 pixels. As you see, the same image appears bigger on the larger monitor, but you do not gain any screen assets. In fact, when the same image is blown up on a screen like that, it appears less sharp, because it is more spread out.

In summary, a *combination* of large viewable area and high screen resolution can provide more screen assets with good readability for on-screen text and images. Both the space assets and readability are important factors in creating digital art.

The on-screen physical dimensions of an image are not meaningful measures. As explained in Figure 2.3, they depend on both the screen resolution and the viewable dimensions of the display. If the image is designed for an on-screen display (such as embedding on a Web page), always think of its size in pixel dimensions, not physical dimensions.

In creating digital art for on-screen display, you also should consider the screen resolution of your target audience. For example, if your target audience uses a screen resolution of 1024 × 768, and you want your image appear to be approximately one-quarter of the screen—about half of both the width and height of the screen resolution—then you should aim for about 512 × 384 pixels. Digital artists often work with a computer display of much higher resolution— for example, 1600 × 1200 or higher. With this resolution, an image of 512 × 384 pixels is only about one-tenth of the screen area or about one-third of both the width and height of the 1600 × 1200 screen resolution. If you create an image that takes up one-fourth of the screen based on your high-resolution display, then the image will be 800 × 600, which is larger than a quarter of the screen size for your target audience.

2.2.3 Printing Resolution

Digital images do not possess any intrinsic physical dimensions. Only a printed copy of a digital image has physical dimensions, such as inches or centimeters. How, then, do the pixel dimensions of a digital image translate into physical dimensions?

The *physical dimensions* of a digital image are defined by two parameters: (1) its pixel dimensions and (2) an output resolution or *printing resolution* (pixels per inch or per centimeter). These two parameters only matter when the image is printed. Just changing the output resolution does not affect your image's on-screen size. In other words, simply changing the output resolution will not affect the size of a Web image.

Many image-editing programs, such as Adobe Photoshop, let you change the output ppi in order to resize the image's pixel dimensions while keeping the output physical dimensions. In Photoshop, this option is called *Resample Image* and found in the *Image Size* dialog box (Figure 2.4). By resampling an image, you alter its pixel dimensions by scaling it up or down. You do not gain detail by resampling it up (*upsampling* or increasing the number of pixels), because the pixels added are extrapolated from the color information stored by the existing pixels. Instead, the image may become blurry. If you decrease the output ppi with the Resample Image option on, you will *downsample* the image (decrease the number of pixels), and information is deleted from the original image.

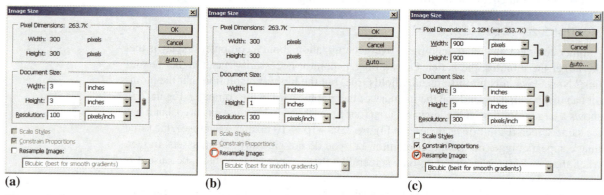

(a) (b) (c)

Figure 2.4 A screen capture of Photoshop's Image Size window, showing the resampling option to change the image's output resolution (a) Original image's pixel dimensions of 300 × 300 and output resolution of 100 ppi; its physical dimensions will be 3 inch × 3 inch when printed (b) Output resolution changed from 100 ppi to 300 ppi without turning on the resampling option (marked with a red circle): its physical dimensions are 1 inch × 1 inch when printed (c) Output resolution changed from 100 ppi to 300 ppi with the resampling option turned on (marked with a red circle) where the pixel dimensions increase to 900 × 900, so when it is printed, it is still 3 inch × 3 inch

When the PPI is increased or decreased with the resample option off (Figure 2.4b), the image's pixel dimensions remain unchanged. You will not see a difference in the image's on-screen size.

The resampling operation (Figure 2.4c) is called scaling and is normally not preferred, unless the image was created to intentionally undergo scaling or resizing for visual effects.

Keep in mind that the information lost as a result of downsampling will not be recovered with upsampling later. Similarly, an upsampled image cannot revert to the exact original by downsampling. To avoid the need to resample an image, it is crucial to understand resolution, to know how to determine optimal scanning resolution, and to correctly set the ppi to translate pixel dimensions into physical output dimensions.

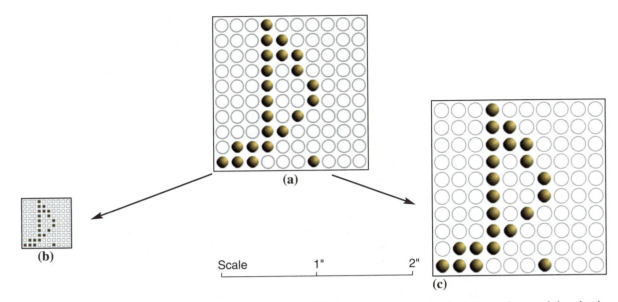

Figure 2.5 The pegboard metaphor illustrates the relationship between an image's pixel dimensions and the physical dimensions of its printed copy (a) A 10 × 10-pixel image is displayed on a monitor (b) Image printed at 20 ppi has physical dimensions of ½ × ½ inch (c) Image printed at 5 ppi has physical dimensions of 2 × 2 inches

Printing Resolution (ppi)—Does It Matter?

Let's use the pegboard metaphor to explain printing resolution (ppi). Here, a peg hole is analogous to a pixel of a digital image. The connection is similar to the one we drew between the pegboard and a monitor display, but now, pixels per inch is the important measure.

Suppose you have an image of on a 10 × 10-hole pegboard (Figure 2.5a) (10 × 10 pixels) and you want to "print" the whole pegboard onto other pegboards with different peg-holes per inch (output ppi). As illustrated in Figure 2.5 and keeping the same pixel dimensions, the output ppi controls the print's physical dimensions. The image printed at lower ppi is bigger but appears blockier than the one printed at higher ppi, but the detail remains the same; you do not lose or gain any detail by altering the output ppi unless you turn on resampling.

If, for some reason, a definite dpi cannot be determined at the time of scanning, then scan the source at the high end of a rough estimate. If an image has to be resampled, downsampling from a higher-resolution image is better than upsampling from lower resolution.

2.3 DIGITAL COLOR

At some point in your art education, you may have been told that you could create nearly any color by mixing red, yellow, and blue media—crayons, watercolors, oils, or acrylics. In theory, to create an orange color, you mix one part of red with one part of yellow. This mixing formula or instruction—1:1:0 of red:yellow:blue—can be thought of as a description of this particular orange color. Digital color is represented similarly—but in red, green, and blue (RGB) values. For a 24-bit color image, each red, green, or blue value ranges from 0 to 255. An RGB value of (255, 255, 0) represents a yellow color; an RGB value of (255, 128, 0) represents an orange color.

2.3.1 Difficulties Reproducing Colors Across Devices

If you have worked in any traditional medium, such as oil paint or watercolor, you have found difficulties when you try to reproduce the colors you see or to translate them across

Color gamut refers to the range of colors that a specific system can produce or capture. See *Digital Media Primer*, Chapter 2, for details.

media. There are many different "red", "yellow", and "blue" paints. For examples, Alizarin Crimson, Cadmium Red, and Venetian Red are all considered "reds", but their specific color differs. Bismuth Yellow, Cadmium Lemon, Indian Yellow, Lemon Yellow Hue, and Naples Yellow are various "yellows"; Cerulean Blue, Cobalt Blue, Ultramarine Blue, and Prussian Blue are "blues". Your choices among red, yellow, and blue paints determine the **color gamut** of your palette.

One artist's palette may use Alizarin Crimson, Bismuth Yellow, and Ultramarine Blue. It will be difficult to reproduce these colors exactly using a palette that is made up with Cadmium Red, Cadmium Lemon, and Cerulean Blue.

Suppose a canvas is covered with a solid orange color. The artist tells you how to reproduce it: by mixing exactly one part red with one part yellow. If you use a different palette, however, you will get a different orange color from that on the canvas. If for some reason, you have to adhere to your palette and still reproduce the artist's orange, what would you do? You probably would experiment with different color mixing ratios to find the closest match and ignore the artist's formula of one part red mixed with one part yellow.

Now, what if you have to reproduce yet another orange color from a different artist using your palette? This color was created with a different red and yellow, although the artist tells you that it is obtained by mixing one part of that red with one part of that yellow. Once again, you experiment by mixing your different colors to produce the closest match.

Such difficulties also exist in the digital realm. There are two main causes.

Cause #1: No computer device, including monitors, printers, scanners, and digital cameras, can reproduce all of the colors visible to humans. For instance:

- A scanner cannot reproduce all the colors in an analog photograph.
- A digital camera cannot capture faithfully all the colors you see in the scene.

Cause #2: Different devices have different color gamuts (palettes). The colors they are capable of producing differ to some extent by device type as well as by individual brand and model. For instance:

- The colors of an image printed by an inkjet printer do not match the colors of the same image displayed on a monitor exactly.
- The same digital image may look different in color on a different monitor.
- The same scene photographed by two different digital cameras may show different colors.
- The colors of an image scanned by two different devices do not match exactly.

2.3.2 The Concept of Color Management

In the previous hypothetical oil painting scenario, wouldn't it be nice if there was a standard reference palette—a *super-palette*—that contained all of the colors visible to humans, and each color was labeled with an ID number? In this case, every palette would have only a subset of the color numbers from the super-palette. Whenever you had to reproduce a color, you would just need its ID number. You would look up the set of color numbers in your palette to see if that ID number is among them. If so, then you know how to reproduce it. If not, you determine the closest color in your palette and use its formula based on your palette. The super-palette concept is how color is managed for digital images.

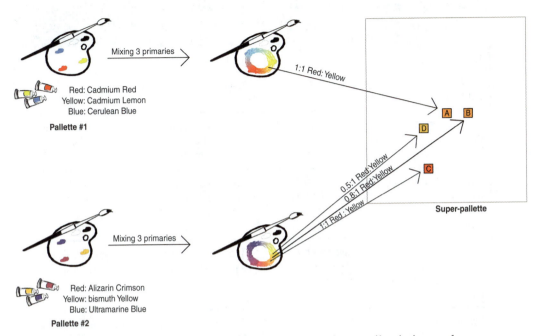

Figure 2.6 The concept of color management illustrated using an oil painting analogy

Figure 2.6 illustrates the idea of color management using the painting scenario. Mapping information to the super-palette is contained in a palette's color profile. For example, 1:1 of red:yellow → Color A is part of the profile of Palette #1. In Palette #2's Profile:

- 1:1 of red:yellow → Color C
- 0.8:1 of red:yellow → Color B
- 0.5:1 of red:yellow → Color D

The same 1:1 of red:yellow produces a different orange using Palette #2. If the orange produced by mixing 1:1 of red:yellow of Palette #1 has to be reproduced using Palette #2, the result may not be an exact match—only the closest match. In this hypothetical scenario, suppose Color B is determined to be the best match. Mixing 0.8:1 of red:yellow using Palette #2 is then used to reproduce the orange color of Color A.

How is Color B selected as the best match? Why not Color D or any other color? Different methods or criteria can be used to determine the "best" match. They pertain to the rendering intents of color management in printing.

A *color management system* (*CMS*) is a software solution intended to reproduce colors across different devices—digital cameras, scanners, computer monitors, and printers—in a predictable and repeatable way. It reads and translates colors between color gamuts of these different devices. A color-management workflow begins by calibrating and creating color profiles for each device. Leading programs for profiling include those from Gretag-Macbeth, Monaco, and Pantone.

Let's return to the painting scenario to explain calibration and color profiles. Table 2.1 summarizes the parallels between digital and traditional media color reproduction methods.

TABLE 2.1	Drawing an Analogy from Painting to Explain Digital Color, Difficulties in Reproducing Colors Across Devices, and the Concept of Color Management
Traditional Media	**Digital Images**
A palette using a particular combination of red, yellow, and blue paints.	Color gamut of a device.
The three primaries (red, yellow, and blue paints) used in a palette.	The primary colors of a device: for instance, the particular cyan, magenta, yellow, and black inks of an inkjet printer.
The formula for mixing the red, yellow, and blue paints to create a particular color: for instance, one part of red mixed with one part of yellow gives an orange color.	The numeric value of a digital color or the color value: for instance, the RGB value of an orange color is (255, 128, 0).
The same formula of color mixing does not produce exactly the same color using one made up from a different set of red, yellow, and blue paints.	The same RGB value does not give exactly the same color appearance across devices.
Hypothetical super-palette.	Standard reference color space that contains all the color human can see: CIE-XYZ or CIELab.
Referencing all of the colors of a particular palette to matching colors on the super-palette.	The color profile of a particular device.

The palette in this scenario is analogous to the color gamut of different devices. Notice that to maintain the analogy, it is limited to color mixing with only three primary colors, because computer devices mix only a limited number of colors in reproducing the colors of digital images. For instance:

- *Monitors use three colors of phosphor*: red, green, and blue (RGB). Different monitor models may have slightly different "reds", "greens", and "blues".
- *Offset printing generates colors by mixing four colors*: cyan, magenta, yellow, and black (CMYK). Some inkjet printers use seven colors: cyan, light cyan, magenta, light magenta, yellow, light gray, and black. Inks with the same name of different printers produce different appearance. For example, "cyan" inks of different printers produce different appearances of "cyan".

Color Profiles

The super-palette for color management in digital imaging uses the CIE-XYZ or CIE LAB color space. These two color spaces contain all of the colors that the average human eye can see. Therefore, they can serve as an objective color reference. For any device, the colors produced by different mixing can be matched to a color in the reference color space. This referencing establishes what is known as the ***color profile*** of that device. In other words, the color profile of a particular device describes how the device can produce a color. There are monitor profiles, scanner profiles, printer profiles, and profiles for digital cameras. Profiles can be embedded in a digital image file and can be assigned in a digital image-editing application.

Color space is a model for representing color in terms of intensity values of certain parameters. For example, in RGB color space, a color can be described in terms of the intensity of each of the red, green, and blue components. In this sense, a color space defines a multidimensional space that constitutes its color gamut. For example, a RGB color space can be represented by a 3-D cube—the red, green, and blue components define its three axes. Each color within this cube can be described by a 3-D coordinate in term of the red, green, and blue intensity values.

See the *Digital Media Primer*, Chapter 2, for information about CIE-XYZ, CIE LAB, and other common color spaces used in digital media.

Rendering Intents

In the previous scenario, when you try to reproduce a color produced from a different palette, you have to find out if the color's ID number is in your palette's profile. If not, your palette cannot reproduce that color exactly, and you will have to pick the closest match that your palette can produce. How do you pick the closest match? Eyeballing works in the painting scenario. However, digital color management relies on methods referred as *rendering intents* which use algorithms based on different criteria. You encounter these rendering-intent decisions in color-managed printing. To help you make an educated decision in selecting a rendering intent, a brief introduction to each method follows.

- *Perceptual*.
  This intent emphasizes human perception—the fact that the human visual system is more sensitive to relative color *differences* than absolute color values. In mapping the colors from one device to another, the relationship between colors is maintained at the expense of preserving color accuracy. This means that some of the original color values may be changed even if there are exact matches. This method works well for photographs.

- *Saturated*.
  This method emphasizes a color's saturation. It tries to map the original color to the best saturated color that a device can produce. This rendering intent is good for business and schematic graphics that usually use big areas of saturated solid colors. The relative color difference becomes less important.

- *Colorimetric (Relative)*.
  In mapping the colors from one device to another, this method compares the extreme highlight of the two devices' color space and shifts all colors accordingly.

- *Colorimetric (Absolute)*.
  The original color value remains unchanged if there is an exact match. The non-reproducible colors are matched to their closest reproducible color. Choose this rendering intent to maintain color accuracy at the expense of preserving relationships between colors.

2.3.3 Producing Consistent Color with Desktop Inkjet Printing

Many consumers print digital photos from their desktop inkjet printers without knowing anything about color management, and the prints look fine. So why must we care about color management in digital art? The color of a digital image that is not color managed and is inconsistent from the monitor to the printer will still not be off in print totally. For

ICC profiles are color profiles that use a cross-platform standard defined by the International Color Consortium (ICC).

Many printer profiles and the new profiles for different types of paper are available on the printer company's Web site.

Creating a Scanner Profile: A color target and a profile-generating software are needed to create a scanner profile. A color target is a print or a slide with well-defined color patches. The color target comes with a reference file describing the colors of the patches. The color target is scanned with the scanner to be profiled. The profiling software uses the color information from the color target's reference file and the resulting scanned colors to create a profile mathematically. The color target and the profiling software are expensive. In digital art where scanned images often undergo extensive alteration, creating scanner profiles may not be necessary.

instance, a skin tone will still look like a skin tone, not blue. But a consumer's expectations for occasional photos and an artist's expectation for a work differ. Color is one of the important elements in art and design, and artists make conscious choices about the colors in their works, which will be under scrutiny. The color in the final print should represent the artist's original intent as accurately as possible.

It is important to understand that color management does not guarantee *exact* color reproduction, because different devices have different color gamuts. One device may produce a color that is simply impossible for another device to reproduce. For instance, the bright, saturated colors producible on monitors are not printable with printers that use cyan, magenta, and yellow inks. Likewise, in analog media, it is impossible to reproduce an oil painting using markers.

Color management for printing a digital image with a desktop inkjet printer involves several steps.

Step 1 Create or Acquire Profiles for Your Devices

- *Monitor profile*: You can calibrate your monitor and create a profile for it using Adobe Gamma in Windows. For MacOS, you can use Monitor Calibrator. You also can use third-party hardware and software for more precision. You do not have to calibrate your monitor every time you need to print; once a year should be sufficient. After you have calibrated your monitor, do not change its brightness, contrast, and color settings.

- *Printer profile*: Some inkjet printers provide profiles. Some printers make available different profiles for different types of paper, because ink color can look different on different papers. For printers or types of paper for which you do not have profiles, you can create custom profiles with color management hardware and software. Without them, you may need to figure out by trial and error what profile produces the best result for your system.

- *Scanner profile*: A scanner profile makes the scanned colors agree as closely as possible with the actual colors of the source document being scanned.

The first color management profile you should create is for the monitor, because it is your working canvas in creating digital art. The display must represent the colors of your working digital images accurately. If the digital image is intended for printing, then a printer profile also is needed to maintain color consistency.

If the digital image is intended for use on the Web, you will have no control over how it will be displayed on other monitors. In this case, color management seems less crucial. However, you should still calibrate and profile your monitor to keep the color as consistent as possible and to represent the actual colors of your images.

If you need the colors of a scanned image to closely represent the actual colors of the source, then a scanner profile is critical. However, in situations where scanned images only are used as a reference or starting point for extensive alterations (which is common in digital art), capturing the actual color becomes less crucial.

Step 2 Set Up Color Management in Your Image-Editing Application

Not all digital-image application programs support color management. Adobe Photoshop lets you set up a color management workflow for image files. Refer to the Help of your application program about color management set up. There are two options in Photoshop: *assign a profile* and *convert to a profile*. Assigning a profile to an image does not change its color values. Converting an image's profile to a different profile will change the color values. To explain the difference, let's return to the painting scenario.

- Assigning a profile to an image is like maintaining the instruction or formula, "1:1 of red:yellow", but using the particular red and yellow of the new palette—not the originals. Therefore, the displayed color may look different when assigned with different profiles, although the RGB values are unchanged. For instance, in Figure 2.6, the orange Color A produced from Palette #1 will become Color B when reproduced on your canvas, although the formula 1:1, red:yellow will not change and will be passed along to the next person who may want to reproduce the color on your canvas.

- Converting to a profile is like changing the 1:1, red:yellow formula to 0.8:1, red:yellow to make the closest match of the color using the particular red and yellow of the new palette. The color values of the image are changed, and the color displayed on screen will look different. This approach is not the common way to work with profiles if you generally want to keep the original color values. The orange Color A produced from palette #1 will be reproduced as Color B on your canvas. The formula of 1:1 of red:yellow will be changed to 0.8:1 of red:yellow and passed along to the next person who wants to reproduce the color on your canvas. In this case, the original color formula is lost.

Step 3 Printer Settings

Some printer drivers (for example, drivers for models of Epson inkjet printers) and some applications (for example, Adobe Photoshop) have color management options. Photoshop does not recommend color managing in both the printer driver and Photoshop at the same time—use either one and turn off the color management of the other.

2.4 ART AND DESIGN ELEMENTS

Line, *shape*, *value*, *color*, *texture*, and *space* are the basis of visual elements across media in art and design. Although space is inherent to any physical artwork and can be considered a result of the interrelationships of the first five basic elements and human perception, artists shape and reconstruct the inherent space to create new space and new meaning. Hence, learning how to read and to shape space is as basic as learning how to read and create lines. Space is also an important factor in critiquing images. This chapter therefore addresses space along with the five basic art elements.

The following subsections examine how each art element works. After you have gained experience with them, they will become part of your artistic instincts. You will use them without having to think about or to analyze them. To help you understand their relationships, each element will be discussed in terms of answers to three questions:

The soft-proof option in Photoshop displays a simulated printed image on the monitor.

1. What is it?

The answer to this question generally defines the element. Some elements have a real and an imaginary representation. *Real* means, simply, physical presence. Each element has a simple and intuitive meaning that can be represented by a *real mark* on a surface. *Imaginary* means that the element's presence is only implied by other visual elements.

2. What are its aesthetic properties and languages?

Each element has its own unique characteristics and can create different aesthetic qualities and statements. The answer to this question intends to give you a basic idea of the element's properties and what you can do with them. The list will be by no means inclusive.

3. How does it work with or relate to the other elements?

Although these elements are introduced one by one, they almost never work alone. They interact to make up the whole. You can use one element to create or to manifest another. In some situations, they may counterbalance each other.

2.4.1 Line

What is it?

- A line can be thought of as a thin, continuous mark made by a pencil, a pen, or a brush on a surface.
- A line also can be imaginary, as it is implied by other visual elements on the surface.

What are its aesthetic properties and languages?

- *Direction and Movement*: A line can impart direction and movement to a piece and direct a viewer's attention within the piece.
- *Artist's Gestures*: A line's width can vary, adding dimension and implying the artist's gestures by giving a sense of varying forces and brush direction. Variable width of a brush stroke sometimes conveys a sense of elegance. (Figure 2.7)
- *Temperament*: A line can be thick, thin, curvy, smooth, jagged, tapered, straight, angular, continuous, and broken. Its different properties can convey different temperaments and movements. A variety of lines are used in the drawing shown in Figure 2.8. The group of lines at the upper left of (Figure 2.8b) conveys a sense of energy and activities.

(a)   **(b)**

Figure 2.7 (a) Constant line width (b) Lines with variable width

How does it work with or relate to the other elements?

A line is the most basic element. It can be grouped to create any other elements. The work shown in Figure 2.9 is made of lines and dots which form the shape and details of the face and create areas of light and shade. The direction of the lines conveys the 3-D form of the head—for example, the lines that form the hair and those in the neck.

(a)

(b)

Figure 2.8 (a) Alix Hitchcock's Spring Thaw, 1996, oil stick
and watercolor, 32" × 40" (b) A close-up view

Figure 2.9 Leah J. Hohman's *Untitled*, 2001, lithograph (Courtesy of John. P. Anderson Collection of Student Art, Wake Forest University)

(a)

Figure 2.10 (a) Alix Hitchcock's *Provincetown*, 1977, oil pastel, 20" × 15" (b) Geometrical shapes are outlined (c) An implied shape of triangle is outlined

(b)

(c)

Figure 2.10 *(continued)*

2.4.2 Shape

What is it?

- In its simplest definition, a shape is an outline or a silhouette of an object. For example, the work shown in Figure 2.10a contains many geometric shapes, as indicated in

Figure 2.10b, while the work shown in Figure 2.11 is made up with many organic shapes.
- A shape does not have to be a closed outline.
- Like lines, shapes need not be confined to a single, physical outline of a continuous area. They can be imaginary and implied by the grouping of other visual elements or objects.

Figure 2.11 Alix Hitchcock's Figure Forms, 2001, pastel, 22" × 30"

What are its aesthetic properties and languages?

- *Abstraction*: A shape is not dictated by exact specifications or its contents. It can be used for abstracting the object or a group of objects.
- *Negative space*: A shape without any content can create a sense of void and mystery, provoking viewers' thoughts. In this sense, it forms a negative space.

- *Inside and Outside*: An outline may be thought of as a shell—an outer surface of an object. The shape's inner content may be in harmony with or in opposition to the meaning of the outer shell (to convey conflicts).

How does it work with or relate to the other elements?

- *Implied shape*: An imaginary or implied shape can be formed by an arrangement of groups of any of the elements. For example, the implied triangular shape in Figure 2.10c is formed by a group of different shapes. The triangular shape draws the viewer's attention back to the center of the drawing.
- *Space*: Overlapping shapes can create a sense of space by creating a foreground and a background.
- *Texture*: Repetition of shapes can be used to create patterns. For example, in the work shown in Figure 2.12, repetition of shapes creates stripes and checker patterns. The patterns fill the larger shapes.

Figure 2.12 Alix Hitchcock's *Through The Mirror*, 1991, pen and ink, 11" × 14".

2.4.3 Value

What is it?

- Value denotes relationships of light and dark. Value is also called *tone*.
- Value is not about the color or *hue*. At the same time, the concept of value is *not* applicable only to grayscale artwork, like black-and-white photographs. Color information has a value, a saturation attribute, and hue. The same hue can have a higher value (lighter color) or a lower value (darker color).

What are its aesthetic properties and languages?

- *Mood*: Lightness and darkness have their implied moods. Value can be used to bring emotion to an artwork. Generally, lighter value conveys positive emotions, such as cheerfulness and hope. Darker values generally introduce a negative mood, such as melancholy or suspense.
- *Relativity of value*: Human perception of lightness and darkness is relative. Placing the same gray tone on a lighter background or a darker background creates a different perception of its value (Figure 2.13). The same gray tone on a lighter background seems darker when set on a darker background. The highlight of the sphere and the front face of the cube appear brighter on the darker background in Figure 2.13b. The shadow of the cube appears darker on the lighter background in Figure 2.13a. In Figure 2.13b, a slight halo seems to appear between shadow area of the sphere (lower right) and the black background, because the darker background makes the adjacent gray on the sphere look lighter, and the sphere's highlight makes the adjacent gray of the shadow area look darker.

> 🖱 **Relativity of Value of Human Visual Perception** A demonstration of relativity of value, as in Figure 2.13. In this demonstration, note how your perception of value of an object changes when you drag the cube and the sphere in and out of backgrounds of different values.

- *Contrast*: Contrast refers to the difference between the light and dark areas of an image. High contrast suggests a dramatic mood and can draw the viewer's attention. Keep in mind the relativity of value perception. High contrast can exist in bright or dark areas.

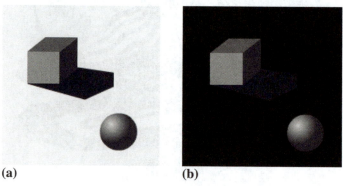

(a)   (b)

Figure 2.13 Demonstration of relativity of value where the same cube and sphere are placed on backgrounds of different values

How does it work with or relate to the other elements?

- *Lines*: A group of lines (as in hatching in drawing) can create different values or tones. For example, in the figure drawing shown in Figure 2.14, the variation of line density

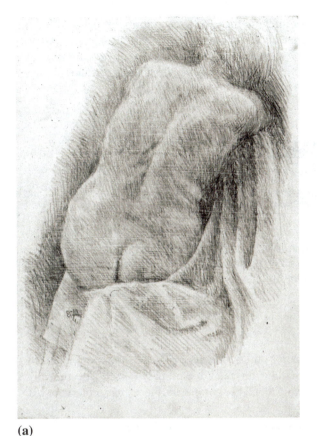

(a)   **(b)**

Figure 2.14 (a) Alix Hitchcock's *Torso Back*, 1972, silver point on board, 8" × 10". (b) A close-up view of the right shoulder

and intensity creates different values. The direction of the lines combined with the modulation of tones depicts the three-dimensional (3-D) form of the back of a human torso.

- *Shape and form*: Lightness and darkness create light and shadow, which can convey a sense of space and dimension for a shape. For example, in Figure 2.13, the light and shade on the sphere create a sense of 3-D roundness; we describe the shape as a sphere rather than as a circle. The shadow cast by the cube conveys its dimensionality.
- *Space*: Humans often perceive lighter-colored objects as closer and darker-colored object as farther away.
- *Texture*: Modulation of light and shadow can create patterns and depict surface texture.

2.4.4 Color

What is it?

- A color can be described by three properties: hue, value, and saturation.
- *Hue*: The seven rainbow colors comprise the hue property of a color.
- *Value*: Value determines the lightness or darkness of a color. Tint and shade also are used to describe a color's value. Tint refers to how much white is added, and shade refers to how much black.

- *Saturation*: Saturation of a color refers to the vividness or purity of its hue. With the same hue and value, a less saturated color appears more grayish. Note that lower saturation does not mean the color is darker or of lower value. A fully desaturated color is a gray of the *same* value. (Figure 2.15). For example, desaturating a color of higher value makes it a light gray and a color of lower value a dark gray.

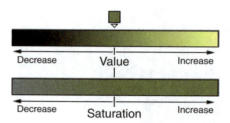

Figure 2.15 Value versus saturation of a color where the top bar shows changes in value and the bottom bar shows changes in saturation of the same color (in the middle of each color bar shown in the small color chip at the top)

COLOR MIXING

Some colors can be created by mixing others. **Primary colors** cannot be created by mixing. In visual art, red, yellow, and blue are the three primary colors. Theoretically, any other color can be created by mixing them. For computers, the primary colors are red, green, and blue.

Secondary colors are created by mixing two primary colors. For example:

orange = red + yellow
green = yellow + blue
purple = blue + red

The *complement* of a secondary color is the primary color that is not used to create it. Therefore, the complementary primary–secondary color pairs are

red : green
yellow : purple
blue : orange

It is easy to determine a color's complement on a color wheel (Figure 2.16). *Complementary colors* are opposite each other.

Analogous colors are colors close to each other on the color wheel. For example, orange is analogous to both red and yellow.

Of course, color mixing does not stop at the three secondary colors. You can mix any combination of the primary and secondary colors to create many more different colors. To help you visualize the color relationship—complementary or analogous—use the color wheel as a reference. For example, to determine the complement of a yellowish-green follow these steps.

Step 1 Imagine placing the color somewhere between yellow and green on the color wheel (Figure 2.17a). If the color is more on the yellow side, then place the color closer to the yellow.

In traditional media, colors are in the form of dyes and pigments. How do computers represent colors? See the *Digital Media Primer*, Chapter 2, for a detailed discussion of light and color mixing, additive and subtractive color systems, and how colors are represented on computers.

Figure 2.16 The color wheel where three primary colors are represented by circles, the secondary colors are squares and each secondary color is positioned between the two primary colors that are mixed to create it

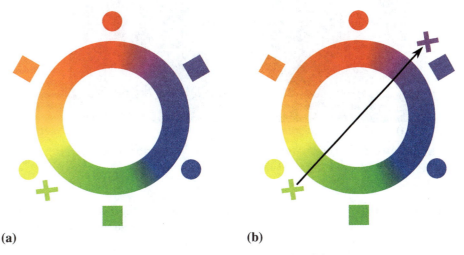

(a)   **(b)**

Figure 2.17 Finding the complementary color of a yellowish-green

Step 2 Draw a line from this yellowish-green through the center of the color wheel to the other side (Figure 2.17b). The color opposite is the complement. In this case, the complement of this yellowish-green is reddish-purple.

What are its aesthetic properties and languages?

- *Complementary color*: When two complementary colors are placed next to each other, they look more vibrant and dynamic than when they are used separately or placed next to their analogous colors.
- *Analogous color*: Analogous colors can give a sense of harmony, because they are made up of the same primary colors, differing only in percentages.
- *Color temperature*: In general, reds, oranges, and yellows are considered warm colors, while blues, greens, and purples are considered cool. Figure 2.18 shows the same

> **Color Wheel** A color wheel helps you to identify complementary color pairs and analogous colors.

Figure 2.18 The same illustration rendered in colors of different temperatures where the one using the red and yellow color scheme seems warm

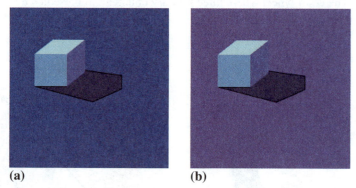

(a)   **(b)**

Figure 2.19 The background color in (a) is a warmer blue than the background color in (b)

illustration rendered in colors of different temperatures. Regardless of the general classification of warm and cool colors, each color has its warmer and cooler versions. For example, Figure 2.19 shows a warm and a cool blue.

- *Relativity of color*: The human visual system can adapt to different lighting conditions. For instance, white paper looks white whether it is placed under incandescent light or fluorescent light. It actually has a yellow cast under incandescent light, but our vision accounts for the yellowish lighting, and we therefore *see* or interpret it as white. Why should we care about this perceptual ability, when digital images are not sculptural objects that will be displayed under different lighting conditions? The relativity of colors tells us that the colors surrounding an object in an image can change how we *see* or interpret the color.

As shown in Figure 2.20b, you perceive the face in light brown color under the dark blue tint. Actually, it is more a grayish color. The highlight in the hair and the red cloth look brighter than the actually colors. To remove the context which may affect your perception, the skin tone colors from Figure 2.20a and Figure 2.20b are now placed against their respective background colors (Figure 2.20c and Figure 2.20d). You perceive a brownish

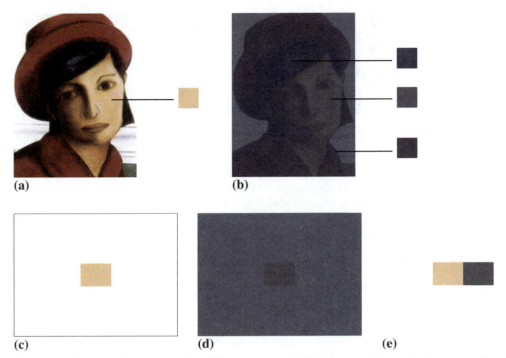

Figure 2.20 Relativity of color (a) An original image (b) Image with a dark blue color tint (c) Skin tone color from (a) against white background (d) Skin tone color from (b) against the dark blue background of (b) (e) Two skin tones placed side by side for comparison

color in Figure 2.20d. When the two skin tones are placed side by side (Figure 2.20e), the darker one does not appear as brownish any more.

- *Color association*: Some colors or combinations of colors carry associations or symbolic meanings. Sometimes, the symbolic meaning is not universal but culturally dependent. For example, for Americans, the use of red, white, and blue may symbolize patriotism, because they are the colors of the flag. People of other cultures may not see them this way. White often is associated with purity and weddings in Western societies, but many Asian cultures associate white with funerals and mourning.

> ⊗ **Relativity of Human Visual Perception of Color**   A demonstration of the relativity of color. You can drag a mask onto the image to help you perceive the actual colors.

How does it work with or relate to the other elements?

- *Shape*: An imaginary shape can be formed by creating an area of a specific color temperature.
- *Value*: Every color has a certain value.
- *Space*: Humans tend to perceive warm colors as closer and cool colors as farther away. Brighter colors seem to project forward in space, while darker colors tend to recede. In Figure 2.21a, the yellow center appears to protrude from the blue color. In Figure 2.21b, the blue center appears to recede, as if we are looking into a long tunnel.

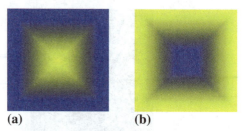

(a)   **(b)**

Figure 2.21 The brighter yellow color, appears to be closer to us than the darker blue (a) The center appears to pop up toward us (b) The center appears to recede, as if we are looking into a tunnel

2.4.5 Texture

What is it?

- Texture refers to the apparent *feel* of a surface.

What are its aesthetic properties and languages?

- *Feeling*: In the physical world, texture is felt by our sense of touch, and we often associate the visual image of a texture with a feeling. In visual art, texture can be used to evoke a feeling through the sense of sight. To convey a feeling using texture, think about the characteristic that imparts that feeling in the physical world. Then use it to guide the visual representation of that feeling. Depending on your work, the texture for an object does not have to always match the reality.
- *Flatness*: Texture does not have to have a dimensional and tactile look. Flat patterns can be used as texture to give a different aesthetic quality—flatness.
- *Detail*: Texture adds visual details that you may not want the viewer to scrutinize. It may build up a feeling of clutter and too much information if overapplied.
- *Contrast*: Placed in juxtaposition, textures of different "feelings" can create psychological contrasts.

How does it work with or relate to the other elements?

- *Line*: Texture can be created by a group of lines, such as hatching. For example, in the work shown in Figure 2.22, a tactile feel of roughness of tree trunks is conveyed through hatching. The work also uses many different styles of hatching (Figure 2.22b through c), adding textural variations.
- *Shape*: Texture adds detail to a shape. A repeated pattern on objects of similar shape can unify the overall image. For example, the work shown in Figure 2.23 demonstrates the use of patterns to create texture. In addition, the repetition of short strokes of blue lines in three different patterns (Figure 2.23b through d) creates a visual unification.

See Human Perception of Depth in the next subsection on space.

- *Space*: Texture can add depth and dimension. Texture appears denser and smaller when it is observed from a farther distance. The change of density of the pattern shown in Figure 2.23 adds a sense of depth.

(a)

(b)   (c)   (d)

Figure 2.22 (a) Alix Hitchcock's *Figure/Tree Rise,* 1998, oil stick and ink, 32" × 40"
(b) through (d) Closeup views

2.4.6 Space

What is it?

We can look at space in three aspects of an artwork:
- Physical size of the work
- Illusion of 3-D space created in the piece
- Positive and negative space relationships of elements within the piece

What are its aesthetic properties and languages?

- *Size of the work*: Size reflects the space of the piece that you can work within. Images
  are often in rectangular format. In traditional media, such as oil painting and watercolor, you decide the exact size and aspect ratio (ratio of the width to height) of the
  canvas. For digital art that is intended for display on a monitor, the size and aspect
  ratio are fixed by the monitor. If those of the image differ from the monitor's, part of

Figure 2.23 (a) Alix Hitchcock's. *The Child*, 1987, pastel, 22" × 28" (b) through (d) Closeup views

the image may be cropped off, or there may be empty space around the piece. The role of this extra space should not be ignored. Think of the monitor as a frame. The extra space around the image is like the mat in a framed artwork. The mat's size, color, and texture should support the image. Sometimes the mat and the frame become part of the artwork.

DISPLAYING IMAGE WORKS

Images often are framed in a rectangle form. However, the work of images does not have to be displayed in a rectangular format. Images physically can be cropped and reassembled. The digital print shown in Figure 2.24 is composed of seven vertical strips of digital prints. Some are images of different recognizable objects. Other strips are made of similar horizontal stripes to unify the work through repetition. The horizontal stripes draw the attention across the piece and create a counterbalance for the strong vertical orientation of other strips.

Figure 2.24 Holly Ivanoff's *Ten* (from *Counterpoint in Eleven Movements*), 2000, digital print on gatorfoam panels, 36" × 26" (Courtesy of John. P. Anderson Collection of Student Art, Wake Forest University)

- *3-dimensionality*: The illusion of 3-dimensional (3-D) space adds depth and can expand the space within the 2-dimensional (2-D) image.
- *Positive and negative space*: These types of space are created by the relationships between elements within the piece. Positive space often is considered the space occupied by the main subject, while all other areas are considered negative space. For example, in portraiture, the person is perceived as the positive space and the background as the negative space. However, negative space is not just the leftover space in a piece. Negative spaces can make the piece more visually interesting by breaking up the positive space. In some situations, the negative space plays a role as

Figure 2.25 Alix Hitchcock's *Model with Fan*, 2001, watercolor and pencil, 20" × 15"

important as—or even more important than—the positive space. For example, we normally consider human figures as foreground and the empty space as the background. In the work shown in Figure 2.25, the white space itself is a figure like the other three main figures. However, it also looks like a void ripping through the painting breaking up the background space into two shapes: one (dark) appears to recede and the other (yellow) to protrude. The adjacent yellow shape appears to project itself forward as a foreground figure. This creates an interesting visual relation between the positive and negative spaces.

How does it work with or relate to the other elements?

- Space works closely with all other elements because it results from their interaction.
- *Perspective*: The illusion of 3-D space is closely related to perspective. Perspective will be covered in Section 2.5.5.

HUMAN PERCEPTION OF DEPTH

For most sighted persons, depth perception is taken for granted. However, when you try to create the illusion of space and depth in a 2-D image, you need to know the various **depth cues** that the human visual system uses to interpret 3-D space. There are two categories of depth cues: physiological and psychological. Physiological cues of depth are related to human binocular vision and how our lens focuses at different depths.

Psychological depth cues include linear perspective, shading and shadowing, aerial perspective, interposition, retinal image size, texture gradient, and color.[*] The more cues, the stronger the sense of relative depth can be conveyed to the viewer.

[*]David F. McAllister, ed. *Stereo Computer Graphics and Other True 3D Technologies*, Princeton, N.J.: Princeton University Press, 1993.

Psychological cues are intuitive. You may have used them in your work without having to stop to think about them. Nonetheless, itemizing these cues provides a guide that will help you analyze illusory space in artworks.

- **Linear Perspective**: Linear perspective refers to the perceived size of an object changing in inverse proportion to its perceived distance from the viewer. In other words, the farther the object is from the viewer, the smaller it seems. Art and design commonly use parallel lines converging to a vanishing point to accentuate perspective and space.
- **Shading and Shadowing**: The shading cue refers to the brightness of an object in relation to a light source. The farther the object is from a light source, the less light it receives from that source, and thus, it will appear darker. In the physical world, an illuminated object casts shadows. The shape of the shadows gives cues of both the shape and depth of the object. The distance between a shadow and the object also provides the cue for the distance between the object and the surface that receives the shadow. As shown in Figure 2.26a, without any shadows, the three gray circles are simply flat circles lining up horizontally in the image. In Figure 2.26a, the middle circle now appears to be sitting on the ground. The gray circle on the right appears to be hovering over the ground and appears to be closer to the viewer. The distance between the gray circle and its shadow provides a cue of the height of the circle from the ground plane. Shading can be added to the lower part of the gray circles to make the lighting and, hence, their dimensions more coherent.

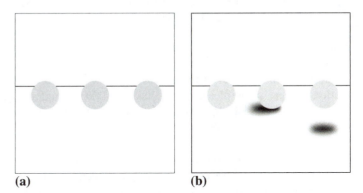

(a)　　　　　**(b)**

Figure 2.26 Shadows convey the illusion of space and spatial relationships as shown between elements (a) without any shadows (b) with shadows

- **Aerial Perspective**: Distant objects often appear to be fuzzy, hazy, bluish, and less saturated.
- **Interposition and Occlusion**: When an object is partially blocked by another object, we perceive the one being blocked as farther away and the blocking object as closer.
- **Retinal Image Size**: When we apply linear perspective to compare the distances of more than one object from us, we often also take a cue from our knowledge of the object's usual physical size. For example, if a depicted mountain appears to be the same size as, or even smaller than, a person, we interpret that we must be much closer to the person than the mountain. It is because we have learned from our experience that mountains are much larger than humans.

Note that our experience influences how we interpret the elements in an artwork, which either may help or counter your intent. Abstracting an object without using its representational form can remove some associative meanings.

- **Texture Gradient**: Texture adds visual details to objects. A distant object appears to be smaller, and its details also become coarser and less distinct. For example, the texture on a tree trunk is less defined at a distance. While you can see individual leaves and branches at a reasonable distance, you do not see these details in a forest on a distant mountain.
- **Color**: Bright-colored objects generally appear closer than dark-colored objects.

 Psychological Depth Cues

This interactive demonstration contains an illustration that uses various psychological depth cues to create an illusory of 3-D space. You can turn the different depth cues on and off separately in order to compare the spatial difference with and without a depth cue.

These basic elements do not work alone. Instead, they often are interwoven to create more complex visual elements in art and design. There are basic visual organization principles for combining basic elements. These principles also are interconnected and work as a whole. Before we look at these organizational principles, let's go over several factors in how we perceive and interpret our environment.

2.5 PSYCHOLOGY OF SEEING—PERCEPTUAL ORGANIZATION PRINCIPLES

In 1920s, a *Gestalt* psychologist[†] suggested several principles of human's perceptual organization in relation to vision. These principles describe how we group or segregate the elements we perceive, and they offer insight into how we interpret our environment. A brief introduction to these principles provides a foundation for understanding the organizational principles of art and design. After all, artworks are intended for human perception and interpretation, and composition is about organizing different elements into wholes.

These principles of visual perception include *proximity*, *similarity*, *common fate*, *good continuation*, *closure*, *figure–ground relationship*, and *past experience*. For illustrative purposes, simplistic examples are used, but these principles can be applied and combined to create complex compositions.

Proximity

Proximity pertains to our tendency to group elements that are closer together in preference to those that are farther apart. Figure 2.27 shows three matrices of 5×5 dots. You may organize them in many different ways, and different people organize them differently. In Figure 2.27b, the dots are closer together in the horizontal direction than in the vertical direction, so we tend to perceive a set of five rows. We see a set of five columns in Figure 2.27c.

[†]For example: Max Wertheimer, "Untersuchungen zur Lehre von der Gestalt," II, *Psychol. Forsch.*, 1923, 4, 301–350. English translated version can be found in: Max Wertheimer, "Laws of Organization in Perceptual Forms" in Willis D. Ellis, A Source Book of Gestalt Psychology, pp.71–88; or online at http://psy.ed.asu.edu/~classics/Wertheimer/ Forms/forms.htm. You also can look up Gestalt psychology in the books and research articles in psychology.

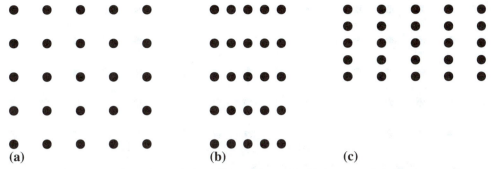

Figure 2.27 Illustration of proximity effects where (a) all dots are placed at an equal distance, (b) dots are closer together in the horizontal direction, and (c) dots are closer together in the vertical direction

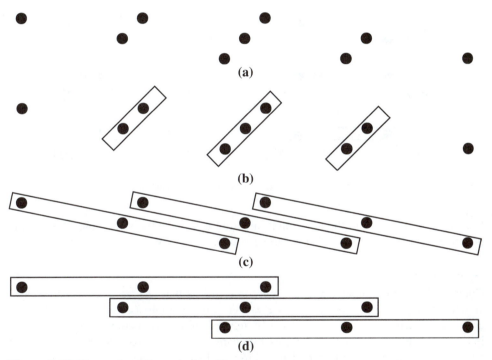

Figure 2.28 Illustration of proximity effects

Figure 2.28 shows another example. The dots are placed closer in one diagonal direction. Again, there are many ways to group these dots. The rectangles in Figure 2.28b through d indicate three alternatives. However, we tend to mentally group these dots as shown in Figure 2.28b.

Similarity

We tend to group elements that are similar to each other in some way. Figure 2.29 shows three matrices of 5 × 5 dots. In Figure 2.29a, all of the dots have the same color. You may organize them in many ways, and different people organize them differently. In

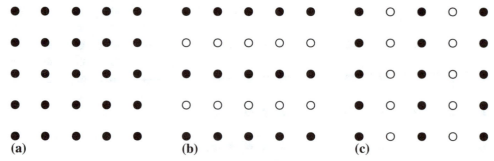

Figure 2.29 Illustration of similarity effects

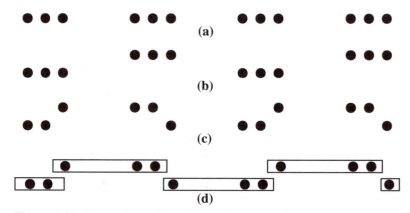

Figure 2.30 Illustration of the effects of common fate

Figure 2.29b, the dots in the horizontal direction now have the same color. We tend to perceive a set of five rows. We tend to perceive a set of five columns in Figure 2.29c.

Common Fate

Common fate refers to our tendency to group elements that change their properties synchronously. For example, in Figure 2.30a, we perceptually group a cluster of three dots that are close to each other. When a change—an upward shift—occurs to some of the dots (as in Figure 2.30b) it seems natural, because the change occurs to perceived groups. However, when the same upward shift is applied to different dots (as in Figure 2.30c) the result is a little discomforting, confusing, and unexpected. The change shown in Figure 2.30c suggests a new grouping that contradicts our natural perceptual grouping, which is illustrated by Figure 2.30d.

Good Continuation

We tend to perceive changes within the same grouping as continuous and gradual in the same direction. Any abrupt change is perceived to result from the introduction of a new group or a branch.

In Figure 2.31a, dots are arranged as straight and oblique segments. We naturally perceive the grouping as shown in Figure 2.31b where the dots in the straight segment are arranged continuously in regular spacing in one direction and are perceived as the same

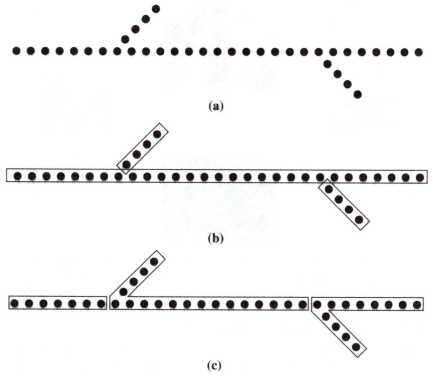

Figure 2.31 Illustration of effects of good continuation

Figure 2.32 Illustration of effects of closure

group. The oblique segments are interpreted as appendages. There are many other ways to group the dots. For example, Figure 2.31c suggests one way to group the dots, but it is not what we naturally perceive.

Closure

Closure refers to our tendency to fill in lost fragments of visual information to make the object seem intact. For example, we mentally fill in tree branches that are hidden by leaves so that we see the tree as a whole. For the example shown in Figure 2.32a, we tend to mentally connect the lines to make the shapes whole (Figure 2.32b).

The photographic work shown in Figure 2.33 arranges four photographs of body parts such that it leaves gaps among the photographs. Although sizes of the body parts and their placements are not in scale, we mentally fill in the gaps to create a whole picture. The imagination that requires us to fill in to connect these not-in-scale body parts makes the piece interesting.

Figure 2.33 Matthew Verga's *Credentials*, 1999, gelatin silver prints, 7 ¼" × 5 ¼" (Courtesy of John. P. Anderson Collection of Student Art, Wake Forest University)

Figure–Ground Relationship (Foreground–Background)

We are able to distinguish the foreground from the background and to direct our attention to the foreground object. In order for us to do so, the object must have relatively distinctive characteristics to differentiate itself from the background; for example, color difference, a clear enclosure boundary, or seeming to move relatively more than the background.

Past Experience

Our experience influences how we interpret our environment. In particular, representational objects and text carry associative meanings that inevitably infuse into our apprehension and perception of object grouping.

Applying Multiple Principles

More than one principle can be applied to the same work. They can work cooperatively or in opposition. Working cooperatively can strengthen the visual perception. When principles work in opposition, they can create interesting illusory effects. As demonstrated in Figure 2.34c, the effects of proximity and similarity are working cooperatively. The perception of five rows is affirmed. In Figure 2.34d and Figure 2.34e, the effects of proximity and similarity are working in opposition. For Figure 2.34d, sometimes the dots may appear to be in rows while other times they seem to be in columns.

The perceptual effects in an artwork are complex. No matter how conscious you are about creating an intended effect, other effects of which you are unaware may compete with your intention. Critique provides a good opportunity to learn what others see. It is not uncommon to discover opposing effects during critique.

2.6 COMBINING ART AND DESIGN ELEMENTS—ART AND DESIGN ORGANIZATIONAL PRINCIPLES

In general, there are several common organizational principles for combining the art and design elements in a composition. They are *unity and harmony*, *balance*, *repetition and rhythm*, *emphasis and focus*, and *perspective*. The visual principles of composition are like

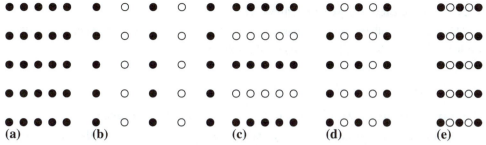

Figure 2.34 (a) Effect of proximity: you see five rows when the dots are horizontally closer to each other (b) Effect of similarity: you see five columns when the equally spaced dots have the same color in the vertical direction (c) Effects of proximity and similarity working cooperatively (d) and (e) Effects of proximity and similarity working in opposition

a glue that holds all of the elements together within a piece. Without a good composition, all of the elements in the piece will seem to be disjointed units that are simply thrown together without a unified purpose.

It cannot be emphasized enough that art and design principles are introduced to students as general guidelines to begin with in both creating and critiquing art. These rules can be bent or broken, but first you must be conscious of what you are bending or breaking, what you intend to accomplish, and what the results will be. Bending the rules for one element often affects the other elements that make up the whole piece. You must ask yourself: Will breaking the rule here serve the overall composition and the intent of the entire piece? Breaking the rules without being conscious of the *what* and *why* may lead to inconsistency in the overall composition and intent of the art, giving the impression of amateurish and careless execution. Don't leave a broken rule unresolved in your artwork only because you do not know how to fix or to create the visual elements that follow the principles.

These principles are given as general guidelines. Note that they do not define the limit to which you can apply them. Excessive application of a principle without considering the piece as a whole will have undesirable side effects. As you read their descriptions, you may find that some principles' intended effects may be in opposition to each other. Proper practice will use each principle to complement the others, but blindly overapplying any one causes conflicts with the others, creating confusion. Think of these principles as the five food groups or the nutrition pyramid. The idea is to give you a guide for a balanced diet. Excessive consumption of any one type of food may cause negative effects and will not compensate for insufficient consumption of the others.

In the following subsections, each basic visual principle will be introduced and explained in terms of answers to three questions:

1. What does it mean, and how can we identify it in a piece?

This answer intends to give a general definition of the concept behind the principle.

2. What are the aesthetics it can create?

This answer intends to give you ideas about the aesthetic qualities that adherence to the specific principle can produce and how it may glue the different elements together. The qualities described here are by no means the only ones that these principles can achieve. Creative ways to make new aesthetic statements remain possible.

Because visual concepts are interrelated and their visual results somewhat overlap, trying to break down the subject of composition into individual principles is problematic. Different artists and textbook authors may have a slightly different list or group these principles differently.

3. What are the ways we can achieve it?

This answer explores some mechanisms for achieving the desired effects through different uses of the art and design elements and provides examples.

2.6.1 Unity and Harmony

What do they mean, and how can we identify them in a piece?

- In a piece that has achieved unity, its different elements work together to convey a feeling that they belong together.
- Imagine a part of the piece in isolation. Do you have the urge to put it back where it was? Do you feel that it belongs with the whole piece?
- *Unity can be visual.* It also can be conceptual, which means that the work expresses a unified idea. Both types of unity are important to make an artwork strong.
- Harmony is about finding a visual rhyme scheme by combining elements that accent their similarities.
- In a harmonious composition, the elements—even standing in opposition—share common visual or conceptual attributes.
- Too much variation or contrast between elements can break up an image's sense of harmony.

What are the aesthetics they can create?

- The piece naturally will appear whole visually and conceptually. All of the individual elements will contribute to the whole effect. Without unity, different parts of the piece will look disjointed.
- Harmony can reinforce unity.
- Harmony makes the work visually pleasing.

What are the ways we can achieve them?

Unity and harmony are closely related principles. But they are different. Unity can be created by visual linking of various elements in a piece. For example, scattered houses can be connected by adding a road. Sharing similar colors and architectural design for the houses adds harmony.

Creating the visual elements coherent with the idea being expressed reinforces the sense of unity. For example, an active and dynamic subject may utilize an oblique design, rough texture, high contrast, and angular lines, while the passive and quiet subject is more consistent with horizontal design, soft texture, low contrast, and monotonous lines. If the active and the passive subjects share enough similar visual attributes—for example, analogous colors—it will convey a sense of harmony.

Most of the ideas here are founded on the perceptual organization principles discussed in the previous section.

- *Line*:
  - Use a line style consistent with the theme of the piece.
    - Variable line width versus the same line width
    - Organic (curved, flowing) versus angular
  - Different elements can be linked together by sharing imaginary lines that imply direction or path of action.

- *Shape*:
  - Use shapes that are visually or conceptually similar.
    - Visually similar: organic versus angular
    - Conceptually similar: repeat objects that carry similar meanings; different shapes can be brought together by their similar conceptual associations
  - Recall that shapes do not have to have a single continuous outline; they can be imaginary as well as made up of multiple elements or objects. Multiple elements arranged to make up a shape will be perceived naturally as a group.

- *Value*:
  - Use light and shadow consistent with the mood of the piece.
  - Use similar values throughout the piece.

- *Color*:
  - Use the color temperature consistent with the mood of the piece.
  - Recall that a color is made up with three components: hue, value, and saturation. Using a palette of similar hue or saturation on different elements can bring them together.
  - Use of analogous colors can create a sense of harmony.

- *Texture*:
  - Different elements with the same textural quality—highly tactile versus a flat pattern—will be viewed generally as related to each other.

It should be emphasized that coherence or consistency does not mean using only one single line style, one texture pattern, or one color throughout the piece. Simply repeating the same component will create a boring result. **Variety** makes the work more interesting. Still, too many unrelated variations will make the work disjointed. Variants of the same component can be connected by sharing some properties. Variants can share similar shapes or concepts but may have a different size and color. For instance, repetition of a pig does not create as strong feeling of a farm as using pigs, cows, horses, chickens, goats, and sheep together.

In the photograph shown in Figure 2.35, the cars basically are facing the same direction. The slight disorders of the cars add variety and make the photograph visually more interesting. In addition, some cars are in motion while others stay still.

2.6.2 Balance

What does it mean, and how can we identify it in a piece?

- Balance refers to the distribution of the visual weight of the different elements in the piece.
- The composition lacks balance when one part of the piece overwhelms the rest. A piece that lacks balance often makes viewers feel uncomfortable, although they may not be able to pinpoint the problem right away. Their attention may keep leaving the piece or stick on one part of the piece and fail to look at the whole.

What are the aesthetics it can create?

- A piece that has balance gives a sense of harmony, while an out-of-balance piece creates tension.
- Tension is not necessarily bad. It can increase interest by breaking the dull quiescence created by a perfect balance. Too much tension, however, can make the viewer uneasy.

Figure 2.35 Marcia Eaddy Baker's *Order in Paris*, 2000, photograph (Courtesy of John. P. Anderson Collection of Student Art, Wake Forest University)

BALANCE, SYMMETRY, AND THE RULE OF THIRDS SYMMETRY

Symmetry may seem like a synonym for balance, but it is not the only way to create balance in an artwork. In some situations, symmetry is viewed as a form of beauty. However, sometimes symmetry makes an image dull and static. For example, making the focal point the dead center of an image may suggest perfect balance, but it often is perceived as a very static and uninteresting composition.

If the dead center is where we try to avoid placing the emphasis, then where should we place it? The ***rule of thirds*** suggests we place it one-third (or two-thirds) of the way from the edge of the image. This rule is used as a guide for a balanced image, while avoiding the dead center. Again, like any rule, this one is just a guide.

What are the ways we can achieve it?

The weight of any part of a piece can be created not only by size but by value, color, space, texture, and the arrangement of groups of elements to convey a sense of density.

- *Line*:
  - The thicker the line, the heavier it looks.
  - How the line spreads across the piece also spreads out its weight
  - A group of lines conveys a sense of density that depends on how closely together the lines are drawn.

- *Shape*:
  - A larger shape looks heavier than a smaller one.
  - Recall that a shape can be imaginary and made up of multiple elements. The arrangement of these elements influences our perception of the size of the shape that they make up. For example, a group of many smaller shapes can be used to balance a single large shape.

- *Value*: Lighter colors look lighter, while darker colors look heavier.

- *Texture*:
  - The rendered texture can have associations with physical objects. For example, a rough, stone-like texture will convey a heavier weight than a linen texture.
  - Whether tactile or flat, texture often is applied as a tiled pattern. The scale of the single unit affects how dense the tiling will be. A denser tiling generally suggests larger weight.

- *Space*:
  - Negative space generally is perceived as empty and weightless, while positive space is perceived to have weight.
  - The illusion of space that gives a sense of depth to the piece extends the balance into the 3-D illusory space, not just the 2-D display space.

- *Implied Motion*: The anticipation of an object's motion in an image can make viewers imagine the space where it should arrive. The imagined motion also implies weight. The implied thrust on the ball in Figure 2.36a creates a mental image of the anticipated space the ball will occupy, as shown in Figure 2.36b. Figure 2.36c removes the implied motion, and the image loses balance as the weight is now concentrated on the right-hand side of the image. In the photograph shown in Figure 2.35, most of the space is occupied by motionless cars. The driving cars occupy only a smaller area on the left. The activities created by the motion of the driving cars add weight to that smaller area, thus balancing the large area of motionless cars.

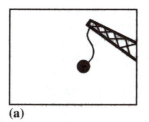 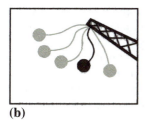 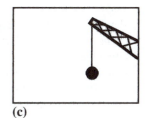

(a)   (b)   (c)

Figure 2.36   Balance by implied motion

2.6.3 Repetition and Rhythm

What do they mean, and how can we identify them in a piece?

- Repetition refers to multiple appearances of a visual element within a piece.
- In music, rhythm is characterized by the pattern of beats repeated *over time*. Similarly, in a visual image, rhythm refers to how the visual elements are repeated *across the space*; that is, the relative placement of the repeated elements.

What are the aesthetics they can create?

- Applying repetition in a piece can often convey an immediate sense of unity.
- Repetition does not necessarily mean exact duplicates. Repeating an exact copy of an object may create monotony. Consider adding variations to the repeated elements.
- Repeating an element can create a sense of grouping. When the repeated elements are arranged in an imaginary line, they can imply motion or direction.

What are the ways we can achieve them?

Repetition can be applied with any of the basic elements—using a similar line style or width, shapes, values, colors, and textures over and over. The rhythm is related to the systematic placement of the repeated elements. Arrange them at spatial intervals that do not have to be equal. Intervals increasing or decreasing in one direction can create a more interesting rhythm and imply motion.

2.6.4 Emphasis and Focus

What do they mean, and how can we identify them in a piece?

- Adding emphasis to a specific part of the piece draws the viewer's attention to it.
- If a piece has a focus or emphasis, viewers often find themselves drawn to it first.

What are the aesthetics they can create?

- Adding a focus to a piece helps to catch the viewer's attention.
- The focus serves as a starting point for viewers' response to your piece.
- If the emphasis is too strong, viewers will be stuck at that specific part of the piece. The emphasis should be prominent enough to attract attention but then release it to the other parts of the piece. For example, an implied line or motion leading out from the focal point helps to direct the viewer's attention.

What are the ways we can achieve them?

- The simplest way to add emphasis is to create differences in line style and width, shape, value, color, texture, and spatial relationships. In the photograph shown in Figure 2.35, the open areas in the middle of the traffic jam and the moving cars become the focal points. In addition, these two areas—being brighter than the rest of the image—draw the viewer's attention.
- Repetition and rhythm can be used to build up or to dispel any unintended focus, so that the intended focus will be more prominent.
- Lines (real or imaginary) can imply motion and direct the viewer's eye within the piece. Converged lines draw attention to the vanishing point.

2.6.5 Perspective

What does it mean, and how can we identify it in a piece?

- Perspective refers to the way something looks from a certain point of view.
- Perspective often aims to create the illusion of 3-D space to simulate our physical world. Because it intends to simulate accurate physical space, the organization principle of perspective has more specific guidelines than the other principles.

- This principle works closely with the space element. To understand perspective, see Section 2.4.6 on the space element and the previous discussion of human depth perception.

What are the aesthetics it can create?

- Perspective creates depth by creating the illusion of 3-D space.
- Bending this principle can create a different kind of reality that only exists in the piece.

What are the ways we can achieve it?

Human perception of depth is the foundation for techniques to create perspective. The size, position, shading, and obscurity of an object influence our perception of its depth. In visual art, several techniques can help you create the illusion of linear perspective. The most basic include either a one-point perspective or a two-point perspective.

- *One-point perspective* uses only one vanishing point. It follows two basic rules.
  - The lines (real or imaginary) that govern the third dimension move away from the viewer and converge to the vanishing point.
  - All other lines that frame the other elements in the piece, vertical and horizontal, remain parallel to each other (Figure 2.37).

- *Two-point perspective* uses two vanishing points to convey depth (Figure 2.38). The rules are similar to those for one-point perspective.
  - The lines (real or imaginary) that govern the third dimension converge to one of two vanishing points.
  - Only the vertical lines that govern the shape of the other elements must remain parallel, not the horizontal ones.

> 🖰 **Two-point Perspective**   A demonstration of two-point perspective construction.

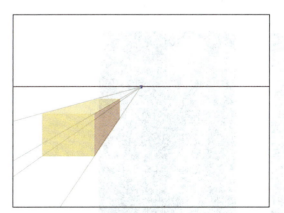

Figure 2.37 A box constructed with one-point perspective where the vertical and horizontal lines are parallel to each other and the lines that govern the third dimension converge to a vanishing point

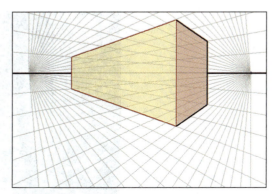

Figure 2.38 An image of a box constructed with two-point perspective (note the two vanishing points on both sides)

- *Isometric perspective* is similar to one-point perspective, except that it does not use a vanishing point. The lines that govern the third dimension are oblique and all of them are parallel to each other (Figure 2.39). Because this technique eliminates the size factor in linear perspective, the illusory space that it creates is less realistic.

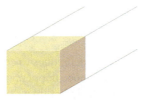

Figure 2.39 An image of a box constructed with isometric perspective

2.7 CRITIQUING DIGITAL IMAGES

Based on the general steps for critique suggested in Chapter 1, this section gives suggestions specifically for critiquing digital images.

1. Describe what you see.

Start with a straightforward factual description of what you see. Imagine you are describing the image to someone over the phone. Your description should give sufficient visual information for that person to sketch it. Let's take an example: How would you factually describe what you see in Figure 2.40a? Perhaps, "The only thing in this image is a

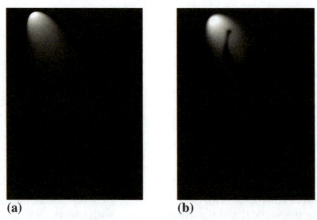

(a) (b)

Figure 2.40 How would you factually describe what you see in these images?

bright spot in a black background. It is placed at the upper left region diffusing toward the lower middle . . . " and so on. You also could describe the size of the spot, its color, and the length through which it fades out. You also might comment what it looks like to you, say, a spotlight in the dark. Try not to describe your emotional or cognitive response, using words like mysterious, enclosed, or isolation. In Figure 2.40b, there is a dark shape in the light area. The factual description may include human-like body parts and gestures seen in the image. Be careful to distinguish between the gesture you see and the non-visible gesture that you only infer from what you see.

2. Describe what you see in terms of the art and design elements and principles.

Use the basic elements and organizational principles as guidelines to discuss the properties of the image's visual components.

- Do you identify any lines, shapes, textures, and spaces?
- What are the values and colors of the elements in the image?
- How are these elements combined in the image?
- Does their interaction convey a sense of unity and balance?
- Is there repetition and rhythm in the piece?
- Is there a focal point in the piece? If yes, where is it?
- Where do your eyes look first? What is your order of looking?
- Is there any part of the image you keep returning to?
- Are there any imaginary lines or shapes?
- Does the composition keep your eyes within the image?
- What is the style of the piece—abstract or realistic?
- Does it seem to bend or break any rules? If so, does it seem intentional? Does the disruption support the intent of the piece?
- What is the perspective created in the piece? How does it place the viewer's position or role within the piece?

You also can start discussing the emotion and meaning these elements convey to you.

- What are the mood and feeling as a whole?
- How are these moods and feelings conveyed? What makes you feel that way?
- Are there different moods in different parts of the image?

3. Discuss the subject matter.

What do you think the image is about? What does it mean to you? What do you think the image is trying to communicate? Do other students' responses change your initial reactions? Discuss how the artist's choices of compositional elements work or do not work with the subject matter.

4. Discuss the execution of techniques.

Scrutinize the image for its craftsmanship. How is the work executed? Here are some sample questions pertaining to technical craftsmanship and professionalism.

- Is the image a bitmap, vector graphic, or a combination of these? Can you identify which part is bitmap and which part is vector graphic?
- Are the edges of the composite objects clean and seamless? If not, do you think it is intentional? Why do you think so?
- Is the image color corrected properly? Is there any color cast or color tint in any part of the image? If so, do you think it is intentional? Why do you think so?

- Does the image have the proper resolution for its intended display method?
- Is there any blockiness or pixelation due to insufficient resolution? If so, do you think it is intentional? Why do you think so?
- Is there any unintentional jaggedness in the vector shapes?
- Are there any unintentional small, crack-like voids or empty spaces between elements?
- Is there any dust or dirt from the scanned image?
- Do the sharpness and contrast of the image look deliberate?
- Are there any non-original or copyrighted materials? Can they be replaced by original materials? If not, why not? Do these materials carry any specific associative meaning? Is being non-original important to the image? For example, if da Vinci's drawings are used, it is because the work uses these drawings to form a commentary.
- If the non-original materials have to be replaced by original materials, can you suggest what they might be?

5. Student artist responses

The student artist can respond to the other students and talk about the original intent, intended subject matter, and any unsolved problems in the image. Students are encouraged to continue responding to expand the discussion, which now has new information about the piece from the artist.

TERMS

aerial perspective, 67
analogous colors, 58
assign a profile, 48
balance, 72
bitmap images, 34
CCD array, 36
closure, 68
color, 49
color management system (CMS), 45
color profile, 46
color temperature, 59
colorimetric intent, 47
common fate, 68
complement of a color, 58
complementary colors, 58
convert to a profile, 48
depth cues, 66
downsample, 42
dpi (dots per inch), 36
emphasis and focus, 72
figure–ground relationship, 68

good continuation, 68
hue, 56
image size, 42
interposition, 67
isometric perspective, 79
line, 49
linear perspective, 67
occlusion, 67
one-point perspective, 79
past experience, 68
perceptual intent, 47
perspective, 72
physical dimensions, 42
pixel, 36
pixel dimensions, 36
ppi (pixels per inch), 36
primary colors, 58
printing resolution, 42
proximity, 68
rendering intents, 47
repetition, 72
resample image, 42
retinal image size, 67

rhythm, 72
rule of thirds, 76
saturated intent, 47
scanning resolution, 36
Secondary colors, 58
shading, 67
shadowing, 67
shape, 49
similarity, 68
space, 49
symmetry, 76
texture, 49
texture gradient, 68
tone, 56
two-point perspective, 79
unity and harmony, 72
upsampling, 42
value, 49
variety, 75
vector graphics, 34

LEARNING AIDS

The following learning aids can be found at the book's companion Web site.

⌐ **Pegboard and Resolution**
An interactive tutorial using the pegboard as an analogy to explain resolution in capturing and displaying digital images.

⌐ **Relativity of Value of Human Visual Perception**
A demonstration of relativity of value, as in Figure 2.13. In this demonstration, note how your perception of value of an object changes when you drag the cube and the sphere in and out of backgrounds of different values.

⌐ **Color Wheel**
A color wheel helps you to identify complementary color pairs and analogous colors.

⌐ **Relativity of Human Visual Perception of Color**
A demonstration of the relativity of color. You can drag a mask onto the image to help you perceive the actual colors.

⌐ **Psychological Depth Cues**
This interactive demonstration contains an illustration that uses various psychological depth cues to create an illusion of 3-D space. You can turn these different depth cues on and off separately in order to compare the spatial differences with and without a depth cue.

⌐ **Two-point Perspective**
A demonstration of two-point perspective construction.

REVIEW QUESTIONS

When applicable, please select all correct answers.

1. What are the six basic art elements discussed in this chapter?

2. What are the five organizational principles of art and design viewed in this chapter?

3. What are the perceptual organization principles introduced in this chapter?

4. What are the psychological depth cues for human perception?

5. What is the main difference between one-point perspective and two-point perspective?

6. What are the two main causes of difficulties in reproducing colors in digital images?

7. Which of the following should be the first profile you create or acquire in color management?

   A. monitor profile
   B. printer profile
   C. scanner profile

8. Which of the following rendering intents works well for photographs?

   A. colorimetric (absolute)
   B. colorimetric (relative)
   C. perceptual
   D. saturated

9. Which of the following rendering intents works well for business schematics?

    A. colorimetric (absolute)
    B. colorimetric (relative)
    C. perceptual
    D. saturated

10. Which of the following rendering intents preserves the most color accuracy?

    A. colorimetric (absolute)
    B. colorimetric (relative)
    C. perceptual
    D. saturated

11. **True/False:** A color management system guarantees *exact* color reproduction.

12. Suppose your computer screen resolution is set to 1600 × 1200, and you want to create an image that will occupy a quarter of a screen based on your monitor screen size.

    i. What are the pixel dimensions of the image?

    ii. You post this image on your Web site. Your target audience's computer-screen resolution is only 800 × 600 pixels. When they look at your image, how big is the image relative to its screen?

    A. one-eight of the screen
    B. one-quarter of the screen
    C. one-half of the screen
    D. three-quarters of the screen
    E. larger than the maximized browser window can fit in

13. **True/False:** A digital image can gain detail if it is displayed on a higher resolution monitor.

14. **True/False:** Displaying a digital image on a high-resolution monitor will increase the image's resolution.

15. **True/False:** Displaying a digital image on a high-resolution monitor will increase the image's file size.

16. **True/False:** A digital image captured by scanning a 1-inch × 1-inch picture will always displayed as 1 inch × 1 inch on a Web page viewed by any monitor.

17. **True/False:** A digital image will gain detail by increasing its ppi during the image editing.

18. **True/False:** A digital image will gain detail by resampling.

19. **True/False:** A digital image can be printed with more detail by increasing its ppi before printing.

20. A digital image captured by scanning will have larger pixel dimensions if _____.

    A. it was scanned using a higher scanning dpi
    B. it was scanned from a bigger photograph

21. Which of the equations given correctly describes the relationships among pixel dimensions, physical dimensions, and scanning dpi?

A. Pixel dimension of the scanned image = Physical dimension of the picture to be Scanned × Scanning dpi

B. Pixel dimension of the scanned image $= \dfrac{\text{Physical dimension of the picture to be scanned}}{\text{Scanning dpi}}$

C. Pixel dimension of the scanned image $= \dfrac{\text{Scanning dpi}}{\text{Physical dimension of the picture to be scanned}}$

22. To ensure a digital image will be displayed in the relative dimensions that you want (say, one-fourth of the screen width) on a Web page, you need to find out _____.

A. the monitor resolution of the target audience to calculate the image's pixel dimensions

B. dpi of the target audience's monitor to calculate the image's pixel dimensions

C. the monitor resolution of the target audience to calculate the image's physical dimensions

D. dpi of the target audience's monitor to calculate the image's physical dimensions

EXERCISES AND ACTIVITIES

1. Sketch a simple piece (on the computer or on paper) that bends one or more art and design principle discussed in this chapter. For example, use a bright color to create a negative feeling and a dark color to create a positive feeling.

2. Look up an artwork—digital or analog. Describe it to another student to sketch. Compare the sketch with the original artwork. How closely the sketch matches the artwork may reflect how detailed your factual description of the artwork is.

3. Look up an artwork—digital or analog, and critique both the work's composition in terms of the art and design elements used in the work and the organizational principles.

4. i. Find out the screen resolution of your computer display.

   ii. The aspect ratio of a computer display is the ratio of the width to the height of the screen. What is the aspect ratio of your computer display based on the resolution settings found in part (i)?

Yue-Ling Wong

Creating Digital Images

CHAPTER

3

GENERAL LEARNING OBJECTIVES

In this chapter, you will learn:

- To get started learning a digital image program.
- Digital imaging tools to aid creating traditional art.
- To create a digital image by combining digital drawing and painting, digital photography, and scanning.
- Technical considerations for creating Web images for portfolio.
- Technical considerations for creating print images for portfolio.
- Possible ways to incorporate the art and design elements and examine the application of organizational principles with digital imaging tools.
- To create a convincing composite.
- To use digital imaging tools to explore ideas for abstract and non-representational works.

3.1 LEARNING NEW SOFTWARE TOOLS

Many digital imaging tools emulate or extend traditional art techniques. For example, the dodge and burn tools in digital photo-editing programs are based on the darkroom techniques of the same names. Therefore, having a background in traditional art will help you understand these digital tools—their concepts and how they are supposed to work.

Some digital imaging tools are unique in the digital realm. Without having an in-depth working knowledge of a digital image program, you may feel at a loss in coming up ideas for realistic "do-able" class projects. Still, many traditional art techniques are not part of the digital imaging tools; technology cannot replicate every single aspect available in traditional art. When you are new to digital imaging, at times, you may feel you are juggling fluency in the software tools and the art. This section intends to provide you with several suggestions in getting started to learn a new digital image program.

Digital Media Primer Chapters 2 and 3 provide background readings for the digital imaging terminology used in this chapter. However, if you prefer finishing this chapter before reading those chapters, mark down the terms that you need more information while you read this chapter. Then, refer to the *Digital Media Primer* chapters afterwards.

3.1.1 Copying

Copying a masters' work is one of the methods of learning art techniques. This approach also can be used with digital imaging tools and to learn digital techniques. The advantage of this approach is that the target image gives you a direction to head in and a destination to reach. It eliminates the juggling of learning the tools and the art, and lets you concentrate on the learning the use of the tools. You often can gain appreciation of the design of the original work when you scrutinize it during copying. It also can broaden your perspective of what effects are possible with a creative use of tools.

After you have learned the basics of a digital image program, try to replicate an existing work—digital or non-digital—that you like. Do not worry about if you are using the right or wrong tool. It is a hands-on practice and a learning experience. Use the tools that you know. When you get stuck and cannot seem to accomplish the effect used in the original, look up Help menu on your computer or resources on the Web. For many beginners, this top-down goal-oriented learning method often is more effective and interesting than the bottom-up approach (learning tools by tools first.)

3.1.2 The Basics—What to Learn First

There are so many things to learn in a digital image program, such as Photoshop. If you feel at a loss in figuring out how to start, here are a few suggestions. Adobe Photoshop is the program that this text based on. However, digital image-editing programs usually have very similar interfaces and features. These suggestions can be applied to learning other digital image programs.

Digital Media Primer Chapters 2 and 3 explain in detail how to determine an image's pixel dimensions or resolution.

1. Workspace.

Be familiar with the workspace first. You need to be able to identify the Tool palette, document window and Layers palette. When you continue learning the program, whether you are reading books or watching tutorial movies, you will encounter these terms. Therefore, the workspace is the basic building block in your learning process.

Of course, one of the very first things is to find out how to create a new file properly. Starting a new file is easy—a standard command of File > New. However, for bitmap images, you need to specify the pixel dimensions or the physical dimensions and ppi for the image. If you only want to start exploring the program and do not have a project in mind, try 1200 × 900 pixels. This corresponds to a 4 inch × 3 inch printed image if printed at 300 ppi.

◇ **Photoshop Workspace** A screen-capture movie introduces the workspace of Adobe Photoshop.

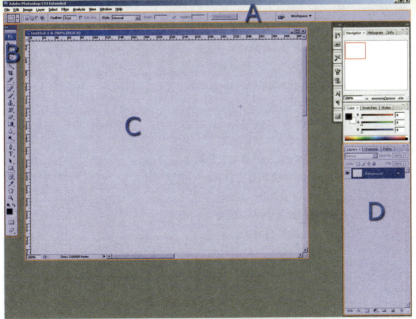

? Self-Test Exercises: Adobe Photoshop Workspace*

Figure 3.1 A screenshot of Adobe Photoshop CS3 workspace

---

*Answers to the self-test exercises: (1) C;   (2) D;   (3); B;   (4) A

In Figure 3.1:

1. Document window is labeled as: **A   B   C   D**
2. Layer palette is labeled as: **A   B   C   D**
3. Tool palette is labeled as: **A   B   C   D**
4. Option bar is labeled as: **A   B   C   D**

2. Tool palette.

The tool icons on the Tool palette are pretty self-explanatory. You also can place the mouse cursor over each icon to find out the name of each tool. Feel free to click on the tool and try it out. The ***Brush tool*** is a good tool to start with. Once you know their names, you always can look up how they work by entering their names in the keyword search in the Help menu.

> ✏ **Photoshop Tool Palette** A screen-capture movie introduces the Tool palette in Adobe Photoshop.

The Tool palette in Photoshop also has color chips that let you set the color for the ***Brush tool***, ***Pencil tool***, and ***Paint Bucket tool***.

> **(?)** **Self-Test Exercises: Photoshop Tool Palette**[†]
>
> Shown in Figure 3.2 is the Photoshop CS3 Tool Palette. Each tool is labeled with a letter. Identify the following tools.
>
> 1. **Brush** tool is labeled as _____.
> 2. **Stamp** tool is labeled as _____.
> 3. **Crop** tool is labeled as _____.
> 4. **Eraser** tool is labeled as _____.
> 5. **Eyedropper** tool is labeled as _____.
> 6. **Hand** tool is labeled as _____.
> 7. **Heal** tool is labeled as _____.
> 8. **Lasso** tool is labeled as _____.
> 9. **Magic** Wand tool is labeled as _____.
> 10. **Marquee** tool is labeled as _____.
> 11. **Move** tool is labeled as _____.
> 12. **Quick Mask** tool is labeled as _____.
> 13. **Zoom** tool is labeled as _____.

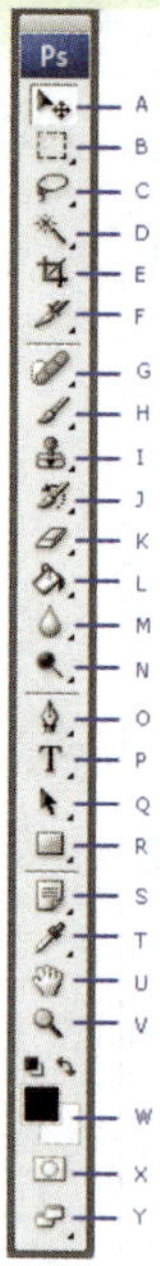

Figure 3.2

[†]Answers to the self-test exercises: (1) H;   (2) I;   (3) E;   (4) K;   (5) T;   (6) U;   (7) G;   (8) C;   (9) D;   (10) B;   (11) A;   (12) X;   (13) V

3. Layers.

The layer is an essential tool in digital imaging. As a start, learn how to create new layers, delete layers, rearrange the order of layers, toggle the visibility of layers, and adjust the opacity of layers.

> ⟡ **Photoshop Basics: Using Layers** A screen-capture movie and a worksheet exercise on the basics of the Layers palette in Photoshop.

4. Learn how to make selections.

Here is an overview of the different categories of selection tools by task. Find out how each of these selection tools work by looking them up the Help menu.

- Geometric shapes: *marquee tools* and *polygonal lasso*
- Making freehand selection: *lasso* and *pen tool*
- Color: *magic wand*, and menu command that lets you select by color
- Painting: *quick mask*

> ⟡ **Photoshop Basics: Selection (worksheet exercise)** A worksheet exercise to identify the different selection tools in Photoshop.

In addition, you can *add, subtract, intersect, exclude and invert selections*. This helps you combine selections or cut selections out of other to make a complex shape.

? **Self-Test Exercises: Photoshop Selection Tools‡**

I. Listed here are selection tools and commands related to selection. Match the best tool with the description in the questions.

    A. Lasso

    B. Magic Wand

    C. Magnetic Lasso

    D. Marquee

    E. Polygonal Lasso

    F. Quick Mask

    G. Select > Select All

    H. Select > Deselect

    I. Select > Feather

    J. Select > Invert

  1. To select all pixels: _____

  2. To deselect any selection: _____

  3. To inverse a selection: _____

  4. To make a rectangular or elliptical shape selection: _____

  5. To make a selection by freehand drawing the selection border: _____

  6. Which lasso tool is the best to make a selection of an irregular object with straight edges? _____

  7. To make a selection of an object with complex edges set against a high-contrast background: _____

---

‡Answers to the self-test exercises: I. (1) G; (2) H; (3) J; (4) D; (5) A; (6) E; (7) C; (8) B; (9) F
II. (1) B; (2) C; (3) D

8. To make a selection based on the similarity in colors: _____

9. To make a selection by painting a mask: _____

II.

ABCD

Figure 3.3

Choose the correct selection adjustment option (found in the option bar, Figure 3.3) for the task:

1. To add to a selection: **A   B   C   D**

2. To subtract from a selection: **A   B   C   D**

3. To select only an area intersected by other selections: **A   B   C   D**

5. Basic image adjustment tools.

The concepts behind adjusting histograms and using the color correction tools are discussed in the Digital Media Primer *Chapter 3.*

The common tools include adjusting the histogram, color balance, color curves, and hue/saturation. Different tools use different graphical representations of the color or tonal values of the pixels in the image and thus offer different types of control.

Adjusting the histogram and color correction is the basic tools. **Adjusting the histogram** lets you define and re-map the shadows, midtones, and highlights using sliders. It is called **adjusting levels** in Photoshop. The ***Color Balance tool*** works by letting you offset one color by moving the corresponding slider towards its complementary color. This is useful for removing color casts of images.

? Self-Test Exercises: Interpret and Predict the Results of Levels Adjustment[§]

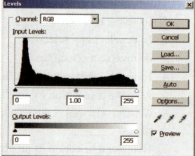

(a)   (b)

Figure 3.4

? Self-Test Exercises: Interpret and Predict the Results of Levels Adjustment (*continued*)

Shown in Figure 3.4 are an image and its histogram. Match the following Levels adjustment settings to the following correct resulted images.

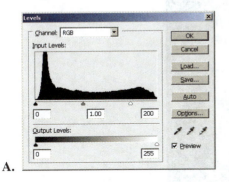

A.

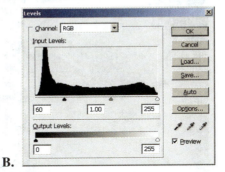

B.

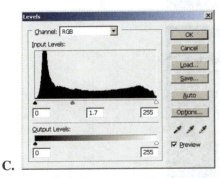

C.

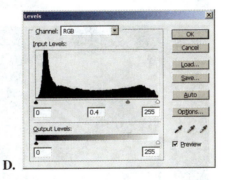

D.

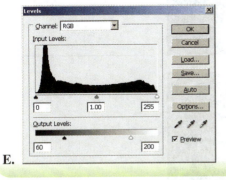

E.

1. _____

2. _____

3. _____

4. _____

5. _____

3.1.3 Methods of Learning

In addition to books, common mediums to learn about a new software program include tutorial movies, hands-on practice, Help menu, and training classes. No matter what methods you choose, it is important for you to take notes and hands-on try out the tools. The notes do not have to be in an electronic format. If you keep a sketch book, you can designate several pages for notes about digital imaging tools.

---

§Answers to the self-test exercises: (1) A; (2) D; (3) C; (4) E; (5) B

Tutorial Movies

These are movies that capture the on-screen activities to show you how to work with the tools. There are tutorial movies available at this book's Web site. Commercial sites, such as lynda.com and adobe.com, also have tutorial movies available.

Just by watching tutorial movies is not enough to become proficient with a digital image program; you need to try out the technique hands-on as soon as possible. Use the techniques while you are watching the tutorial movies. You do not have to wait until the whole movie finishes before trying out the techniques demonstrated in the movie; you can always pause the movie while you are trying out the technique. Open the digital image program and arrange its window side-by-side with the tutorial movie. When you try out the technique in your digital image program, you still can see the paused movie on-screen and use it as a visual reference of what to do.

Tutorial movies often are designed around tools, not by task. These movies are like a multimedia user reference. If you just watch the movies without applying the techniques in a hands-on project, you probably will forget the techniques soon. It also is important to take notes of what you have learned from each movie—even just the tool name, what it does, and how to find the tool.

Hands-On Practice

Hands-on practice is essential to learn any form of studio art for any media. There are tutorial books available. You learn by following the project lessons. *Adobe's Classroom in a Book* is an excellent source. There also are many project lessons available on the Web. Learning-by-doing projects takes more time than watching the tutorial movies, but it guides you through hands-on experience with a combination of tools and techniques. It may inspire creative ideas for your own projects.

Help Menu

In addition to listing the help content by topics, the Help menu in almost all programs allows you do keyword searches. This is a handy tool to look up information about a tool. After all, you easily can find out the names of the tool or icon by placing the mouse cursor over it.

Training Classes

Many schools provide students informal training sessions on digital imaging tools. You may want to check out these services at your school. Many art centers and community colleges also offer Photoshop courses.

3.1.4 Moving Onto the Next Level

After you have learned the basics, the next level of useful tools is the various image-adjustment tools and those that support non-destructive image editing.

More Image-Adjustment Tools

The Curves adjustment tool is a powerful color and tonal adjustment tool available in many image-editing software. You can specify different amounts of adjustment and control different contrasts for different ranges. Hence, manipulating curves to make color or tonal adjustment gives you more control than adjusting the histogram or color balance.

CURVES ADJUSTMENT TOOL

In a 2-D plot, there are two axes: *x*-axis (horizontal) and the *y*-axis (vertical). The line or the curve shows the relationship between the *x*- and *y*-values. For adjustment curves, both the *x*- and *y*-axes represent the spectrum of the tonal values from darkest to brightest. Conceptually, each axis is similar to the horizontal axis in a histogram—except that now you have both the vertical and horizontal axes representing the tonal range shown as a gradient bar next to each axis.

So, how are the *x*- and *y*- axes different? In Photoshop, by default, the *x*-axis is input and the *y*-axis is output. Think of the input as "before" and the output as "after"—as in before and after applying the adjustment using the Curve tool.

Above or Below the Diagonal Line—Darker or Lighter

The default diagonal straight line shown in Figure 3.5 does not alter the tonal value of the image.

A curve that like in Figure 3.6 lowers the tonal value of the original image (i.e., the image becomes darker). As you see, the corresponding gray on the output axis is darker than the input gray value.

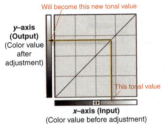

Figure 3.5 A diagonal straight line in the Curves adjustment tool

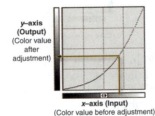

Figure 3.6 This curve specifies lowering the original tonal value

To help you tell whether the resulting tonal value will be darker or brighter, you can imagine the presence of the default diagonal straight line—a straight line drawn from the upper-right corner to the lower-left corner—like the colored diagonal line shown in Figure 3.7.

- If the portion of the curve is above the default straight line, then the resulting color will be brighter.
- If below, then the resulting color will be darker.

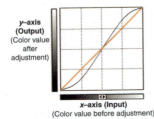

Figure 3.7 Imagine a diagonal straight line, like the colored line shown here

Because the direction of lightness on the axes can be reversed, be careful which direction you are using. No matter which direction is used it will give the same result if you adjust the curve correctly. For this example:

- Figure 3.8a: The *y*-axis goes from dark to light upward. The portion of the curve is below the default straight line. The resulting color will be darker.
- Figure 3.8b: The *y*-axis goes from light to dark upward. The portion of the curve is above the default straight line. The resulting color will be darker, as Figure 3.8a.

Either representation gives the same result—in this example, the tone of the image will become darker. The orange-colored line is included to help you visualize the diagonal line.

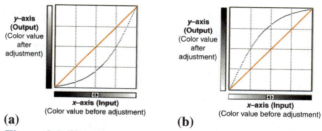

(a)   **(b)**

Figure 3.8 The same curve shown with different directions of the *x*- and *y*-axis (a) Axes with default direction from black to white (b) Axes with a reversed direction from white to black

Curve Steepness and Image Contrast

The curvature of the curve controls the contrast. If a region of a curve is steeper than the default straight line, then the contrast of the tonal range within that region will be increased. In the example shown in Figure 3.8, the contrast of the highlight areas is increased, but the contrast of the shadow areas is lowered.

In summary, two properties of the Curves adjustment tool that determine the color adjustment are

- Being above or below the diagonal line determines the brighter or darker adjustment.
- The slope controls the contrast.

Understanding and Applying Curves for Color Adjustments An interactive tutorial and exercises help you understand the Curves tool for image adjustment.

I.

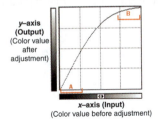

Figure 3.9

The following questions are based on the adjustment curve shown in Figure 3.9.

1. After the adjustment, the overall tonal value will be _____.

    A. brighter

    B. darker

2. _____ of the curve is steeper than the default diagonal line, and thus after the adjustment, the contrast for the tonal range within that region will be _____.

    A. Region A, higher

    B. Region A, lower

    C. Region B, higher

    D. Region B, lower

II. **The "S-curve"**
    The "S-curve" often is used to boost the contrast of an image. Let's see why.

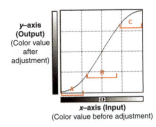

Figure 3.10

The following questions are based on the adjustment curve shown in Figure 3.10.

1. After the adjustment, the **highlight** area (Region C) will become _____.

    A. brighter

    B. darker

2. After the adjustment, the **shadow** area (Region A) will become _____.

    A. brighter

    B. darker

3. The curve in _____ is steeper than the default diagonal line, and thus after the adjustment, the contrast of the image in that region will become _____.

   A. Region A, higher

   B. Region A, lower

   C. Region B, higher

   D. Region B, lower

   E. Region C, higher

   F. Region C, lower

III.

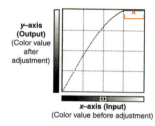

Figure 3.11

The following questions are based on the adjustment curve shown in Figure 3.11.

1. After the adjustment, the **highlight** area (Region A) will become _____.

   A. all white

   B. all black

2. After the adjustment, the overall tonal value other than in Region A, will become _____.

   A. brighter

   B. darker

3. The curve other than in Region A is _____ than the diagonal line, and thus after the adjustment, the contrast of the image (except the highlights in Region A) will be _____.

   A. steeper, higher

   B. steeper, lower

   C. less steep, higher

   D. less steep, lower

IV.

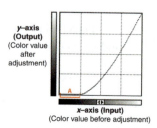

Figure 3.12

The following questions are based on the adjustment curve shown in Figure 3.12.

1. After the adjustment, the **shadow** area (Region A) will become _____.
   A. all white
   B. all black
2. After the adjustment, the overall tonal value (except that in Region A) will become _____.
   A. brighter
   B. darker
3. The curve other than in Region A is _____ than the diagonal line, and thus after the adjustment, the contrast of the image (except the highlights in Region A) will be _____.
   A. steeper, higher
   B. steeper, lower
   C. less steep, higher
   D. less steep, lower

V.

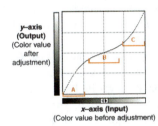

Figure 3.13

The following questions are based on the adjustment curve shown in Figure 3.13.

1. After the adjustment, the **highlight** area (Region C) will be _____.
   A. brighter
   B. darker
2. After the adjustment, the **shadow** area (Region A) will be _____.
   A. brighter
   B. darker
3. The curve in _____ is **less steep** than the default diagonal line, and thus after the adjustment, the contrast of the image in that tonal region will be _____.
   A. Region A, higher
   B. Region A, lower
   C. Region B, higher
   D. Region B, lower
   E. Region C, higher
   F. Region C, lower

For examples
of these non-
destructive image
adjustments, refer
to the *Digital
Media Primer*,
Chapter 3.

? Self-Test Exercises: Interpreting Curves (*continued*)

4. After the adjustment, the **contrast** of the **highlight** area (Region C) will be _____.
   A. higher
   B. lower

5. After the adjustment, the **contrast** of the **midtone** area (Region B) will be _____.
   A. higher
   B. lower

6. After the adjustment, the **contrast** of the **shadow** area (Region A) will be _____.
   A. higher
   B. lower

Non-Destructive Methods in Image Editing

There are three common non-destructive methods in image adjustments: adjustment layers, a layer mask, and a clipping mask. Non-destructive means that the original color information of the pixels is not lost after the adjustment. The original color can be recovered by removing the adjustment at any time.

Adjustment layers are for applying image adjustments, such as Levels and Color Balance, to a layer without altering the pixel color information on that layer. Instead, an image adjustment layer is a separate layer by itself. It applies the adjustments to all of the layers below it—unless you create a clipping group. The advantage of using an adjustment layer instead of applying the adjustment on an individual layer is that it allows you to change the adjustment settings. It is like you can reapply a different adjustment to the original image. In addition, you can delete the adjustment layer to remove the adjustment or hide the adjustment effect temporarily by turning off the visibility just like any other layers.

A *layer mask* is associated with a layer and lets you obscure—just obscure, not delete—part of the image on that layer. This non-destructive method of editing offers the advantage of preserving the original image in that layer. Later if you change your mind in how you want the image on that layer to show, you can always revert back to the original image on that layer and start over.

A *clipping mask* works very similarly to a layer mask. While a layer mask is associated with a single layer and only masks that one layer, the clipping mask works like a cookie cutter cutting through multiple layers that are in the same group. A clipping mask can act as a mask for multiple layers.

3.2 DIGITAL IMAGING TOOLS—CREATING TRADITIONAL ART

There are at least two ways that digital imaging tools can be used to aid in creating traditional art: getting image references and exploring composition.

Digital imaging and digital video are the common media for artists to get image references. The composition for an oil painting can be experimented with using digital images before transferring to the canvas. Photographing each state of the oil painting is not new to artists. Many have been doing so with film cameras. With the digital technology, the state of a painting can be captured with digital photography directly into digital images, which then can be manipulated to test out ideas for the next step. It is like a sketch book in a sense, but now the sketches can be made directly on a digital replica of the current state of the painting.

There are several features of the digital imaging program that make it such a good "sketch book" to aid in creating traditional art.

- *Rapid reproduction*. The current state of the work can be captured instantly with digital photography.
- *Ease of manipulability of digital images.*
- *Undo*. The capability to "undo" encourages experimentation. At the time of writing, Photoshop allows only one step "undo". However, it also has a History palette (Figure 3.14) that keeps a log of the changes you have recently applied to the image. The bottom one is the one most recently applied. You can step backward or forward. You can also select any of the states to revert the image to that state.

(a)   (b)   (c)

Figure 3.14 Adobe Photoshop History palette (a) A list of commands applied to the image (b) Click on any one on the list to revert to the previous stage—notice the items below the selected one are dimmed, but you can select any of them if you change your mind (c) If you revert to the previous stage by deleting the items, you cannot return to a stage below it

3.2.1 Layers

You can create layers to test out different ideas by putting each possibility onto separate layers. You can turn on the visibility of layers in different combinations.

For example, the first state of a painting can be photographed as a digital image (Figure 3.15a). A series of layers are created on top of the painting image layer to explore

(a)

(b)

Figure 3.15 (a) A work-in-progress oil painting photographed as a digital image then opened in Photoshop (b) Layers created to explore different visual content and composition for the next step (c) The finished oil painting

(c)

Figure 3.15 (*Continued*)

the composition for the next step (Figure 3.15b). Each layer contains a single item—for example, one layer for power lines, one for birds, one for the car body color, one for the car shadow, and two layers for trees. This way the items can be more manageable. You can resize or reposition the car shadow without altering the appearance of the trees. These items can be quickly sketched out using a paint brush or a pencil tool. They do not have to be a perfect rendition—after all, they are intermediary sketches for yourself; your final product is an oil painting on canvas.

Figure 3.15c shows the finished oil painting. As you see, many of the elements are incorporated in the final painting. However, the final painting does not have to be a faithful reproduction of the digital exploration. It is your decision on the level of spontaneity when you transfer sketches to a canvas—regardless of the medium of the sketches.

What if you want to resize or reposition the items in different layers together? You can Control-select the layers before you apply changes to the layers.

Another tool called *Layer Comps* in Photoshop is particularly useful when you have multiple versions of a layout or compositions of an image. The multiple versions are often created by various combinations of layer visibility.

Figure 3.16 shows another painting example in which two composition possibilities are explored—one with an oval mirror with a window shadow (Figure 3.16b), and the other with a rectangular mirror and no cast shadow (Figure 3.16c).

Each possibility involves a different combination of layers being visible. One composition requires that the shadow layer, the oval mirror, and reflection in the mirror being *visible*, while the rectangular mirror and its reflection are *invisible*. The other composition requires that the shadow layer, the oval mirror and oval mirror reflection are *invisible*, while the rectangular mirror and its reflection are *visible*.

Here, each of these possibilities is created as a layer comp given the names "oval mirror" and "rect mirror no shadow". This lets you quickly switch between these two compositions with just one click on the proper layer comp in the Layer Comps palette.

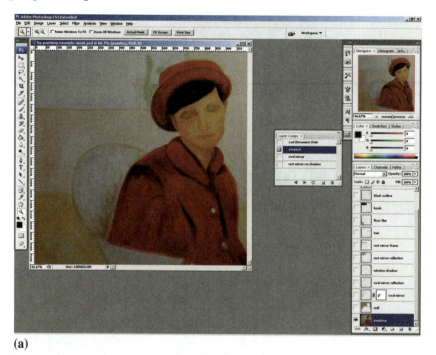

(a)

(b)

Figure 3.16 (a) Using Layer Comps where "original" shows the digital image of the work-in-progress oil painting (b) "oval mirror" (c) "rect mirror no shadow" (d) The finished oil painting incorporates the ideas of the second layer comp but is not just a faithful reproduction of the digital version

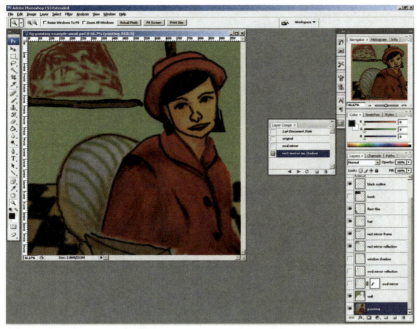

(c)

(d)

Figure 3.16 (*Continued*)

LAYER COMPS

A layer comp is a snapshot of a state of the Layers palette in Photoshop. As you see in Figure 3.17, the New Layer Comp dialog box has three types of layer options you can set the layer comp to be recorded at

- Visibility
- Position
- Appearance (Layer Style)

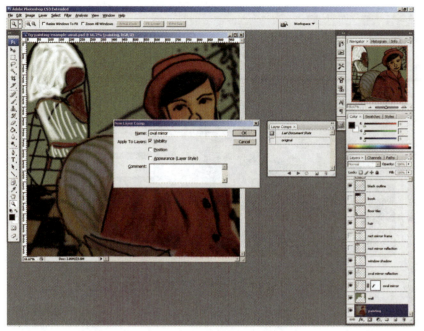

Figure 3.17 Create a new layer comp in Photoshop

The Appearance (Layer Style) setting includes whether a layer style is applied to the layer and the layer's blending mode.

To create a layer comp in Photoshop, first set the visibility, position, and layer style of all of the layers you want recorded in the layer comp, and then click on the New icon in the Layer Comp palette. The New Layer Comp dialog box will come up.

3.2.2 Filters

Commands (such as posterize) and some filters (such as Artistic > Cutout in Photoshop) remove details by reducing the number of colors in an image. The resulted effect is like squinting your eyes to look at the scene. Squinting helps you visualize the light and dark in a scene. Therefore, when a scene or object has so much intricate detail that you find yourself lost in trying to block out the light and dark areas, take a digital photo of the scene or the object and apply the Cutout filter at different settings. It may help you see past the details and isolate the light and dark regions.

Let's look at an example. As shown in Figure 3.18, the texture of a basket in a still life contains quite intricate details. When applied with the Cutout filter, the details quickly are simplified. Setting the options at different values gives you various views of blocking out the light and dark (Figure 3.19). As you see, despite the intricate details, only a few different values of brown oil paint would be sufficient to depict this basket.

Figure 3.18 Digital photo of a still life

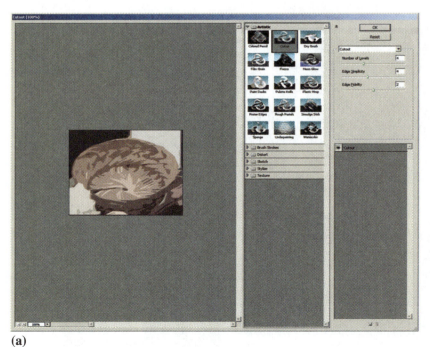

(a)

Figure 3.19 Applying the Cutout filter to the basket to reduce the details (a)using default settings (b) further reducing details by simplifying the edge and lowering the edge fidelity, and (c) using a different set of settings

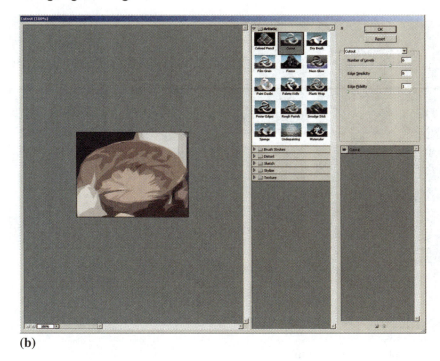

(b)

(c)

Figure 3.19 (*Continued*)

(a)   **(b)**

Figure 3.20 (a) Final oil painting of the still life (b) Close-up of the basket in the final oil painting

The final oil painting of the still life is shown in Figure 3.20. Only three different values of brown—a light brown, a medium brown, a deep dark brown—and white oil paint were used to paint the basket. The natural mixing of the paint on the canvas and the revealing of the brush strokes make the final work unique from the digital image generated by the filter. In this example, the digital filter is used only as an aid to visualize the light and dark in a difficult situation. It is not intended to make the oil painting into a faithful reproduction of the digital version.

3.3 DIGITAL IMAGING TOOLS—CREATING DIGITAL ART

There are several ways that digital images can be created: digital photography, scanning objects or pictures, and digital painting and drawing. These different methods often are combined.

3.3.1 Digital Photography

The concepts, aesthetics, and techniques of analog film photography still apply to digital photography. Although the shutter speed and aperture can be set to automatic, you still need to understand how they affect the results, because automatic settings do not always produce the intended results, especially in creative works or for scenes under extreme lighting conditions. So, first let's review some photography terms: shutter speed, aperture, and ISO. Then, we will discuss file types of digital photos.

Shutter Speed

Shutter speed controls how long the shutter of the lens is open to allow the projected image onto the film in the camera. For digital cameras, the "film" would be the electronic sensor that records the image.

Standard speeds for mechanical cameras are 1, 2, 4, 8, 15, 30, 60, 125, 250, 500, 1000, and 2000. The number represents the number of seconds in reciprocal. For example, a

Electronic and Digital Cameras: Many SLR film cameras, such as Nikon F-100, are electronic cameras. Unlike mechanical cameras, the shutter speed and aperture of these cameras are controlled electronically. Digital cameras are also electronic cameras, but they shoot images in digital format.

value of 125 means that the shutter will open for 1/125th of a second. The larger the number, the faster the shutter speed, and the total amount of light received by the camera's sensor will be less. Cameras with an electronic shutter also allow intermediary numbers:

1, 1.3, 1.6, **2**, 2.5, 3, **4**, 5, 6, **8**, 10, 13, **15**, 20, 25, **30**, 40, 50, **60**, 80, 100, **125**, 160, 200, **250**, 320, 400, **500**, 650, 800, **1000**

When the shutter speed is relatively slower than the movement of the object, the object will look blurry or smeared. This effect can add a feeling of movement to a still image. However, for some situations, this is not desirable, and it is difficult to remove the smear from a blurred image. On the other hand, simple motion blurs can be added digitally by applying image filters—for example, a Motion Blur filter in Photoshop. However, not all motion blurs can be recreated by digital imaging.

How slow the shutter should be to cause the blurring (so you can avoid it or intentionally capture it) depends on the speed of the motion. For a sporting event, if you do not want to have a motion blur, you may want to keep the shutter speed at as fast as 1/500 or 1/1000 second. If you want to experiment with the motion blur, start with 1/30 second. After reviewing the shot (with a digital camera), you can decide if you want to increase or decrease the shutter speed.

Aperture

Aperture refers to the size of the lens opening that allows the light of the projected image onto the camera's sensor. It is measured in f-stops. Standard f-stops are 1, 1.4, 2, 2.8, 4, 5.6, 8, 11, 16, 22, and 32. Like the numbers for the shutter speed, the f-stops and the size of the lens opening are in a reciprocal relationship. Larger numbers mean a smaller lens openings. Making the lens opening smaller by one step (say, from f/8 to f/11) is called **stopping down** one stop. Making the lens opening larger by one step (say, from f/11 to f/8) is called **opening up** one stop. Digital cameras also provide intermediary apertures:

1, 1.1, 1.25, **1.4**, 1.6, 1.8, **2**, 2.2, 2.5, **2.8**, 3.2, 3.6, **4**, 4.5, 5, **5.6**, 6.3, 7, **8**, 9, 10, **11**, 13, 14, **16**, 18, 20, **22**

Decreasing the size of the lens opening (i.e. increasing the f-number) can increase the depth of field. Depth of field refers to the distance range within which the subject appears sharp in the photograph. Hence, by decreasing the size of the lens opening, more subjects may appear sharp in the photograph.

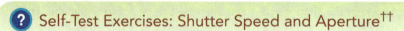

⑦ Self-Test Exercises: Shutter Speed and Aperture[††]

I. **What Shutter Speed and Aperture Mean**

_____ 1. **True/False:** A shutter speed of 250 is faster than 500.

_____ 2. **True/False:** An aperture setting of f/16 means a larger opening than f/8.

II. **Determining Shutter Speed and Aperture**

Suppose your camera shows a light meter reading of **f/8 250** on its on-camera LCD display (the figure in the center) for a given scene. You may override the setting manually by opening up or stopping down the f-stop and/or increasing or decreasing the shutter speed (Figures A through H). Choose the best matches for the following questions. (*Hint:* There may be more than one possible setting as an answer.)

? Self-Test Exercises: Shutter Speed (*continued*)

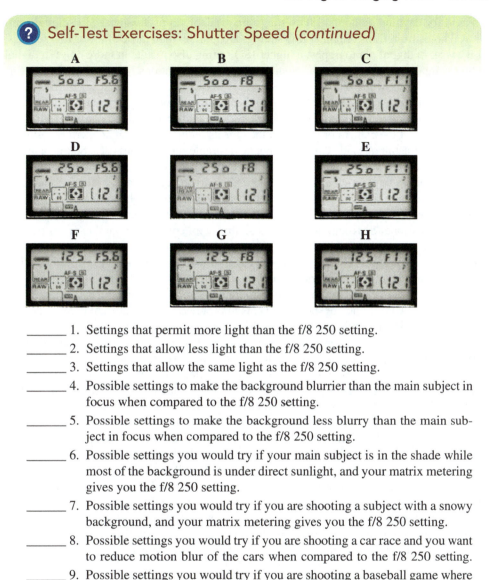

Matrix metering uses the overall lighting from the scene to calculate the f-stop and shutter speed settings. This works well for most situations. However, if your subject of interest is relatively small in the picture and its lighting condition is very different from the rest of the scene, then your subject will be either too bright or too dark in the image. With matrix metering, a skier against a vast white snowy background will make the camera set the f-stop and shutter speed for a very bright scene. This will make the skier darker than you may have desired.

_____ 1. Settings that permit more light than the f/8 250 setting.

_____ 2. Settings that allow less light than the f/8 250 setting.

_____ 3. Settings that allow the same light as the f/8 250 setting.

_____ 4. Possible settings to make the background blurrier than the main subject in focus when compared to the f/8 250 setting.

_____ 5. Possible settings to make the background less blurry than the main subject in focus when compared to the f/8 250 setting.

_____ 6. Possible settings you would try if your main subject is in the shade while most of the background is under direct sunlight, and your matrix metering gives you the f/8 250 setting.

_____ 7. Possible settings you would try if you are shooting a subject with a snowy background, and your matrix metering gives you the f/8 250 setting.

_____ 8. Possible settings you would try if you are shooting a car race and you want to reduce motion blur of the cars when compared to the f/8 250 setting.

_____ 9. Possible settings you would try if you are shooting a baseball game where the subjects of interest are spread out, a large distance from the camera, and you want most of the subjects to be in focus.

ISO

ISO numbers progress in terms of light sensitivity or speed of the film. With film cameras, you choose the film with the ISO that best suits your shooting situations. You can use the same rules of thumb as analog films in setting the ISO for digital photography. For example, a higher ISO (such as 800) is used for night scenes or indoors and lower (200)

---

††Answers to the self-test exercises:

I. (1) F;   (2) F

II. (1) D, F, G;   (2) B, C, E;   (3) A, H;   (4) A, D, E;   (5) C, E, H;   (6) D, G, H;   (7) D, F, G;   (8) A, B, C;
    (9) C, E, H

is used for daytime outdoors. ISO settings are available in professional SLR digital cameras. Photos from films of higher ISO settings are grainier than those of lower ISO settings. Likewise, in digital photography, a higher ISO setting also results in more noise in digital photos. Image noise manifests as small random color variations in the image. Its appearance is similar to film grain.

Why would one use a higher ISO setting then? In low-light situations, you would need to use a slower shutter and/or a larger aperture. Slower shutter is prone to blurry imaging due to movement of the camera or motion of the objects in the scene. Larger aperture results in a decrease of depth of field. These may not be desirable for your purposes. Setting a higher ISO setting allows you to shoot photos at low-light situations with reasonable aperture and shutter speed, so that the subject will be more likely to be in focus and without motion blur. While with analog film cameras you have to change films to switch to different film speed, digital cameras allow you to switch the ISO setting any time through its menu settings.

All professional SLR digital cameras and almost all consumer digital cameras have an instant review of shots. This gives you instantaneous feedback that helps you decide on settings for the next shot. Professional digital cameras also have an option to display the histogram of the photo. The histogram gives you statistics of the tonal range of the shot. Tonal range problems are easier to spot in the histogram than by eyeballing the photo preview on the camera's LCD. If you are shooting events in progress and do not want to miss the next shot, you may want to hold off reviewing the shots and keep shooting while you can.

> **⌂ Light Metering Emulation** An emulation of photographing a still life. It lets you see how spot-metering different parts of the scene affects the overall tones of the resulted image.

For studio shootings where you have more control over the set up, you should take time to compose your shots—arrange the objects, pose the subjects, look for interesting angles, and set up desired lighting. Although digital photography allows much more freedom in retouching and editing, a well thought out shot with advanced planning will save you a lot of time and give a better result in the end. For example, if you intend to extract an object from the shot to use in a montage, then it would be better to shoot the object against a solid color background with minimal texture. This will make selecting the object in an image-editing program easier—you can select the background by color and then invert the selection to select the object. The color of the backdrop should be very different from the object. In addition, watch out for the reflected light from the backdrop onto the object. A white or light-colored object placed on a bright green backdrop will very likely get a tint of green color from the backdrop and a green matt around the object.

File Format and Image Quality

The common file formats that a digital camera shoots in are *JPEG, TIFF,* and **camera *RAW***. JPEG format is the most commonly available. You often can set a different quality for JPEG. JPEG uses a lossy compression to reduce the file size. A higher-quality JPEG is less compressed and has a larger file size. In general, the file size of a JPEG file is much smaller than a TIFF or RAW file.

Digital cameras have their in-camera image-processing software to convert the electronic signals from the camera's image sensor into pixel information in the resulted digital photo. If you choose JPEG or TIFF settings, the pixel information of the digital photos is processed. A camera RAW file contains unprocessed picture data from a digital camera's image sensor. Most interchangeable-lens SLR digital cameras let you save digital photos in camera RAW format. Figure 3.21 shows the menu for setting the digital photo format to the camera RAW on a Nikon D70s.

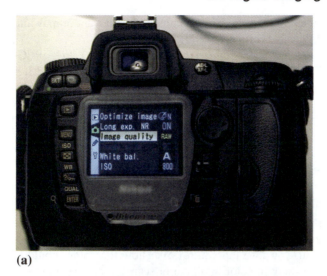

(a)

(b)

Figure 3.21 An example of the menu of a Nikon D70s digital camera (a) Image quality menu lets you set the image file types that determine the image quality and size (b) Raw file format is chosen

Many photographers prefer shooting in RAW file format because it offers at least two advantages.

- *Original data:* Photographers can manipulate the image data based on their own interpretation instead of letting the camera make the automatic adjustments and conversions. The adjustments that you can edit include the white balance, tonal range, contrast, color saturation, and sharpening. Think of the RAW files as the photo negatives in films. The negative, not the processed print, contains the most original information of the image. The same negative can be interpreted to produce prints with a different look and feel. You may argue that digital imaging allows you to edit and adjust a digital photo no matter what file format they are. However, the automatic in-camera

Each pixel in a RAW file contains one data—the original electronic signal from the camera's image sensor. On the other hand, in a TIFF file, each pixel has been processed into RGB values—one data for each of the red, green, and blue channels. Hence, the file size of a TIFF file is about three times that of a RAW file.

processing may remove some information that you want or may alter the image such that it would make it difficult to edit.

- *Lossless and smaller file size than TIFF*: JPEG uses lossy compression and has visible artifacts on an image. It is not a preferable format intended for further editing. The camera's TIFF and RAW do not apply compression. The file size of a TIFF file is about three times as large as a RAW file. Hence, even if you do not care about getting original data with RAW, a RAW file type still offers an advantage of smaller file size of lossless format, allowing you to shoot more pictures in a single storage card.

> ⌐ **JPEG Compression Artifact (worksheet exercise)** Look at the impact of JPEG compression artifact on different digital images, and learn when and why an image may be or should not be saved in JPEG format.

Black-and-White Digital Photography

Some digital cameras are capable of capturing images in black-and-white directly by converting color images into grayscale images. However, by letting the camera do the automatic conversion for you, you lose the control over how the color should be mapped to the grayscale. You can shoot in color in digital or scan color slides/transparencies first. Color images then can be converted to black-and-white (grayscale) using imaging-editing programs such as Adobe Photoshop. There are several ways to convert an image into grayscale:

- Change the image's color mode to grayscale (Image > Mode > Grayscale)
- Use the Desaturate command (Image > Adjustments > Desaturate)
- Use the Hue/Saturation command to turn the saturation to minimal
- Use Channel Mixer (Image > Adjustments > Channel Mixer...) and turn on the monochrome option.

The first three methods allow you to quickly convert an image into grayscale. However, you do not have much control over how the colors are mapped into different grays. *Channel Mixer* provides more control of how the colors are mapped to grays.

Figure 3.22 shows resulting grayscale images using the different methods. The text at the two ends in the color image (Figure 3.22a) stands out pretty well from the background.

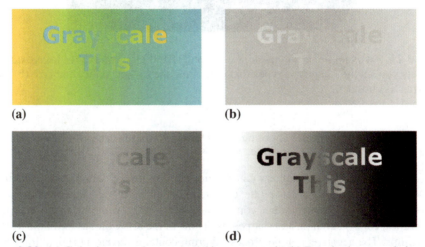

(a)   (b)

(c)   (d)

Figure 3.22 (a) Color image to be converted into grayscale (b) Resulted grayscale image using Image > Mode > Grayscale (c) Resulted grayscale image using Desaturate or Hue/Saturation (d) Resulted grayscale image using Image > Adjustments > Channel Mixer . . .

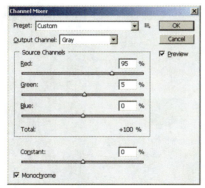

Figure 3.23 Settings in the Channel Mixer used on the image shown in Figure 3.22a to produce the one shown in Figure 3.22d

However, the resulting images using the first three methods (Figure 3.22b through c) do not maintain such distinction between the foreground and background anymore. The resulted grayscale image using Channel Mixer (Figure 3.22d) preserves such distinction. Figure 3.23 shows the Channel Mixer dialog box. The Monochrome option is turned on. Think of the red, green, and blue sliders as a way of specifying the weight of each red, green, and blue in mapping to grays. Let's look at several simple examples of single colors:

- A red color of (RGB 255, 0, 0) would become white if you set the following values for the sliders:

  Red: 100%   Green: 0%   Blue: 0%

- The same red color would become black if you set the following values for the sliders:

  Red: 0%   Green: any   Blue: any

- The same red color would become mid-gray if you set the following values for the sliders:

  Red: 50%   Green: any   Blue: any

- The yellowish color in Figure 3.22a has a value of (RGB 255, 208, 7). Therefore, setting the red slider to a high percentage (95%) in the Channel Mixer (Figure 3.23) pushes this yellow color to white.
- The cyan color in Figure 3.22a has a value of (RGB 0, 255, 247). Therefore, leaving the Green and Blue channels at only 5% total (Figure 3.23) pushes this cyan color to black.

Figure 3.24 shows another example of using different methods to convert a color image into grayscale. The colors in the color version (Figure 3.24a) are distinct from one another. The Channel Mixer, using the settings shown in Figure 3.25, gives an image that maintains such distinction (Figure 3.24d) while other methods produce images that are rather flat (Figure 3.24b through c).

> ⌨ **Channel Mixer (worksheet exercise)**
> This exercise helps you understand how Channel Mixer works and how to customize a conversion of a color image to a black-and-white (grayscale) image.

Figure 3.24 (a) Color image to be converted into grayscale (b) Resulted grayscale image using Image > Mode > Grayscale (c) Resulted grayscale image using Desaturate or Hue/Saturation. (d) Resulted grayscale image using Image > Adjustments > Channel Mixer...

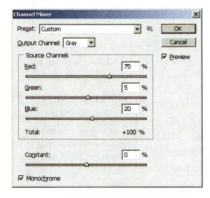

Figure 3.25 Settings in the Channel Mixer applied to the image shown in Figure 3.24a to produce the one shown in Figure 3.24d

WHY STILL SHOOT IN COLOR WHEN YOU WANT A BLACK-AND-WHITE PRINT?

With film, it in general is preferable to shoot with true black-and-white film rather than color film and print on black-and-white paper later. For digital imaging, however, it actually is preferable to shoot in color—even if you are aiming for a black-and-white print.

When you shoot in black-and-white mode, the digital camera still shoots in colors but converts the color information into grays using the in-camera image-processing software. This raises at least two issues.

1. **Automatic versus custom control by the photographer:** There are digital adjustment tools available to convert color images into grayscale. These tools (such as Channel Mixer) give you more control in interpreting the image by letting you determine how to convert the color into gray tones. With the color image, you can experiment and produce different black-and-white interpretations of your own.

2. **256 versus 16 millions of color:** Most grayscale images are stored in 8-bit-format (i.e. the image can have 256 different grays). Some are 16-bit, (i.e., 2^{16} or 65,536 different grays). Most color images are 24-bit (i.e., 2^{24} or over 16.7 millions of colors) offering more color details. Hence, when a color image is converted to a grayscale image, it certainly will lose some color distinctions whether it is by automatic conversion or custom control by the artist. However, working from a color image gives you more color differentiation to start with. The number of grays in the final black-and-white photo is determined by its bit depth of the grayscale version. Nonetheless, adjustment tools (such as Channel Mixer) offer you many more possibilities to interpret your image than an automatically converted grayscale image. You control what information will be lost.

ANALYZING RGB CHANNELS BEFORE CONVERTING AN IMAGE TO GRAYSCALE

Analyzing the RGB channels of a color image before using Channel Mixer to convert it to grayscale will give you useful information in determining the relative setting for each channel. The following example demonstrates what information you may get by looking at each channel.

The ***Channel palette*** in Photoshop lets you look at each of the red, green, and blue color information of a RGB image. You can show or hide each color channel. In each color channel, the color information is represented with grays. Darker grays mean less intensity of that color component, while the lighter grays mean higher intensity of that color component.

Figure 3.26b through d show the red, green, blue channels, respectively, of a color image (Figure 3.26a). The red channel is the sharpest. The blue channel is fuzzy, and there is minimal shadow detail in some areas and no shadow detail in others, such as in the area circled in red in Figure 3.26d. This quick analysis can give you ideas on setting

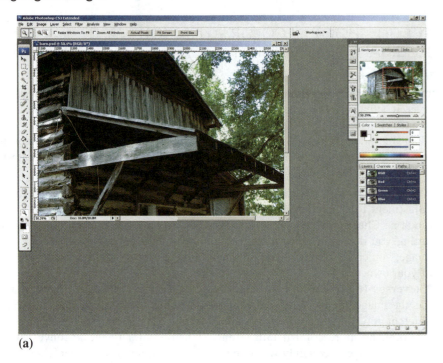

(a)

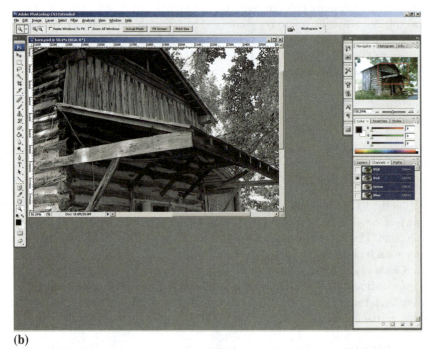

(b)

Figure 3.26 Analysis of color information using the Photoshop Channel palette before converting it to grayscale (a) All RGB channels (b) Red channel only (c) Green channel only (d) Blue channel only.

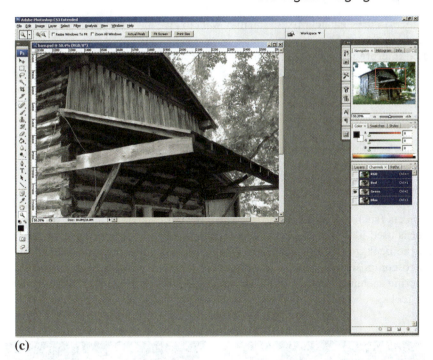

(c)

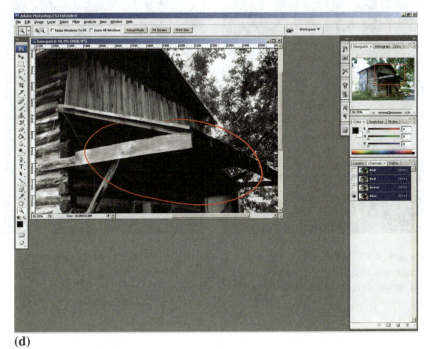

(d)

Figure 3.26 *(Continued)*

the sliders in the Channel Mixer. You may want to give more emphasis for the red channel and less for the blue channel.

The interpretation of a color image into black-and-white is certainly a creative and expressive process. However, the objective analysis of color information can give you an idea of how to start manipulating the sliders to get the intended result.

3.3.2 Scanning

Scanning is another way of obtaining digital images to use in a project. Flatbed scanners are used commonly, and the analog source is normally in sheet form, (such as pictures, documents, and books). However, digital artists have been using flatbed scanners to scan 3-D objects (such as fabrics, keys, dried plants, and hands). In these cases, the flatbed scanner is used like a focus-free camera. When an object is scanned without the flatbed cover, the background appears black (Figure 3.27a), allowing easy extraction of the object to compose with others in a project. Moving the physical object on the glass plate during scanning will result in distorted images (Figure 3.27b), giving an interesting surreal feel.

(a)   **(b)**

Figure 3.27 (a) An image obtained by scanning a physical object on a flatbed scanner without closing the lid (b) Object moved slowly along the scanning direction during scanning to create distorted elongation

Pen and pencil sketches also are good scanning sources. Scanning allows you to incorporate the visual content of the traditional media (such as your own sketches or artworks) into a digital project. Even simple, broad strokes of charcoal on a textured paper can be scanned to serve as a basis for a texture element.

3.3.3 Digital Painting and Drawing

There are a variety of software application programs for digital drawing and painting—for example, Corel Painter, Alias Sketchbook, and Adobe Illustrator. Although Photoshop is a digital photo-editing program, it has tools for drawing and painting. In addition to software, there are hardware devices designed to use for digital drawing—for example, tabletPC and Wacom tablets.

Corel Painter

Corel Painter (Figure 3.28a) is called a natural-media painting application because it simulates many traditional art tools—for example, oil paints, watercolor, charcoal, pastel, colored pencils, and felt pens. Figure 3.28b shows a list of available media. A wide range of options are available for each medium. Figure 3.28c shows the brush options for the oil medium.

Don't forget to return the Brush's Opacity to 100% when you don't need to lower the opacity. If you can't get your brush color as intense as the color set in the color chip, check the Brush's Opacity option and make sure it is returned to 100%.

Adobe Photoshop

Adobe Photoshop is a digital photo-editing and compositing program, but it also has painting and drawing tools, such as brush and pencil tools. There are different brush styles available, and you can define custom brushes. Another useful tool for painting and drawing is the Brush tool's Opacity option. By default, the Opacity option is 100%. However, if you lower the opacity, you can build up the color by brushing on top of the existing strokes, mimicking traditional painting media.

◇ **Photoshop: Defining Custom Brushes**
A screen-capture movie demonstrates how to define custom brushes in Photoshop.

Pressure-Sensitive Tablets

TabletPCs and Wacom tablets let you use a stylus (instead of a mouse) to paint and draw. These devices are useful in creating freehand strokes. Wacom tablets and most tabletPCs are also pressure sensitive. This means that when it is used with a software program that supports this feature, the appearance of the brush stroke responds to the stylus's pressure on the tablet. Adobe Photoshop supports pen pressure, and you can set many different properties (such as color, values, and size) of a brush to be controlled by the pressure (Figure 3.29).

Figure 3.30 shows a comparison of different brush strokes created with a pressure-sensitive tablet and a mouse. The brush strokes shown in Figure 3.30a through b use the Shape Dynamics settings shown in Figure 3.29a. The brush strokes shown in Figure 3.30c through d use the Shape Dynamics and Color Dynamics settings shown in Figure 3.29b.

Adobe Illustrator

Adobe Illustrator also comes with a variety of artistic brush styles, such as ink, chalk, and paintbrush (Figure 3.31a). The paths can be applied with these artistic brushes (Figure 3.31b).

3.3.4 Mixing Different Techniques and Images

Digital images from different sources often are combined in an artwork. To compose the different images into a single work, selected areas of an image will need to be extracted from the original image. The subsequent material will discuss the techniques for extracting images and compositing multiple images.

(a)

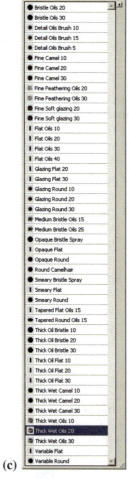

(b)

(c)

Figure 3.28 Corel Painter 10 (a) workspace, (b) list of brush choices, and (c) list of the oil brush options

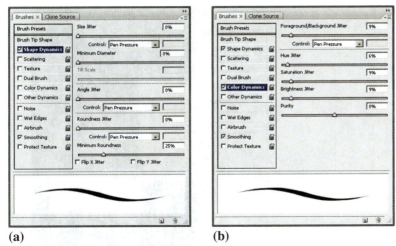

(a)   **(b)**

Figure 3.29 Adobe Photoshop Brushes palette provides many options for adding dynamic properties to the preset brushes, and you can set some options to use pen pressure to vary (a) size, angle, and randomness of the brush shape and (b) color jitter between the foreground and background colors

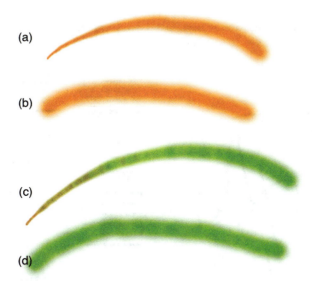

Figure 3.30 Brush strokes created using (a) pressure-sensitive tablet with brush size set to vary with pen pressure, (b) a mouse, (c) pressure-sensitive tablet with brush size and color set to vary with pen pressure, and (d) a mouse

Extracting Image Content

The techniques discussed previously—using digital tool as an aid, digital photography, scanning, and digital painting and drawing—are used often in combination in a project. To combine different images, you often need to be able to selectively extract only a portion of

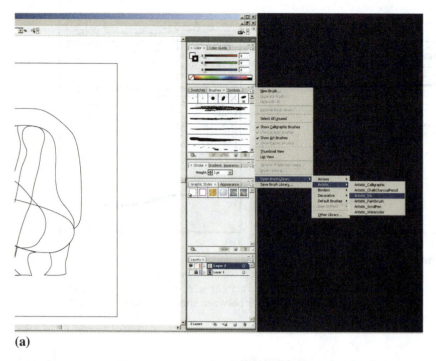

(a)

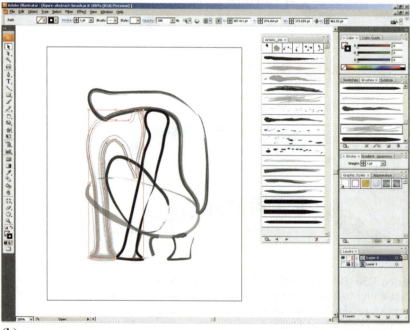

(b)

Figure 3.31 (a) Adobe Illustrator's lists of different brushes (b) Paths are applied with different brushes

Figure 3.32 There are several small specks of unselected areas within the big selection of the white window frame where the red rectangles show some of these specks

the content from each image. The shape of the content you want to extract is not always rectangular. Your proficiency in the selection tools plays an important role in your craftsmanship. The extracted content should not contain any unintended areas nor leave out any areas that are supposed to be in the selection. Scrutinize your selection inside, outside, and around the edges before copying the selected content. Check if there are any small areas within the selection left out from the selection. You can tell by looking for the sign of any "marching ant" selection edge within the selected area. For example, the entire white frame in Figure 3.32 is intended to be selected, but some specks are left out. You can tell by the "marching ant" selection edges within the larger selection. In Photoshop, to add those specks to the selection, you can hold down the Shift key while selecting them. When adding to a selection, you can include the area that is already in the selection. In this example, you do not have to select each individual speck by their exact shapes. The rectangular marquee tool can be used.

The selection tools are reviewed in the first section of this chapter. A detailed discussion can be found in the Digital Media Primer.

Don't forget to examine the edge of the selection too. The edge should be clean. A clean edge means it does not have any unintended jaggedness and it encloses the content you want, no more and no less. To refine the edge, **Quick Mask** is a useful tool. It lets you paint the mask with black to add to the existing selection and with white to remove the area from the selection.

By default, the selection has a hard edge. You can soften the edge by applying feathering to the selection before you copy the selected content. For objects with fuzzy and undefined edges, you may need to use the **Extract filter**.

> ✍ **Photoshop: Extract Filter** A screen-capture movie demonstrates how to use the Extract filter in Photoshop to extract an object with fuzzy edges.

Figure 3.33 Margaret Campbell, *Untitled*, 2007, digital print, 20" × 15" (Courtesy of John. P. Anderson Collection of Student Art, Wake Forest University)

Compositing Multiple Image Contents

Layers are indispensable in compositing multiple images. Each image content can be organized on a separate layer so that altering one does not affect the rest of the content. However, layers are more than just a stack of acetate sheets. Layer features (such as opacity, blending mode, and layer styles) let you create sophisticated effects for the composite. The digital print shown in Figure 3.33 is made of images of various opacity layered on top of each other.

Opacity controls the transparency of the content on the layer. A layer's blending mode specifies how its pixels blend with those pixels in the layers underneath it. Look up the list of blending modes in Photoshop Help for more information. Also, experiment with the blending modes. You will need at least two layers to see the effect. In addition, the layer applied with a blending mode needs to have at least a layer below it in order to show the effect. One of the most commonly used blending modes is *Multiply*. This blending mode always results in either a darker color or the same color. Multiplying any color with black produces black. Multiplying any color with white leaves the color unchanged.

3.4 CREATING DIGITAL IMAGES FOR A PORTFOLIO

Portfolios of digital images can be in print or in electronic format. Different formats require different considerations. This section examines these issues.

3.4.1 In Print

These discussions about paper selection and printing dpi are based on common inkjet printing.

Getting the File Ready—Setting Print Resolution

For printing, it is crucial that your image has a high enough resolution for your printing purpose. You need to set up the proper resolution for your image file before you start the project. The resolution of your image can be higher than you need for the final print. You can lower the resolution if needed. If the resolution is not high enough for your printing purpose, it is not possible to raise the resolution without negative impact on your image quality.

The resolution of your bitmap image should have been set up properly at the start of your project. The following steps for setting print resolution are used to confirm the printing resolution and dimension before printing.

PRINT PPI

The common printing ppi (pixels per inch) for images is 300 ppi. However, just setting 300 ppi alone is meaningless, because the physical size of the print is also a determining factor.

A detailed discussion and determination of resolution can be found in the *Digital Media Primer.*

Let's use a car's gas mileage as an analogy of an image's print ppi. The gas mileage is measured in miles per gallon. Simply knowing the number of miles per gallon does not tell you how many miles your car can go, nor how many gallons your car has (or needs to have).

Suppose your car's gas mileage is 20 miles per gallon. To determine how many miles your car can go (with the current tank), you need to know the number of gallons of gas in the tank. If it has 5 gallons, then your car can go 100 miles (20 miles per gallon $\times$ 5 gallons).

To determine the number of gallons your car needs, you need to know the number of miles you want to drive. If you want to drive 120 miles, then your car will need to have 6 gallons (120 miles / 20 miles per gallon) of gas in the tank.

In this analogy:

- A car's gas mileage (miles per gallon) is analogous to an image's ppi (pixels per inch).
- The total miles a car can drive (with the current tank) is analogous to the pixel dimension of an image.
- The number of gallons of gas in the tank is analogous to the physical dimension of an image.

If you want to print an image at 300 ppi and you know that it needs to be printed as 8 inch $\times$ 10 inch, then your image's pixel dimensions need to be 2400 $\times$ 3000 pixels.

If your image's pixel dimensions are 1200 $\times$ 1500 pixels and you want to print it at 300 ppi, then it will be printed as 4 inch $\times$ 5 inch.

In Photoshop, choose Image > Image Size. . . . A dialog box like the one shown in Figure 3.34 appears. It is important for you to understand how to read the information in this dialog box and be able to determine whether the Resample Image option needs to be enabled or not for your purpose. Inadvertently turning on the Resample Image

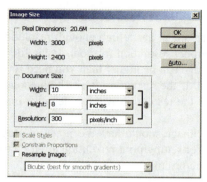

Figure 3.34 Photoshop's Image Size dialog box

option while you make changes on the Document Size settings will degrade the quality of your image.

Here is a brief explanation the settings in the Image Size dialog box.

- The ***Document Size*** means the physical print size of your image. The relationship between the settings in the Pixel Dimensions section and the Document Size section can be represented by the equations:

$$\text{Pixel width} = \text{Width of document size (in inches)} \times \text{ppi}$$
$$\text{Pixel height} = \text{Height of document size (in inches)} \times \text{ppi}$$

In the example shown in Figure 3.34, the pixel width is 3000 pixels, because the physical width is 10 inches and the resolution is 300 ppi:

$$10 \text{ inches} \times 300 \text{ ppi} = 3000 \text{ pixels}$$

- The ***Resample Image*** option has the following uses.
  - If *unchecked*, the pixel width and pixel height will be kept constant in the above equation—no matter how you change the document size or the ppi. If you change the document size, the ppi will change accordingly so that the product of width of document size (in inches) times ppi will always the same.

    In summary, *unchecking* Resample Image allows:
    - *No* resizing of the *pixel* dimensions
    - Resizing of the *document* dimensions (physical dimensions of the print)

    If you only want to change the print size, uncheck the Resample Image option. This should be the case if your image has been set to a high enough resolution at the start of the project. Changing any of the settings with Resample Image unchecked will not alter the image quality.
  - If *checked*, the pixel width and pixel height will not be kept constant anymore. The pixel dimensions increase or decrease according to your changes in the document size and ppi. Such resizing will have negative impact on the image quality.

The following exercises will help you to understand how to interpret the settings in the Image Size dialog box and to apply your knowledge.

❓ Self-Test Exercises: Interpretation of the Information in Photoshop's Image Size Window[‡]

I. According to the Image Size window shown in Figure 3.35,
1. The pixel dimension of the image is _____ × _____ pixels.
2. The physical size of the image, if it is printed out, is _____ inches × _____ inches.
3. The printing resolution of the image is _____ ppi (pixels per inch).

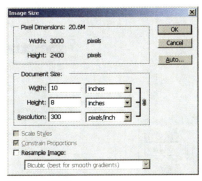

Figure 3.35

II. Suppose a class assignment requires an image print size of 10 inches × 8 inches at 300 ppi (pixels per inch). The image should have the pixel dimensions shown in Figure 3.35. However, a student notices his image's pixel dimensions do not match the expected pixel dimensions; they are much larger than the correct pixel dimensions. Figure 3.36 shows the Image Size information of the student's image. Identify the incorrect setting that causes such a discrepancy in pixel dimensions.

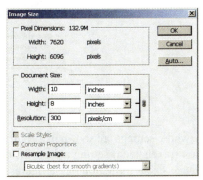

Figure 3.36

[‡]Answers the self-test exercises:
I. (1) 3000 × 2400 pixels; (2) 10 inches × 8 inches; (3) 300 ppi
II. The unit for the resolution is set to pixels/cm; it should be pixels/inch.

> **?** Self-Test Exercises: Resample Image versus Not Resample
> Image: Predicting Information in Photoshop's Image Size
> Window[§§]

I. Starting with an image whose settings are shown in the left dialog box in Figure 3.37,
    lowering its resolution (pixels/inch) setting affects the other image size information.
    Fill in the new image size information in the figures on the right—the top one refers
    to changing the resolution without resampling the image and the bottom one with
    resampling the image.

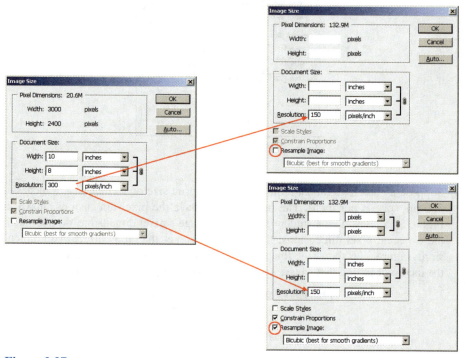

Figure 3.37

II. Starting with an image whose settings are shown in the left dialog box in Figure 3.38,
     increasing its resolution (pixels/inch) setting affects the other image size informa-
     tion. Fill in the new image size information in the figures on the right—the top one
     refers to changing the resolution without resampling the image and the bottom one
     with resampling the image.

? Self-Test Exercises: Resample Image versus Not Resample Image: Predicting Information in Photoshop's Image Size Window (*continued*)

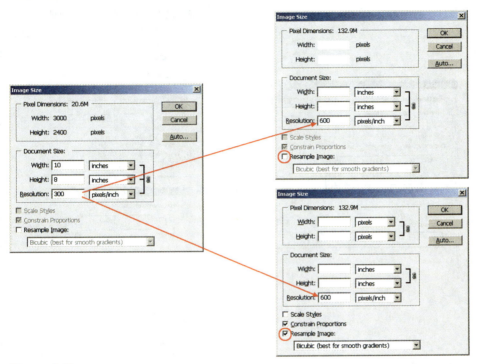

Figure 3.38

III. Starting with an image whose settings are shown in the left dialog box in Figure 3.39, changing its print width (inches) setting affects the other image size information. Fill in the new image size information in the figures on the right—the top one refers to changing the print width without resampling the image and the bottom one with resampling the image.

? Self-Test Exercises: Resample Image versus Not Resample Image: Predicting Information in Photoshop's Image Size Window (*continued*)

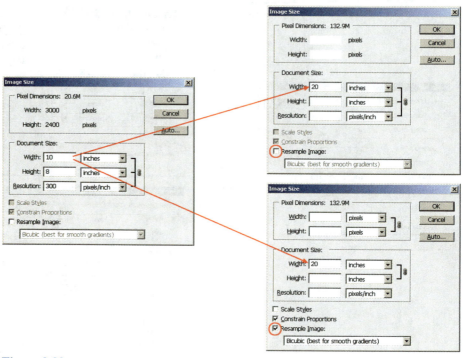

Figure 3.39

---

§§Answers to the self-test exercises:

I. Top: Resample Image *unchecked*:
  Width = 3000 pixels, Height = 2400 pixels
  Width = 20 inches, Height = 16 inches
Bottom: Resample Image *checked*:
  Width = 1500 pixels, Height = 1200 pixels
  Width = 10 inches, Height = 8 inches

II. Top: Resample Image *unchecked*:
  Width = 3000 pixels, Height = 2400 pixels
  Width = 5 inches, Height = 4 inches
Bottom: Resample Image *checked*:
  Width = 6000 pixels, Height = 4800 pixels
  Width = 10 inches, Height = 8 inches

III. Top: Resample Image *unchecked*:
  Width = 3000 pixels, Height = 2400 pixels
  Width = 20 inches, Height = 16 inches, Resolution = 150 pixels/inch
Bottom: Resample Image *checked*:
  Width = 6000 pixels, Height = 4800 pixels
  Width = 20 inches, Height = 16 inches, Resolution = 300 pixels/inch

? Self-Test Exercises: Application to a Scenario***

Suppose you have created an image (with size information shown in Figure 3.40) and you want to print it on a 10" × 8" paper with at least a half-inch margin all around. In the dialog box on the right, fill in the correct image settings that can accomplish this task with the maximum printed area for the image without affecting the image quality.

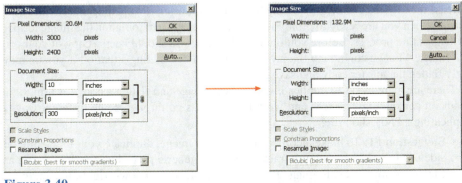

Figure 3.40

Unlike bitmapped images, vector graphics (such as Illustrator files) are resolution independent. There is no ppi setting for printing vector graphics. However, if you are going to export the vector graphic to a bitmapped image, you will need to determine the proper ppi.

Figure 3.41 shows Illustrator's Export Options dialog box. You can set the export resolution in terms of ppi. The physical dimension of the file is set in your Illustrator document. If you want to double the width and height of the physical dimension, you will need to set the export ppi to be double the intended printing ppi. For example, if your vector graphic

Figure 3.41 Adobe Illustrator's Export Options dialog box

***Answers to self-test exercise:
Resample Image *unchecked*
Width = 3000 pixels, Height = 2400 pixels
Width = 8.75 inches, Height = 7 inches
Resolution = 343 ppi

document is set up to be 4 inch × 5 inch but you want to export it to a bitmap file that will be printed at 300 ppi as 8 inch × 10 inch, you will need to export your vector graphic at 600 ppi. Then, open it in a bitmap image-editing program and change the ppi from 600 to 300 while keeping Resample Image unchecked.

Getting the File Ready to Print—Flattening

Working on a digital image project, you often have many layers in the image file. Layers increase the file size and the processing time (such as during file opening and saving) of the image. When you are ready to print your image, you may want to flatten the image to speed up the printing process. Before you flatten the image, you should keep a copy of your original (master) image containing the layers. It can be a devastating situation if you unknowingly flatten the master copy and save over it.

There are many ways to duplicate your master image and flatten a copy for print; it depends on personal preferences and work habits. Let's go through some different ways of duplicating a Photoshop file.

- **Suggestion #1:** To make a copy of your master image, duplicate your image file outside of the image-editing program. This is the generic procedure for duplicating any file and is not limited to image files. For example, in Windows, right-click on the file and choose Copy. Then, right-click anywhere outside of the filename and choose Paste. Rename the copy so that you know it will be used for printing. In Mac OS X, select the file and choose File > Duplicate.
- **Suggestion #2:** Open the master image in Photoshop, save the image with another name. This is not preferable if your master image file has so many layers that it takes a long time to save.

After you have duplicated the master copy, flatten the duplicate. You can do so by selecting Flatten Image from the Layers palette (Figure 3.42), and save again.

> Naming the Printing Copy: You can append "for-print" to the filename, so you can tell from the filename that this is a printing copy of which file.

Figure 3.42 The Flatten Image option is one of the Layers palette options

There is a more efficient, one-step procedure of duplicating and flattening an image. While your master image is open in Photoshop, you can choose File > Save As . . . , and in the Save As . . . dialog box, set the Save Options as (Figure 3.43)

- *Check the option*: As a Copy
- *Uncheck the option*: Layers

Figure 3.43 Saving without layers

Make sure the filename is different from the original master image. Otherwise, your master image will be replaced with this new flattened copy!

Paper Selection

Inkjet papers have different finishes. The most common ones available in traditional photo papers (such as gloss, matte, and semigloss) also are available for inkjet printing. There are also fine-art papers and canvas. Fine-art papers have heavier weight and acid-free archival quality. They come with different textures. Epson is one of the major carriers of inkjet papers. At the time of writing, Arches also has inkjet papers available in smooth and textured finishes.

When you make an inkjet print, make sure you are printing on the correct side—the coated side—of the paper. Printing on the non-coated side produces uneven smearing of the ink on the paper. The color of the print will be off, and the image will be blurry. The fine-art papers are difficult to tell which side is coated. You will need to pay attention to the instructions in the box.

The color of an image differs slightly on different papers. Color profiles for specific printer and paper combinations often are available from the paper company's Web site.

3.4.2 On the Web

The image file types that are currently supported by Web browsers are .jpg, .gif, and .png. Because the Web medium is intended for on-screen viewing, the way you determine a proper resolution for the image is different from that for the image intended for print.

The physical dimensions (inches) and the ppi of the Web image are not relevant anymore. Pixel dimensions of the image are the dimensions that you need to consider. How

JPG *versus* GIF *versus* PNG: See *Digital Media Primer* Chapter 3 for detailed discussion and a worksheet on optimizing images for the Web.

large a Web image appears on a screen should be thought in relative to the viewer's screen resolution—not in an absolute sense of inches. Because the Web viewer's screen resolution is not something you can control, you should use only the most common screen resolution of your target audience. At the time of writing, the most common screen resolution is 1024 × 768 pixels but higher resolutions are becoming more common. So, let's use both 1280 × 1024 and 1024 × 768 as examples to demonstrate how to estimate the pixel dimensions for a Web image.

The Web browser window that a Web page is displayed in can be any size, but it normally is no larger than the screen resolution. In the following discussion, let's suppose the browser window is maximized. A test image marked with different pixel dimensions (Figure 3.44) is displayed in a Web browser with maximized browser window at two screen resolutions: 1280 × 1024 pixels (Figure 3.45b) and 1024 × 768 pixels (Figure 3.45c).

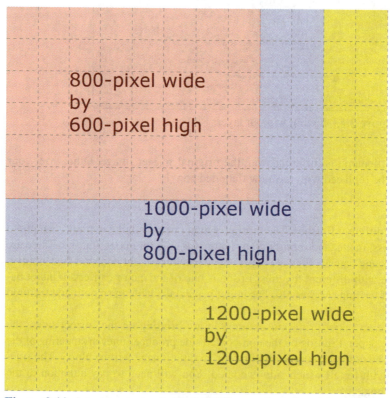

Figure 3.44 A test image marked with different pixel dimensions used to demonstrate how much of the image can be displayed in a Web browser on different screen resolutions

The Web browser window has menu and tool bars that take up screen space (Figure 3.45a). Different browsers' menu and tool bars take up different amounts of space. In addition, the preferences set in the viewer's browser also determine the size of the menu and tool bars. Hence, even if the Web browser window is maximized to full screen size, the image needs to be smaller than the full screen resolution to fix in the browser window without having to scroll to see the full image.

(a)

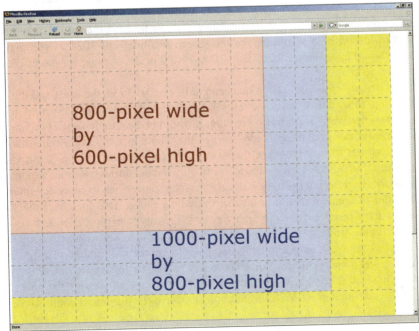

(b)

Figure 3.45 (a) An example of a Web browser window where the Web content is displayed in the large white area (b) The test image is displayed in the Web browser with window maximized to full screen of a resolution of 1280 × 1024 pixels (c) The same test image is displayed in the Web browser with window maximized to full screen of a resolution of 1024 × 768 pixels.

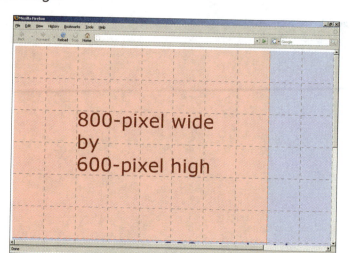

(c)

Figure 3.45 (*Continued*)

As shown in Figure 3.45b, for the screen resolution of 1280 × 1024 pixels, the image size should be no larger than about 1200 × 800 pixels in order for the whole image to be displayed without scrolling. Of course, if you include the title of your work on the same page, the image would need to be even smaller in order for both the title and the image to be viewed in full without scrolling. For the screen resolution of 1024 × 768 pixels, the image size should be no larger than about 1000 × 600 pixels in order for the whole image to fit in one screen.

When an image is too big to fit in one screen, its composition, the flow, and the motion that you design to lead the viewer's eyes will be disrupted. Hence, in general, if an image is displayed on the Web for portfolio viewing, it would be best to make it fit on one screen so that the viewer does not have to scroll to see the whole image. On the other hand, only allowing the viewer to see part of the image at a time can be used for artistic purposes in a digital artwork itself. Each view seems to allow only a view through a small window to the whole artwork. It creates a mystery—puzzle that the viewer has to piece together of the views in order to create a mental image of the whole piece. This increases the viewer's involvement in the piece and can raise the viewer's curiosity to explore the work.

The traditional, printed book form of a portfolio arranges artwork sequentially. The viewer looks at the work by going from one page to another. Of course, like reading any books, the viewer always can jump directly to any page. The former way of viewing is linear, and the latter is nonlinear. When these two different ways of viewing the book form of a portfolio is translated into a Web format, you also have the linear and nonlinear design to consider.

- **Linear design**: In this design, each page that contains your artwork always has a **link** or **button** to continue to the next page, and a link of button to move back to the previous page.
- **Non-linear design**: This design often has a main page (like a table of content) that lists all of the links to your artwork pages. **Thumbnails** often are used on this page. A thumbnail is a smaller image representing the full artwork. Thumbnails provide the

viewer a preview of your work. Loading multiple thumbnails is faster than loading multiple full images. Grouping thumbnails on a Web page provides the viewer an overview of your body of work. Some Web sites also make all the thumbnails available alongside each full view page so that the viewer can go to any individual artwork page any time.

Linear design seldom is used alone for the Web. Nonlinear design is more common. However, the two designs can be used in conjunction if you want to preserve the simulation of sequential viewing of a printed book.

You can have:

- a main page listing all of the links to your work,
- each individual page of your work including links or buttons to the next and previous pages,
- a navigation menu to any of your work.

CREATING THUMBNAILS: AESTHETICS AND TECHNICAL CONSIDERATIONS

A thumbnail can be a partial view of the artwork; it does not have to be the full view of the art. Because thumbnails are smaller in size, a full view of the artwork will not display well.

A thumbnail for each artwork should be created as a separate image with the proper pixel dimensions that does not require redefining its size in HTML. Technically, the display size of an image embedded on a Web page can be set to be different from the original size in the HTML code. However, this is not a good practice, because it will still take the same amount of time as the full image to load. The download time required for an image depends on the actual file size—which in turn depends on its pixel dimensions. Even if you decide to use the full view of your artwork in the thumbnail, the thumbnails still should be separate images with smaller pixel dimensions. Do not use the full image and redefine its width and height in HTML code to make it appear smaller. It will take a longer time to load many of these full images than smaller, resized thumbnails on the same Web page.

3.5 DIGITAL IMAGE TOOLS—ART AND DESIGN FUNDAMENTALS

Digital technology allows you to experiment with ideas and possibilities in your artwork but is by no means divorced from the aesthetics of traditional art. This section discusses common digital imaging tools that can help you incorporate the art and design elements—in terms of shape, line, value, color and space—and examine the application of the art and design organization principles in your artwork. Examples of tools and techniques will be discussed in this section, however, the intention is to give you pointers to the tools that you can look up in the Help of your digital image program. It is *not* the intention of this text to provide step-by-step how-to's of all the tools.

3.5.1 Shape

Tools such as brush, pencil, and pen let you create an outline freehand to create a new shape. In most situations, you probably want to create a shape based on an existing content in an image (usually a digital photo). The selection tools are useful. You first need to identify the best selection tools for your purpose. Often, you will need to use a combination of selection tools, not just one tool.

Selection

Making a selection in an image often is used to copy the content to paste into another image—for example, a collage. However, making a selection based on a visual content in an image does not mean you have to use the visual content in the selection. Think of the selection as a cookie cutter that you mold out of an object. That cookie cutter can be used to cut any type of cookie dough, but this does not mean that it can be used only to cut out the exact same object that it was modeled from. With a selection made, you can apply the selection to another image by making the layer of the new image active.

Let's look at an example of taking a shape from the visual content of one image and applying the shape to another image. Figure 3.46 shows a scanned picture with visible brush strokes. Suppose you want to use the shape of the brushed area but not the visual content inside it. This is a very irregular shape, and there is a wide range of tones in it. Hence, it is hard to use the Lasso tool or to select by color. You may notice that the shape you want to select here basically contains any non-white color. You easily can select the white area and then invert the selection.

The picture shown in Figure 3.46 originally was created by exposing a paper brushed with liquid light—a silver-based emulsion—to a film negative.

Figure 3.46 A scanned picture where the shape revealing the brush strokes will be used as a clipping mask in another image

Figure 3.47 shows a technique that may be useful for situations where the color between the areas you want to select and those you do not want to select is not as distinctive. You can exaggerate the color or tonal difference by moving either the highlight or shadow slider (depending on what you want to select) to one side or the other. Now, it becomes much easier to select the shape. The visual content inside this shape is destroyed, but in this example, it is the shape that you are interested in—not the visual content.

Figure 3.47 The color levels in the image shown in Figure 3.46 are reduced by using Adjust Levels to exaggerate the color difference, making the selection of the shape easier

Masking with a Shape

So, now it is easy to make a selection of the shape by using tools (such as magic wand tool) that allow selection by color. Once you get a selection, it can be used for many different purposes. Here we will show you using the shape as a clipping mask in Photoshop.

A clipping mask works so that the transparent pixels of a layer mask the content of the layer above it. It will be clear to you after you see the result in this example.

Step 1 The black shape shown in Figure 3.47 is copied to another image (Figure 3.48a). It is rotated 90° for this example.

Step 2 The layer of the pasted black shape is moved beneath the layer containing the image (Figure 3.48b).

Step 3 To create a clipping mask, select the image layer. Then select Layer > Create Clipping Mask or hold down the Alt key (Windows) or the Option key (Mac OS) and then click on the line dividing two layers in the Layers palette. Figure 3.48c shows the result of creating a clipping mask.

The content in the lower layer (the one containing the black shape) now clips the content in the layer above it. Think of the shape as a cookie cutter and the layers above it in the clipping group as the cookie dough. But unlike a cookie cutter, Clipping Mask is a non-destructive tool—the image being clipped or masked still is intact. You can reposition the image or the mask at any time to explore different variations in your composition.

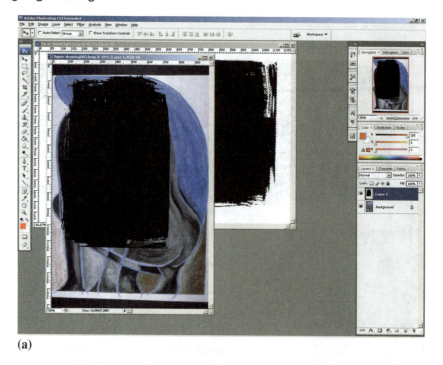

(a)

(b)

Figure 3.48 (a) The black shape from Figure 3.47 copied and pasted into another image (b) The layer containing the black shape moved beneath the image layer (c) A clipping mask is created

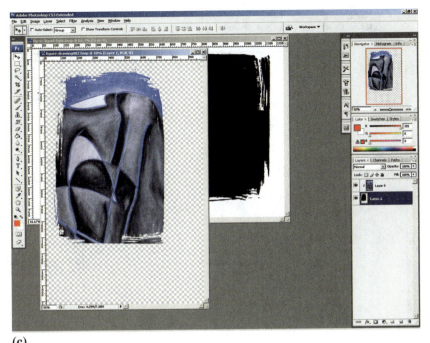

(c)

Figure 3.48 (*Continued*)

Edge of the Shape

The edge of the selection by default is hard. In some situations, you may want to soften the edge to give a more natural look. To soften the edge, you can apply a feather to the selection. A higher value of feathering makes the edge softer. After you have applied a feather to a selection, the shape of the selection may become smoothed out. The visual content that is under the selection will not change at this point. You only see the visual difference after you cut or copy the selected content and have pasted it into another image. Recall the cookie cutter analogy—this selection also is, like a cookie cutter. When you apply a feather to a selection, it is like you make the edge of the cookie cutter a little blunt—it does not affect the cookie dough until you make the cut and separate the cut-out piece from the cookie dough.

Creating Complex Shapes in Vector Graphics

In vector-graphic programs, the concept of selection is different from that in bitmap programs which make selection by pixels. When you make a selection in a vector graphic program, you select an *object,* such as a shape or a line. You can create shapes using the Pen tool or by freehand drawing a path but most vector graphic programs also let you combine different shapes to create complex shapes. For example, in Illustrator, a tool called ***Pathfinder*** lets you divide, trim, crop, outline, and subtract shapes to create more complex shapes. Figure 3.49a shows an example of applying the Divide option to three overlapping shapes. After ungrouping the divided shapes, each divided shape now can be selected individually (Figure 3.49b) to re-position or to apply different fills and strokes (Figure 3.49c).

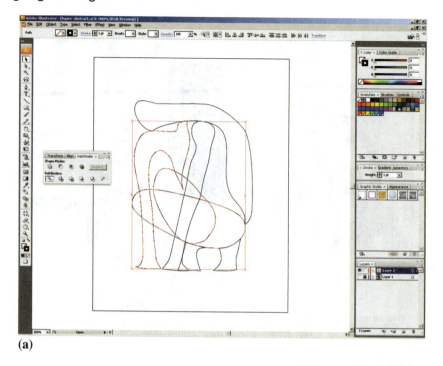

(a)

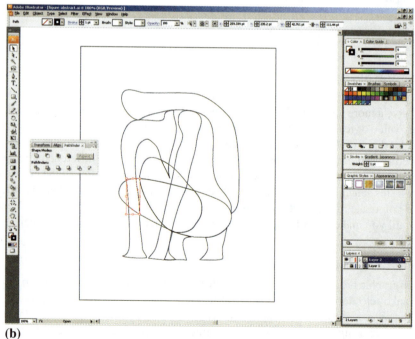

(b)

Figure 3.49 Pathfinder in Adobe Illustrator where Shapes to be combined are selected and then apply a Pathfinder action (a) Divide option is applied, (b) shapes are divided and can be selected independently after ungrouping, and (c) Divided shapes can be applied with different colors and patterns

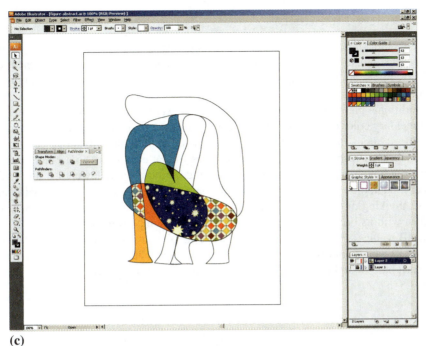

(c)

Figure 3.49 (*Continued*)

3.5.2 Line

As discussed in the section on digital drawing and painting, the brush tool lets you paint freeform lines. You can adjust the brush width and brush style. With a pressure-sensitive drawing tablet, you also can vary the brush width by pressure you apply to the tablet with the stylus.

Stroking a Selection

You can create lines by stroking a selection (Edit > Stroke . . . in Photoshop). This will give an outline of a closed shape. You always can use the eraser tool to remove the un-wanted part of the stroke to open up the shape. You can use a combination of selection tools to create and refine a selection before applying a stroke. Hence, by stroking a se-lection, you have more control on refining the shape than by freeform painting.

Pen Tool in Vector Graphics

In vector-graphic programs, you can use the pen tool to create paths. Then, you can apply a stroke style and width to the paths to create lines. Unlike bitmap-image programs, you can easily change the stroke style and width of the lines in vector graphics at any time later. Some examples are shown in the section on digital drawing and painting.

3.5.3 Value and Color

Value and color (hue) are discussed as two art and design elements in Chapter 2. In digital imaging, the adjustment of these two elements often coexists with color adjustment tools. Therefore, this section combines these elements and examines how digital imaging tools can work with them.

In traditional painting and drawing media, you lower the value of a color by mixing its complimentary color or by adding black. Colors in the digital realm are described in terms of RGB (red, green, and blue). To lower the value of a color, all of its red, green, and blue values will need to be lowered. In a sense, it is like adding black to a color. However, figuring out how much each of the red, green, and blue should be lowered is not intuitive. Another model, the HSB model (Hue, Saturation, and Brightness), works well with human intuitive thinking of colors. If you have a color in mind, you would first identify it with a hue, then with its brightness and saturation. The program converts the H, S, and B values into RGB values. For example, if you want to pick a color like the one shown in Figure 3.50, you would first identify it as a green color. Then, you decide that it is a light green (brightness) and not very intense (saturation). Its HSB an RBG values are shown in Figure 3.51a.

Figure 3.50 A green color.

Selecting Color Using Color Picker

Digital image-editing programs have visual color charts that you can use to choose among RGB, HSB, or other color modes. In Photoshop, the ***Color Picker*** is by default in the HSB mode.

You always can set the HSB or RGB of a color by entering the color value numbers without having to switch between options.

- When you click on the color chip on the Tool palette, the **H** option (hue) is selected in the Color Picker by default (Figure 3.51a). The vertical color slider bar displays all hues. You can choose a hue from the slider. Then, you can visually and simultaneously select the saturation and brightness of the hue from the big color field box on the left.
- If you select the **S** option (saturation), the vertical color slider bar will display the maximum to minimum saturation of that hue (Figure 3.51b). You then can choose a saturation from the vertical slider bar and the hue and brightness simultaneously from the color field box.
- If you select the **B** option (brightness), the vertical color slider bar will display the maximum to minimum brightness of that hue (Figure 3.51c). You then can choose a brightness from the slider bar and the hue and saturation from the color field box.

You can pick a color within any one of the H, S, or B options. You then can select one component from the color slider and the other two components from the color field box next to it. This is useful in picking a new color.

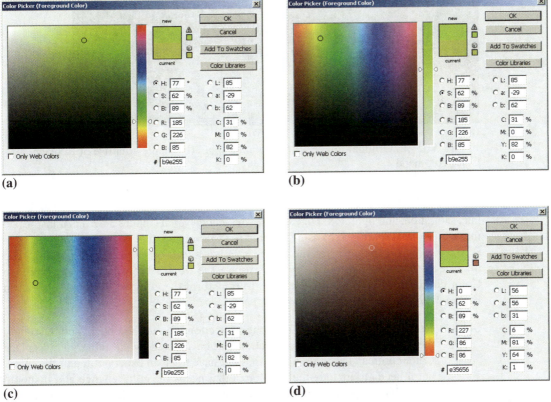

(a) (b) (c) (d)

Figure 3.51 Photoshop's Color Picker in HSB mode (a) H option displays all hues in the color slider (b) S option displays the maximum saturation to minimum saturation for the same color (c) B option displays the maximum brightness to minimum brightness of the selected color in the color slider (d) Changing the hue to red while preserving the saturation and brightness of the green color

When you want to modify only one property of a color—say just lowering its value—it would be better to select the B option to lower its brightness. By doing so you can change the brightness while preserving the hue and saturation of the original color.

In situations where you want to maintain a certain color scheme or mood within a project, you may want to maintain the same saturation and brightness of specific existing color in the project when picking a new color. In this case, you first use the Eyedropper tool to pick the existing color, and in the Color Picker, you then choose the H option and only change the hue in the color slider. Figure 3.51d shows that a green color is first selected and then its hue is altered to red. This new red color maintains the saturation and brightness of the previous green color.

Replacing Colors

There are situations that you want to replace a color in an image. Photoshop's **Replace Color** command lets you select a range of multiple colors and replace those colors by altering the

(a)   **(b)**

Figure 3.52 (a) Original image with an orange spool (b) Image after use of Replace Color command

hue, saturation, and lightness. For example, the orange spool (Figure 3.52a) is transformed into a blue one (Figure 3.52b) using the Replace Color command.

Depending on the color of the object relative to the other part of the image, you may need to make a rough selection around the object before using the Replace Color command. Let's discuss the steps to transform the color of the orange spool in Figure 3.52a.

Step 1 Use the Lasso tool to make a rough selection around the orange spool, so only the orange color within the selection will be affected by the subsequent Replace Color command. The selection does not have to be an exact outline of the spool, but it needs to include the spool area that needs the color change and it should not include extra areas that have similar colors such as yellow or red—its analogous colors.

Step 2 Once you have made a selection, you can select the Replace Color command (Image > Adjustments > Replace Color . . .) Use an Eyedropper tool, and click on the preview box in the Replace Color dialog box (Figure 3.53) to specify the color you want to replace. There are different Eyedropper tools that let you select, add, or remove colors that you want to replace. The orange spool is made up of a wide variety of different orange colors. You can use the Eyedropper tool (the one with an "+" sign) to add multiple orange colors as the target colors to be replaced.

Adjust the Fuzziness slider to specify the range of the related colors to be replaced. To specify the resulting color, you can adjust the Hue, Saturation, or Lightness sliders or click on the Result color chip to pick a color from the Color Picker.

The ***Match Color*** command is another color replacement tool. It matches the colors in one image with those in another. The two images can be different images or different layers in the same image. This is useful when you're trying to make the colors consistent across multiple images.

Another tool for modifying colors is the ***Variations*** command (Image > Adjustments > Variations . . .) (Figure 3.54). Unlike the Replace Color command which allows you specify colors to be replaced, the Variations command will alter all of the colors within a selection or the whole image if no selection is made. You can select whether the shadow, midtone, highlight, or saturation is adjusted. This tool is more intuitive to use—you pick

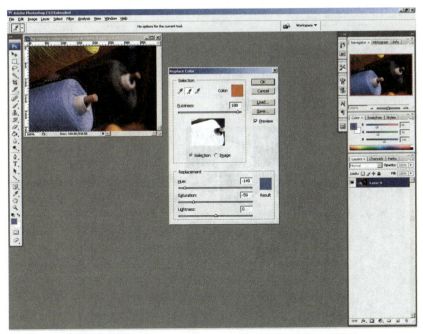

Figure 3.53 Photoshop's Replace Color command used to transform the orange color of the spool into blue

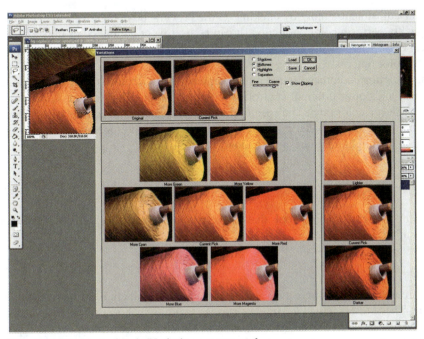

Figure 3.54 Photoshop's Variations command

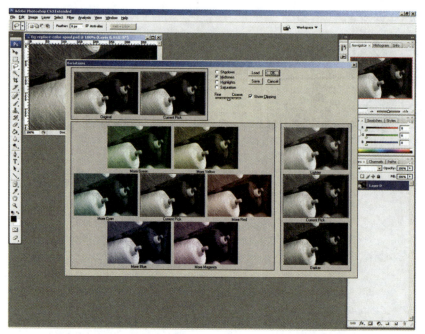

Figure 3.55 Photoshop's Variations command used to quickly apply a color tint to a desaturated image

the color adjustment simply by clicking on the preview box (Figure 3.54). This tool lets you quickly perform color correction. It can be useful for adding color tints to grayscale images. Figure 3.55 shows how to apply the Variations command to a desaturated image to add a color tint.

The Variations command is not a replacement of the Replace Color command. These two commands offer different controls of color alteration. The Replace Color command lets you select a color range and specify the new hue, saturation, and lightness. The Variations command lets you alter color by shifting the color and tone and by targeting areas defined by highlight, midtone, and shadow.

3.5.4 Texture

The common digital imaging tools that can help you create texture include filters, patterns, and scanning.

Filters

There are many *filters* for creating textures. In Photoshop, there is a filter category called Texture. These filters intend to simulate surface textures such as canvas, tiles, and stained glass. Texture as an art and design element is not limited to the meaning of the appearance of natural surface texture. Many other filter categories (such as Distort, Noise, Artistic, and Brush Strokes) can be used to add texture.

Patterns

A *pattern* contains a repetitive image. Photoshop includes a variety of preset patterns. You also can define your own patterns following these steps:

Step 1 Select the image content that you want to define a pattern.

Step 2 Select Edit > Define Pattern . . . and enter a name for your pattern (Figure 3.56).

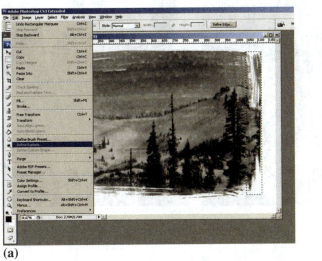

(a)   **(b)**

Figure 3.56 Defining custom patterns in Photoshop (a) Selecting an area for the unit of a new pattern and choosing Edit > Define Pattern . . . (b) Selected area as a new pattern

There are two ways you can apply your pattern on an image: by simple fill or by painting.

- *Fill*: To fill an area with a pattern, select Edit > Fill . . . , select Pattern as the content, and choose the pattern you want to fill the area with. Figure 3.57b shows the resulted image after the blue areas in Figure 3.57a are filled with the custom defined pattern (Figure 3.56b).
- *Painting*: The **Pattern Stamp tool**—a tool that is grouped with the **Clone Stamp tool** in the Tool palette—lets you choose a pattern, brush size, and style to paint the pattern on the image.

> ✏ **Photoshop: Defining Custom Patterns** A screen-capture movie demonstrates how to define custom patterns in Photoshop and then fill a selection with the custom pattern.

When the pattern is placed in a separate layer, layer blending can be applied to the pattern layer to let the pattern mix with the layers beneath it to create interesting effects. Figure 3.57c shows the result of the pattern-filled layer being set to the Hard Light blending mode. This makes the pattern color change to blend with the original blue color.

Digital image filters and patterns often give a canned and mechanical appearance, especially when you apply a filter indiscriminately to the whole image. When you choose to use filters and pattern filling, try to use them creatively and for a specific purpose. You can mix and blend different areas of your images with the filters with different opacity. You also can apply the filter or pattern to a selected area and alter the area further later.

(a)

(b)

(c)

Figure 3.57 (a) The image to be filled with a pattern (b) Blue areas are selected and filled with the custom defined pattern (Figure 3.56b) (c) The pattern-filled layer is set to the Hard Light blending mode

Scanning

You can acquire the texture of a natural object by scanning. The object is not limited to those that have an intrinsic surface texture, like fabric, paper, or tree bark. Texture can be created by the way how you arrange or "sculpt" the object on the scanner, for examples, a nylon net, tangling cables, a piece of wrinkled paper, or plastic wrap.

You always can add textures by drawing hatching on your digital images by using the pencil or brush tool. You also can create texture in traditional media and convert it into digital images by scanning or using digital photography.

3.5.5 Space

The several psychological depth cues discussed in Section 2.4.6 give you guidelines in creating an illusion of space and depth in a 2-dimensional (2-D) image. Now, let's examine digital image tools that can help you to create these depth cues.

Linear Perspective

This refers to the phenomenon that the farther object appears to be smaller than the object closer to the viewer. A simple scale tool will help you size the object. In Photoshop, the Scale tool can be found under Edit > Transform > Scale. You can scale a selected area or a whole layer.

Shading and Shadowing

This refers to the phenomenon that farther objects often appear to be darker than the objects closer to the viewer. Tonal adjustment tools let you adjust the shading of the image content. For example, adjusting the midtone in the level adjustment can shift the image to lighter or darker tone. The Dodge and Burn tools also let you brighten or darken the image by brushing on the areas.

The direction of the object's shadow and the way the shadow bends and shifts provide powerful cues of depth and space. The common way of creating shadows is to replicate the shape of the object, fill it with dark color, and distort it. A Blur filter often is needed to apply to the shadow to soften the edge.

Aerial Perspective

Distant objects often appear to be hazy, bluish, and less saturated. The Blur tool from the Tool palette is useful for blurring smaller areas that need a little more blending with the surrounding area. To blur a larger area, select the area and apply the Gaussian Blur filter.

The Hue/Saturation command lets you adjust the saturation and the degree of bluish color. Applying noise to the object also can help add a feeling of haziness. On the other hand, if you want to make the object appear closer to the viewer, use the Hue/Saturation command to boost the saturation, and then use a sharpening filter (Unsharp Mask) or the Sharpen tool in the Tool palette to make the object look crisper.

Interposition and Occlusion

When you want to create an illusion of an object in front of another, try to simulate an overlapping of objects. It is a good practice to organize different image content in separate layers so that you can arrange the layer of the front object on top of the layers of the objects below.

Retinal Image Size

Using recognizable objects can give the viewer a point of reference for the relative sizes of the objects. This depth cue is not applicable in a nonrepresentational work. However, an abstract work—still having reference to the natural world—can use this cue to create an interesting spatial relationship that bends the rule to depict visual ambiguity and distorted reality.

Texture Gradient

See Section 3.5.4 for creating texture in Photoshop.

How the coarseness of an object texture changes visually can imply a spatial difference. The coarseness of the texture can be created by scaling the area that is applied with texture. You also can define custom patterns to represent different coarseness.

Color

See Section 3.5.3 for example techniques to alter colors and values of objects.

Objects with bright colors (such as yellow and orange) often appear closer than objects with dark colors. When you compose an image, you many find that the color of the object may not always match your vision of their placement in the illusionary 3-D space. You may need to digitally alter the color of the object. Color adjustment tools are useful for this situation.

3.5.6 Composition

Layers are very useful tools that let you explore different composition by setting the visibility of each layer. You also can experiment with different positions of the image content by repositioning the layer. The Layer Comp feature in Photoshop lets you define different combinations of layer visibility, position, and style. You then can quickly switch between layer comps to compare different composition possibilities.

See Section 3.3.1 on black-and-white digital photography for the different methods.

Non-destructive editing tools, such as layer masks and adjustment layer tools, discussed at the beginning of the chapter are useful in experimenting with different compositions while allowing you to revert to the original stage of a layer or to change the adjustment settings any time.

Removing color information often can help you see the overall composition of your image. Removing color information means converting the images into grayscale.

3.5.7 Repetition

There are several digital imaging techniques that are useful for repeating visual content.

- *Copying and pasting*: The simplest way to repeat visual content is by copying and pasting.
- *Cloning*: With cloning, you copy part of the image by painting. The brush size, brush style, and softness can be adjusted. Thus, this can give the duplicated content a more freeform and organic appearance than simple copying and pasting.
- *Defining patterns*: Once you have defined a visual content as a pattern, you can create repetition of the content by filling an area with the pattern.

Refer to Section 3.5.4 for defining and applying patterns in Photoshop.

Whenever you duplicate the image content, make the content into separate layers if possible. The new content will not destroy the original image, and you can reposition the repeated content later if needed, allowing you to experiment with different compositions.

Repetition does not necessarily mean a straightforward duplication. Repetition also may have variations in size, value, color, and orientation. By separating the duplicated content into layers, you easily can add variations to individual duplicates.

3.5.8 Balance and Emphasis

Balance and emphasis are discussed together here as many single digital imaging tools can be used to help you to examine these two elements in a digital image.

Zoom Tool

When you draw or paint with traditional media, you often stand back to look at your work. With digital images, you can use the zoom tool to quickly bring your image to almost any size. Viewing your work at a small thumbnail size often helps you identify the emphasis and visual balance of your work.

Mirror

Digital images can be flipped or mirrored. This will allow you to see your work at different perspectives and break away from some preconceptions that may have prevented you from objectively analyzing the composition of your work.

Grayscale

Removing color information from an image may reveal its emphasis and balance better through lights and darks. This will help you identify problems with the emphasis and balance of the image.

Selection Tools and Layers

The simplest way to add visual emphasis is to create differences from the surrounding—line style and width, shape, value, color, and texture. In order to alter an area, you need to be able to isolate the area—for example, by selection or by organizing the visual content in layers.

Lines (real or imaginary) can imply motion and direct the viewer's eye within the piece. You can use a separate layer to sketch out these lines to use as guidelines for placement of visual content.

3.5.9 Perspective

There are several tools that may help you create perspective.

Transform Tool

The Transform tool in Photoshop lets you apply a one-point perspective to the selected image content. You also can combine the use of rotation, distortion, and skew to create the perspective that you want.

Scale

The effect of perspective can be created by applying a linear-perspective visual cue—the perceived size of an object gets smaller as it is farther away from the viewer. Thus, a group of objects with a progressive change in scales can be used to imply perspective.

Vanishing Point

In the recent editions of Photoshop, a tool called *Vanishing Point* lets you preserve correct perspective in editing images that contain apparent perspective planes. For example, to remove the metal siding on the far side of the side wall in Figure 3.58a, the Stamp tool may be used to clone one half of the side wall to cover the other half. However, direct cloning will duplicate image content in the same size which is undesirable. The Vanishing Point filter lets you define a perspective plane for the side wall (Figure 3.59a). The Stamp tool will then follow the perspective defined by the plane. Figure 3.59b shows the cloning in progress so that part of the metal siding on top has been replaced. Figure 3.58b shows the final result when the half of the side wall has been cloned over completely.

(a)

(b)

Figure 3.58 (a) Before altering the side wall of the barn (b) After cloning the half of the side wall using Photoshop's Vanishing Point command to cover the metal siding that is farther from the viewer

(a)

(b)

Figure 3.59 Photoshop's Vanishing Point filter using (a) the Create Plane Tool to define the perspective plane of the side wall to be cloned and (b) the Stamp Tool to clone the content based on the perspective defined by the plane

3.6 MAKING CONVINCING COMPOSITES

This section introduces several concepts, tools, and techniques for composing digital image content originated from different sources into a convincing composite. Here, *convincing* refers to the effect that the combined images look integrated and seamless as a whole. The result is not necessarily a faithful reproduction of the reality. Although the two examples provided in this section are composed using digital photos, the techniques can be applied not only to photorealistic works but also to abstract and nonrepresentational works. The technical craftsmanship often depends on making selections, using blending, matching colors and tones, and creating shadows.

Creating a believable composite requires understanding of perspective, space, light, shade, and shadows. A combination of tools and techniques often are needed. Many tools and techniques that are useful in creating convincing composites already have discussed in this chapter.

Selection is the tool used most commonly in the composite creation process. It is crucial to make a good selection when you need to extract the object or to contain the subsequent modification within the selection. Feathering often is applied to the selection to soften the edge; hard edges often make it look disjointed.

Keep in mind that if objects coexist in the same scene, they often manifest visual impact (such as shadows, reflection, and overlapping) on one another and on the environment. These elements often will need to be created, but they can be based on the objects in the source images. For example, shadows can often be created by distorting the duplicate of the original object, filling in spaces with dark color, blurring, and applying a layer Multiply blend. Such visual influences may be subtle at times, but they add the believability to the final composite.

This section uses two examples to demonstrate the process and the selection of the tools. The names of the tools used to produce the effect are referenced. The intention of these examples is to give you an idea of the composite process and what is possible. Once you have the names of the tools, you easily can find more information about them by looking them up in the Help menu.

The settings for each tool require experimentation. It is not the intention of this text to give you a step-by-step recipe to faithfully reproduce the examples discussed here. Hence, no detailed settings for each tool will be provided. The source images for both examples are available at the book's Web site. You are encouraged to follow the steps and experiment with the settings.

3.6.1 Example 1: Replicating an Object in Its Environment

In this example, the final image (Figure 3.60b) contains an extra duplicated object—a humanoid chain sculpture—which is not in the original image (Figure 3.60a). This example demonstrates the following aspects.

- Application of selection
- Scaling with the perspective in mind
- Creation of shadows

Step 1   **Selecting the Object of Interest for Duplication: Quick Mask**

Quick Mask is chosen to make a selection for the standing chain sculpture (Figure 3.61). Although it is made up of dark colors, there are many small, bright

(a)

(b)

Figure 3.60 (a) Original digital photo of a sculpture (Will Garin's *Link (3 Figures)*)
(b) Final composite with an extra chain sculpture

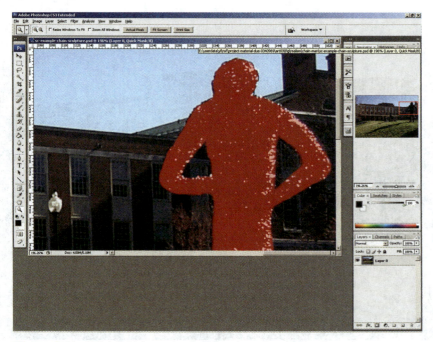

Figure 3.61 Quick Mask mode showing the selected area in red

sparkles that prevent you from quickly making a contiguous selection by color (as by using the Magic Wand tool.) You can use any selection tool to make a rough selection first and then refine the selection using Quick Mask.

Save Selection: Because making the selection is not trivial and takes some time and effort, it would be preferable to save the selection (Select > Save Selection . . .) frequently during the selection-making process. You always can overwrite the same selection name or load the selection later to refine. In this example, the edge around the head of the sculpture has a blue matt because of the sky. The blue matt becomes very visible when the duplicate of the sculpture later is placed against dark background. The saved selection indeed has been reloaded and refined a few times to contract the selection of the head area until the blue matt is excluded from the selection.

Step 2 **Scale the Duplicate:** Transform > Scale
The selected chain sculpture is copied and pasted into a new layer. The duplicate is scaled. Its size is determined by its new location and the linear perspective in the scene (Figure 3.62).

Step 3 **Creating Shadows**
Without the shadow, the duplicate would look pasted and disjointed from the environment (Figure 3.62). To demonstrate how shadows can affect the perception of the object in its environment, Figure 3.63 shows a vertical separation of the shadow from the duplicate, giving an illusion that the sculpture is floating in mid-air.

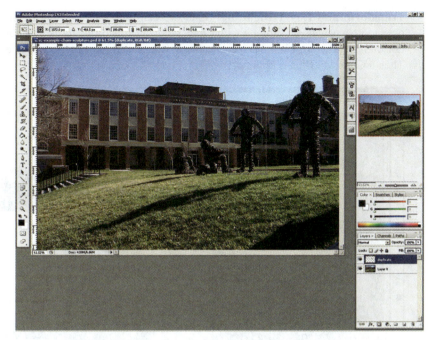

Figure 3.62 The chain sculpture copied and pasted into a new layer then scaled in accordance to its location and the linear perspective in the scene

Figure 3.63 When the shadow is offset vertically from the sculpture, it causes an illusion that the sculpture is floating

Transform and Layer Blending: Shadows can be created by duplicating the object into a new layer, filling it with a dark color, and distorting it (using a combination of Scale, Distort, Warp, Perspective, Skew, Rotate, and Flip options) (Figure 3.64). Then a Gaussian Blur is applied.

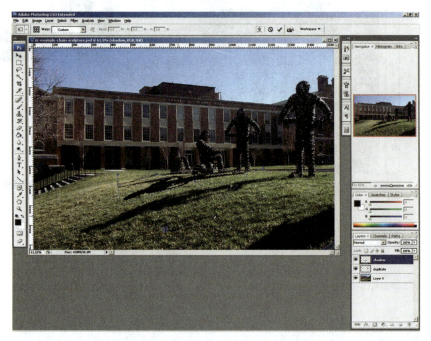

Figure 3.64 The shadow for the pasted sculpture is created by warping the duplicate of the sculpture after a series of transformations

The Warp tool (Transform > Warp) is handy to bend the shadow and distort different areas unproportionally. Many other tools that may not be obvious for shadow creation can be used as you see fit. For example, the Stamp tool also can be used to elongate some part of the shadow. You also can use the Eraser tool to further refine the shape of the shadow. Color tint also can be applied to the shadow—for example, a dark green tint is applied here because the shadow is on a green lawn. The original shadows also have a green tint. Finally, layer blend and transparency are applied to the shadow layer to let the grass texture show through.

> ✎ **Source Image for Example 1**
> You can download the source image to try out the tools discussed to reproduce the final composite as shown here.

3.6.2 Example 2: Recreating a Sky Background

In this example, the final image (Figure 3.65c) contains an artificial sky and is created by compositing two digital images (Figure 3.65a and b). The tools used to make the composite include:

- Layer blending mode
- Layer mask
- Layer style
- Filters
- Stamp tool
- Dodge tool

(a)

(b)

(c)

Figure 3.65 (a) Digital photograph of a lighthouse at dusk (b) Rendering of a 3-D model (c) Final composite

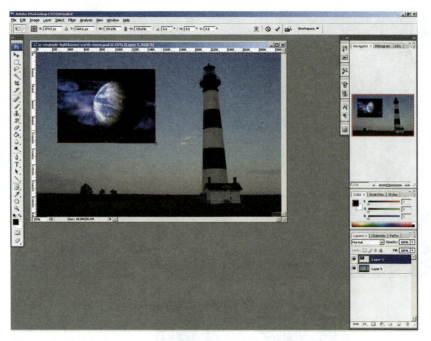

Figure 3.66 Placing the two source images in separate layers and scaling the moon image

Step 1   **Combining Two Images: Layers and** *Transform > Scale*
The moon image is pasted into the lighthouse photo (Figure 3.66). The moon image has much lower resolution than the lighthouse photo. When the moon image is scaled to cover the sky area of the lighthouse photo, it becomes less defined. This would match the intent here to give the planets a distant, hazy appearance.

Layer Blending Mode: The Layer Blending mode of the layer with the moon image is set to Screen in this example. The original sky of the lighthouse photo is blended nicely with the moon image.

Step 2   **Masking the Area the Moon Image will not Cover**
The moon image is now covering the lighthouse and the ground. To make it only occupy the sky area, you need to make a selection of the sky first. Because the sky is made up of very smooth and continuous colors, tools that allow selection by color would be useful. The **Magic Wand** tool is used in this example—multiple selections with Magic Wand are added together to make one big selection for the sky (Figure 3.67). A slight feathering is applied to the selection to soften the edge. This reduces the pasted-in look after the lighthouse and the ground areas have been masked on the moon image.

Layer Mask: Instead of inverting the selection and deleting the pixel content of the moon image, a non-destructive method (Layer mask) is used (Figure 3.68). This keeps the moon image intact, allowing further manipulation (such as repositioning the moon image, if needed). For example, if you unlink the moon image from its Layer Mask, the moon image can be repositioned while the mask for the lighthouse and the ground stays in place.

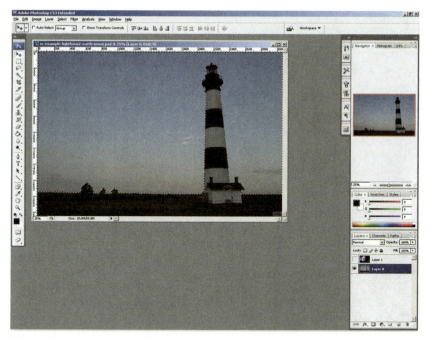

Figure 3.67 Make a selection of the sky area in the lighthouse image

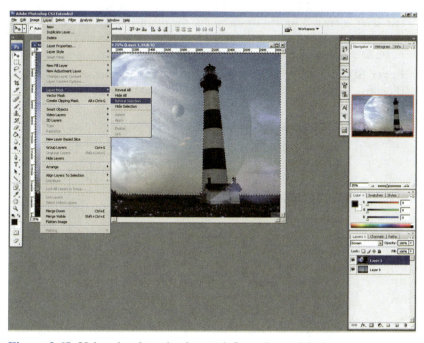

Figure 3.68 Using the sky selection to define a Layer Mask
for the moon image

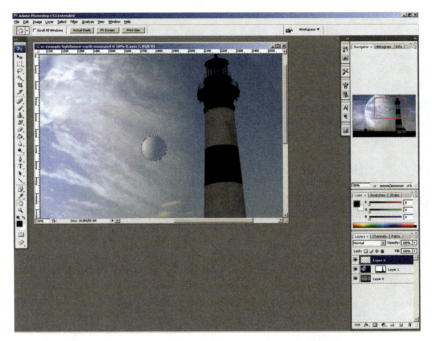

Figure 3.69 Select the moon using the Oval Marquee tool and create a new layer

Step 3 **Applying Effects to the Moon**

Layer and Filters: You need to make a selection of the moon first. In this case, the Oval Marquee tool is perfect, because the moon is circular (Figure 3.69). A separate layer is created for the moon so that the original image preserved in case you want to revert back to the original. Filters > Render > Clouds is applied to fill the moon selection with an orange to white texture.

Layer Style: This layer then is applied with a combination of Layer Styles (Figure 3.70), such as Outer Glow, Inner Glow, and Color Overlay.

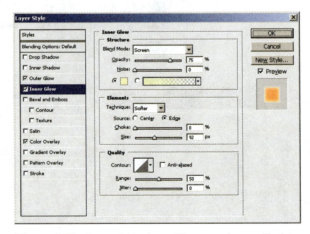

Figure 3.70 A combination of layer styles applied to the new moon layer

Step 4 **Refining by Removing Distractions and Enhancing Realism**

Stamp Tool: After examining the image, a distraction is found—a gray block at the lower right-hand corner of the lighthouse image. It can be removed using the Stamp tool to clone the nearby ground to cover it.

Dodge Tool: The windows on the lighthouse are dodged to add light reflection. Lightening up the windows on the lighthouse also draws some of the attention to the foreground. The ground in the lighthouse image is dodged to give an impression of light from the moon. These subtle changes create the visual influence of the object in one image on the other—an object has certain visual influence (whether by reflection or shadow) on other objects if it really coexists with these other objects.

> ✏ **Source Images for Example 2**
> You can download the two source images to try out the tools to produce the final composite as explained.

3.6.3 Example 3: Tools in Vector-Graphic Application Programs for Organic Look

Vector graphics are used well for producing hard-edged shapes. The general gradient fill interpolates color changes in a defined gradient—often giving a smooth, mechanical appearance. Thus, it is harder to achieve photorealistic effects with vector graphics than with bitmap images. However, vector-graphic programs have added tools that help you add an organic feel to the graphics. For example, the Blur effect in Illustrator lets you soften the edge of a shape (Figure 3.71).

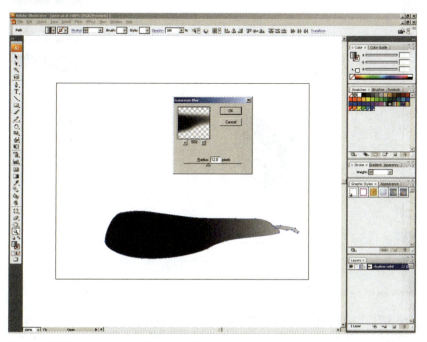

Figure 3.71 Applying a Gaussian Blur effect to a shape in Adobe Illustrator

The starting shape shown is filled with a gradient from gray to black. A larger radius value will soften the edge more. The resulted blurred shape is the pear shadow shown later in Figure 3.74b through c.

Blend Tool: Gradient and Repetition

The Blend tool or Blend command (Object > Blend) lets you blend colors, opacities, and shapes between objects. You can select two objects to define the beginning and ending shapes, opacities, and colors of the blend. Applying a blend (Object > Blend > Make) will create the intermediate steps that interpolate the colors, opacities, and shapes of both ends of the blend to create a softening effect.

Figure 3.72 demonstrates the effects of different blending options. Although a smaller step size or larger distance lowers the smoothness of the blend, it also may give interesting effects. In this example, lowering the smoothness depicts an appearance of an onion.

The example shown in Figure 3.72 blends four shapes that are stacked on top of another. However, the shapes to be blended do not have to be stacked. Figure 3.73 shows the four shapes are separated. A small step size or large distance makes each intermediate step in the blend a distinct object that morphs between two shapes. The blending in this case does not produce smoothness. However, it creates repetition with variations.

The *Gradient Mesh tool* in Illustrator also allows you to create a soft color blending, such as the pear shown in Figure 3.74. A gradient mesh can be created on a shape (Figure 3.74a). It is made up of points and patches. Specifying the color and position of the points or patches on the mesh creates color blending (Figure 3.74b).

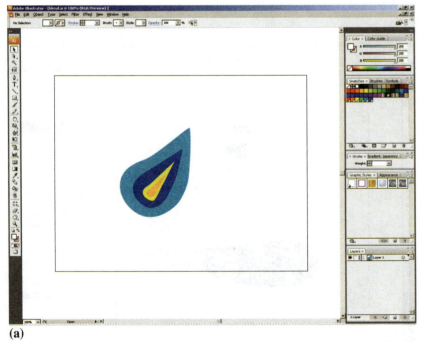

(a)

Figure 3.72 Blending in Adobe Illustrator (a) Four shapes to be used for blending (b) using Smooth Color option, (c) setting the number of steps between shapes to 3, (d) setting the distance between each step to 14 points

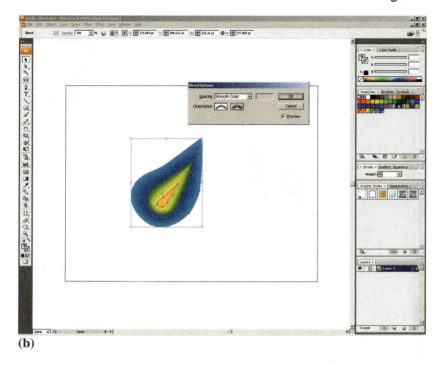

(b)

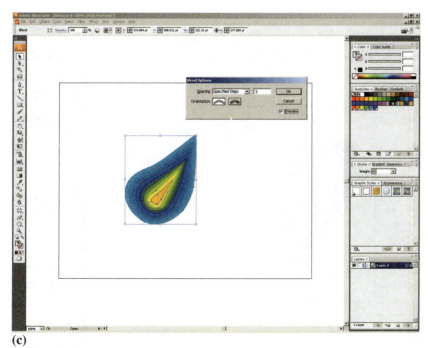

(c)

Figure 3.72 (*Continued*)

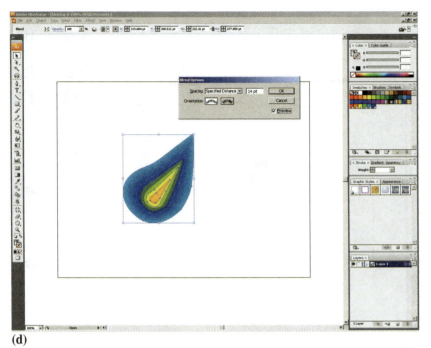

(d)

Figure 3.72 (*Continued*)

Figure 3.73 Blend by setting the number of steps between shapes to 3. So that the starting four shapes are separated instead of being stacked on top of another.

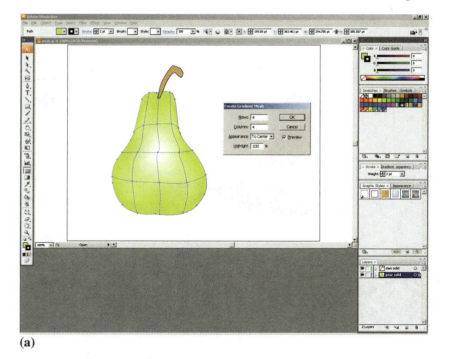

(a)

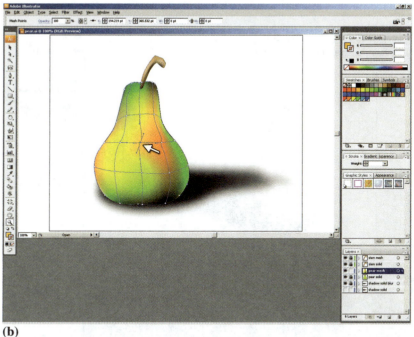

(b)

Figure 3.74 Adobe Illustrator's Gradient Mesh used to create soft color blending. (a) A 4 3 4 gradient mesh for the pear shape (b) An orange color is assigned to one of the mesh point (indicated by the white arrow) (c) A light green color is assigned to another mesh point (indicated by the white arrow) (d) More rows are added with the Mesh tool in the Tool palette to the top of the pear shape

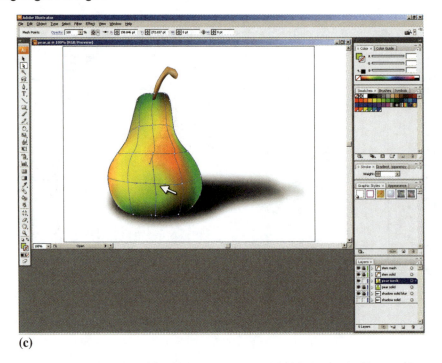

(c)

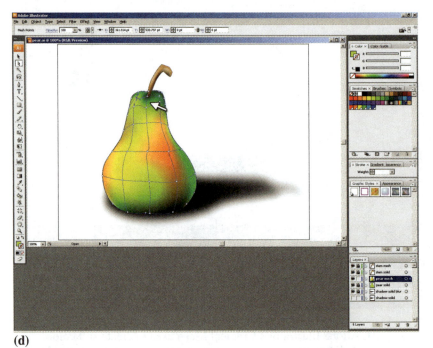

(d)

Figure 3.74 (*Continued*)

To start a grid by specifying the number of rows and columns, you can select the shape and choose Object > Create Gradient Mesh . . . (Figure 3.74a). You also can use the Mesh tool on the Tool palette to create a mesh or add more rows and columns to an existing mesh. It would be best to start with a minimal number of rows and columns using the ***Create Gradient Mesh*** command to block out the overall color blending of the shape. Then use the Mesh tool to add rows or columns to the areas that needs more color details.

In the pear example shown in Figure 3.74, the pear shape starts with a 4 × 4 mesh (Figure 3.74a). Points are specified with colors to create a color blending. For this example, a mesh point near the top is assigned with an orange color (Figure 3.74b) and one of its adjacent points is assigned with a light green color (Figure 3.74c). The color chip in the Tool palette shows the color assigned to the selected point. Color blending of the orange and light green colors occurs between these two points. Then, two more rows are added to the top of the pear near the stem area where finer color details are needed to create the shading to depict the dip at the base of the stem (Figure 3.74d).

Importing Bitmapped Images

Although vector-graphics programs are not designed to create and edit bitmapped images (such as digital photographs), most of these programs let you import bitmapped images. You can use vector shapes to clip bitmap images.

For example, you can import bitmapped images by choosing File > Place . . . Figure 3.75 shows a bitmapped image—a scanned fabric—imported in the Illustrator file of the pear example. The imported image shown in the figure is tilted because it has been rotated.

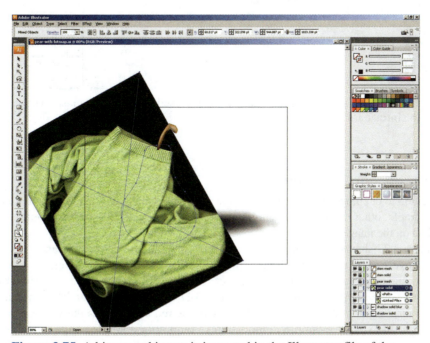

Figure 3.75 A bitmapped image is imported in the Illustrator file of the pear example

Clipping Mask

If you are not using Illustrator, search in your vector-graphic program Help menu using the keywords "clipping" or "mask" to find out if there is a feature similar to the Clipping Mask command.

The pear shape is then used to clip this image using the clipping mask command. While the path of the pear and the imported image are selected (the path layer being on top of the image layer), select the Clipping Mask command (Object > Clipping Mask > Make). The image will show through the pear shape (Figure 3.76). The clipping is non-destructive (i.e., the content in the image outside of the pear shape is not deleted), it is just hidden or masked. You can still drag to reposition the image. Such flexibility allows you to explore different composition.

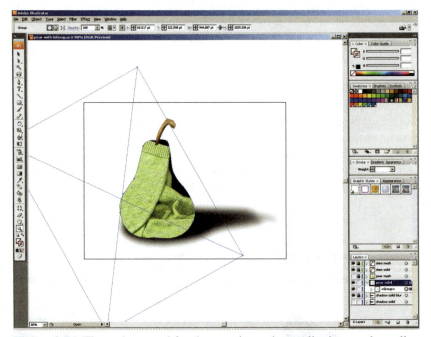

Figure 3.76 The path created for the pear is used as a clipping mask to clip the bitmap image

Overlay Using Transparency

In addition to clipping, other vector objects in the file can interact with the imported image. For example, other shapes set to semitransparent (using the Transparency palette) can be overlaid on the image.

Figure 3.77 shows the gradient mesh created in the previous example and set to 55% opacity overlaid on the clipped image. In this particular example, the overlay of the gradient mesh seems to remove the flatness of the clipped image because the flow of the color and value in the gradient mesh depicts a 3-D volume of the pear. The way the fold of the fabric in the red area follows the flow of the red accentuates the volumetric feel. Although this simple example demonstrates combining a single shape with a single image, more complex composites can be created with multiple images and perform multiple clippings.

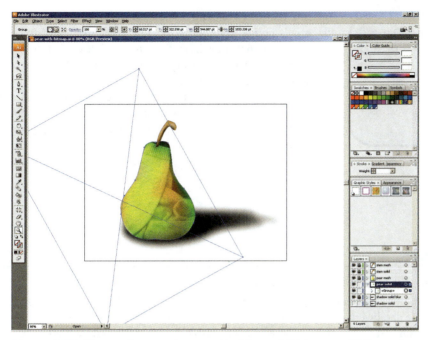

Figure 3.77 The gradient mesh created in Figure 3.74 is set to 55% opacity and overlaid on the clipped image

3.7 ABSTRACT AND NONREPRESENTATIONAL IMAGES

Representational objects often have their connotations. While some connotations may be common to the majority, they are not universal—some may be personal to the individual viewer and some differ by cultural and religious background. These connotations may be advantageous to you when the interpretation by the viewers matches the intended message of your work. However, some hidden connotations may exist that diverge from the intention of your message.

Removing the representational aspects of objects lets you convey your messages free of viewers' predisposed judgments that may be associated with the objects. Such expression of feeling can be rested on a different awareness that encourage viewers to think deeper, draw from their inward experience, and use their imagination to interpret the work beyond the immediate meaning of representational objects.

Abstract art has reference to the known natural form of the object that it depicts, but its reality is distorted. You often can tell what the reference is, but it is obvious that the work is not trying to reproduce an exact visual reality of the object.

Nonrepresentational art has no reference to the natural form and often uses shapes, lines, and colors to convey emotions.

Digital image filters are objective in extracting visual content into shapes or different forms based on pure visual criteria, such as colors. Hence, they can be effective in abstracting visual content into shapes, dismissing their connotations. Filters are useful *aids* to help you look past the associated meaning and visualize the object in its basic, neutral visual form. Because of this, a plain application of filters to an image often results in a feel of

Project Aid: Making Sense Out of Random Words This Web page randomly generates a set of words—one adjective, one emotion, one noun, one phrase, and one verb. Use the whole set or select your own to construct a unified and coherent idea, story, or emotion by connecting these words. Create an artwork based on your choice.

"generic dazzling" but emotionless effect, lack of depth, and loss of the artist's unique style. Filters can be good visual aids to help you explore ideas, but they should not be used "as-is". Filters can be used more creatively by being applied to selected areas which are digitally manipulated before or after the application of the filter. Such further manipulation rests on your consciousness to express your message in your own way and hence can make your work richer than a plain, computational conversion of the pixel color information.

TERMS

abstract art, 177
add, subtract, intersect, exclude and invert selections, 91
adjustment layers, 102
aperture, 112
Brush tool, 90
Channel Mixer, 116
Channel palette, 119
clipping mask, 102
Clone Stamp tool, 153
Color Balance tool, 92
Create Gradient Mesh, 175
Curve adjustment tool, 96
document size, 130
Dodge tool, 169
filters, 152
Gradient Mesh tool, 170

histogram, 92
ISO numbers, 113
JPEG, 114
layer blending, 164
Layer Comps, 105
layer mask, 102
layer mask tool, 166
Layer Style tool, 166
Layers, 91
levels, 92
marquee tools, 91
Match Color command, 150
multiply, 128
Nonrepresentational art, 177
opacity, 128
opening up, 112
Paint Bucket tool, 90
Pathfinder tool, 145

pattern, 153
Pattern Stamp tool, 153
Pen tool, 91
Pencil tool, 90
Polygonal Lasso tool, 91
Quick Mask tool, 91
RAW, 114
Replace Color command, 149
Resample Image, 130
Save Selection command, 162
shutter speed, 111
stopping down, 112
TIFF, 114
Tool palette, 90
Vanishing Point tool, 158
Variations command, 150

LEARNING AIDS

The following learning aids can be found at the book's companion Web site.

Photoshop Workspace
A screen-capture movie introduces the workspace of Adobe Photoshop.

Photoshop Tool Palette
A screen-capture movie introduces the Tool palette in Adobe Photoshop.

Photoshop Basics: Using Layers
A screen-capture movie and a worksheet exercise on the basics of the Layers palette in Photoshop.

🖰 **Photoshop Basics: Selection (worksheet exercise)**
A worksheet exercise to identify the different selection tools in Photoshop.

🖰 **Understanding and Applying Curves for Color Adjustments**
An interactive tutorial and exercises help you understand the Curves tool for image adjustment.

🖰 **Light Metering Emulation**
An emulation of photographing a still life. It lets you see how spot-metering different parts of the scene affects the overall tones of the resulted image.

🖰 **JPEG Compression Artifact (worksheet exercise)**
Look at the impact of JPEG compression artifact on different digital images, and learn when and why an image may be or should not be saved in JPEG format.

🖰 **Channel Mixer (worksheet exercise)**
This exercise helps you understand how Channel Mixer works and how to customize a conversion of a color image to a black-and-white (grayscale) image.

🖉 **Photoshop: Defining Custom Brushes**
A screen-capture movie demonstrates how to define custom brushes in Photoshop.

🖉 **Photoshop: Extract Filter**
A screen-capture movie demonstrates how to use the Extract filter in Photoshop to extract an object with fuzzy edges.

🖰 **Test Image for Web Browser Display**
The test image (Figure 3.44) is available marked with different pixel dimensions.

🖉 **Photoshop: Defining Custom Patterns**
A screen-capture movie demonstrates how to define custom patterns in Photoshop and then fill a selection with the custom pattern.

🖰 **Source Image for Example 1**
You can download the source image to try out the tools discussed to reproduce the final composite as shown here.

🖰 **Source Images for Example 2**
You can download the two source images to try out the tools to reproduce the final composite as explained.

🖰 **Project Aid: Making Sense Out of Random Words**
This Web page randomly generates a set of words—one adjective, one emotion, one noun, one phrase, and one verb. Use the whole set or select your own to construct a unified and coherent idea, story, or emotion by connecting these words. Create an artwork based on your choice.

ASSIGNMENTS

Assignment 1. Learn by Copying—Vector Graphics
Choose a master painting and obtain a digital image of the painting. Import it into a vector-graphic program, such as Adobe Illustrator. Replicate the painting into a vector graphic. Identify the lights and darks, and block out these areas into shapes using the Pen or Pencil tool. (Use the Pen tool if possible, as it takes a little more practice to than the pencil tool. The

Pencil tool allows freehand drawing, but it may create too many anchor points, making the whole file bigger and slower at the end.)

To find master paintings, look up on the Web such sites as http://www.artchive.com/ftp_site.htm or http://www.worldimages.com or art resources (such as the visual resources library of the Art Department) at your institution.

Assignment 2. Learn by Copying—Bitmap Images

Choose a master painting and get a digital image of the painting. This time, use a bitmap program (such as Photoshop) to replicate the painting. Identify the lights and darks. Use the Brush tool to block them out. Use layers to group the brush strokes of different parts of the image.

To find master paintings, look up on the Web such sites as http://www.artchive.com/ftp_site.htm and http://www.worldimages.com/ and art resources (such as the visual resources library of the Art Department) at your institution.

Assignment 3. Still-Life Digital Painting

Construct a physical still life. If you have a pressure-sensitive tablet, make a digital sketch of the still life in Photoshop. (Suggested resolution is about 8" × 10" at 300 ppi, or 2400 × 3000 pixels.) If you do not have a tablet, draw a pencil sketch of the still life and then scan your sketch into a digital image.

In Photoshop, create new layers on top of your sketch. Use the Pen tool to create paths to represent shapes of objects in your still-life sketch. Load one path at a time as a selection, and paint in the selection. Make sure you are painting on the intended layer.

Tips: (1) When you paint inside a selection, feel free to stroke outside of the selection edge to make sure that the stroke covers the selection to the edge. Only the selected area can be modified by the paint stroke. The purpose of making a selection before you paint is to help you paint freely while only the pixels within the selected area are affected.

(2) If the selection edge seems too hard, you can soften the edge of the selection by feathering before you paint. Alternately, you also can apply the Gaussian Blur filter or use the Blur tool to selectively blur the edge after you have painted the shape.

Assignment 4. Digital Filter Overflow

Abstract works often are thought to be easier than realistic ones because there are no physical models to use as a standard to judge for details and accuracy. However, good abstract paintings are not easy to create. They still require thought, time, care, and control. Digital image filters also are thought to be easy to use to create abstract effects. However, effective use of filters or effects to convey an intended message is not trivial.

In this assignment, choose the message you want to convey through the work. You can choose an emotion you want to express or several words to connect them into a story. (*Tip:* Use the online project aid, "Making Sense Out of Random Words".) Start with one or more image sources, and apply as many filters as you can to create a meaningful abstract image.

One objective of this assignment is to let you explore and experiment with as many filters as you desire. Another objective is to have you think about how to use non-representational visual content to transcend an emotion. (Review Sections 2.4 and 2.5.)

If this is a class assignment, let's see who can use the most filters and still convey the message—without the distractions of "dazzling effects."

PROJECTS

Project 1. Digital Montage
Create a montage using different image sources:
> Digital photography
> Scanned objects
> Scanned sketches
> Digital painting and drawing

To get ideas for this project, look up photomontage and the works by John Heartfield, Hannah Höch, Johannes Baader, Raoul Hausmann, and George Grosz on the Web or art resources (such as the visual resources library of the Art Department) at your institution.

Project 2. Inside and Outside
A shape and its visual content within can be used to represent different things—meanings, emotions, or expressions. It can be filled with a solid color or a pattern that implies an inner emotion of the object being represented by the shape. Filling with white or black often creates a sense of negative space—a void or an absence, as demonstrated in Figure 2.25. Depending on the context of the work, the absence can accentuate the presence of the missing subject. It also can help viewers think deeply while trying to understand the work and use their imagination to fill in the gap.

In this project, based on an image, create a selection that has a recognizable shape. The image that you start with can be a digital photograph or a scanned image of your artwork in traditional media. Fill in the selection with visual content that is not part of the representation of the shape. The content filling in the shape does not have to be one single, intact image; use a montage of images from various sources (such as digital photography, digital drawing and painting, or digital images of your artwork in traditional media.)

Project 3. Who Am I?
Before you make a self-portrait, start some self-exploration by writing down your thoughts about yourself. How do you see yourself—personality, character, physical appearance? How do you think others see you? What kind of a person do you want others to see in you? How do you want to be represented in a self-portrait? What will be the facial expression, posture, and clothing? Do you want to abtract yourself using lines, shapes, and color? What is the surrounding? What will you be doing in the portrait? If you want to portray yourself actively doing something, what will it be? Does the action reflect who you are?

Look up and study self-portraits of artists*—for example, Albrecht Dürer, Frida Kahlo, Rembrandt van Rijn, Vincent van Gogh, Paul Gauguin, Egon Schiele, Leonardo da Vinci, Pablo Picasso, Jan van Eyck, Mary Cassat, Andy Warhol, Norman Rockwell, Milton Avery, Henri Matisse, or Jacob Lawrence. What do their portraits tell you about their personalities and characters? What are the cues in the artwork that make you think so about them? Many artists created more than one self-portrait in their lifetime. It is interesting to look at an

---

*Useful resources can be found at the following Web sites:
http://www.nga.gov/education/classroom/self_portraits/act_intro_self.shtm
http://www.artchive.com/tours/selfport.html

artist's self-portraits created at different times, because they reflect a different person and the evolution of his/her artistic style.

Project 3. Personal Map[†]

Create a map representing a slice of yourself or your life.

Traditional maps intend to document physical locations. A map is a means of interpreting complex information in a way that makes it easy to comprehend. Your map may reconfigure, compress, or interpret information in any way you see fit. Remember that maps generally deal with three-dimensional reality but result in a two-dimensional surface diagram.

For this project, a personal map may refer to many different things. Rather than simply being a map in the sense of a road map or a street guide of where you live, the personal map is an embodiment of an expression of a personal experience or attitude regarding a place, a space, an object, an event, or a moment.

Here are some questions to help you start thinking and getting ideas for this project by identifying your emotional responses.

- Write a list of words or short phrases that describe your life. Write down why you choose these words and phrases. What are the specific events or moments that embody these words?
- How did you resolve various conflicts over your lifetime?
- What events have been landmarks in your life?
- What is the most exciting moment in your life? What is the most dangerous thing you've ever been seriously tempted to do? What is the most embarrassing or humiliating situation you have ever been in?
- What is something that makes you really angry? Why?
- How have you grown and changed?
- What had the most influence on your life? Who had the most influence?
- Think about your relationships with others. Again, write a list of words or short phrases to describe these relationships?
- How might your life story have meaning for other people?
- Has there been a special place in your life?

What makes your map unique is you. Without your voice and passion, the message you try to deliver will lack force and an emotional tone.

When searching for ideas or a central theme for this project, you should keep in mind a statement of a general concept that you feel passionately about. Try to embody your message with specific events or moments.

For example, you may want to include struggling to find your place in life living in a crime-infested neighborhood. This is a general concept, a general feeling. Can you pick or create specific events during a short period of time to focus on against this backdrop? Then, create an image around these events. This project is not about creating a documentary nor a news report of your life. You can use your imagination to create or bend situations based on real life experiences to embody your message. The message you want to convey is the main focus.

If you want to include how a childhood experience influenced your relationships with others, then can you focus on a particular situation in your life? Compose an image around this situation, weaving in the childhood experience.

[†]This project is based on a class project from Jym Davis.

Technical considerations:

- You may use Illustrator and/or Photoshop for this project. If you plan to use photo-related materials, start with Photoshop first.
- All of the materials used in the final image must be created by you. You are welcome to scan in others' images for reference but do not include the works by other people. Exceptions may apply. For example, a sketch, closely related to the concept of your project, by a family member may be used provided that you re-interpret the image by making a modification or clipping a selected part of it for your purpose.
- If your instructor requires you to print the final image and you are working with bitmap images, you need to determine the proper resolution at the start.

Stella Priscilla Poco, *Heartbeet*

Fundamentals of Digital Audio in Digital Art

CHAPTER **4**

GENERAL LEARNING OBJECTIVES

In this chapter, you will learn:

- Distinctions between sampled audio and MIDI.
- To determine the optimal sampling rate and bit depth for an audio file.
- Principles of perceptual organization of sound.
- To apply basic art and design organizational principles to audio.
- The general framework of a narrative model.
- To critique digital audio in a classroom setting.

4.1 WHAT IS DIGITAL AUDIO?

Digital audio (in its simplest definition) is sound stored in digital format. Before digital technologies, audio information could be recorded:

- On tapes, which retain any sound that can be recorded using a microphone.
- As sheet music, on which musical compositions can be described with special notation.

There are two types of digital audio: *sampled audio* and *MIDI*. Their characteristics are summaried in Table 4.1. In the following sections, these two types of digital audio are compared in terms of their general characteristics, creation process, editing method, file size and type, and playing and using them with other media.

This section summarizes sampled audio and MIDI. These topics are explained in detail in the *Digital Media Primer*, Chapter 4, as are many terms, such as sampling rate, bit depth, and waveform, which you also will encounter in this chapter.

4.1.1 Sampled Audio

General Characteristics

It can capture and store actual sound—speech, music, or any sound that can be generated with a pressure wave and recorded with a receiver, such as a microphone.

Factors Determining the Quality of Sound

- The quality of the original source being digitized.
- The sampling rate and bit depth for the digitized audio; higher sampling rate and bit depth produce higher fidelity to the original audio but increase the file size.

These two factors affect the actual audio data stored in a file. The perceived sound quality upon playing also depends on the quality of the speakers or headphones.

Creation Process

The sound can be captured by recording with a microphone or via the line-in port on a computer. The computer must have proper hardware and software installed.

- *Hardware*: In general, all computers now have a sound card that supports recording as well as playing sound.

TABLE 4.1	A Summary of Sampled Audio versus MIDI
Sampled Audio	**MIDI**
General Characteristics	
Actual sound, whether speech or music.	Music.
Creation	
• Recording with a microphone into a computer. • Digitizing an analog audio source, such as an analog audio tape.	• Recording MIDI messages while playing on a MIDI keyboard. • Entering notation using MIDI creation application programs.
Factors Affecting Sound Quality	
• Original source. • Sampling rate and bit depth. • During playback: the quality of the sound card, speakers, or headphones.	• Musical composition. • Does not use sampling rate and bit depth. • During playback: the quality of the MIDI synthesizer.
Editing	
• Working with waveforms. • Application programs: e.g., Adobe Audition, Sony SoundForge.	• Working with, for example, notation, timing of notes, and musical instrument assignments. • Application programs: e.g., Cakewalk, Cubase, and Finale.
File Size and File Type	
• Larger file size than MIDI: .wav and .mp3. • Audio data stored in the file: amplitude values of samples.	• Smaller file size than sample audio: .midi and .mid. • Audio data stored in the file: MIDI data.
Playing	
• Hardware: computer with a sound card, speakers, or headphones. • Software: a digital audio player program.	MIDI synthesizer.
Use in Digital Art	
Commonly used in digital video and interactive work.	May require plug-in to import MIDI files in digital video and multimedia authoring projects.

Sampling and Quantization: You do not encounter these terms explicitly in digital audio programs. However, the settings of the sampling rate are obtained from the sampling process and the bit depth setting from the quantization step. See the *Digital Media Primer*, Chapter 1, for a detailed explanation of the concepts of sampling and quantization for digital media and Chapter 4 for specific discussion of sampling and quantization of digital audio and the impact of the sampling rate and bit depth on audio quality and file size.

- *Software*: Digital audio-editing application programs (such as Adobe Audition and Sony SoundForge) also support sound recording. Operating systems often come with a basic sound-recording program (for example, Sound Recorder in Windows and iMovie in Mac OS). These built-in recording programs have limited editing capability.

The microphone or line-in signal is digitized through a two-step process: sampling and quantization.

Editing Method

You work with audio *waveforms* in editing. A waveform is a graphical representation of a sound wave which is produced by the changes in air pressure or electrical signals over time. The vertical axis of the waveform represents the amplitude of the sound wave. The horizontal axis represents time.

For example, you can cut and paste a selection of a waveform to rearrange the audio content (Figure 4.1a through c). You also can alter the volume by changing the waveform's

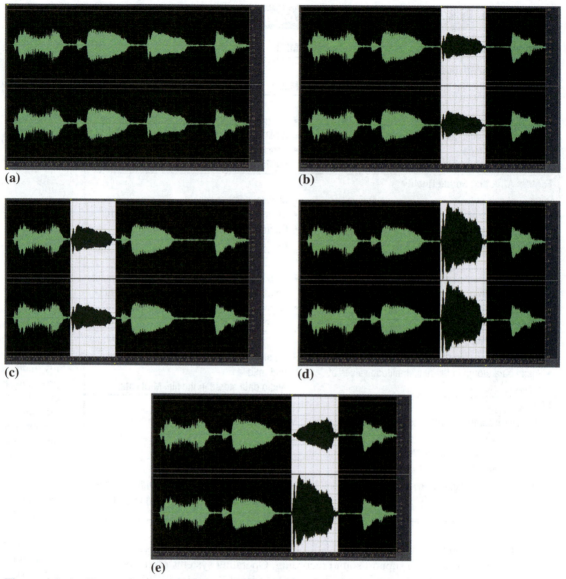

Figure 4.1 Audio waveform representations of a stereo recording (a) Recording of speech saying "1 2 3 4" (b) Waveform segment corresponding to the word "3" (c) The Selected segment "3" is cut and pasted between segments "1" and "2", resulting in an altered audio saying "1 3 2 4" (d) The amplitude of the selected waveform segment in (b) is increased, and (e) the left channel is applied with a fade-in effect

amplitude (Figure 4.1d through e). In some cases, you may want to perform a frequency analysis to determine the frequency range of the audio.

Editing features include the following.

- The audio can be resampled and bit depth can be changed to decrease the file size.
- Special effects (such as noise reduction, echo, and pitch change) can be applied.
- Software application programs (such as Adobe Audition and SoundForge) are available.

File Size and Type

- A file with a higher sampling rate is larger.
- A file with a higher bit depth is larger.
- Sampled audio often has a much larger file size than MIDI. For example, for a 1-minute 44.1 KHz, 16-bit, stereo digital audio file, the file size (uncompressed) is about 10 MB.
- .wav and .mp3 files are the most common file types of sampled audio.

Playing and Using Audio with Other Media

- *Hardware*: Playing digital audio on a computer requires a sound card. Speakers or headphones are needed to output the sound. Most (if not all) computers now have sound cards installed. Some computers and computer monitors even have built-in speakers.
- *Software*: You need a digital audio-player program to play digital audio. The most common digital audio players are Windows Media Player, Real Player, Winamp, QuickTime, and iTune. Most digital audio players play .wav and .mp3 files.
- The .wav file is a common file format that can be imported into video-editing programs and multimedia authoring programs to add audio content to the project.

4.1.2 MIDI

General Characteristics

- MIDI deals with music and synthesized sound—not with any actual sound that a human can hear.
- MIDI music creation does not involve capturing or digitizing analog sound waves or any analog information. Therefore, it does not involve sampling and quantization; there is no sampling rate or bit-depth option when storing a MIDI file.
- MIDI signals are not digitized audio sample points but note *information* played with a virtual instrument. Such information includes the instrument being played, the note being played, when the note begins, when it ends, how hard the key is pressed, and how long the key is held down. Such information is called a ***MIDI message***.

Many video-editing programs and multimedia authoring programs allow the import of .mp3 files, but .mp3 files use lossy compression, which means some original data will be lost or altered. If the audio will be recompressed in the final export using either a video or multimedia authoring program, you may want to use uncompressed .wav files as the original source files.

Factors Determining the Quality of Sound

The perceived sound quality depends on the ***MIDI synthesizer*** that plays back the MIDI file. Even the same note of the same instrument can differ among different synthesizers.

Creation Process

You need a MIDI controller and a MIDI sequencer.

- A ***MIDI controller*** is a device that generates MIDI messages.
- A ***MIDI sequencer*** allows you to receive, store, and edit MIDI data. It can be a hardware device or software application program.
  - *Hardware device*: A "stand-alone" hardware sequencer works independently from a personal computer.
  - *Software*: Software application programs (such as Cakewalk, Cubase, and Finale) can be installed on a computer to create and edit MIDI music.

Editing Method

The notation and instrument assignment in a MIDI file can be edited using a MIDI sequencer. For example, Figure 4.2a through c shows different views available in Cakewalk SONAR for different editing methods.

- *Staff view* for working with notation and staff.
- *Piano Roll view* for visualizing the notes as they would appear on a player-piano roll.

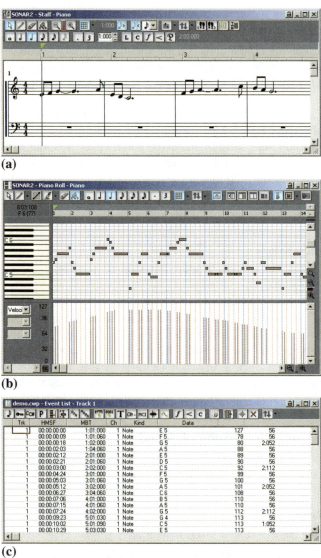

(a)

(b)

(c)

Figure 4.2 Screen captures of workspace windows in Cakewalk SONAR. (a) A Staff view of a MIDI track (b) A Piano Roll view of a MIDI track where the bottom pane shows the notes' velocity, which corresponds to how hard the key is hit and, thus, the note's loudness (c) An Event List of a MIDI track (d) Assignment of harmonica as an instrument for a MIDI track

(d)

Figure 4.2 (*continued*)

- *Event List* for working with a sequence of MIDI information or MIDI messages. Figure 4.2d demonstrates the assignment of a harmonica to a MIDI track.

Examples of software application programs are Cakewalk SONAR, Steinberg Cubase, and MakeMusic! Finale.

File Size and File Type

MIDI files often have a much smaller file size than sampled audio files. The common file extension is .mid or .midi.

Playing and Using with Other Media

Playing the music composed with a MIDI file requires a synthesizer.

- Most MIDI keyboards that can play and generate MIDI messages serve as both controller and synthesizer.
- Computer sound cards that support MIDI audio playback have a software synthesizer. A *soft synth* (short for software synthesizer) is a software program that generates various sounds through the sound card when it receives MIDI messages.

MIDI is not a common file format that can be imported into video or multimedia authoring projects. Some programs may require a third-party plug-in to import MIDI files. MIDI-to-WAV file converters are available to convert the MIDI files into sampled audio, but doing so will lose both the notation and instrument data and, thus, the editability of the original MIDI file.

4.2 EXAMPLES OF DIGITAL AUDIO WORKS

The Prix Ars Electronica has been an interdisciplinary platform for media artists. Its digital music category does not just include music creation but all types of sound productions, computer compositions, voices and instruments, and electronica.* You will find many digital audio works from the Prix Ars Electronica.

Many digital audio works are intended for experiencing through audiovisual performance. The Sancho Plan's *Spacequatica* (Figures 1.12 and 4.3) is a 12-minute piece that combines sound, music, and technology with animated fantastical sea creatures (Figure 4.3a through b) which react to the performers' drumpads. Here is an excerpt of the performance description.

"As we perform both the music and characters live using our drumpads, the sounds of the various characters move around the audience in 3D space through . . . 16-speaker immersive audio system. Visually and sonically, the performance takes us on a journey down through a musical ocean—from the surface, where schools of small exotic creatures are performed like phasing xylophones, through the deeper waters populated by dangerous robotic sharks, and on to the pitch black depths, where all we see and hear are rare self-illuminating species occasionally blinking out of the darkness."

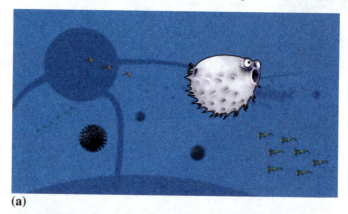

(a)

(b)

Figure 4.3 The Sancho Plan's *Spacequatica* (Courtesy of The Sancho Plan—http://www.thesanchoplan.com)

---

*Prix Ars Electronica Digital Music Category: http://www.aec.at/en/prix/cat_digital_musics.asp

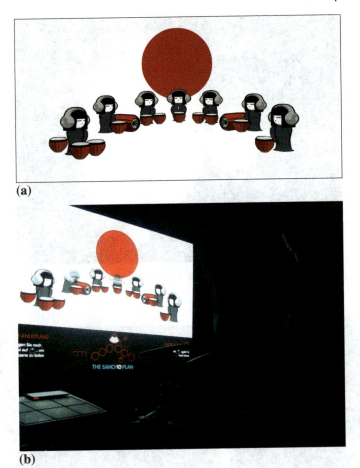

(a)

(b)

Figure 4.4 The Sancho Plan's *Drum Machine* (Courtesy of ToykoPlastic.com and The Sancho Plan— http://www.thesanchoplan.com)

In *Drum Machine* (Figure 4.4), another audio-visual performance of The Sancho Plan, music and the animated characters (the drummers, created by ToykoPlastic.com) are synchronized. The animated characters (who never show their hands) perform creatively with their drums. This piece also won the People's Choice Award at the Sundance Online Film Festival in 2004. Its Flash version is available on The Sancho Plan's Web site.

3-D sound can give the listener a sense of spatial orientation. Obtaining the sound usually involves the installation of a multi-speaker audio system. The *Audio Fraktal*[†] (produced by Joachim Goβmann at the Institute for Music and Acoustics at ZKM, Germany) is an interactive audiovisual installation. The audience can navigate a visual image of a fractal on a computer by zooming in and out. Figure 4.5 shows an example of the fractal. The spatalized sound (if activated by the audience) will be produced corresponding to the navigated location within the image. The edge areas of the fractal produce a more chaotic sound.

Alex Baker's *A Recurring Sequence of Events* (Figure 4.6) is a site-specific sound installation created for the historical building St. Augustine's Tower—the oldest building in

A fractal refers to an object that displays similar patterns at any level of magnification. The fractal phenomena can be observed in nature, for example, shapes of snow flakes, branching of trees, and fern fronds. Fractals also can be generated mathematically.

[†]Joachim Goβmann, "Towards an Auditory Representation of Complexity," Proceedings of ICAD 05-Eleventh Meeting of the International Conference on Auditory Display, Limerick, Ireland, July 6–9, 2005.

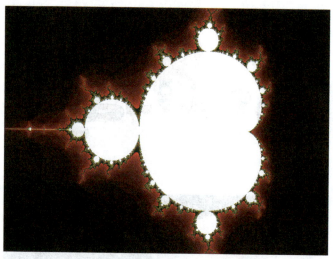

Figure 4.5 An image of a Mandelbrot fractal with a colored environment

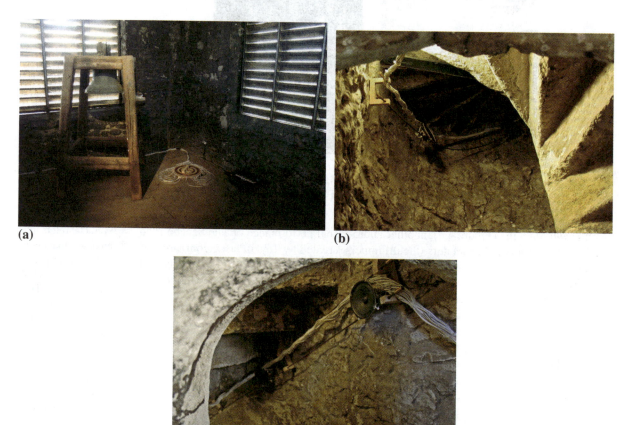

Figure 4.6 Still photographs of Alex Baker's instillation, *A Recurring Sequence of Events*, St. Augustine's Tower, London, 2007 (Courtesy of Alex Baker—http://www.alexbaker.co.uk)

Hackney, London. The building dates back to the end of the 13th Century. The set up involves 72 speakers and allows a sound of a D-minor chord to move through the tower. Here is an excerpt of the description:

> "The gentle, urgency of a D-minor chord ripples away from you following its course through the tower becoming almost imperceptible before racing back down the shaft and cascading over you chasing its route back around the staircase again.

> The speakers connect through several kilometres of wire to a customised turntable with 72 individual contacts located on the top floor in the Bell room. As it revolves it connects to each of the 72 speakers in turn, creating the effect of a continuously moving D-minor chord and activating the building with sound.

> . . . This new version takes advantage of the physically and historically resonant space of St. Augustine's Tower. The cyclical movement of the sound both relates to the physical shape of the building and also to the building's function as a clocktower—timekeeping and rotation."

In this installation, the content of the sound is a simple chord. The feeling and emotion evoked through the combination of the historical aspects of the site and the auditory effects are specific to the site's physical construction.

4.3 BASIC ELEMENTS OF DIGITAL AUDIO

Sound is characterized by three perceptual properties: pitch, loudness, and timbre. Pitch is related to the sound's frequency—loudness to its amplitude. Sound frequency and amplitude are not specific to digital audio; analog sound waves possess these physical properties, too.

4.3.1 Perceptual Properties of Sound

Pitch

The perception of the relative highness or lowness of a tone is pitch. The physical attribute of pitch is the audio's frequency. In visual arts, tone refers to a color's value—lightness and darkness—which have their implied moods. Higher pitch, like lighter value, may convey positive emotions, such as cheerfulness and hope. Lower pitch, like darker values, may convey negative moods, such as melancholy and fear.

Loudness

Loudness is related to the audio's amplitude. A loud sound can grab a listener's attention, but silence also can draw attention by creating a sense of void—an absence—like the negative space in images. Silence can enrich the sense of the sounds that come before and after it. It can create anticipation and suspense. Silence or cadence also can be used to break up a long audio into sections.

Timbre

Timbre refers to the perceived difference between two sounds of identical pitch and loudness. In music, timbre refers to the quality of a note that distinguishes different types of instruments. For example, the same note played on a piano sounds different when played on a flute. Figure 4.7 shows the waveforms of these sounds. The different shapes of the waveform reflect the difference of these sounds. In principle, timbre is not limited to musical

The audio waveforms in the example shown in Figure 4.7 were not obtained by recording a note played on an actual piano or flute. They were produced by a MIDI synthesizer and converted to the sampled audio to obtain the waveform. The MIDI synthesizer produces the sounds to create the sensation of the actual musical instrument. The audio examples illustrate different timbres, regardless of how these sounds were captured.

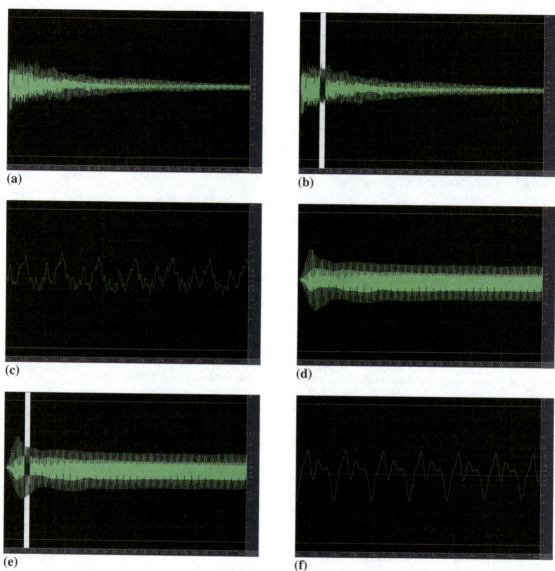

Figure 4.7 Audio waveform representation of the same note played on a piano in (a) through (c) and a flute in (d) through (f) (a) 1.2-second piano sound of a note (b) 0.025 second of the waveform (a) (c) Zoom-in view of the selected segment of the waveform (b) (d) The same note played for 1.2-second on a flute (e) 0.025 second of the waveform (d) (f) Zoom-in view of the selected segment of waveform (e)

notes. Anything that produces sound can be considered a musical instrument—for instance, the human voice.

Almost all of the sounds we encounter in everyday life are complex, as they are made up of various frequencies at different intensities—for example, speech (Figure 4.1) and the notes generated on different musical instruments (Figure 4.7). These ordinary sounds are in contrast to a single tone that contains a single frequency (Figure 4.8). Unlike pitch and loudness, which can be measured on a one-dimensional scale, no simple, single scale can compare or order the timbres of different sounds.

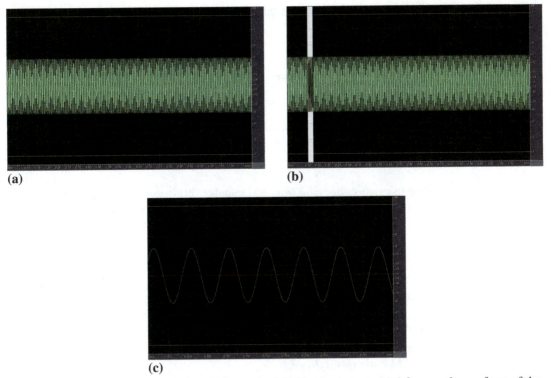

Figure 4.8 Audio waveform representations of a 261-Hz single tone (a) 1.2-second waveform of the tone (b) 0.025 second of the waveform (a) is selected (c) The zoom-in view of the selected segment of the waveform (b)

The expression ***tone color*** often is used to describe timbre. Although colors on a color wheel are not explicitly associated with particular timbres or instruments, the sound of an instrument (like colors in imagery) may be associated with feeling like warm or harsh.

> 🖱 **Single Tone, Timbre, and Complex Sound** Hear the sound of a single tone (Figure 4.8) and the same note played on a piano, a flute (Figure 4.7), a cello, a glockenspiel, a guitar, a harp, a trumpet, a tubular bell, a violin, and a synthesized voice. The waveform for each of these sounds also is available for comparison.

4.3.2 Properties of Sampled Audio Files

In working with sampled audio files, you have to set two properties: sampling rate and bit depth. For example, in Adobe Audition, when you start a new file, it prompts you for sampling rate, channels, and resolution (that is, bit depth) settings (Figure 4.9). A higher sampling rate and bit depth always give the digitized audio file better fidelity but also generate a larger file. Large files require more storage space, longer processing time, and longer transfer time. If the digital media files are created for use on the Internet, the network transfer time of a file is often a more important consideration than the storage space, which is becoming less expensive.

For an uncompressed .wav file which is one of the most common file types for sampled audio, the sampling rate, bit depth, duration, and number of channels are proportional directly to the file size. For instance:

- Doubling the sampling rate from 22,050 Hz to 44,100 Hz will double the file size.
- Doubling the bit depth from 8-bit to 16-bit will double the file size.

Figure 4.9 Adobe Audition prompts you for sampling rate, channels, and resolution (i.e., bit depth) settings

- Doubling the audio's duration from 30 seconds to 60 seconds will double the file size.
- Doubling the number of channels from one (mono) to two (stereo) will double the file size.

The uncompressed .wav file of a 1-minute, CD-quality (44,100 Hz, 16-bit) stereo audio will be about 10 MB. Lowering the sampling rate from 44,100 Hz to 22,050 Hz will reduce the file size from about 10 MB to about 5 MB. Lowering the bit depth of this file from 16-bit to 8-bit will reduce the file size further—from 5 MB to 2.5 MB.

Sampling Rate

The most common sampling rates you will encounter in a digital audio editing program are

11,025 Hz AM radio quality/speech
22,050 Hz near FM radio quality (high-end multimedia)
44,100 Hz CD quality
48,000 Hz DAT (digital audio tape) quality
96,000 Hz DVD-audio quality
192,000 Hz DVD-audio quality

Bit Depth

The most common bit-depth settings you will encounter in a digital audio-editing program are 8-bit and 16-bit. 24-bit, 32-bit, and 48-bit audio also are supported in some digital audio application programs. Typically, 16 bit or higher is used for music. 8-bit resolution usually is sufficient for speech and short sound effects, such as the sound of an explosion. For music, 8 bit is too low to accurately reproduce the sound. Our ears usually can notice the degradation in playback.

4.4 PERCEPTUAL EXPERIENCE OF DIGITAL AUDIO VERSUS DIGITAL IMAGES

Audio, unlike imagery, is a time-based medium with a linear presentation. The experience spreads out over time and the meanings unfold over time. The audience perceives the whole picture or boundaries of the piece only in retrospect. In addition, because of the temporal and dynamic nature of audio, its interpretation relies on the listener's short-term memory. If a long audio is used as a stand-alone medium, you should consider placing reference points to help listeners situate themselves in the piece and grasp its ideas. A reference point might be a short stop or a gradual or sudden accent of loudness or pitch. Think of points of reference as landmarks that enrich and punctuate the memory of a long road trip.

See the *Digital Media Primer*, Chapter 4, for how to calculate the uncompressed audio file size.

Upsampling an existing digital audio file (say, from 22,050 Hz to 44,100 Hz) does not recover the audio's original fidelity but will increase the file size.

Changing an existing 8-bit audio file to 16-bit will not recover the audio's original fidelity but will increase the file size.

Visual art is perceived in 2- and 3-D space. Audio is heard consecutively in time. However, audio also can be thought of in two dimensions. It is organized horizontally across the page—as melody in music. Vertically, simultaneous events form chords and harmony. Simultaneous organization also exists in non-musical sound, for example, clapping sound playing simultaneously with speech.

4.5 DIGITAL AUDIO IN DIGITAL ART

The content of digital audio in digital art varies from music to sound effects to speech. They commonly are created for audiovisual work, combining the visual media. They also are created as standalone pieces.

4.5.1 Combining Visual Elements

In digital art, audio often is used in combination with visual components—for example, still images, videos, and animation. In many cases, audio is used to supplement and to enrich visual information. However, in cases such as musical pieces, the visual components often assume a supporting role to enrich the auditory experience. When used in combination with audio, the visual components can provide the audience an additional sensation in interpreting the artwork. Points of reference can be created in the visual component in addition to the audio.

Audio may have to synchronize with other media. In thinking of audio's two-dimensionality, the visual components may be one of the events in the vertical dimension and integral to the whole work.

4.5.2 Content

Digital audio used in a digital artwork can be a short sound clip (such as clapping or a door slamming), speech, music, ambient background noise, or a combination of these. The use of spoken words is analogous to the use of text in images. Like text, speech can be a clear, direct, articulate message (such as voice-over instructions). It also can be a whisper or indistinct words used to raise questions and stimulate the audience's interest.

4.5.3 Ending

Depending on the intent, digital audio used in digital artwork can have a distinct ending or loop seamlessly. For an interactive work that by nature is not linear, the digital audio (especially background sound) may loop seamlessly to maintain the audience's sense of continuity, despite the different paths it may take to navigate the work.

4.6 PRINCIPLES OF PERCEPTUAL ORGANIZATION— THE PSYCHOLOGY OF HEARING

The perceptual grouping principles discussed in Chapter 2 also apply to hearing. In this section, we will revisit these psychological factors and examine how they may govern our auditory grouping.[††]

[††]For a comprehensive essay comparing visual and auditory pattern perception, see Bela Julesz and Ira J. Hirsh, "Visual and Auditory Perception—An Essay of Comparison," in Edward E. David, Jr., and Peter B. Denes, eds., *Human Communication: A Unified View* (New York: McGraw-Hill, 1972).

Before we discuss these factors, we must explain two terms that will be used in the rest of this section: source and stream.

- A *source* is a physical entity that causes the acoustic pressure wave—for example, a guitar string being plucked.
- A *stream* refers to the perceptual grouping of the auditory elements into a whole. In a stream, these auditory elements may not be emitted from the same physical source but are *perceived* to emanate from the same source.

Most of the principles discussed in this section are based on studies pertaining to the fusion of sequential or simultaneous auditory components into a single stream or to the segregation of audio units in a single stream. Some examples used to demonstrate the principles are laboratory experiments using discrete, simple tones. Digital audio is seldom used this way (discrete, single tones) in digital art. However, these principles provide insights and inspirations of how we may extrapolate from these studies to arrange audio segments for artistic communication.

4.6.1 Proximity and Similarity

We tend to group auditory elements that are similar or proximal in pitch, timbre, loudness, and time as a stream. For example, a sequence that repeats two tones with the same pitch but alternating loudness is perceived as a single stream if the two tones are similar in loudness. When the loudness difference increases, the two-tone sequence is perceived as two separate tones in parallel—the softer tones grouped in one stream and the louder tones in another. In a sequence of simple clicks, we naturally group those closer in time together.

In another experiment, listeners were presented with a sequence of six repeating tones—three in the high range and three in the low range. The high and low tones alternated—that is, high, low, high, low, high, low. When the tones were played slowly, listeners heard the alternating high and low tones. When the tones were played faster, listeners started to perceive two separate streams of tones—one high and one low—playing in parallel.

Although using simple tones to create an auditory illusion is not a very common practice in digital art, using audio similar in content, pitch, loudness, and timbre and proximal in time may help the audience make connections between audio units heard at different times.

Composers have exploited this phenomenon. By playing a series of tones drawn from different pitch ranges at a fast tempo, listeners hear multiple melodic lines in parallel, which makes the music richer.

4.6.2 Common Fate

If different auditory components of a sound undergo synchronous changes—for example, if they start and end at the same time or change in loudness and pitch together—they may be perceived as emanating from the same source.

4.6.3 Good Continuation

We perceive abrupt changes in sound as a new source coming in, but continuous and gradual changes are perceived as the same source changing. It is easier to attend to and follow a sound that changes smoothly than one that changes unexpectedly or discontinuously.

4.6.4 Closure

Closure refers to our tendency to fill in lost fragments of sound to make the stream seem intact. For instance, when you are conversing with a friend on a busy downtown street, speech often is drowned out by short bursts of noise, but you perceptually restore the speech fragments to perceive it as continuous instead of a number of fragments from different sources.

4.6.5 Figure–Ground Phenomenon

We normally cannot attend to every aspect of our sensory input consciously, including the auditory input. Complex sound may be grouped perceptually into separate streams, and we primarily attend to one stream at a time, although still aware of the other sounds. For instance, at a party, we may pay attention to one conversation and let others fall into background. We still are aware of the other voices conversing, but we often think of them as background noises. The attended stream of sound stands out as the *figure* or ***foreground***, and the unattended streams become ***background***. The foreground and background streams may switch roles as the audio progresses. For example, we can switch our attention from one conversation to another at a noisy party. Then the new conversation emerges as the foreground, while the sound from the previous conversational group falls into the background.

For sounds that you intend to present as background sounds, you may want to make it softer, faded, and muffled. On the other hand, to make a sound stand out as foreground, make it loud and clear. Sometimes, the length of a sound influences whether it is perceived as foreground or background. For example, a balloon popping is more likely to be heard as a foreground sound than the longer buildup and decay of a passing airplane.

TABLE 4.2	Examples of Contrasting Sounds
Foreground	**Background**
Sad: Cars skidding and crashing	Happy: Children playing in playground
Tense: Two people arguing	Peaceful: Gentle ocean waves and seagulls

Layering emotional contrasting sounds together—one as the foreground sound and one as background—can build tension and suggest underlying conflicts. Table 4.2 shows examples of contrasting sounds. Although two contrasting sounds may play together, the listener is situated in the foreground. The emotion evoked will not be the same when the foreground and background sounds are swapped.

> **Contrasting Sounds** Examples of contrasting sounds. Even with the same contrasting sounds, how you designate the foreground and background for these sounds will evoke different mood and emotion.

4.6.6 Past Experience

Our past experience influences our apprehensions. Sometimes, arbitrary meaning can be made to connect with the sensory input. Connection between a sound and a visual image can be established by repetitious, simultaneous presentation of the sound and the image.

4.7 GENERALIZATION OF ART AND DESIGN ORGANIZATIONAL PRINCIPLES

The temporal nature of sound may require creation and evaluation approaches that differ from those for images. However, some general organizational principles exist across media types. The organizational principles of art and design enumerated in Chapter 2 are derived from the nature of human perception. Despite the media used, art has the common purpose of stimulating and sustaining the audience's interest and conveying emotions and meanings. Human perception is the common platform for reception, absorption, retention, and interpretation. For instance, unity is a fundamental property of artistic structure whether in imagery or music. Rhythm and harmony describe musical properties but are used as organizational principles in visual art.

There are intrinsic differences in the way that humans use acoustic and light information to interpret their environment. Light travels in a straight line and does not bend around objects. An object in your line of sight blocks your vision of other objects behind it. However, low-frequency sound can bend around obstructions and corners, while high-frequency sound bounces around them. We hear a *mixture* of sound that pertains to the immediate and distant environment—even from elements that we do not see. The principles of perceptual organization deal with how people sort out the mixture of auditory information to make sense of it. Unlike images, the information delivered by sound does not supply detailed information about shapes, sizes, and textures of objects. The spatial localization of sounds is not as precise as visual localization.

Digital art often combines various media. By finding the common ground across media types and formulating principles based on that common ground, we can make connections and weave different media coherently in an artwork. The organizational principles discussed here combine the general principles of art and design with general concepts of musical composition. Musical composition is beyond the scope of the book. The intention of this section is to explore new ideas for digital audio by generalizing principles from art and design and musical composition. Not all of these organizational principles are required for every digital audio work. These principles only serve as a starting point for artistic exploration and aspiration. As with any medium—digital or traditional—following all of the principles does not guarantee great art. New and creative approaches always remain possible.

4.7.1 Unity, Harmony, and Variety

Having *unity* means that the different elements of the piece work together to make a whole. Adding variety can create interest. Unity and *variety*, while appearing to be two opposing concepts, emerge as a similar concept of different implementation. An audio work without variation becomes dull. Too much variety will break up the coherence. Unity and variety work together. Adding variety by altering only one auditory element or property—pitch, loudness, timbre, or pacing—at a time can make it sound familiar and give listeners a sense of gradual evolution.

Harmony in music refers to the relation of notes in a chord—how a simultaneous combination of notes form a chord pleasing to the ear. In the 2-D sense of audio, harmony pertains to the relation of events happening in the vertical dimension. For a nonmusical digital artwork, tonal harmony is not applicable, but you still may have more than one simultaneous audio unit. An illustration of a 2-D representation of an audio sequence is shown in Figure 4.10. This sequence starts with a traffic sound. Muffled speech begins in the middle of the traffic sound and continues for a while after the traffic sound has ended. Then, there is a period of silence followed by a sound of footsteps. There is another period of silence. A musical instrument playing is heard. A woman talking is heard during the playing of the instrument and continues after the playing of the instrument has subsided.

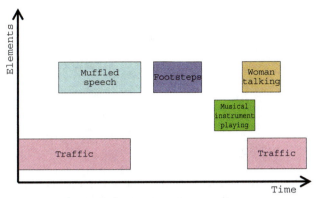

Figure 4.10 An example of a 2-D visual representation of an audio sequence.

Then the traffic sound similar to the beginning of the audio starts and continues to the end. The 2-D representation helps you plan and visualize an audio sequence.

Conceptually, you can think of harmony in terms of the relationship between these simultaneous audio units. The sound of pebbles rubbing or soft speech may be in accord with the sound of a running brook, but simultaneously combining the noise of a machine shop and the sound of a running brook will create discord.

When visual elements are integrated with the audio in a digital artwork, visual elements become one of the events in the vertical dimension. They must work together harmoniously to create a unified meaning. For example, a video of a slow running brook and an audio of a poem being read convey a harmonious feeling, while machine shop noise would clash with the running brook imagery.

4.7.2 Balance

In musical composition, **balance** refers to the harmonious adjustment of volume and timbre among instruments. Applying this concept to digital audio used in conjunction with visual components in digital art, balance can be thought as the relative dominance of various auditory and visual elements in a harmonious way.

Another notion of balance pertains to the **overall balance** which also can be thought of as the relative proportions and durations of the elements conveying different feelings. One way to help visualize the audio's feature development and direction is to use curves or lines to depict them and sketch them out (Figure 4.11). The sketch is only a qualitative representation to help you visualize and plan the development of the audio's different properties or features. A feature refers to the idea of the work, its emotion, and its meaning. It also can refer to more tangible properties, such as loudness, pitch, number of different timbres, or richness. For example, the overall balance of the feature represented in Figure 4.11a is more balanced than that represented in Figure 4.11b, because the development represented in Figure 4.11a allows the level of the feature to come down after its

✎ **Overall Balance in Concept Development of Digital Audio** Two examples of audio, each demonstrating a feature development represented in Figure 4.11a and b. The feature in these examples is the feeling of wet versus dry. Both audio examples use various water sounds to convey a feeling of wetness. One audio returns to dryness at the end while the other keeps building up the watery sound throughout the piece. Listen to both audio pieces and compare the different feelings you have—do you feel satisfied at the end of the journey?

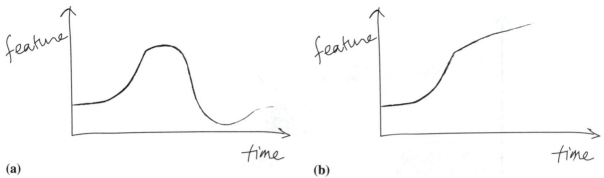

(a)   **(b)**

Figure 4.11 Simple sketches of trajectories of how an audio feature, such as emotion, will develop throughout a given piece (a) The feature is more balanced overall (b) The feature has no resolution

climax. The development represented in Figure 4.11b keeps building up without a resolution, perhaps leaving listeners with an unsatisfied feeling and the question: "Now what?"

If an audio piece is not well-balanced, the audience may feel it is too short, too long, or has too much or too little of certain auditory components.

"The piece is too short . . ."

There may be too many changes and activities in the piece. You may consider lengthening it to allow more time to elaborate each segment and for transitions between changes. You also may reexamine the following aspects.

- The importance of each activity for your intent. Trim off the less important activities to allow more time for others.
- The ending of your audio. Does the ending provide a release or resolution of the tension that has built throughout the piece? For example, the development represented in Figure 4.11b does not have a release and may make the audience feel that it ends too soon.

"The piece is too long . . ."

There may not be enough changes and activities in the piece to sustain the audience's interest. You may consider shortening the piece to tighten up the ideas.

4.7.3 Repetition and Rhythm

Repeating elements can give listeners a sense of familiarity and stimulate their memory. Familiarity often draws attention and thus creates emphasis. As in imagery, repetition in audio also can convey a sense of unity.

Repeated elements do not have to be exactly the same audible sound. They can be variants of different pitch, loudness, pace, or length. If the repeating audio is composed of a variety of elements—natural sounds or musical tones—then keeping one or more element the same in the variant will connect the variants. To avoid boredom, try not to simply repeat an element or its variant. The repetition should carry and develop previously established ideas farther along in a coherent flow.

Rhythms and beats play an important role in human perception of emotion in an audio work. They give a direct sense of speed. A slow rhythm can sound relaxing. Rapid beats—like a flickering image—may convey irritation or stress.

4.7.4 Emphasis and Focus

In imagery, emphasis and focus can be added by creating visual differences. Audio may have to build up similarity before difference can be noticed. Loudness and silence can draw the audience's attention. Emphasis and focus also can be created by repeating a similar audio unit.

4.7.5 Perspective

Sound can be used to convey a sense of location and environment. Acoustics is the study of how sound transmission in space is influenced by the way different places reinforce, absorb, and reflect different parts of sound. Surround sound, 3-D sound, and stereo sound technologies create the illusion that a sound is coming from a certain place and is moving in a certain direction.

Perspective also can be created by generating a sense of foreground and background. One option is to mix the digital audio intended for foreground and background in separate tracks. Assign the tracks with different emphasis or priority. The most engaging element at any given moment will be perceived as the foreground, while the secondary element will become the background (see Section 4.6.5). A sporadic giggle or a bell may take the foreground against a background that is comparatively softer, slower, relatively steady, and less recognizable in detail, like whispering or ambient noise. Audio elements that constitute the foreground and background also gradually can reverse their roles and dominance, directing the listener's attention in and out of different tracks of sound.

The pitch of a car's horn increases as the car approaches and lowers as the car moves away from the observer. This is called the **Doppler effect**. By creating this auditory experience, one can create a mental, spatial moving image.

4.8 USING A NARRATIVE MODEL

For a longer piece of time-based artwork (either audio or video) a narrative model may be used as a framework for idea development. In general, a *narrative model* is characterized by three stages: beginning, development, and ending. However, not all long, digital audio pieces find the narrative model applicable; it depends on the intent of the piece.

4.8.1 Beginning

The goal of the beginning is to engage the audience, which can be achieved by either posing a question or making the audience ask a question. For instance, withholding some information and not giving away the whole picture will enhance audience interest and help in experiencing more of the piece. Breaking audio passages up may elicit curiosity—wanting to piece them together to gain meaning. The broken-up passages may be repeated later in the audio to convey a sense of unity and to set up long-range associations that give interest and depth to the whole.

4.8.2 Development

In the development stage, the ideas of the piece elaborate and intensify. Ideas or passages are bridged by *transitions*. Depending on your intention, transitions might be constructed subtly to disguise a change or emphatically to clearly signal an upcoming change to the listener. The simplest and most common technique for constructing a transition in a nonmusical piece is a simple cross fade or gradual change in volume between two separate segments. Transition also can be achieved by gradual emotional changes or adjusting the auditory elements of pitch, timbre, or rhythm.

4.8.3 Ending

A time-based medium may end with a gradual fade out or an abrupt stop at a climax. The ending is a critical point in any time-based medium, because it is the part that is most likely to remain in the audience's memory. The ending becomes the starting point for the audience to interpret the piece in retrospect.

4.9 CRITIQUING DIGITAL AUDIO

Although based generally on the steps for critique suggested in Chapter 1, because of its temporal nature, critiquing time-based media is more difficult than critiquing images. The audio may be kept playing while it is being critiqued to get a complete response of the work.

1. Describe what you hear.

Start with a straightforward factual description of what you hear.

- What is the length of the piece?
- Is it music, speech, a natural sound, or a combination of these? If a combination, how are they combined and arranged in the audio?
- If it is music, can you identify the instruments?
- If it is speech, can you hear the words clearly? Can you identify the gender and age of the speaker?
- If it is a natural sound, can you identify what it is?
- Are any segments distinct in style, content, or loudness? How long does each distinct segment last?

2. Describe what you hear in terms of the art and design organizational principles.

Use the principles of art and design and perceptual organization as a guide to discuss the properties of the audio. Feel free to extend the discussion beyond the questions given here.

- What are the pitch, loudness, and timbre of the sound at any particular time?
- Are there any repetitions in the piece? Are the repeated units exactly the same? How do they vary? Can they still be connected as the same group?
- Does the overall audio convey a sense of unity and balance?
- Does the piece have a focal point or climax? If so, where is it? How is the climax built up?
- Which part of the audio remains in your memory after your first listening? After more listenings?
- Does the audio keep your attention? If not, in which part does your attention wander?
- Do you perceive a foreground and background? If so, describe the sound of each. Why do you assign one as the foreground and the other as the background?

- What is the listener's position or role within the piece (in the first person or third person)?
- Does the audio use a narrative model? If so, can you identify the beginning, development, and ending?
- How are changes bridged?
- Are there any periods of silence? How long do they last?
- If the audio is playing along with a visual medium (such as video):
  - How do the audio elements (such as pitch, loudness, and timbre) synchronize with the visual elements (such as value, color, shape, and texture)?
  - Does repetition occur at the same time in both the audio and visual elements?
  - Does the video or the audio attract or lose your attention?
  - What is the visual element during a silence?
  - Is there any segment containing audio only, without visual elements?

Discuss the emotion and meaning that you pick out from these elements.

- What are the mood and feeling of the whole?
- How are these moods and feelings conveyed? What makes you feel them?
- Do different parts of the audio convey different moods? How are they bridged?
- If the audio is playing with a visual medium (such as video):
  - Are both the audio and visual elements integral to the whole?
  - Would the mood and feeling change without the visual element?
  - Would the mood and feeling change without the audio accompaniment?

3. Discuss the subject matter.

- What do you think the work is about?
- What does it mean to you?
- What do you think the piece is trying to communicate?
- Does the order of the audio units support the subject matter? Does any part of the audio seem out of order? Could any parts be rearranged to enhance communication of the intent?
- If the work employs a narrative model, what do you think the story is? Does it tell a series of events, an abstract journey, or an emotional journey?
- Do other students' responses change your initial thoughts about the piece?
- Discuss how the artist's choices of audio properties and transitions work or do not work with the subject matter.

4. Discuss the execution of techniques.

Here are some sample questions pertaining to the technical aspects of the work, craftsmanship and professionalism.

- Is the audio sampled audio or MIDI?
- What is the intended delivery method of the audio? How is it being presented during critique? Describe the software and hardware. Does the current presentation method reflect how the intended audience will experience the piece? If not, how will the audience play the piece?
- Does the audio sound clean—without noise? If not, is the noise part of the message?
- Is the audio's volume equalized throughout? Is there any sudden burst or drop in volume in some segments? Do you think this is intentional?
- Is there any distortion caused by clipping—the audio being too loud during recording?

- If the audio is a sampled audio, are its choices of sampling rate, bit depth, and channel number appropriate for its intended use?
- Are there any artifacts caused by insufficient sampling rate and bit depth or the low quality of the original source?
- Are there copyrighted materials? Can they be replaced by original materials?

5. Student artist responses.

The student artist now can respond to the other students' responses and talk about the original intent, intended subject matter, and any unsolved problems in the piece.

Students are encouraged to continue responding to expand the discussion, because they now have new information about the piece from the artist.

TERMS

LEARNING AIDS

The following learning aids can be found at the book's companion Web site.

Single Tone, Timbre, and Complex Sound
Hear the sound of a single tone (Figure 4.8) and the same note played on a piano, a flute (Figure 4.7), a cello, a glockenspiel, a guitar, a harp, a trumpet, a tubular bell, a violin, and a synthesized voice. The waveform for each of these sounds also is available for comparison.

Contrasting Sounds
Examples of contrasting sounds. Even with the same contrasting sounds, how you designate the foreground and background for these sounds will evoke different mood and emotion.

Overall Balance in Concept Development of Digital Audio
Two examples of audio, each demonstrating a feature development represented in Figure 4.11a and b. The feature in these examples is the feeling of wet versus dry. Both

audio examples use various water sounds to convey a feeling of wetness. One audio returns to dryness at the end while the other keeps building up the watery sound throughout the piece. Listen to both audio pieces and compare the different feelings you have—do you feel satisfied at the end of the journey?

REVIEW QUESTIONS

When applicable, please choose all correct answers.

1. For each of the descriptions, identify the correct digital audio type as sample audio or MIDI.
    i.   It can be captured by recording with a microphone into a computer.
    ii. Musical notation information is stored in the file.
    iii. .wav and .mp3 are example file types.
    iv. It requires sampling rate and bit depth settings.
    v.   In general, any sound that can cause air pressure changes can be captured in this type of digital audio.
    vi. This type of digital audio is mainly musical composition.
    vii. It is most commonly supported in digital video editing programs and multimedia authoring programs.
    viii. It may need a third-party plug-in to use digital video editing programs and multimedia authoring programs, if supported at all.

2. Sound is characterized by three perceptual properties: _____, _____, and _____.

3. Give two types of audio content, besides music, that are commonly used in digital art.

4. The three general stages in a narrative model are: _____, _____, and _____.

5. If a long audio is used alone, adding _____ can help listeners situate themselves in the piece and grasp the ideas.

6. Audio is heard consecutively in time, but it can be thought of as two dimensional—horizontal and vertical—like musical sheets. Horizontal refers to _____. Vertical refers to _____.

    A. the organization across the page—as melody,
       the simultaneous events that form chords and harmony
    B. the simultaneous events that form chords and harmony,
       the organization across the page—as melody

7. _____ can give listeners a sense of familiarity and thus simulate their memory.

    A. Harmony
    B. Variety
    C. Balance
    D. Repetition
    E. Perspective

EXERCISES AND ACTIVITIES

The following activities serve as a preparation for projects suggested in the next chapter. Only descriptions and sketches are expected at this point. After you have learned more about the practical and hands-on aspects of digital audio creation and editing in the next chapter (and in the *Digital Media Primer*, Chapter 5), you will be able to produce an audio based on this preparation.

1. Describe what you would use for several short clips of natural sounds to convey a feeling for each of the following.

    i. Closed space
    ii. Open space
    iii. Empty space
    iv. Crowded space
    v. Orderliness
    vi. Chaos
    vii. Hot
    viii. Cold
    ix. Hope
    x. Melancholy
    xi. Jaggedness
    xii. Flow
    xiii. Nostalgia
    xiv. Futuristic thoughts

    The sounds used in the audio need not be musical. In fact, it would be best not to use musical pieces for this exercise.

2. Sketch out a plan for a longer audio by composing the different short sound clips that you described previously to convey two contrasting feelings in the same piece.

    i. Closed space versus open space
    ii. Empty space versus crowded space
    iii. Orderliness versus chaos
    iv. Hot versus cold
    v. Hope versus melancholy
    vi. Jaggedness versus flow
    vii. Nostalgic versus futuristic thoughts

    Tip: The plan may include

    - Horizontal placement, like a timeline (Figure 4.10), of different sound clips to show when they should occur.
    - Vertical placement, like multiple sound tracks (Figure 4.10), of different sound clips to show how they could be mixed.
    - Several plots that develop various features of the audio, like those shown in Figure 4.11.

3. Sketch out a plan for a longer audio composition that is suggestive of a narrative or a sequence of events (such as a part of your day).
    Tip: The sketch may include

    - Horizontal placement, like a timeline (Figure 4.10), of different sound clips to show when they should occur.
    - Vertical placement, like multiple sound tracks (Figure 4.10), of different sound clips to show how they could be mixed.
    - Several plots that develop various features of the audio, like those shown in Figure 4.11.

4. If the timbre of a sound is analogous to color in imagery, describe how you would use this analogy to create an audio that conveys

   i.   a black-and-white photograph of a tulip
   ii. a field of colorful wild flowers

Describe what sounds you would use and how you would combine these various sounds. Sketch out the horizontal and vertical placement of these sounds.

5. If the pitch of a sound is analogous to brightness and darkness in imagery, describe how you would use this analogy to create an audio that conveys

   i.   a high noon
   ii. a starry night

Describe what sounds you would use and how you would combine these various sounds. Sketch out the horizontal and vertical placement of these sounds.

Thomas Whaples, *International Relations,* pen and ink

Digital Audio Manipulation for Digital Art

GENERAL LEARNING OBJECTIVES

In this chapter, you will learn:

- How waveform editors work in general.
- How multitrack editors work in general.
- How to use digital audio tools to help create audio composition.
- How to use digital audio tools to help create perceptual organization elements.
- The basic steps to start a multitrack session in Adobe Audition.

5.1 INTRODUCTION

Capturing and editing of digital audio are discussed in the *Digital Media Primer* Chapter 5, which introduces several commonly used editing tools.

There are two types of digital audio: sampled audio and MIDI music. This chapter focuses on the manipulation of sampled digital audio. We will discuss how the various digital audio-manipulation tools can be exploited to create intended effects based on the perceptual organization and the organizational principles of art and design that are discussed in the previous chapter.

5.1.1 What Can Be Manipulated?

To manipulate any digital media file to create intended effects, you need to know the perceptual properties that define the media element. Then, you need to identify the available tools in an application program that allow you to operate on the file to give the desired perceptual effects.

There are three perceptual properties for sound, as discussed in Chapter 4: pitch, loudness, and timbre. Chapter 4 also showed that an audio can be thought of as having two dimensions: (1) time as the horizontal axis and (2) the simultaneous combination of sound elements (like chords for music) in the vertical direction. The idea of the vertical dimension can be realized by the multitrack feature of a digital audio editor (such as Adobe Audition) that allows you to mix different audio segments to play simultaneously.

5.2 ELEMENTS SHARED IN AUDIO-EDITING APPLICATION PROGRAMS

Although there are many different audio-editing application programs, they share many similarities in workspace and audio-manipulation tools. Chapter 5 in the *Digital Media Primer* gives an overview on the basic workspace elements in digital audio programs. In this text, we are going to discuss those ideas by detaching from any particular application program. This will help you build a general foundation to help learn new digital audio programs. Specific examples will be given using Adobe Audition and Apple GarageBand.

5.2.1 Waveform Editor—One Audio at a Time

Waveform editors are generally designed for working on mono or stereo files one at a time. You can record and edit audio files. They are good for simple assembling of audio and for audio enhancements (such as noise reduction). Working with a waveform editor is a good way to start learning digital audio editing. Example application programs of waveform editor include Adobe Audition, Sony Sound Forge, Audacity (a freeware), and Apple Sound Studio Pro. Here are some commonalities in these editors.

- Audio files are displayed one at a time.
- Audio is represented as a waveform. The horizontal axis is time and the vertical axis is the amplitude.
- You can record audio.
- The common controls include: play, pause, stop, rewind to beginning, forward to end, and zoom in/out of the waveform. You can click within the waveform window to place the playhead location.
- You can click and drag to select part of the waveform. You can delete, copy, and paste the selection to reassemble the waveform. For example, Figure 5.1a shows a waveform of a voice recording saying "a", "b", "c". The waveform segment corresponding to the voice "c" is selected, cut, and pasted in before the waveform segment for "a" (Figure 5.1b). Now, the waveform is reassembled as "c", "a", "b".
- For a stereo audio, two waveforms will be displayed (Figure 4.1)—one for each channel. Mono audio is shown with one waveform.

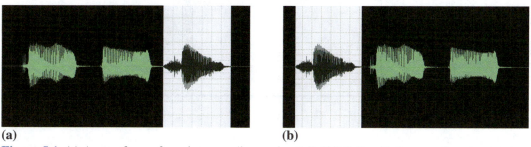

(a)   **(b)**

Figure 5.1 (a) A waveform of a voice recording saying "a", "b", "c", with the waveform segment corresponding to "c" selected (b) Segment "c" is cut and pasted before segment "a", resulting in the waveform "c", "a", "b"

5.2.2 Multitrack

As the name implies, *multitrack editors* allow you to work with multiple audio tracks. Multitrack editing embodies the concept of audio composition in two dimensions: the horizontal axis as time and the vertical axis as the audio elements. Figure 5.2 illustrates this concept.

The multitrack editors' workspace often seems a little busy and overwhelming at first sight. We will use this illustration to serve as a basis to help you understand the concept behind the multitrack editor interface.

A multitrack editor lets you work with multiple audio segments at one time. It allows you to mix different audio segments. As illustrated in Figure 5.3a, at 10 seconds, clips of violin 1, cello 1, and piano 1 are mixed together; at 21 seconds, only piano 1 is playing.

In Chapter 4, a similar illustration is used to explain the idea of simultaneous playback of different sound clips. Musical sound clips are used in the example here. A multitrack editor lets you work with any types of sound.

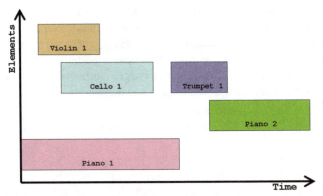

Figure 5.2 Illustration of the multitrack concept

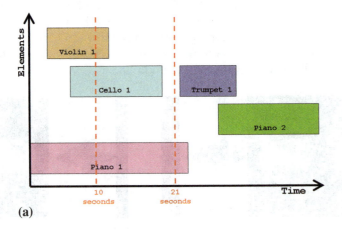

(a)

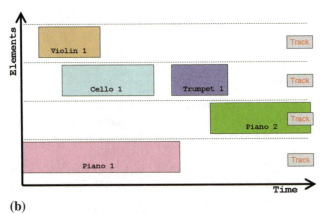

(b)

Figure 5.3 Illustration of the concept of using
a multitrack editor for audio mixing

In multitrack programs, each audio clip often is represented as a rectangle block on the track (Figure 5.3b). Now if you think of the placement of audio elements in the vertical direction as stacking them on a shelf or layers of images in Photoshop, it is easy to understand the concept of tracks.

Let's also draw a parallel with image editors, such as Adobe Photoshop. Tracks are like layers in Photoshop. In a sense, working with tracks to compose an audio is like working with layers to create an image composition. Similar to placing multiple visual elements on a layer in Photoshop, you can place multiple audio clips in a track—as long as the clips are not occupying the same time frame. If clips overlap in time, you can place them in different tracks.

Like applying layer effects to a layer, you can apply audio effects (such as reverb) to a track. The audio effects (like layer effects) applied to a track are non-destructive. This means that the effects do not alter the original clips on the track. Like applying opacity to a layer, you also can adjust the volume and pan for a track. In audio, you also can adjust the volume and pan over time. Table 5.1 summarizes these comparisons between layers and tracks.

TABLE 5.1	Parallels between Audio Editing in Multitrack View and Image Editing Using Layers
Audio	**Images**
Tracks	Layers
Clips	Visual elements
FX or effects	Layer effects
Audio mix down	Flatten image

When you are satisfied with the mixing results, you can export the audio as an audio mix down. *Mixing down* means combining all of the tracks with effects. This is analogous to flattening an image in Photoshop. When you open a mixed down audio piece, there are no separate tracks.

The layer's ability to organize visual elements for independent manipulation and apply non-destructive effects makes it a valuable tool for image composition. Similarly, the multitrack is a valuable tool for audio composition.

You can adjust the volume and *pan* of a clip over time. Panning refers to spreading the audio signal in multiple channels. In other words, if you adjust the pan of a stereo (i.e. two channels—left and right) you spread the audio signal into the left and right channels. Audio panning can create an impression of the sound source moving across from one side to the other. The common representation of the volume and pan controls is as horizontal lines within the block that represents the clip. In some programs, you may find a horizontal volume line located at the top of the clip's block, such as in Figure 5.4a. The height of the line represents the volume level. You can alter the shape of the line to control the volume change over time. For example, the volume line shown in Figure 5.4b creates a fade-in at the beginning of the clip and a fade-out at the end.

(a)   (b)

Figure 5.4 An audio clip's volume change over time can be adjusted by altering the shape of it volume line (a) A straight horizontal line means the volume remains constant over time (b) This line defines a fade-in effect at the beginning of the clip and a fade-out at the end

Figure 5.5 An audio clip's pan change over time can be adjusted by altering the shape of it volume line (a) A straight horizontal line positioned in the middle means there is no bias for the two channels over time (b) The result of this line is a pan from left to right

Similarly, you can specify panning using a line, except now the height of the line corresponds to the bias of the volume level for two different channels: left and right. By default, the pan line is placed in the middle, which does not have a bias for the channels (Figure 5.5a). Figure 5.5b shows a panning from left to right. The volume for the left channel starts at the maximum while the right starts at zero. The line gradually moves away from the bottom (left channel) towards the top (right channel). This means that over time the volume of left channel decreases while the volume of the right channel increases.

5.3 MULTITRACK IN ART AND DESIGN ORGANIZATIONAL PRINCIPLES

Multitrack is invaluable for creating audio composition. Table 5.2 lists how multitrack editing may help you incorporate the organization principles that are discussed in Chapter 4.

TABLE 5.2	How Multitrack Becomes Useful for Composition
Organizational Principles	**How Multitrack Becomes Useful**
Unity	Create Coherency by allowing you to apply same effect settings to multiple clips on either the same track or on multiple tracks.
Harmony	By layering different audio clips that are harmonic in nature using tracks.
Variety	Being able to work with multiple clips and to reuse clips with altered properties.
Balance	Help you to explore the balance of the overall audio by allowing you to visualize the relative temporal positions of the audio clips on a track and relocate the clips.
Repetition	Being able to loop audio clips and reuse clips at a different time.
Emphasis/focus	Allowing a curve/line shape to visually control volume change over time, so you can create bursts easily.
Perspective	Panning and reverb effects can be used to create an illusion of space.

5.4 AUDITION MULTITRACK BASICS

The basic steps of working with a multitrack session are

Step 1 Place clips on tracks. You can always add and remove clips any time during the process.

Step 2 Apply effects; adjust volume and pan, if needed.

Step 3 Export the final audio by mixing down the tracks.

Audition 2.0 Multitrack View (Figure 5.6) and Apple GarageBand 3.0 (Figure 5.7) are used as examples to demonstrate the basics in multitrack editing.

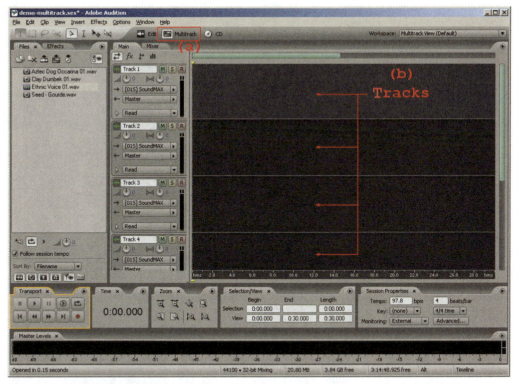

Figure 5.6 Adobe Audition 2.0 Multitrack view showing (a) button to switch to Multitrack view and (b) horizontal tracks for audio clips

Figure 5.7 Apple GarageBand '08 indicating tracks for audio clips

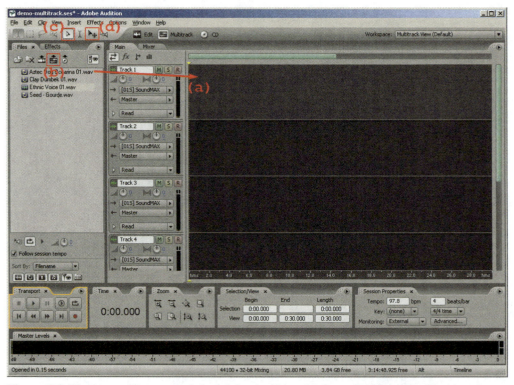

Figure 5.8 Placing a clip on a track in Adobe Audition (a) from the Files tab, (b) using the Insert button, (c) using the Hybrid tool, or (d) using the Move/Copy Clip tool

5.4.1 Placing Clips on a Track

There is more than one way to place an audio clip on a track. Here are two possible ways.

1. You can drag a clip file onto a track (Figure 5.8 for Audition and Figure 5.9 for GarageBand).
2. You can click the Insert button in Audition to insert the clip at the playhead position (Figure 5.8b).

To move the clip to another time on the track:

- *Audition:* Right-click and drag the clip if you are using the Hybrid tool (Figure 5.8c). If you are using the Move/Copy Clip tool (Figure 5.8d), you can simple click and drag the clip.
- *GarageBand:* Click and drag the clip.

5.4.2 Applying Effects in Multitrack

Audition

To apply an effect to a track, turn on the Effect (*fx*) button (Figure 5.10a). In the drop-down menu (Figure 5.10b), select the effect that you want to apply to the track. The effect will

Figure 5.9 Placing a clip on a track in Apple GarageBand (a) by choosing a clip file from the Loops browser and (b) dragging it onto the track window

Figure 5.10 Apply an effect to a track in Audition using (a) the Effect button, (b) a track's drop-down menu, and (c) the Effect Power button

Figure 5.11 GarageBand track effect settings found in the Track Info pane (a) Click the Details triangle to show the settings (b) A reverb effect is applied

apply to the whole track (i.e. to all of the clips that are placed on that track). The effect can be toggled on and off by clicking the *fx* Power button (Figure 5.10c). This allows great flexibility for experimentation. In addition, the effect can be deleted any time.

GarageBand

The track effect settings can be found in the Track Info pane (Figure 5.11). To display the Track Info pane, choose Track > Show Track Info. In the example shown in Figure 5.11, the second track is selected, and, as indicated by the checked box for Reverb and the non-zero setting, a reverb effect is applied to this track.

5.4.3 Using Sends and Busses to Apply Same Effects to Multiple Tracks in Audition

A *bus* is a special track. Unlike the normal audio track, a bus track does not have audio clips. Busses allow you to apply the same effects to a group of tracks. This feature is very helpful in ensuring consistency of the audio. Thus, it is helpful in creating unity, similarity, and common fate.

Shown here are only the "bare-bones" steps for creating a new bus in Adobe Audition and assigning multiple audio tracks to this new bus. This is to give you a basic idea of how to create and set a bus track. There are many adjustment options that you can use to refine the audio. Once you have tried out the basics, look up the program's Help menu to find out more options.

Step 1 Create a bus if there is not an existing one you want to use.

One way to create a bus is to select Insert > Bus Track. A bus track is added by default near the bottom of the track list. You can drag the track to another location. Figure 5.12 shows a new bus track which has been moved to below Track 2.

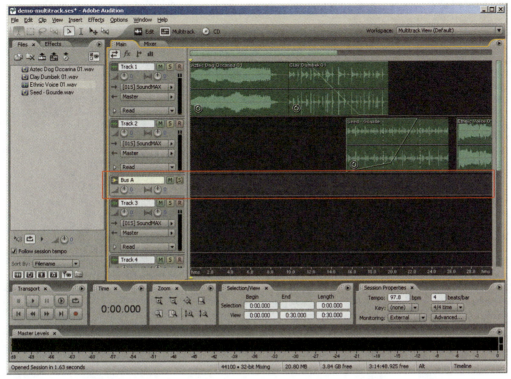

Figure 5.12 A new bus track below Track 2

Step 2 **Assign effect(s) to the bus track.**

You can assign effects to the bus track (Figure 5.13) like you would for a normal audio track.

Step 3 **Send audio tracks to the bus track.**

Just creating a bus track does not affect any audio track. To assign multiple audio tracks with the same effects that are specified in the bus track, you need to *send* these audio tracks' signals to the bus. To do so:

1. Click the *Sends* button (Figure 5.14a) to see the settings for sends.
2. For each track that you want to apply with the effects of the bus track, click on the output drop-down menu (Figure 5.14b), and select the bus track. In this example, the name of the bus track is Bus A.

To make the sends take effect, enable it using the Send Power button (Figure 5.14c). The Send Power button toggles on and off the track's sends. You also will need to adjust the Sends Level knob (Figure 5.14d). The *sends level* controls the signal level of the audio to be sent to the bus. By default, the sends level is set at $-\infty$ decibels, which means that no signal is sent to the bus track. A higher sends level will produce stronger effects on the audio.

5.4.4 Creating Repetitions Using Loops

An audio or music *loop* refers to an audio segment that can be repeated seamlessly. Seamless playback of an audio clip is not a technical requirement of the loop music-

Figure 5.13 Applying effects to a bus track (a) Turn on the effect button (b) Select the effect (c) Turn on or off the effect for the bus track

creation program. Technically, you can designate any audio clip as a loop, regardless of whether its audio content at the beginning and end is consistent enough to produce the seamless effect; the program will not prevent you from doing so.

Audition

A multitrack view allows you to create repetition by looping an audio clip. When you enable the loop property of a clip, you can drag the lower-right edge of the clip to extend the clip to create repetitions.

To toggle the loop property of a clip, right-click on the clip on the track, and select Loop Properties. . . . In the Audio Clip Looping properties dialog box (Figure 5.15), check or uncheck the Enable Looping check box.

If a clip's looping is enabled, you will see a circular arrow within a circle at the lower-left corner of the clip (Figure 5.16a). When you extend the clip, it automatically will create repeats for the duration you have specified. For example, the clip in Figure 5.16b has been set to repeat about 3.5 times.

GarageBand

To extend the clip to create repetitions in GarageBand, simply click-drag the upper-right edge of the block that represents the clip. In Figure 5.17, the clip in the first track is set to loop twice, and the clip in the fourth track (in blue) is extended to have about 2.5 repetitions.

Figure 5.14 (a) Sends button (b) Sends output of Track 1 assigned to Bus A
(c) Sends Power button (d) Sends Level knob

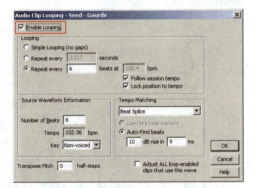

Figure 5.15 Audio Clip Looping dialog box

5.5 DIGITAL AUDIO TOOLS IN PERCEPTUAL ORGANIZATION

This section discusses some of the tools and techniques that may help you to develop perceptual organization in an audio piece.

5.5.1 Proximity and Similarity

Proximity in Time

Proximity in time can be controlled easily by reassembling the audio waveform. You can select a segment of an audio waveform and then copy and paste it at various times either in the same track or in a different track (if working in multitrack).

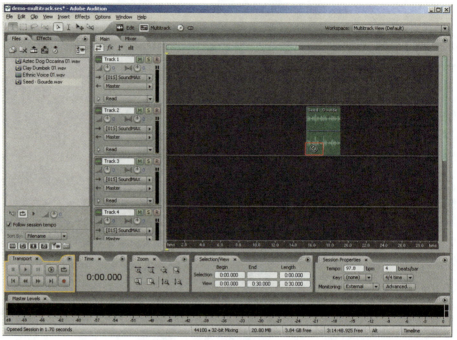

(a)

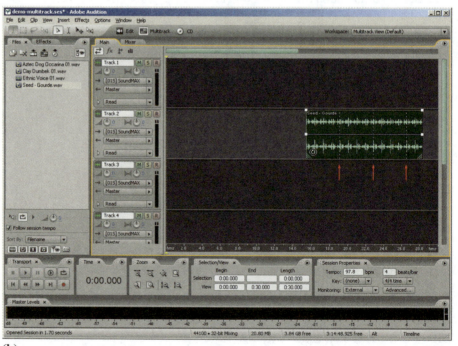

(b)

Figure 5.16 Audition looping of a clip (a) The circular arrow inside a circle at the lower-left corner of the clip indicates looping is enabled (b) The clip has been extended to create about 3.5 repetitions

Figure 5.17 GarageBand looping of clips where the red arrows mark the end of cycle of the loop

Figure 5.18 Adobe Audition's
Normalize dialog box

Similarity in Loudness

To create similar levels of loudness for different audio segments, you can normalize the amplitude of the different audio segments to be the same level. The *Normalize function* will boost or attenuate the amplitude so that the peak amplitude of either the entire audio piece or the selected segment is the specified value. For example, Adobe Audition's Normalize function, found under Effects > Amplitude > Normalize, lets you normalize audio amplitude to a specified percentage or amount of decibels (Figure 5.18). You can normalize different audio files or selected segments to the *same* amplitude to create the similarity of loudness.

Audition also has a function called *Group Waveform Normalize* (Edit > Group Waveform Normalize . . .) that makes it easier to normalize multiple files at once. It analyzes the audio's loudness and provides you with statistical information about it. This helps you to make an informative decision for creating similarity in loudness. Here are some general steps of how to use this function.

Step 1 Open the files that you want to normalize together.

Step 2 Choose Edit > Group Waveform Normalize . . . .

Step 3 In the Group Waveform Normalize dialog box, hold down the Ctrl or Shift key to click to choose the files that you want to normalize together (Figure 5.19a).

Step 4 Click on the tab labeled "2. Analyze Loudness" at the bottom of the dialog box.

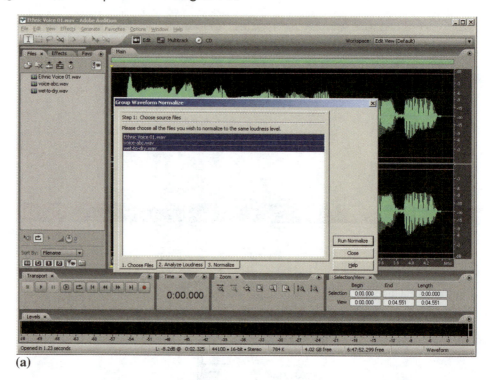

(a)

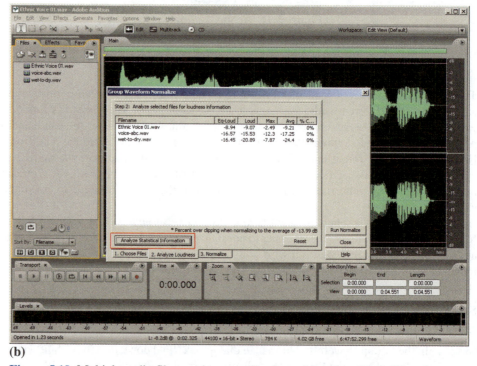

(b)

Figure 5.19 Multiple audio files can be normalized together using Group Waveform Normalize in Adobe Audition

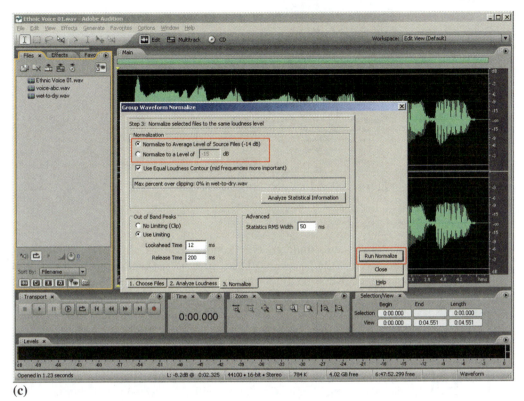

(c)

Figure 5.19 (*continued*)

Step 5 Click the Analyze Statistical Information button (Figure 5.19b). Audition will analyze each of the selected files and give you the loudness information.

Step 6 Click the tab "3. Normalize" to go to the normalization step.

Step 7 Here, you can set the normalization level based on the information from the statistical analysis (Figure 5.19c). You can choose to normalize the files to their average level or to specify a different level.

The option Use Equal Loudness Contour should be checked for best perceptual results. It takes into account that human hearing has different sensitivity to different audio frequencies. For example, with the same amplitude, a lower frequency sound is perceived to be softer than a mid-range frequency sound.

Similarity in Pitch

To change the pitch in Audition, you can use the ***Stretch function*** (Effects > Time/Pitch > Stretch). Select the Pitch Shift option in the Stretch dialog box (Figure 5.20a). There are presets (Figure 5.20b) of pitch shifting to choose from. You also can custom adjust the amount of pitch shift (Figure 5.20c).

Multitrack's sends and busses features also can be used to apply effects such as pitch shift and reverb to multiple tracks.

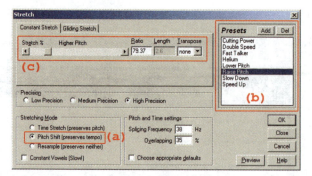

Figure 5.20 Adobe Audition's Stretch dialog box

5.5.2 Common Fate

When different audio elements undergo synchronous changes (such as in loudness or pitch), they may be perceived to be related. There are tools in Audition that allow you to change loudness and pitch over time. Like many other tools, they let you save the changed audio pattern as a preset so you can reuse the pattern to apply it to multiple audio clips using the idea of common fate.

Change of Loudness Over Time

To define how the loudness of an audio piece varies over time in Audition, you can use Effects > Amplitude > Envelope. The ***Envelope function*** allows you to use a curve (Figure 5.21a) to define how the amplitude of the audio (either a selected segment or the entire work) changes over time.

The horizontal axis of the graph represents time and the vertical axis the amplitude level (in percentage). The curve can be a straight line or a smooth curve. By checking the option Spline Curve (Figure 5.21b), you get a smooth curve which creates a smooth transition of pitch changes. The shape of the curve or the line is defined by the control points represented as white square dots (Figure 5.21c) in the graph. You also can drag the curve segment to reshape it, and new control points automatically will be created for the new shape. To remove any control point, simply drag the point off the graph.

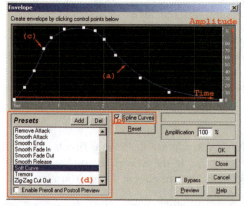

Figure 5.21 Adobe Audition Envelope dialog box for adjusting changes of audio amplitude over time

Figure 5.22 GarageBand Track Mixer changes the track volume over time

You can save the curve as a preset Envelope (Figure 5.21d) by clicking the Add button in the Presets box. Then you can reuse the changed pattern to apply it to other audio files or segments to create the effect of common fate in loudness.

In GarageBand, the volume level of each track can be changed over time in the Tracks Mixer. For example, in Figure 5.22, the fourth track is expanded to show its Tracks Mixer. The volume of the fourth track (Percussion) is set to fade out after the first loop. The triangle button (marked with a red rectangle in Figure 5.22) toggles between show and hide features of the Track Mixer.

Change of Pitch Over Time

Effects > Time/Pitch > Pitch Bender works very similarly to the Envelope function, but it is used for changing audio pitch over time. Like Envelope, *Pitch Bender function* allows you to use a curve (Figure 5.23a) to define how the pitch changes over time.

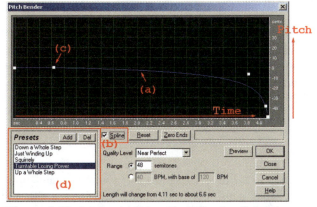

Figure 5.23 Adobe Audition Pitch Bender dialog box for adjusting changes of audio pitch over time

The horizontal axis of the graph represents time and the vertical axis the pitch level. The curve can be a straight line or a smooth curve. Manipulation of the curve works the same way as for the Envelop effect. By checking the option Spline (Figure 5.23b), you get a smooth curve which allows a smooth transition of pitch changes. The shape of the curve (or the line) is defined by the control points represented as white square dots (Figure 5.23c) in the graph. You also can drag the curve segment to reshape it and new control points automatically will be created. To remove any control point, simply drag the point off the graph.

Again, you can save the curve as a preset Pitch Bende (Figure 5.23d) by clicking the Add button in the Presets box. You then can reuse the setting to apply it to different audio segments to create the perception of common fate.

5.5.3 Good Continuation

We often perceive continuous and gradual changes as the same source and abrupt changes of sound as an introduction of a new source. This section discusses methods that allow you to apply gradual and abrupt changes of loudness and pitch.

Gradual Change in Loudness

Effects > Amplitude > Envelope discussed in the previous section allows you to create gradual change in loudness. If an audio piece is made up of different audio segments, you may need to normalize the different segments to be a similar loudness before applying the Envelope. This way, the Envelope effect will be more prominent. For example, the audio segment shown in Figure 5.24a has a consistent amplitude throughout. When an Envelope Soft Curve (see Figure 5.21) is applied to this audio, the gradualness is apparent (Figure 5.24b).

However, when each different audio segment differs widely in amplitude or the audio has many long discontinuities (Figure 5.25a), then the Envelope effect will not be noticeable anymore (Figure 5.25b). The discontinuities in the audio due to long, abrupt changes in amplitude can break up the gradual effect.

Gradual Change in Pitch

Effects > Time/Pitch > Pitch Bender (discussed previously) allows you to create a gradual change in pitch. Like loudness, the gradual change may not be noticeable if the audio has large discontinuities in pitch.

Abrupt Change

To make an abrupt change, you simply can delete a segment of a continuous audio. You also can select a short segment of the audio at the time you want to make an abrupt change, then apply the Envelope or Pitch Bender effect with an abrupt curve shape, such as the one shown in Figure 5.26. This will create a quick (abrupt) fall off but retain certain transition characteristics.

5.5.4 Closure

To exploit our tendency to fill in lost fragments of sound to maintain an intact piece of audio, you can create small gaps or short discontinuities in an audio. Deleting the audio fragments is a simple way to create discontinuities. However, silence is not the only form of discontinuity. Think about when you are conversing with a friend on a busy street and

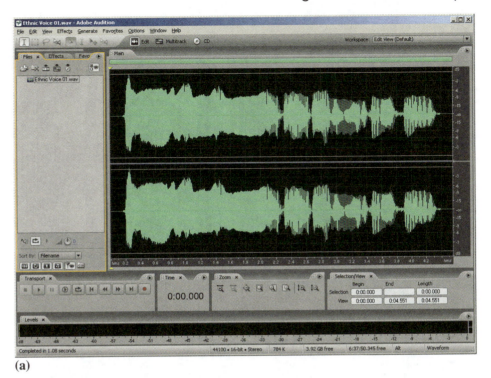

(a)

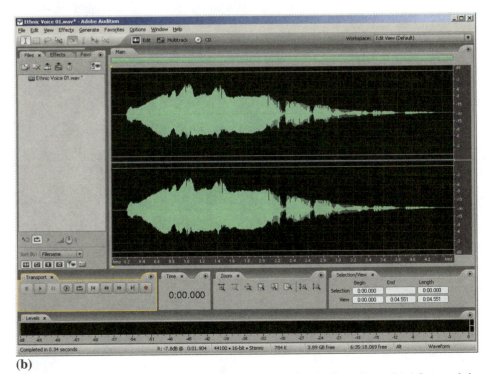

(b)

Figure 5.24 (a) An audio with quite consistent amplitude throughout (b) After applying the Envelope Soft Curve to the audio, the gradualness becomes apparent

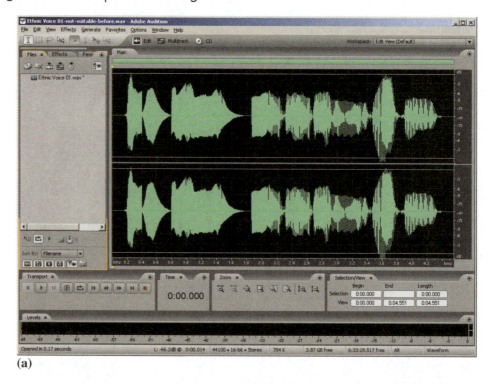

(a)

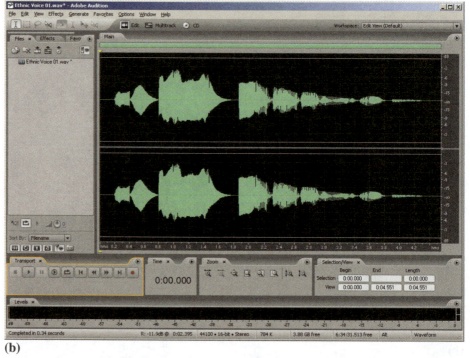

(b)

Figure 5.25 (a) An audio with long discontinuities (b) The Envelope Soft Curve is applied to the audio, but the gradualness is severed by the large discontinuities

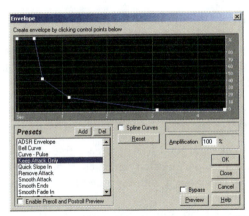

Figure 5.26 The Envelope effect preset of Keep Attack
Only has a curve indicating an abrupt change

some of the speech is drowned out by short bursts of noise. You can distort a short segment of the audio where you want to insert a disruption. Distortions can be created by very high amplitude, an unusual pitch shift, or an exaggerated reverb.

You also can overlay another audio with occasional short bursts. The Multitrack view lets you mix multiple audio segments. The volume level of each track of audio can be adjusted independently. Figure 5.27 shows two tracks of audio in the multitrack mode.

Figure 5.27 Two tracks of audio in Multitrack View where the volume level of audio in Track 1 is adjusted to have intermittent bursts (a) A line representing the volume level of the clip (b) A control point

The volume of the audio in Track 1 is adjusted to create intermittent short bursts. By default, the line representing the volume level located at the top of each track is 100%. There are two control points for the line: one at the beginning of the audio and the other at the end. You can drag the control points to control the change of the volume. You also can click on the line to create new control points to create changes of volume.

5.5.5 Figure–Ground Phenomenon

It is easy to see how multitrack is a good tool to create figure–ground phenomena. Background sounds usually are softer and muffled compared to the foreground sounds. The foreground and background can be assigned with separate tracks. You then can adjust the sound properties individually.

The line shape of the volume and pan controls are helpful in visualizing the change of audio's role over time—for example, changing from foreground to background or vice versa at different times.

TERMS

bus, 222
Envelope function, 230
Group Waveform
  Normalize function, 227
loop, 223

mixing down, 217
multitrack editors, 215
Normalize function, 227
Pan, 217

Pitch Bender function, 231
Sends function, 223
Stretch function, 229
waveform editors, 215

ASSIGNMENTS

1. Create short clips of natural sounds. Each sound should convey a feeling based on the following concepts.

   i.   Closed space
   ii.   Open space
   iii. Empty space
   iv.   Crowded space
   v.   Orderliness
   vi.   Chaos
   vii. Hot
   viii. Cold
   ix.   Hope
   x.   Melancholy
   xi.   Jaggedness
   xii. Flow
   xiii. Nostalgia
   xiv. Futuristic imagination

   The sounds used in the audio need not be musical. In fact, for this exercise it would be best not to use musical clips.

2. Create an audio that contrasts two feelings in the same piece.

   i. Closed space versus open space
   ii. Empty space versus crowded space
   iii. Orderliness versus chaos
   iv. Hot versus cold
   v. Hope versus melancholy
   vi. Jaggedness versus flow
   vii. Nostalgic versus futuristic

   Construct a sketch first. See the description about the sketch in the Activities section in Chapter 4.

3. Create an audio that is suggestive of a narrative or a sequence of events (such as part of your day). Construct a sketch first. See the description about the sketch in Activities section in Chapter 4.

4. If the timbre of a sound is analogous to color in imagery, create an audio that convey a feeling based on the following.

   i. A black-and-white photograph of a tulip
   ii. A field of colorful wild flowers

   What sounds would you use? How you would combine these various sounds? Plan for the sounds to be recorded for the project, and sketch out the horizontal and vertical placement of these sounds before working with the software.

5. If the pitch of a sound is analogous to brightness and darkness in imagery, create an audio that conveys a feeling base on the following

   i. High noon
   ii. A starry night

   What sounds would you use? How you would combine these various sounds? Plan for the sounds to be recorded for the project, and sketch out the horizontal and vertical placement of these sounds before working with the software.

6. Create a voice-over audio piece with background music using the following methods.

   i. Record a voice over segment. Apply noise reduction to clean up the audio. Remove any unwanted pauses. Add pauses by inserting silence to where it is needed.
   ii. Use a loop music program to create a background music.
   iii. Use multitrack to mix the voice over with the background music. Adjust the volume of the background music so that it does not compete with the voice over.

A still from Erin Regan's *Fast Forward*, digital video

Video as a Time-Based Medium in Digital Art

GENERAL LEARNING OBJECTIVES

In this chapter, you will learn:

- To apply basic art and design organizational principles to video.
- The general framework of a narrative model.
- To analyze your video ideas in space, time, and narrative.
- To critique digital video in a classroom setting.

6.1 WHAT IS DIGITAL VIDEO?

Throughout this text, the terms videos, movies, and films are used interchangeably. The creator of the work is referred to as the filmmaker or artist.

Video in its simplest definition is a sequence of images that are played in succession. When these images are played at a sufficiently high speed, an illusion of motion is created although the intent of video is not *always* to create an illusion of motion. Digital video refers to the video stored in a digital format. Before digital technologies, video could be stored and shot on film and on analog tape.

Video, whether in digital or analog format, is a time-based medium. When you think of movie making, you naturally may think of drama and fiction. However, video has been used for various creative purposes—for example, entertainment, storytelling, instructions, documentary, and fine art. Not all videos are narrative. In the textbook *Film Art**, the authors classify five types of films regarding their narrative and non-narrative natures.

1. Categorical Films.

In these films, the subject of the film is presented by cataloging a set of information. The film presents individual examples. For example, if the film deals with ants as an overall category, it could go through each genus of ant.

2. Rhetorical Films.

Unlike categorical films, these films do not simply present information about the subject but go further to provide a persuasive argument (like a thesis statement in a paper) in an attempt to convince the viewer of some insights about the subject.

3. Abstract Films.

These films present the subject in an abstract form. They rely on abstract visual and audio elements, such as color, graphic composition, movement, editing, sounds, and visual distortion.

4. Associational Films.

Instead of presenting the direct meaning of the subject, these films elicit the viewer's emotional response to the subject through juxtaposition and metaphorical audiovisual materials that may have their own symbolic meaning.

---

*David Bordwell and Kristin Thompson, *Film Art An Introduction*. New York, NY: Newbery Award Records, Inc., 1986, pp. 44–5.

5. Narrative Films.

These films present "a chain of events in cause-effect relationship occurring in time . . . A narrative begins with one situation; a series of changes occurs according to a pattern of causes and effects; finally, a new situation arises which brings about the end of the narrative."[†] The characteristics of these films are the causal and temporal relationships among the events presented in the film.

In many situations, the classification of films may not be very clear-cut. Almost every narrative film uses a mixture of narrative and non-narrative elements. It is not uncommon that fine-art styles of films present a narrative or express a message in a combination of abstract and associational film formats. These works rely on the viewer's imagination and interpretation—more so than the drama made for entertainment purposes in TV or Hollywood movies—in order to make sense of the narrative and the message that the artist intends to communicate.

The general scope of this chapter focuses on the narrative and fine-art aspects of video. Many of the ideas in this chapter are based on the concepts of form found in the visual arts. This chapter also will use some fundamental concepts and techniques established for dramatic structure.

6.1.1 Properties of Digital Format

Video captures motion as a sequence of pictures at a constant time interval. Each picture is called a *frame*. How fast the pictures are captured or how fast the frames are played back is determined by the *frame rate* which is measured in *frames per second (fps)*.

The *frame size* also is referred to as the resolution. It is measured in pixel dimensions of a frame—its width by its height expressed in number of pixels. For NTSC *standard-definition DV* (one of the standard definition digital video formats) format, the frame size is 720 × 480 pixels. The frame size for a PAL standard definition DV frame is 720 × 576 pixels. For the *HDV* format (one of the *high-definition digital video* formats), there currently are two frame sizes: 1280 × 720 pixels and 1440 × 1080 pixels. The format of 1440 × 1080 pixels is displayed at the resolution of 1920 × 1080 pixels. Table 6.1 summaries the properties of the standard definition and high definition digital video formats.

The *frame aspect ratio* is the ratio of its width-to-height dimensions. For standard definition DV format, there are two formats: standard format and widescreen format. The frame aspect ratio for the standard format is 4:3, while the widescreen format is 16:9. The frame aspect ratio for high definition digital video is 16:9.

Some video formats use pixels that are *not* square to make up the frame. The shape of the pixel can be described by an attribute called the *pixel aspect ratio*. For a square pixel, the pixel aspect ratio is equal to 1. A pixel aspect ratio of less than 1 depicts a tall pixel, while a pixel aspect ratio of greater than 1 depicts a wide pixel. A video should be displayed on a system with the same pixel aspect ratio, otherwise the image will be distorted.

For the standard-definition DV format, the pixel aspect ratio for the standard format is 0.9, while for the widescreen format, the pixel aspect ratio is 1.2. For high-definition digital video of 720p (i.e., 1280 × 720 pixels, progressive), its pixel aspect ratio is 1.0. The pixel aspect ratio of high-definition digital video of 1080i and 1080p is 1.33 during playback to give a frame size of 1920 × 1080. In the notations 1080i and 1080p, i stands for *interlaced* and p stands for *progressive*.

NTSC and PAL are broadcast standards for analog color televisions. These standards pertain to the technical details of how color television pictures are encoded and transmitted as broadcast signals. NTSC was named after United State's National Television Systems Committee, which designated this standard. It is used in North America, Japan, Taiwan, and parts of the Caribbean and South America. PAL stands for Phase Alternating Line, which refers to the way the signals are encoded. It is used in Australia, New Zealand, and most of Western Europe and the Asian countries.

For a detailed introduction to digital video format, see *the Digital Media Primer* Chapter 6.

[†]Ibid, p. 83.

The final video can be exported for DVD playback, Web, CD-ROM, or DVD-ROM. High-definition digital video also can be output to high-definition discs (BluRay) for playback.

TABLE 6.1	A Summary of Properties of Digital Video Format			
	Standard Definition DV Format		**High Definition HDV Format**	
Types of Format	Standard Format	Widescreen Format	720p	1080i and 1080p
Frame rate	• NTSC: 29.97 fps • PAL: 25 fps			
Frame size	• NTSC: 720 × 480 pixels • PAL: 720 × 576 pixels		1280 × 720 pixels	1440 × 1080 pixels
Frame aspect ratio	4:3	16:9	16:9	
Pixel aspect ratio	0.9	1.2	1.0	1.33

VIDEO RESOLUTION

Higher resolution provides more details in the image. However, the image definition depends on the intention of the work. Blurriness and obscurity evoke a different mood and experience (Figure 6.1).

Pixelvision (PXL 2000) was a toy black-and-white video camera manufactured by Fisher Price in 1987. It recorded videos on analog audio cassette tapes. There have been film festivals dedicated to films shot by this camera, for example, the PXL THIS film festival at http://www.indiespace.com/pxlthis/.

Information of the video examples cited in this chapter can be found at the end of the chapter.

Figure 6.1 An example video still shot with a Pixelvision Fisher Price camera (PXL 2000) (Courtesy of Jym Davis)

6.2 FORM AND CONTENT

For visual art, *form*—in its simplest term—refers to the way it looks—how the content (the work of art) is presented and how it embodies the idea. Form includes everything from the physical materials and medium of the work to the use of the basic elements of art, such as lines, shapes, values and colors. It also includes the composition—how these different elements are put together to make the whole piece of art work into a unified whole.

A video, a film, or a movie is a collection of elements put together to convey an idea—whether an expression or a story—with an additional dimension—time. In the subsequent sections, we will introduce three formal aspects of video work: space, time, and narrative.

Like in an art work, how a collection of elements are put together in a video work is governed by the artist's intention and the relationships between these elements. There are general guidelines or principles for these relationships. They are very similar to the organizational principles of art and design. They will be discussed later in this chapter by drawing parallels to those of art and design.

6.3 SPACE, TIME, AND NARRATIVE

In a narrative movie, there exists a three-dimensional (3-D) world that relies on the filmmaker to create out of two-dimensional (2-D) images—spatial relationship. These two-dimensional images that depict objects and events are presented to the viewer in a certain sequence—temporal relationship.

The sequence of events that a movie presents to the viewer is not necessarily in the same order as the actual story the movie is trying to tell. In addition, the viewing time (time taken for the story to be told) does not necessarily match the actual time. A movie may last from 60 to 90 minutes, but the time within the story itself can be decades or only 30 minutes.

It is useful to introduce the concept of *diegetic* and *non-diegetic*. The diegetic world is the *world* that is seen on-screen where the story's events occur and the characters exist. The viewer presumes (or is led to presume) that this diegetic world is governed by a set of rules and contains many other characters and objects (whether depicted on-screen or not).

Non-diegetic elements are addressed to the viewer only and are not accessible to any of the characters. They can be used to provide viewers additional information to help them understand the diegetic world and the sequence of events.

Sounds of footsteps, a door closing, or a gun shooting created by the characters in the story are diegetic sounds, whether the actual sound source is depicted on-screen or not. On the other hand, the background music and a narration are non-diegetic sound. Most of the visual representations on-screen (such as the characters and the props) are diegetic elements. Examples of non-diegetic visual elements include on-screen text that commonly is used to tell the viewer the time and location status of the diegetic world, for example, "Two years later. . . ."

The diegetic world of most movies is based on our realistic world and contains everyday objects. Abstract movies, however, may use abstract shapes that are not everyday objects. Even when everyday objects are used, they may be filmed in such a way that they become unrecognizable by being reduced into abstract shapes. In these cases, it is not the space of the diegetic world that the movie is going after.

Other useful concepts to be introduced here are story versus plot. The events and actions that are presented to the viewer constitute the *plot*. The *story* constitutes emotions that cannot be seen or heard but are felt by seeing and hearing the actions presented—the plot. Think of the plot as *physical* actions and the story as an emotional journey. The plot embodies the story, while the emotion of the story motivates the actions, i.e., the plot. For example, the movie synopsis you read on the DVD-movie packaging describes the *plot* summary of the movie; it is a straightforward *description* of the actions and what happens.

The space and time of the story are not necessarily the same as those of the plot. The ***story space*** refers to the spaces where the story actions and events occur. The ***plot space*** refers to the spaces where those actions presented to the viewer occur. The viewer may not see all of the story space in a movie but is given an understanding of these unseen story spaces through the plot.

Similarly, the ***story time*** refers to the time span in which the story events occur. The ***plot time*** refers to the time during which those actions are presented to the viewer. Further discussions in space and time are given in subsequent sections.

6.4 SPACE

There are different types of space in movies: story space, plot space, and screen space. We have explained story space and plot space in the previous section. But what is screen space?

Movies are made up of a sequence of images; each of the images is called a frame. ***Screen space*** refers to the space that is depicted within the frame. Each frame has a composition within it, just like a painting or a still photograph. The basic art and design principles for image composition also apply to composition within a movie frame. For abstract films, the visual quality within the flat screen space plays an important role. For narrative films, the screen space provide a view of the three-dimensional diegetic world.

6.4.1 On-Screen and Off-Screen Space

Paintings and drawings frame the image in two dimensions. However, the space that they depict is not necessarily confined within the rectangular frame. Likewise, in a movie, there is always space outside the frame—*off-screen space*—at any moment. The visible space within the frame is the ***on-screen space***.

The space off-screen at one moment may be shown on-screen at different moments in the movie. In many situations, off-screen space of a particular moment may never appear on screen in the movie, but it is acknowledged to make the viewer aware of the existent of the off-screen space.

Off-screen space can be acknowledged by using off-screen sound, such as the sound of footsteps or a door closing. Hearing a sound whose source is not depicted on-screen can generate certain emotions such as tension and suspense and get the viewer involved in the story by inducing their imagination. Off-screen space also can be implied through dialogue between characters. For example, having a character talk about his childhood experience in a park creates the park in the viewer's mind without actually showing it.

The camera controls what is seen on-screen. Thus, camera movement deals with how the on-screen space is presented. The camera can remain static to create a still shot but also can scroll through the scene by panning or tracking. A ***pan*** is a shot created by rotating the camera horizontally while remaining at the same location. A ***tracking shot*** is created by moving the camera (often alongside, in front of, or behind a moving subject).

In early films (early 1900s), the camera often was set up to point at the action and remain static for the entire action or even the entire film. People in the film are seen going and off the frame. The off-screen space is implied but not necessarily shown. Static camera shots still are used commonly today, although it is rare to have one static camera shot for the entire movie. There certainly are some exceptions—such as time-lapse videos, for example, showing germination of a seed and those intending to mimic surveillant videos or Web cams.

Each camera shot depicts just a part of the diegetic world. The space depicted in the different shots may contain overlapping space. If it is not showing any overlapping space, the shot may be showing the adjacent (or non-adjacent) space of the previous shot. Video editing also plays an important role in presenting the on-screen space, because it determines how these different shots are shown: one at a time or simultaneously.

One at a Time

Static camera shots of adjacent space can be used for a one-at-a-time display. A character on-screen often moves off-screen in one direction followed by immediatly cutting to the next shot of the adjacent space. For example, Figure 6.2a through d shows static camera shots. When the girl moves off the frame, it cuts to the next shot (Figure 6.2e) of the adjacent space.

In this new shot (Figure 6.2e), the character then reenters the screen from the side opposite the one that she has moved from off-screen in the previous shot (Figure 6.2d). The character continues to move in the same direction (Figure 6.2f). The space depicted in these two shots (Figure 6.2d and e) are perceived as being adjacent to one another.

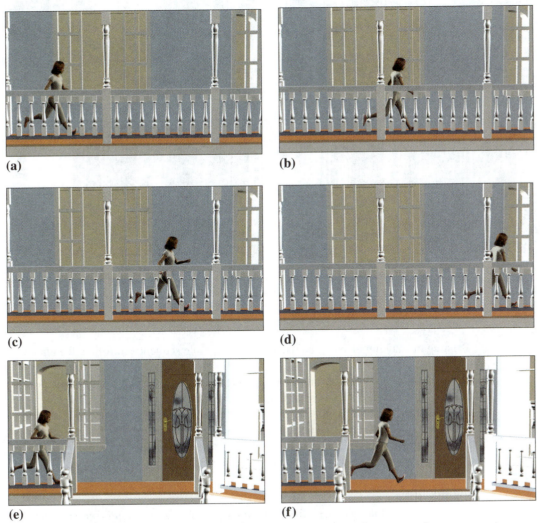

(a) (b) (c) (d) (e) (f)

Figure 6.2 Static camera shots are used to display adjacent space in one at a time sequences

Figure 6.3 Use of tracking to follow the character and slowly reveal the space

Panning or tracking also can be used for this example sequence to follow the character (Figure 6.3).

While both techniques—cutting to different shot and panning or tracking—can be used to display adjacent space, they build anticipation and suspense differently. Panning allows the slow revealing of the space, while cutting to a different camera shot one at a time creates an abrupt change of scene. A new shot to be cut to will replace the whole frame. This creates a larger unknown than the continuous pan does. The uncertainty of something coming up suddenly once the new shot comes up heightens the tension.

Simultaneously

One technique of simultaneously displaying multiple shots is called *split-screen*. The split-screen technique often is used to show simultaneous events or actions of characters. This divides the viewer's attention among the images in the split screens. Split-screen sequences have been used in Abel Gance's *Napoleon* (1927), *Timecode* (1999), and *The Hulk* (2003).

Max Negin's *Observe* (Figure 6.4) examines growth and change during life over time. The video uses a split-screen technique in some segments in which each split screen plays a time-lapse video of a different perspective.

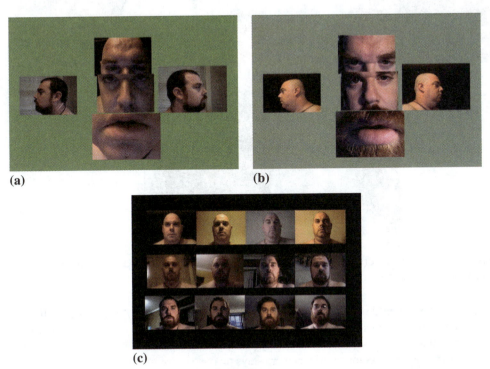

(a)   **(b)**

(c)

Figure 6.4 Video stills from Max Negin's *Observe*

Another technique for displaying multiple shots on the same screen is by ***superimposing*** one on another to allow overlapping. Superimposing without image overlapping will produce the effect of split-screen technique.

> ◇ **Video Example: Split-screen and Time-lapse Video** You can see the split-screen techniques combined with time-lapse effect in this short segment of video from Max Negin's *Observe*.

6.4.2 The Line and the 180-Degree Rule

A video is made up of multiple camera shots. The viewer sees only part of space of a scene within a frame. In order to help the viewer make sense of the 3-D spatial relationship of your scene, the shots and their order need to create a sense of spatial continuity.

For example, in a sequence of two characters facing each other conversing (Figure 6.5a), cutting two shots like Figure 6.5b and c together will cause confusion on their spatial relationship. It looks like one character is talk to the back of another character. The confusion is due to the change of screen direction. ***Screen direction*** is the direction that the characters and things face when viewed through the camera.

The ***180-degree rule*** is a commonly used principle to help you avoid confusion by determining the locations of the camera that create a logical sense of spatial continuity of your scene. In this rule, it uses a line to determine on which side the camera should be to

The term *cut* is commonly used to describe the relationship between shots. Cutting two shots together refers to instantaneously changing from one shot to another.

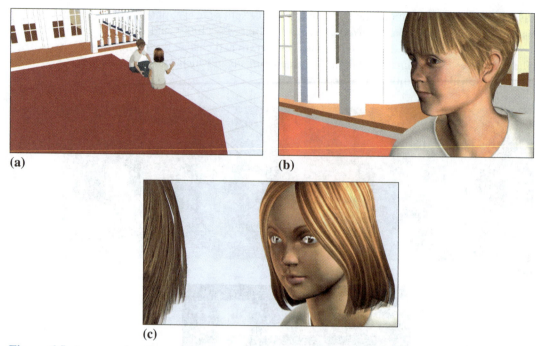

Figure 6.5 An example of reversing screen direction (a) Two characters are actually facing each other (b) A shot of one character (c) A shot of another character

maintain the screen direction. The *line* also is known as the ***axis of action***. Basically, the rule is that the camera stays on the same side of the line to maintain the screen direction. It does not matter which side the camera stays on. Aesthetic factors often determine the side the camera stays on. As long as the camera stays on one side of the line, the screen direction is maintained. If the camera crosses the line in creating two shots, the subjects who are facing each other will appear to be looking at the same direction on-screen.

So, how is the line constructed? There are two types: sightline and direction of action. Both are imaginary lines. The ***sightline*** is a line that depicts the *facing* direction of a character or object. The ***direction of action*** represents the subject's direction of *movement*.

Sightline

Figure 6.6a through d shows shots corresponding to different camera locations (Figure 6.6e through h). The red line in Figure 6.6e through h represents the sightline for the boy. The camera is represented by the red outline of a camera icon in a black circle. For the shots shown in Figure 6.6 a through c, the camera stays on the same side of the line. The boy is facing left within the frame in all shots. When cutting two of these shots together, the spatial relationships of the characters in the scene still make sense.

When the camera crosses the line (Figure 6.6h), the boy is now facing right—the opposite direction—on-screen (Figure 6.6d). When cutting two shots together in which the camera crosses the line—for example from Figure 6.6c to d—the characters look like they have somehow switched places, although nothing in the scene has moved but the camera.

> 🖱 **Camera Location, Sightline, and Screen Direction** This interactive demo lets you examine the screen direction on different sides of the sightline by looking at shots from 36 different camera locations surrounding the two characters in the example shown in Figure 6.6.

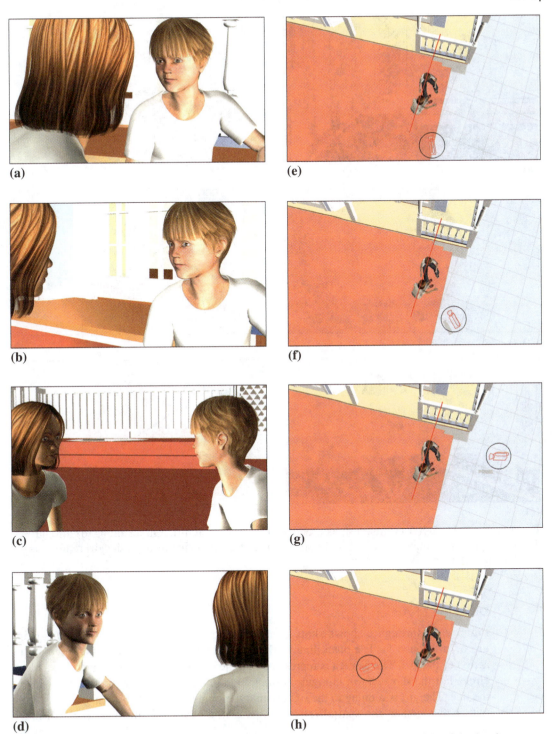

Figure 6.6 (a) through (c) Camera shots produced by shooting on the same side of the boy's sightline (d) Camera shot produced by shooting on the other side of the boy's sightline (e) through (h) The corresponding camera locations in the scene

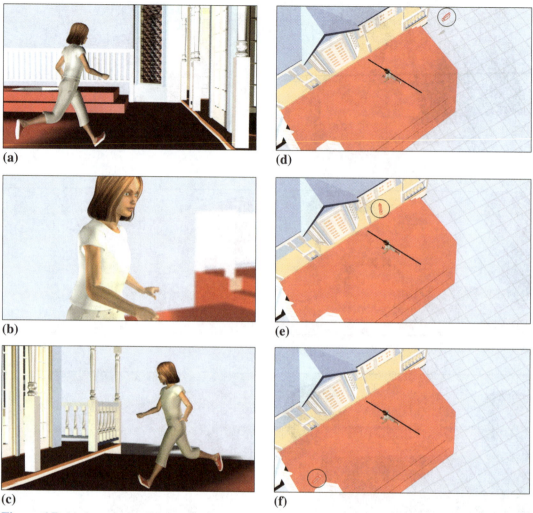

Figure 6.7 (a) through (c) Camera shots produced by shooting at different locations (d) through (f) The corresponding camera locations in the scene where the black line through the girl represents the direction of action

Direction of Action

Figure 6.7a through c shows shots corresponding to different camera locations (Figure 6.7d through f). The black line in Figure 6.7d through f represents the direction of action of the girl. The camera is represented by the red outline of a camera icon in a black circle. For the shots shown in Figure 6.7a through b, the camera stays on the same side of the line. The girl is running to the right within the frame in both shots. When cutting these two shots together, the spatial relationships of the characters in the scene still make sense.

When the camera crosses the line (Figure 6.7f), the girl is now running to the left on screen (Figure 6.7c). When cutting either Figure 6.7a or b with this shot together in which the camera crosses the line, the girl appears to have changed the direction.

6.4.3 Establishing Shot

An *establishing shot* is a shot that is wide enough to help your viewers establish the spatial relationships of the subjects in their mind. It usually is used at the beginning of a scene to tell viewers where they are. The shot does not have to include everything—just everything that is necessary for the viewer to get an idea of the type of environment that the subject is situated in and the spatial relationship of the subjects. For example, Figure 6.8 shows an example shot of two characters conversing on the deck of a house.

Figure 6.8 An establishing shot showing two characters conversing on the deck of a house

6.5 TIME

Time often is manipulated in movies. This includes the duration of the story and the temporal order of events depicted in the movie.

6.5.1 Duration: Movie Time versus Story Time

In most movies, time is compressed. This means that the story takes place over a much longer time period than the actual running time of the movie itself. The compression of time is achieved by the use of *ellipses*, where certain durations of time are left out between cuts or scenes so that the film only consists of certain key stretches of the story.

Some movies do present stories in real time (i.e., the story takes place in the same amount of time as the movie's running time). Examples of this include Alfred Hitchcock's *Rope* (1948), Fred Zinnemann's *High Noon* (1952), Louis Malle's *My Dinner with Andre* (1981), John Badham's *Nick of Time* (1995), Mike Figgis's *Timecode* (1999), Andy Warhol's *Empire* (1964), and the TV series *24* (2001).

Andreas Müller-Pohle's *Yumiko*[††] (2001–02) captures the eye movement of a Japanese dancer, Yumiko, for over four minutes in real time. A sequence of alphanumeric code that represents the video image moves at the bottom of the video. Its speed is synchronized with the move movements. The dancer's face represents an "analog interface" and the sequence of digital code is now "read as linear noise."

Time-lapse videos compress time. They present events in a shorter period of time than the events normally do in real life. For example Amy Purcell's *Diurnal Rhythm: Head in the Clouds* (Figure 6.9) compresses a single day into a 15-minute video.

[††]http://www.muellerpohle.net/projects/yumiko.html

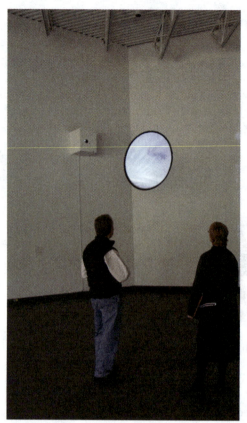

Figure 6.9 An installation still of Amy Purcell's
Diurnal Rhythm: Head in the Clouds, 2007–08

Usually, the compression of time in time-lapse videos is achieved by removing frames. However, in Christopher Cassidy's *Atlantic Flyway* (Figure 6.10), the images of the removed frame remain in the video. The video captures birds in flight during migration for long durations. Adjacent frames were then collapsed by superimposing so that the images of all the frames remain after frames have been reduced to compress time. The superimposed film reveals the patterns and lines developed over time.

6.5.2 Temporal Order

A story or the flow of the artist's message is not necessarily presented to the viewer in chronological order. Flashback and foreshadowing present the story out of its chronological order. They also are techniques used to alter the pacing of the plot. In a *flashback*, it travels back in time to introduce the events that occurred before the story began. It slows down the pace of the plot development and gives the viewer a chance to learn about the backstory. *Foreshadowing* can be used to allude to future events. It makes the pace of the plot seem to go faster. By giving the viewer a glimpse of the future event, it builds anticipation, making the viewer wanting to find out how it could have happened and what could have led to the event.

Actions happening at the same time at different spaces each have to be presented at a differ-ent movie time—unless these simultaneous actions are presented in split-screens. The order of

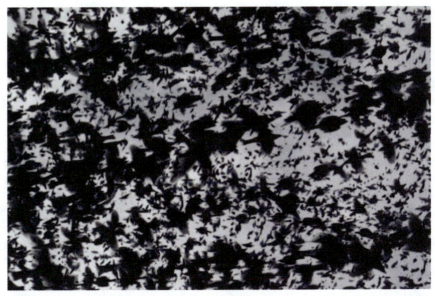

Figure 6.10 A video still from Christopher Cassidy's *Augury video series, The Atlantic Flyway, Pinckney Island, SC,* 2006

presenting these actions therefore does not imply their actual chronological order in the story. Thus, the actions taking place in the movie time can be longer than their actual time.

The relationships between the temporal order of the actions in the story and how they are presented to the viewer can be intricate. To make sense of the story, the viewer has to reconstruct the story timeline out of what actions are presented. These include the logical order and the duration of the events in the story. The plot needs to provide the viewer cues about the temporal order and duration of events.

The pliability of temporal ordering in video was exploited creatively in a 1996 music video called *Sugar Water*, directed by Michel Gondry. The temporal ordering plays with the idea of a palindrome—a word or any text that reads the same forward or backward. The entire video applies split-screen technique. Both sides of the screen show the same footage, which was shot in one shot. The first half of the footage follows one of the two singers and the second half the other singer. The two singers cross paths in the middle of the video. One side of the screen plays forward from the beginning of the original footage. The other side of the screen plays the footage backwards from the ending. The side that plays backward also is flipped horizontally to become a mirror image of the original footage. The timing of both sides meets in the middle—where a dramatic event occurs when the two singers cross paths.

> **◇ Video Example: Time-lapse Video with Superimposed Frames** You can see the time-lapse effect with superimposed adjacent frames in this short segment of video from Christopher Cassidy's *The Atlantic Flyway, Pinckney Island, SC.*

Sugar Water was published on *DVD, The Work of Director Michel Gondry,* by Palm Pictures in 2003. The DVD includes an interview of the director and the singers explaining the making of the video. More information about the video also can be found on the Web.

6.6 NARRATIVE

Narrative involves use of space, time, and causality. It typically has an initial situation (the beginning). As the plot unfolds (the middle), the situation will undergo changes to reach its final stage (the end). Therefore, the beginning and the ending often are related, although it does not mean the beginning and the ending situations have to be different. For example, in

The Wizard of Oz, the main character, Dorothy, runs away from home to avoid some conflict, but in the end, she returns home and realizes that "There is no place like home."

In general, in writing novels and drama screenplays, a narrative model is characterized by a *3-act structure*: beginning, development, and ending. Not all narrative videos find this model applicable, however; it depends on the intent of the piece.

6.6.1 Act 1: Beginning

The opening introduces the viewer to the setting of the story and the characters. It also introduces a situation that drives the main character from his/her normal life towards a different, conflicting situation, which is what the story is about. The goal of the plot in the opening intends to arouse the viewer's curiosity to seek answers to questions, such as what has happened, why it has happened, how it has happened, how it is going to end, and who is responsible.

Let's use the familiar classic movie *The Wizard of Oz* (1939) as an example to explain the concepts of this 3-act structure. First, let's look at a synopsis of the movie in case you are not familiar with the story.

"Dorothy lives on a farm in Kansas until a cyclone arrives, and picks her, her house, and her dog up and deposits them in the land of Oz. Things in Oz are strange and beautiful, but Dorothy just wants to get back home. She's helped by the Good Witch of the east, but she's also in trouble with the Wicked Witch of the West, who seeks revenge for the death of the Wicked Witch of the North, for which she blames Dorothy."[§]

The movie begins with Dorothy running towards her Auntie Em and Uncle Henry's farm. This implies to the viewer that Dorothy is an orphan. The opening also tells the viewers the space and time of the story. Miss Gulch, a mean lady, threatens to take Dorothy's dog away from her. This creates a situation motivating Dorothy to run away from home. This establishes the character of Dorothy—running away from trouble instead of facing it. This is a key trait of Dorothy that is going to change at the end of the story. Dorothy stops by Professor Marvel's place. There, the viewer is given a chance to learn more about Dorothy's life—the backstory. Professor Marvel talks her into going home. But when Dorothy gets home, her house is lifted up by a tornado and lands in Munchkinland, killing the Wicked Witch of the East. There, Dorothy meets the Good Witch of the North, Glinda. The sister of the Wicked Witch of the East, the Wicked Witch of the West, then threatens to kill Dorothy.

Dorothy running away from home and being talked into going home are not the direct cause of her getting lost and killing the witch—it is the tornado. However, these events function to introduce the viewer to the setting of the story and the character of Dorothy. If the movie skipped this establishment and began with tornado lifting up the house to Munchkinland, the viewer would not have known the backstory of Dorothy and would not have been able to contrast her character changes (being more mature in facing crisis) at the end of her journey.

6.6.2 Act 2: Development

Here, the protagonist undergoes an emotional crisis and encounters increasingly greater obstacles to resolve a conflict. As the plot unfolds, the protagonist will then come to a realization of what has been preventing him/her from resolving the conflict.

[§]http://www.amazon.com/Wizard-Oz-Two-Disc-Special/dp/B000ADS63K

Let's return to *The Wizard of Oz* example. In Act 2, Dorothy (the protagonist) and her dog, Toto, follow the Good Witch's advice and journey along the Yellow Brick Road to see the Wizard of Oz. She wants to ask him to help her get home. During the journey, she meets with three friends: the Scarecrow, the Tin Man, and the Cowardly Lion. Each of them is in search of something missing from their lives. They finally find the Wizard. But there have to be new obstacles for the protagonist to struggle with, or the ending would come too easily. The Wizard asks them to bring him the broomstick of the Wicked Witch of the West. However, in order to do so, they have to kill the witch. During this journey, the danger and fear that the witch creates for Dorothy intensifies. It escalates to such a point—seeing her friend Scarecrow on fire—that would push Dorothy to take a big step out of her fear and realize that she has to take action to save the Scarecrow.

6.6.3 Act 3: Ending

The protagonist now works out a plan to resolve the conflict and then carries out the plan to confront the antagonist. This final confrontation between the protagonist and the antagonist is the climax of the film. The climax leads to a resolution of the conflict, giving the viewer a sense of relief or catharsis.

Again returning to *The Wizard of Oz* example, Dorothy grabs a bucket of water and pours it onto the Scarecrow's burning arm. This is instinctive, but she carries it out after she realizes that she has to take action during this crisis. Here comes the climax: The spilled water hits the Wicked Witch of the West (the antagonist) and melts her. The witch's guards are happy that they are free. Everyone, including the viewer, feels relief.

Unlike the protagonist in most films, Dorothy does not really premeditate a plan, and in fact, she never has any intention to kill the witch. This is reasonable, because Dorothy is a little girl. The throwing of water is arranged to be simply an action to save her friend in distress. The killing of the witch is arranged as an accident—an accident that is caused by the Wicked Witch's own wicked act.

Now that the antagonist is gone, the viewer would anticipate the four characters—Dorothy and her three friends—will get what they have been searching for in this quest. The Wizard, who turns out to be a fake, is able to give each of the three friends what they are searching for, while Dorothy is told by the Good Witch that she has had the power all along to get herself home. So, she taps her ruby slippers together three times and says, "There is no place like home." Then she wakes up in her own bed, surrounded by family and friends. She has become more mature and confident in dealing with a crisis than before.

In *The Wizard of Oz*, the space and time of the beginning and the end remain the same. However, the character of Dorothy undergoes great changes. It would not have felt satisfying to the viewer if nothing had changed and Dorothy had not come to any realizations in her journey.

ANIMATION

Animation is also a time-based medium. Time, space, and storytelling of live-action video apply to animation. In Dave Jones' *Teetering*, a Web-based Flash animation, two stick figures are on a teeter-totter hinged on top of a mountain. The situation is introduced as an establishing shot (Figure 6.11a) at the beginning the animation. The tension

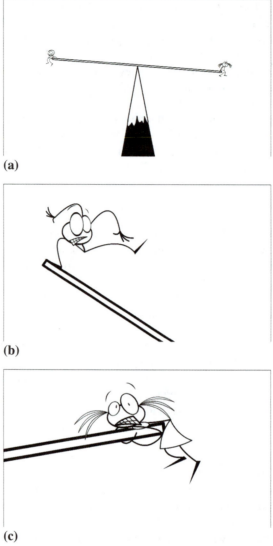

(a)

(b)

(c)

Figure 6.11 Stills from Dave Jones' Flash animation, *Teetering*—http://www.transience.com.au/

slowly builds up by cutting between the two stick figures trying to balance the teeter-totter (Figure 6.11b through c). Then the story ends right after the climax.

The cutting of the scene follows the 180-degree rule. The animation uses off-screen space. Not everything is visible on-screen all of the time. At times, the stick figure is moving off the screen or into the screen from off-screen. When one figure moves off-screen, it cuts to another figure moving into the screen. The animation also makes use of off-screen sound—the sound of the teeter-totter and the background wind blowing. The wind sound positions the viewer at the mountaintop without having to actually show the mountain all of the time.

MACHINIMA

As real-time 3-D video-game technologies become more popular, a new form of movie-making, called Machinima[¶] is growing in popularity among video-gamers. According to the Web site of the Academy of Machinima Arts & Sciences, *Machinima* uses "real-world filmmaking techniques applied within an interactive virtual space where characters and events can be either controlled by humans, scripts or artificial intelligence." Basically, Machinima is 3-D animation but, its production process is different from the existing 3-D animation used for those short film or feature-length animations. Because of Machinima's real-time aspect, the 3-D models and lighting are not as refined as in feature-film animation. The story and the script play a key role in holding the audience's attention.

One way to create Machinima is by recording a video game into video footage. Another way involves creating your own custom characters, props, and scenes first. Either way the recorded footage are captured onto the computer for digital video editing and post-production processing.

6.7 PERCEPTUAL EXPERIENCE OF VIDEO AS A TIME-BASED MEDIUM

Time-based media (such as video) have characteristics that influence the viewer's perceptual experience. Understanding these characteristics will help you develop your video projects. Let's first consider how a viewer will experience non-time-based artworks.

When looking at a painting or a drawing, a viewer is free to look at any area on the painting in any order. It allows the viewer's attention to have random access. There is no time limit, and the viewer's eyes can revisit certain areas in the painting at any time. The viewer can piece together the story or message in a painting through his/her self-directed sequence of visual scrutiny. For example, if after a first look at the painting something interesting catches a viewer's attention and make him/her feel that it is making an interesting reference to another area that he/she has just glanced at, the viewer can look at both areas back and forth multiple times to verify his/her feeling before moving on to look at the rest of the painting.

However, watching a video limits such freedom of random access because of the ephemeral nature of video. Although when you are watching a movie on disc or tape you can always rewind and forward, the intended way of presenting the story in a time-based medium is temporally progressive. Just as you always have a choice to skip over to the ending when you are reading a novel, you choose not to do so. You choose to let the author lead you to progress and discover the ending.

6.7.1 Train Viewers to Form Expectations

Despite such freedom in examining a painting, the artist still wants to direct the viewer's eyes. This can be done by exploiting a variety of composition techniques in a painting. Visual artists also use cues and symbols to elicit certain feelings from the viewer. However, how the viewer interpret the same cue or symbol depends on the viewer's past experience

---

[¶]For more information and examples of Machinima, visit the Academy of Machinima Arts & Sciences Web site at http://www.machinima.org/

For examples of Machinima work, visit: http://www.machinima.com/; http://www.redvsblue.com/; http://www.illclan.com/

as well as the painting's style, theme, and cultural and historical background. A video exists in its own reality guided by rules that may or may not be the same as those the viewer perceives in real life. Some of the laws of the real world do not operate in the video's reality. The viewer needs to know the rules of this different world in order to understand the film content.

Unlike a painting, video is a time-based medium with a linear presentation. The experience spreads out over time, and the meanings unfold over time. The filmmaker controls the order of events the viewer sees. The viewer is given information about the story (if it is a narrative) or the message one piece at a time in the order set by the filmmaker. Only at the end of the film does the viewer get all of the information to perceive the whole picture.

Some of the information only can be interpreted in retrospect. If one point of the film is making reference to an event or action that is presented at another time of the film, the viewer has to rely on his/her short-term memory to look back. Therefore, it is important for the filmmaker to provide the viewer with cues of how different segments of the film are related.

To help viewers understand the cues leading them to form specific expectations, you need to develop patterns and train the viewers to recognize the patterns. One of the techniques to develop patterns is repetition. We will discuss repetition later in this chapter.

Sometimes, false cues are intentionally given to make the viewer build false expectations. It serves to heighten the suspense and the viewer's curiosity in finding out the truth when (as the story unfolds) the viewer's speculation based on the cues starts to fall apart.

Film is not the only medium that uses patterns to help the audience to learn the rules of the film's diegetic world. If you have played computer games, you may understand this concept. For example, you may notice an enemy follows a fixed schedule patrolling an area. It helps you build expectations. After you have watched the enemy moving for a while, you will learn the rules and be able to figure out the best timing to sneak out or strike.

6.8 PRINCIPLES OF PERCEPTUAL ORGANIZATION

How the viewer groups information to make sense of your video and form expectations relies on their being able to *see* the connections and relationships amongst the information. How you organize the information to present to the viewer affects the viewer's ability to do so.

Gestalt principles were introduced in Chapter 2, Section 2.5. These principles describe the way we naturally group objects—how we perceive the totality and interconnection amongst individual units by detecting patterns. Gestalt principles have been used in the medium of visual design, and there have been research studies of Gestalt principles in auditory medium, as well. Some of these principles also can be borrowed for video production.

A film is a time-based medium presented to the viewer linearly in time. Different elements and actions are organized in time, not just spatially within a frame. The following principles can be applied to the spatial organization of visual elements within an individual frame just as in a single still image. In this section, we will generalize these principles to the temporal aspect of the time-based visual media, and discuss the possibilities of how they may provide you with ideas for organizing the order of the different elements (actions and events) in your video project. There are virtually an infinite number of ways to organize actions and events in a time-based work. Instead of using trial-and-error, these principles serve as a perceptual strategy you can use to explore different possibilities to form relationships among the elements. These principles are by no means meant to be a set of prescriptive rules.

6.8.1 Proximity and Similarity

When we look at a 2-D image, we tend to group elements that are spatially closer in preference to those that are farther apart. In a film, similar actions, events, or graphical shapes presented at different times during the film can signal the viewer that they are related. If these similar elements are subtle, they may need to be shown in closer succession to help the viewer notice the similarity and make the connections before the viewer forgets.

6.8.2 Common Fate

Common fate refers to our tendency to relate elements that change their properties synchronously. If the behaviors of characters or certain properties of the elements in the film change in the same direction at the same time, we would expect they are related. For example, in a mystery movie, when you see two characters react suspiciously to the same types of events, you would probably expect both are accomplices in some kind of cover-up.

6.8.3 Good Continuation

Changes are what make a story. There are changes in space, time, flow of events, chain of thoughts, and point of view. The visual elements on screen constantly change; the audio also changes throughout the video. Some changes are gradual and continuous, while some are abrupt.

We tend to perceive changes within the same grouping as continuous and within the same direction as gradual. Any abrupt change can be perceived as a result of the introduction of a new group or a shift of attention. Keeping this idea in mind helps you create connection or disconnection between different elements in your video.

6.8.4 Closure

Closure refers to our tendency to fill in the gaps to make fragmented information into a perceived whole. All of us perform closure daily. We only see parts of the world, but we perceive the world as a whole. For example, you order something online, and few days later you receive your order. You do not get to see what has happened in-between, but you trust that your order has been processed and shipped to you.

It may seem trivial, but it is our understanding that life goes on for everyone—even you do not see the person. If your friend is happy one day and upset the next day, you imagine that something must have happened in-between that time period. Before you ask your friend about it, you may have started to imagine and speculate about what could have happened—you are performing closure.

Storytellers of various media—movies, novels, and comics—have been exploiting closure by withholding information and letting viewers to fill in omitted information. The viewers use their imagination and the rules they have learned from the patterns built up in your story world to fill in the gaps. Leaving gaps also can raise the viewer's curiosity to verify if their speculation matches the reality of the film. By doing so, the viewer becomes actively engaged in the film instead of being a passive spectator.

6.8.5 Figure–Ground Phenomenon

We are able to distinguish the foreground objects from the background by their relatively distinctive characteristics that differentiate them from the rest. We tend to identify foreground as having brighter color, clear enclosure, larger distinct shapes, and more active movement.

Recall the discussion of figure–ground in Gestalt's principles. Here, the figure or foreground refers to activities that the viewer is directed to focus his/her attention on. The ground or background refers to the rest of the things happening on screen.

In films, the term *planes* is used to refer to the overall relation of foreground and background distance.

🖰 **Shifting Camera Focus Distance** See how your attention is directed with the focus by shifting the focus from one character to another and then to the railing.

In a camera shot, the color and shapes may have been set. The play between soft and sharp focus in a camera shot can direct the viewer's attention and define different planes of action.

For example, Figure 6.12 shows a shift of focus in a shot. Your attention is directed to the characters or objects in focus. The object's size and the physical distance of the subject from the camera is not necessarily the dominant factor in defining the figure–ground relationship. As the railings are brought into focus (Figure 6.12c), they become the plane of action.

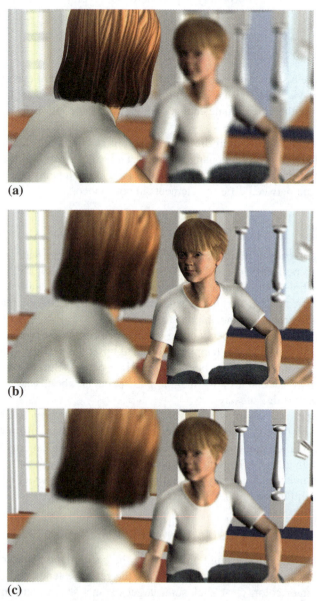

(a)

(b)

(c)

Figure 6.12 Shifting focus in a shot to direct the viewer's attention

6.8.6 Past Experience

The prior experience of the viewer affects his/her understanding and interpretation of the film content. Prior experience includes the viewer's real-world experience and the viewer's experience with similar films. Because it is accepted that the reality in the film can be different from the everyday life, the conceptualization of the reality in the film often is influenced by the viewer's experience of similar films more than those derived from daily life.

For example, in a comedy, the main character slipping on a banana peel may make you laugh. However, if this happens in real life, you may not laugh but hurry to help the person. In musical films, you expect the characters throughout most of the film to sing and dance about their feelings and the situation. However, you would feel pretty odd or may be even funny when someone actually does that in real life. In love stories, you expect an answer at the end about whether the two main characters turn out to be together (happy ending) or go their separate ways (sad ending).

Returning to the analogy of trying to speculate what has happened to a friend who becomes sad, your inference is formed based on your friend's behavior patterns in the past. You form different speculations for different friends. It is hard to form an opinion about a stranger or a new friend, because you do not have enough past experience to draw from.

Thus, it is understandable that a new, unfamiliar, or experimental work often may seem incoherent and its story or message hard to grasp. The viewer may lack the prior experience with similar work to help them grasp the unique reality of the new work and thus fails to form the expectations on the right track. Failure to form speculations that match the reality in the film makes it confusing to the viewer, causing frustration and dissatisfaction. This is not to say that all work has to adhere to the same old conventions, but the viewer's past experience should be taken into consideration. If a new and creative work can guide the viewer to some extent to learn to recognize its new conventions and to respond emotionally, the viewer will be able to form expectations that match the reality of the work. When a viewer is able to do so, conceptualizing the reality of the work can be so revelational that, to the viewer, these new concepts could be more rewarding than those that follow existing conventions.

OBJECT RECOGNITION WITH AND WITHOUT INFORMATION GIVEN

In an object recognition experiment,[||] images of a human face were presented to 28 subjects. The images were photographs converted into high-contrast pictures with just black and white colors (similar to Figure 6.13). The final images were composed of abstract shapes of just solid black and white colors. The sequence of the images corresponds to the 3-D rotation of the face. 17 subjects out of the 28 could not identify the face in at least one photograph. These 17 subjects were then shown two images (again corresponding to the 3-D rotation of the face) in alternation. 16 of them perceived random chaotic motion. However, when they were told that it was a human face, all of them finally saw the 3-D rotation of a human face.

The point that we learn from this study is that when the visual elements become too abstract or non-representational, the viewer may have hard time connecting them and thus fail to interpret your work. One may argue that for some artistic works, it is not the

---

[||]V. S. Ramachandran, C. Armel1, C. Foster and R. Stoddard, "Object recognition can drive motion perception," *Nature*, **395**, 852–853 (29 October, 1998)
http://www.nature.com/nature/journal/v395/n6705/full/395852a0.html

Figure 6.13 Two black and white images of a human face

point whether the viewer's interpretation of the work matches the artist's original intent; it is about the viewer getting something out of the work. However, when the viewer sees the work as just a series of random, chaotic, and unrelated units, he/she would be confused and not be able to interpret your work at all.

This is not to suggest that you have to tell the viewer explicitly what the abstract content is supposed to be—but consider providing cues. Cues do not have to be explicit. When cueing the viewer to learn your conventions, consider withholding information to let the viewer use his/her imagination to fill in the gaps, i.e., perform closure.

Let's say you are using the abstract images similar to the ones in Figure 6.13. The cues do not have to be showing a photo of the face in your work directly. The cues can be indirect and implicit. To search for ideas for cues, first you need to analyze the intentions of the abstract face images. Try to identify the keywords to describe the intentions, and then elaborate the keywords in many different ways.

- *The subject:* Why human? Why face? Does the human face constitute a significant meaning to your work? Is it about human identity? If so, then *identity* is a keyword. What are other ways to represent the ideas of human identity besides the face? To generalize further, what are ways to represent the ideas of identity—not just human identity? How about repeating these similar representations to cue the viewer?
- *The visual presentation:* Why is the image reduced to just two colors and abstract shapes? What does that mean? If *reduced* is a keyword here, then what are other ways to represent the ideas of reduced? Brainstorm as many possibilities as possible. Then, narrow down the possibilities that are or can be connected to the core idea—human identity. For example, the product barcode is a way to identify a commercial product. It is made up of black and white lines. Both the idea and the visual representation relate to the central idea in this example.
- *The motion or temporal changes:* Why 3-D rotation of the face? Does the 3-D rotation of the abstract face have any significant meaning? Is the rotation about one of the changes in perspective in humanity or human identity? If so, the *perspective* is a keyword. Try to come up many different possible ways to represent perspective and then narrow down the possibilities. To cue the viewer about the rotation, how about creating a pattern or rotating objects by repeating the rotation of different objects (primitive shapes that do not change as drastic in the rotation)?

6.9 ART AND DESIGN ORGANIZATIONAL PRINCIPLES

A video is made up of a series of images, each constituting a frame. The art and design organizational principles thus still apply to the image (spatial) composition in a frame—static composition. In this section, we will generalize these principles to the temporal organization of video work.

See Chapter 2 for a detailed discussion of the art and design organizational principles.

For video, new challenges emerge due to its dynamic nature. In a typical video, there are constant movements of subjects and objects in a shot. A balanced composition may become unbalanced when a person or object leaves or enters the frame. This may require reframing. However, reframing is not always possible in the middle of a shot.

In addition, there also may be camera movement; the camera angle and distance from the subjects may change. In a shot that has camera movement, it would be best, in general, to begin and end the segment with a good static composition.

6.9.1 Repetition and Rhythm

Repetition refers to multiple appearances of an element within the work. *Rhythm* describes how they are repeated over time. Repetition is a useful and common technique, because repetition in a piece often can convey an immediate sense of unity. For time-based media, repetition can create patterns to guide the viewer to form expectations from the work.

Repetition does not mean repeating the exact duplicate of an element–doing so may create monotony. Consider adding variations to the repeated elements. *Variety* or *variation* makes the work more interesting. It prompts the viewer to recognize the similarities by comparing and contrasting related elements. Variants of the same element can be connected by sharing some properties. Repeating an element also can create a sense of grouping, thereby forming relationships between elements.

Returning to the example of the movie *The Wizard of Oz*, you can see a strong presence of repetitions or similarities in the following examples.

- The three friends in Kansas homeland versus the three friends (Scarecrow, Tin Man, and Cowardly Lion) that Dorothy meets along the Yellow Brick Road
- Professor Marvel in Kansas versus the Wizard in Oz
- The mean lady (Miss Gulch) in Kansas versus the Wicked Witch of the West, as both threaten Dorothy of taking away something precious from her—her dog Toto and her life, respectively.
- Dorothy's journeys are caused by her dog Toto. The first time in Kansas, at the beginning of the movie when Miss Gulch is threatening to take Toto from her. This causes Dorothy to run away from home. The second time happens when Toto goes chasing a cat, disrupting Dorothy's balloon ride, and thus making her miss her chance to return home.
- Dorothy causes the death of two Wicked Witches, both by accident.

The first three examples are of parallelism. In writing, parallelism means using words or phrase patterns that are similar. You can reinforce similarities—in meaning and by level of importance—between two or more ideas through the use of parallel structures. Effective parallelism in writing can also create symmetry in sentences, add force and rhythm to your writing. Similarly, effective parallelism in time-based work can achieve these effects.

Although these examples from *The Wizard of Oz* all involve characters in a story, repetition is not limited to characters and storytelling. Repetition can be applied to basically any elements of the work. Examples include the use of camera angles, camera movement, colors, dialog, and music.

6.9.2 Unity and Harmony

Like any artwork, each element or action included in a video has to have a purpose. Otherwise, they would become random and the work loses coherence. Irrelevant actions and unrelated events may even contradict with other actions and events causing distraction to the viewer. Because film is a linear presentation and the viewer relies on their memory of the presented actions to make sense of the whole story or the message of the film, a seemingly random element would be harder for the viewer remember.

Related elements that the viewer is able to justify on some ground are more likely to be recalled later. The more association between actions that the viewer can make, the more likely the viewer will make sense of the film, form correct expectations, and fill in the gaps of omitted information. In addition, a random element may mislead the viewer's expectations, further preventing them from making sense of the film.

6.9.3 Balance

In 2-D artwork, the visual balance is evaluated based on the weight of emphasis and focus in its spatial dimension. This also applies to the composition in framing a video shot.

If this concept is generalized to time-based media, the weight of the emphasis and focus in the temporal dimension can be thought of as the temporal placement of the climax—where the climax occurs in the sequence.

Generally, in a dramatic structure, the climax of the plot—when the protagonist confronts the antagonist to resolve the conflict—appears at the end of the movie. The plot builds up the tension right up to the climax. The viewer experiences emotional release once the conflict is resolved. Usually, the movie then concludes very quickly.

This idea of distributing the weight of elements in the temporal dimension also can be a useful guideline for sequencing non-narrative work. Think about the progression of building up your intended message. Think of the climax as the moment when you present your strongest material or when the viewer "gets" your message.

- *Rhetorical work*: Throughout the video, you are building up a persuasive argument to support your thesis about a subject matter or a situation. You can think of the climax as your strongest material or your proposed solution to the situation. If using the dramatic structure as a guideline, then your video may need to conclude (by summarizing what has come before) soon after that.
- *Abstract work*: In the video, you may be using repetition and juxtaposition to present a subject in abstract form. The level of the repetition and juxtaposition may progress to increase viewers' understanding of your work. Think about at what level of the progression that you use to conclude your video.

- *Associational work*: You try to elicit the viewer's emotional response to a subject using metaphorical audiovisual materials. Think about the progression of the material's level of association and level of emotional response.

If the climax—the most exciting part of the video or your strongest material—is presented too early, then the segment after the climax may seem to be simply reiterating the same point. It may stretch too long before the video ends. The video may leave the viewer with an impression of being anticlimactic. If the climax appears too late or there is not enough progression moving toward building up the climax, the video may seem to drag and circle around in the development stage.

6.9.4 Emphasis and Focus

Within a video shot, emphasis can be changed by shifting the camera focal distance to direct the viewer's attention from one subject to another in a frame.

Temporally, repetition of an element can be used to create emphasis. Other ways to add emphasis are to create difference, contrast, and variation. Repetition also can be used to build up rhythm or to remove any unintended focus before presenting the difference, so that the difference will be more prominent.

6.9.5 Perspective

Different types of camera shots give the viewer different perspectives and levels of details about the subject. Some have a narrative and psychological connotation, while others are relatively neutral. Different shots are used to create variation and provide viewers with different types information needed to understand the video.

In terms of the viewing distance from the subject, there are three basic types of shots: long (Figure 6.14a), medium (Figure 6.14b), and close-up (Figure 6.14c). There are also variations of shots within and beyond the range defined by these three types.

- A *long shot* is a shot that includes the full body of a character (Figure 6.14a). It shows the subject in relation to its overall surroundings. A long shot can be used to give the viewer a sense of where the subject is situated. Because a long shot includes many other elements and things going on in addition to the main subject, the viewer may not be able to distinguish the key subject.
- A shot in which the subject is very far away from the camera is called an *extreme long shot*. It often is used to convey a sense of isolation and diminishment of the subject.
- A *medium shot* of a person (Figure 6.14b) is a shot from the waist up. It shows the subject in relation to its immediate surroundings. This shot approximates the perspective of how we interact with people in life.
- A *close-up shot* of a person (Figure 6.14c) is basically a head shot, usually from the neck up. It places the viewer at close range, giving a sense of in-your-face kind of closeness with the character. The viewer can see the character's detailed facial expression, but the shot shows little or no surroundings of the subject.
- An *extreme close-up* is an even closer shot.
- The shot between medium and close-up is called a *medium close-up*, which is usually from midchest up.

(a)

(b)

(c)

Figure 6.14 Three viewing distance examples using
(a) long, (b) medium, and (c) close-up camera shots

In terms of the orientation and height in relation to the subject, camera shots are: low-angle, high-angle, eye-level, bird's eye view, oblique and point-of-view.

- A *low-angle shot* (Figure 6.15) is created by placing the camera below the subject and aiming it upward. This shot tends to make the main character or object look powerful, superior, and intimidating.
- A *high-angle shot* (Figure 6.16) is created by placing the camera above the subject and pointing downward. This shot tends to make the subject look powerless, subordinate, insignificant, and intimidated.

Figure 6.15 Low-angle camera shots

Figure 6.16 High-angle camera shots

- An *eye-level shot* is shot with the camera near the eye-level of the subject. This shot places the viewer at the same footing as the subject. It does not have the distortion or psychological effect (diminishing or superiority) of the low-angle and high-angle shots.
- A *bird's eye view* is shot from very high above looking down.
- An *oblique shot* (Figure 6.17) is taken with the camera tilted. In an oblique shot, the vertical lines of the frame are diagonal. This effect often is used to give a sense of chaos and unbalance.

Figure 6.17　An oblique camera shot

- A *point-of-view shot* simulates the viewpoint of a character. It is commonly seen in thriller and detective movies to represent the perspective of either the stalker or the detective.

6.10 STUDENT PROJECTS AND ANALYSES

This section examines three student projects by applying the concepts that have been introduced in this chapter. The length of the student projects allows a sequence of selected stills from the entire video. Having stills from the entire video facilitates the analysis.

6.10.1 Example 1: You're It!

About the Work

Title: *You're It!*
Length: About 1.9 minutes
Color: Grayscale
Frame Aspect Ratio: 4:3
Student Artist: Bill Brown (Wake Forest University)
Videographers: Bill Brown and Jessica Vogel

Description of the Plot

The video starts with two individuals standing apart and facing each other (Figure 6.18a). Then the female character hits the male character on the shoulder (Figure 6.18b) and says "You're it!" (Figure 6.18c) From that point on (Figure 6.18a), the screen is split into four

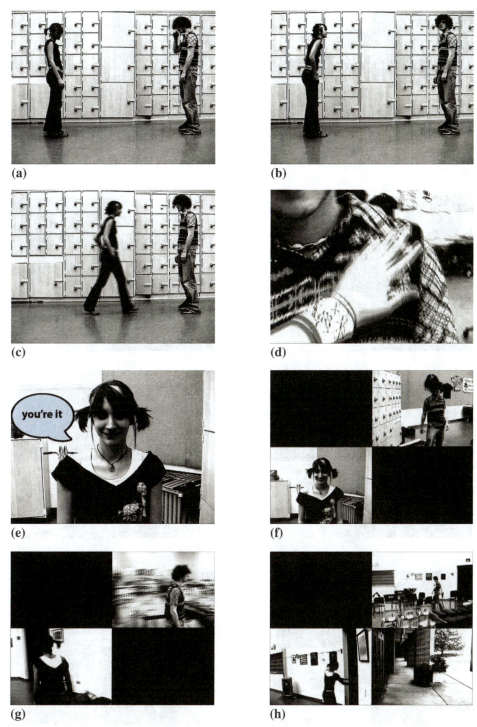

Figure 6.18 A sequence of stills from the student video project *You're it!* by Bill Brown

(i)

(j)

(k)

(l)

(m)

(n)

(o)

(p)

Figure 6.18 (*Continued*)

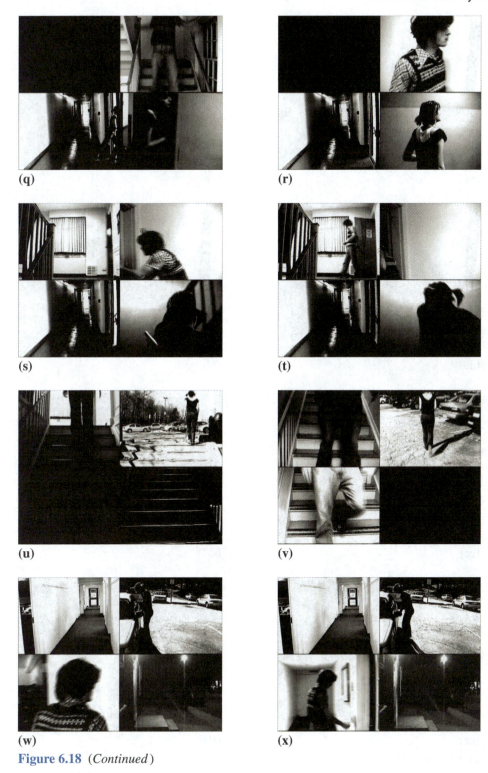

(q)   **(r)**

(s)   **(t)**

(u)   **(v)**

(w)   **(x)**

Figure 6.18 (*Continued*)

(y)

(z)

(aa)

(bb)

(cc)

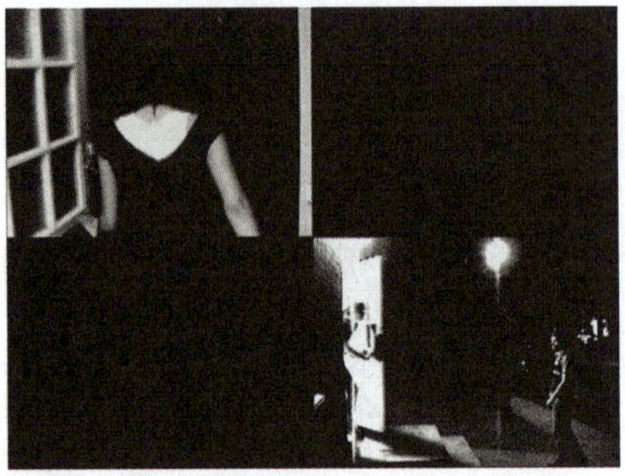

(dd)

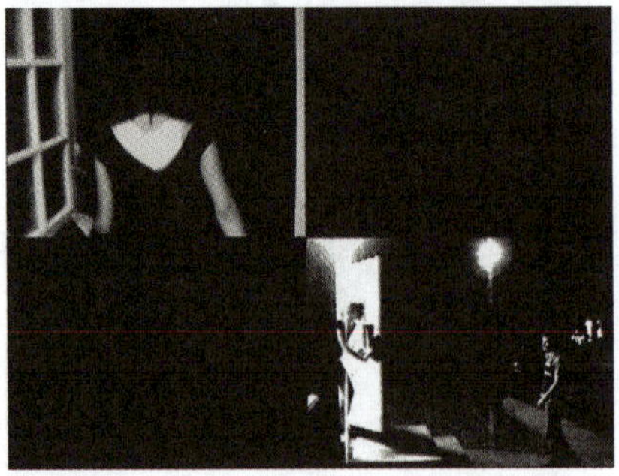

(ee)

(ff)

Figure 6.18 (Continued)

(gg)   **(hh)**

Figure 6.18 *(Continued)*

quadrants, each showing a view of either character. Each view shows the character navigating indoors and outdoors. The characters seem to be playing tags. The video ends once the two characters meet.

Narrative

This video is not a drama, and thus, it does not have all of the elements of the 3-act drama structure discussed previously. However, some of the elements normally in a drama can be found in this video. In addition, this video does have a beginning, development, and an ending. It also contains causal relationships.

- *Act 1: Beginning*: Act 1 of this video starts from where the two characters separate to start playing tags. Let's analyze what the Act 1 does to arouse the viewer's curiosity to seek answers to the questions: What is going to happen? How it is going to end?

    The video begins with the two characters standing—each on one side of the screen. There basically is no activity or interaction between them. The larger lockers in the middle of the screen creates a visual division between the two characters. The placement of the two characters creates a static, symmetrical composition. But this also causes us to scan across the whole frame by encouraging our sight to bounce back and forth between the two standing characters. The regularity of the lockers creates a distinct static pattern in the background and accentuates a sense of stillness. The prolonged and heightened stillness arouses viewer's curiosity.

    Unlike drama movies—and this is *not* a drama movie—here the viewer does not know much about the two characters—their names or their backgroud. However, this scene does help the viewer form an expectation that these two characters will be interacting. The lockers in the background give the viewer a sense of the setting of the *story*—it is in a school or gymnasium which can infer an idea of play. Although play is not the only possible expectation from such setting, it can certainly help the viewer eliminate many possibilities in forming anticipation about the video. The opening has introduced the viewer to the setting of the story and the characters.

    The female character's initiating playing tag is the trigger that is going to change the stillness—put the story in motion. The conflict situation in this narrative is that the two characters are going to separate and have to find each other again.

- *Act 2: Development*: This segment starts with the two characters separating and continues up to the moment right before they meet again at the ending. Here, the two characters are moving around indoors and outdoors. Their activities are shown using a split-screen technique.

- *Act 3: Ending*: In this piece, the climax and the resolution do not have apparent distinctions. One may argue that the climax is when the female character sees the other character outside and pushes open the door at the end, and the resolution is only when both characters meet up outside. The video ends immediately after the resolution.

When comparing and contrasting the beginning and ending situations, it is easy to see that in this video, the ending state returns to the beginning state. First, both characters are back together at the end. Second, it is interesting to note that the female character remains the active role at the beginning and in the ending—she initiates the game at the beginning and finds the other character at the end. It is coming full circle, but there are variations in time and place: It ends at night outside of the building.

Space

The most prominent visual features in this video are

- It is in black-and-white.
- The majority of the video splits the frame into four quadrants.

Every element has a purpose.

Why split screen?

The split-screen technique often is used to provide the viewer with multiple points of view simultaneously. There are only two characters, but why does it need to split into four quadrants? This video exploits split screen for a purpose different from the tradition.

Here, the split screen is not used simply to follow the two characters' journeys. It is exploited to connect the 3-D spaces onto 2-D screen spaces. This means that conceptually the characters are moving in 3-D spaces, but their movements appear to be crossing the planar four quadrants on screen. For example, when the character exits or enters a hallway through a door, the character goes off screen in one quadrant and enters into another. The character appears to be moving across the conjoint quadrants. Here are some example scenes:

- The upper two quadrants from Figure 6.18s to Figure 6.18t
- The lower two quadrants from Figure 6.18h to Figure 6.18i
- The lower two quadrants from Figure 6.18x to Figure 6.18y
- From the upper-left quadrant in Figure 6.18cc to the lower-right quadrant in Figure 6.18dd
- The two right quadrants in Figure 6.18m
- The two right quadrants in Figure 6.18o

The perspectives in the conjoint screens are intentionally different. On one hand, the synchronized exiting one screen and entering the other connects the space. On the other hand, the change in perspective breaks up the space and helps eliminate monotony.

The four quadrants allow the horizontal and vertical arrangement of the character moving across the conjoint screens. The use of the split screen in this video conceptualizes the 3-D spaces changing into flat 2-D screen spaces. The movement of the characters is depicted within the 2-D screen space.

This video was not shot in real time. It required extensive planning and editing in order to achieve the synchronicity of characters moving across conjoint screens.

Why black-and-white?

First, it removes the color differences between conjoint screens. Second, it reduces the visual content into *shapes* of lights and darks. By reducing the color to grayscale, the representational 3-D background objects are flattened into abstract geometrical shapes. Hence, both visual and denotational differences between conjoint screens are reduced. This helps in connecting the conjoint screens into 2-D screen space—an idea that this video explores using the split-screen technique.

Time

The time at the beginning of the video is not revealed to the viewer. The only hint of time the viewer can sense is when the characters are outdoors. It is shown to be day in the middle of the video and night at the conclusion of the video. Time is compressed in this video—few minutes of video time spans from day to night.

This video is presented as if the viewer has been following the two characters continuously in real time. It has been during the day for most of the video. The outdoor scene at the ending is the only night time indication. The large time lapse comes as a surprise. This arouses curiosity about the temporal progression of the *story*. In fact, human *perception* of time passage depends on the spectator's emotional state and thus does not always match the actual duration. For example, a half hour with your dentist may feel like hours. Time flies when you are having fun. Time flies also when you are highly concentrated on a task, for example, working intensely on an exam. The way this video handles temporal progression embodies the interesting notion of human perception of time passage versus the actual duration. Here, it manifests the perception: "Time passes faster than I thought."

Organizational Principles

Repetition is used extensively in this video. Throughout the video, the two characters are moving around in hallways and walkways to search for each other. Some shots are planned to synchronize to make it look like that the characters are crossing from one panel to another. Variations are added by using different types of camera shots—from medium close-up to long shots. The directions of the characters crossing the panels also vary.

Visual balance is created dynamically through the direction of the motion across panels.

6.10.2 Example 2: Untitled

About the Work

Title: *Untitled*
Length: About 2.1 minutes
Color: Color
Frame Aspect Ratio: 4:3
Student Artist: Sasha Gee Enegren (Wake Forest University)

Description of the Plot

The video starts with another video showing on a projection screen on a stage. There are imageries of abstract patterns, shadows of two people fighting, a musical instrument, empty theater seats, and a blurring mouth that seems to be speaking (Figure 6.19a through o). While this projected video is showing, performers (silhouetted against the projection screen)

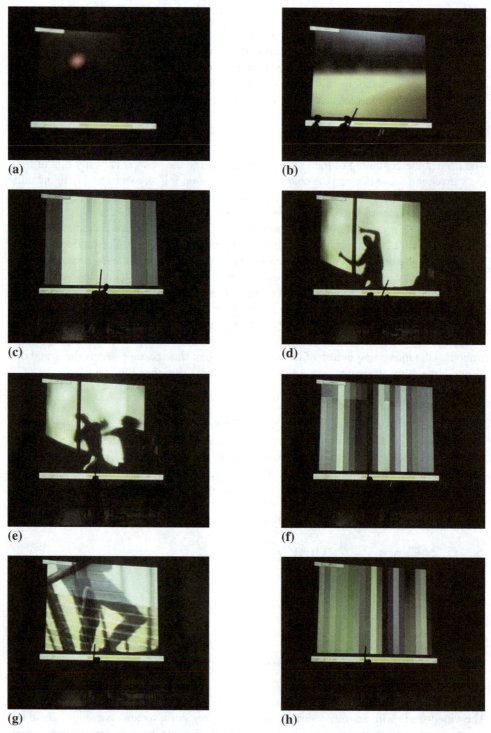

Figure 6.19 A sequence of stills from the student video project. *Untitled* by Sasha Gee Enegren

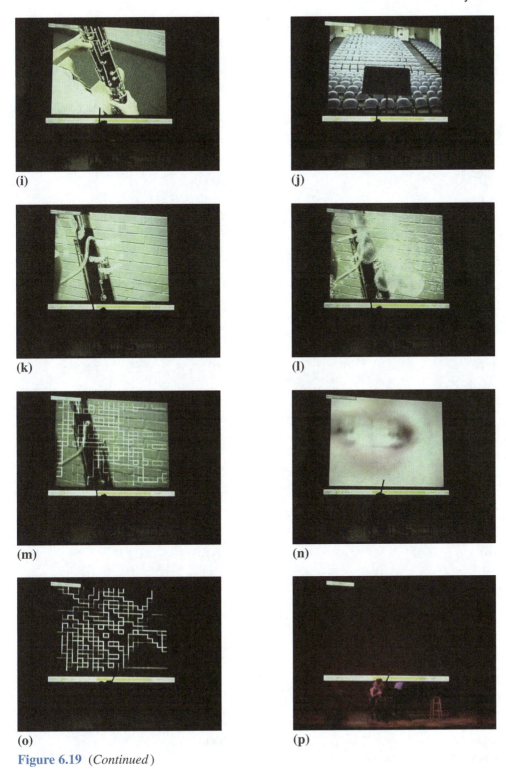

(i)   **(j)**

(k)   **(l)**

(m)   **(n)**

(o)   **(p)**

Figure 6.19 (*Continued*)

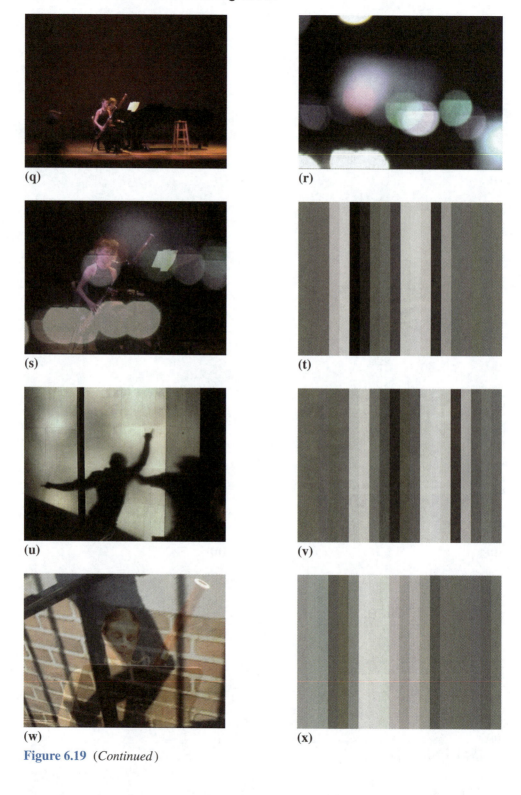

(q)

(r)

(s)

(t)

(u)

(v)

(w)

(x)

Figure 6.19 (*Continued*)

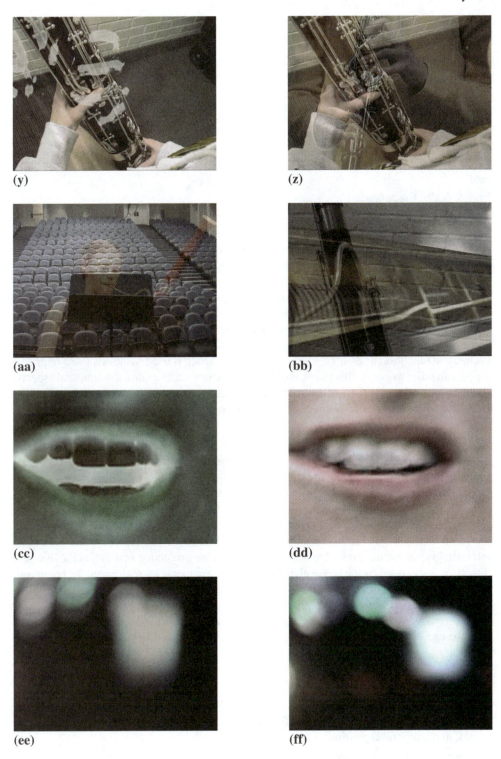

(y)   **(z)**

(aa)   **(bb)**

(cc)   **(dd)**

(ee)   **(ff)**

Figure 6.19 (*Continued*)

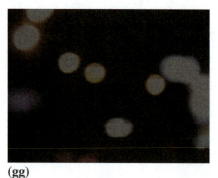

(gg)

Figure 6.19 (*Continued*)

slowly come on stage. After the projected video ends, the lights are turned on, and the live performers on stage start performing (Figure 6.19p). Imageries from the previously projected video reappear in the second part of the video—not by projecting it on the screen but by superimposing it on the live performance (Figure 6.19q through gg). The video ends with the conclusion of the live performance.

The temporal aspects in this video are the key that manipulate how the narrative is being communicated. These temporal aspects include the chronological order of events, duration of events, and repetition of images. The way the screen space is used manifests these temporal aspects. In other words, in this video, the screen space is used to control the temporal aspects, and the temporal aspects in turn control the cues for the viewer to make sense of the narrative. Hence, to discuss this video, we will start with the topics of space and time before narrative.

Space

The physical space shown in this video is a theater stage. Abstract imageries also are superimposed in the video.

In the opening, the use of the projection screen divides the screen space. The projection screen acts like a picture-in-a-picture. On this screen is another video, which has its own screen space. In terms of the physical space in the scene, the projection screen is a flat backdrop on the stage. The live performers are in front of the projection screen. However, interestingly, the figure–ground relationship between the projection screen and the live performers is not defined by the physical distance from the camera—at least not at the beginning of the video. The projection screen has role of figure (foreground, where the focal activities is) and the live performers are the ground (the background). The stage is dark at the beginning. The viewer sees the performers' silhouettes moving across the front of the screen. Then, after the projected video ends, the stage lights come on and the live performers become the foreground.

Time

The interesting temporal aspects of this video are also originated from the use of the projected video. It is provides the cues for the chronological order of events, duration of events, and temporal repetition.

- *Temporal Repetition*: Many of the imageries in the projected video reappear later in this video, intermingling and superimposing with segments of the live performance.

Recall the discussion of figure–ground in Gestalt's principles. Here, the figure or foreground we are referring to is determined by the activities that the viewer is directed to give his/her attention to. The ground or background refers to the rest of the things happening on-screen.

The repetition prompts the viewer to relate the projected video with the live performance—to draw parallels with the live performance and what the projected video is trying to express.

- *Duration*: The solo performance shown in the video is running in real time. The progression of the performance gives a sense of time passing. The projected video uses abstract elements to elicit emotion, but does not provide clues of time passing.

- *Chronological Order*: The repetition prompts the viewer to speculate the relationship between the projected video and the performance. But what is the relationship? It is the temporal ordering of events.

The live performance is presented in a real time. Hence, the performance is seen as one linear, continuous action. What the projected video shows appear to be in different time. It may be inferring a backstory, a flashback, a flashforward, or a foreshadowing. The video does not provide a clear answer. It is up to the viewer to make sense of the type of the temporal order. We will look at how different speculations may lead us to make sense of the chronological order of the underlying narrative.

Speculation #1: The projected video is a flashforward or foreshadowing.

If we infer it as flashforward event the imageries in the projected video would be a preview of what is to come in the live performance. The time of reappearance of the imageries during the performance may be suggestive of their actual time when these imageries are taken from.

Foreshadowing usually alludes to future events implicitly, for example, by using symbols or metaphors. The repeated imageries in this video are basically exact duplicates. This makes foreshadowing an unlikely possibility.

Speculation #2: The projected video is a backstory or flashback.

If it is a backstory, then all of the repeated imageries later in the video would infer flashbacks from the backstory.

If we infer the projected video itself as one long flashback, then the reappearance of these imageries would be a repetition of bits and pieces of the flashback, reinforcing the flashback events. The reappearance of the imageries in the second part of the video—during the performance—does follow the order in the projected video at the beginning.

Both a backstory and a flashback cue you the causal relationship of events. This helps you to understand why you see what you see overlapping the performance segment. If two events at different times have a causal relationship, then the event in the past must be the cause for the more recent one. Based on this logic, you form the expectation that the clues lie in the projected video. Hence, it is more satisfying to think of the projected video as either a backstory or a flashback when you try to make sense of the content of the video. On the other hand, it may feel less satisfying to speculate the projected video as a flashforward, because if the projected video is simply a prediction, then it is only a "trailer" of what is to come. It does not provide any additional information to make sense of the whole piece.

Narrative

The narrative aspects of this piece are less apparent. The video conveys a journey where there are changes of situations or states over the course of the progression of the video. The 3-act structure—a beginning, development, and end—can still be identified in this piece. However, when exactly each act begins and ends depends on your interpretation of the narrative. There is no right or wrong answer. It is up to the viewer to interpret the piece.

The original intent of the projected video was to allude to the emotional states in auditions. The second part of the video is showing a live performance, and thus, it is reasonable to assume that the projected video makes references to the past (auditions then and live performance now). In other words, the projected video can be either a backstory or a flashback.

Given the information that the original intent of the projected video was about the emotional states in auditions, the *story* starts with auditioning for a performance.

- *Beginning:* The video starts with showing a video projected on a screen set up on a performance stage. While the video is being shown, the performers slowly march onto the stage. As discussed previously, speculating about the projected video as a back-story or a flashback makes making sense of the story more satisfying. So, if we maintain this speculation, then the story could be traced back to the time that the projected video is making reference to.
- *Development:* Although this video is not a drama, we still can find some parallel developments of a typical drama, for example, struggles and conflicts. The projected video conveys a sense of struggling in chaos and confusion. The shadow of a person punching another person creates a sense of conflict. If you interpret it literally, it is the feeling of being punched in the face.

  In order to make sense of the struggles and conflicts inferred in the projected video, you may need to do so in retrospect—after watching the whole video. The live music performance in the second part of the video cues you that they are related to the stage performance.
- *Ending:* This analysis leads to a story about struggling to take part in a stage performance. In this case, the climax of this story would be when the performer starts playing solo on the stage. The performers coming out on the stage while the projected video is playing builds up anticipation.

  The video ends with the imagery of fuzzy, moving light spots. It gives a feeling of driving at night—traveling. This imagery first appears at the beginning of the solo, which infers traveling to the performance. The second appearance (at the ending) infers concluding the performance, packing up, and going home.
- *Character:* In the video, the performer is so concentrated on playing her instrument that there is no eye contact with the viewer. What is presented on-screen seems to be a visual representation of the performer's state of consciousness, memories, thoughts, and feelings.

Organizational Principles

Repetition, both temporally and spatially (composition within a frame), is used quite extensively in this video.

- Within a frame, the performers' profiles are juxtaposed with the shadow imageries on the projection screen (Figure 6.19d and e).
- The blurry light spots (Figure 6.19r, ee, ff, and gg); chaotic movement of vertical stripes (Figure 6.19c, f, h, t, v, and x); and maze-like patterns are repeated throughout the video to convey confusion and a chaotic feeling.
- The imageries in the projected video at the beginning are reused throughout the whole live performance in the second half of the video.

6.10.3 Example 3: Fast Forward

About the Work

Title: *Fast Forward*
Length: About 1.8 minutes
Color: Color
Frame Aspect Ratio: 4:3
Student Artist: Erin Regan (Wake Forest University)

Description of the Plot:

The video starts with a series of words—alone, no time, responsibility, too fast, work, pressure, future, fate—appearing one at a time on a black background. Then you see a young woman standing in front of the pumps at a gas station (Figure 6.20a). Everything in the background seems to be in fast motion. A card with a letter "I" written on it pops up in the woman's hands for few seconds (Figure 6.20b). After she looks down at it, the card disappears (Figure 6.20c).

The woman then walks slowly to the left, exiting the frame (Figures 6.20a through o) while entering another frame of a laundromat, where she is doing laundry. She stands still and looks at her watch (Figure 6.20q). A card with the word "AM" written on it pops up in her left hand (Figure 6.20r). As in the previous scene at the gas station, everything in the background, including another customer, is moving at a higher speed. When the card disappears, the character walks to the left, exiting the frame and entering a downtown scene (Figures 6.20v through cc).

Again, everything in the background, such as the traffic and the pedestrians, is moving in fast motion. The character walks at a normal speed and stops at a corner, near a traffic light. Another card with the word "NOT" pops up in her hands, replacing the newspaper that she was holding (Figure 6.20ee). After she reads the card, it disappears, and she is again holding the newspaper (Figure 6.20ff). She then continues crossing the street, walking to the left of the frame and enters the dairy section of a grocery store (Figures 6.20gg through kk).

She is taking her time to look at the items on the shelves (Figures 6.20ll through mm) while other shoppers move at fast speed in the background. A card pops up in her hand again. This time the word on it is "READY". After the card disappears, she resumes looking at the items on the shelves. The video fades to black, and the credits appear.

Narrative

This video does not have three clear-cut acts. However, the fast motion of the backgrounds and the mysterious appearance and disappearance of the cards arouse the viewer's curiosity. We seek answers to such questions as why the background is moving at high speed, why a card magically appears, what the letters on the card mean, why the character is standing in the gas station or the laundromat, and why she looks confused.

Text is used extensively to convey the message. The series of words at the opening hints at the artist's feeling that motivates the work. In the video, a short sentence unfolds slowly, one word at a time, on cards that suddenly appear in the character's hands. By the time the first three words, "I am not", are revealed, the suspense reaches its height. The viewer speculates about the next word based on the visual hints provided so far. Once the last word is shown, the video ends quickly.

Space

The character moves across the frame through alternating outdoor and indoor scenes. In each location, the camera remains static. The character walks off the frame to the left to enter the next location. A transition effect slides the frame of the next location from left to right to put the character at the right edge of the frame so that the direction of her movement is consistently to the left. Through this creative use of transition, the physical spaces are linked as a continuous "panorama". In addition, the scale and vertical position of the character relative to the frame are maintained in all locations to augment the effect of spatial continuity.

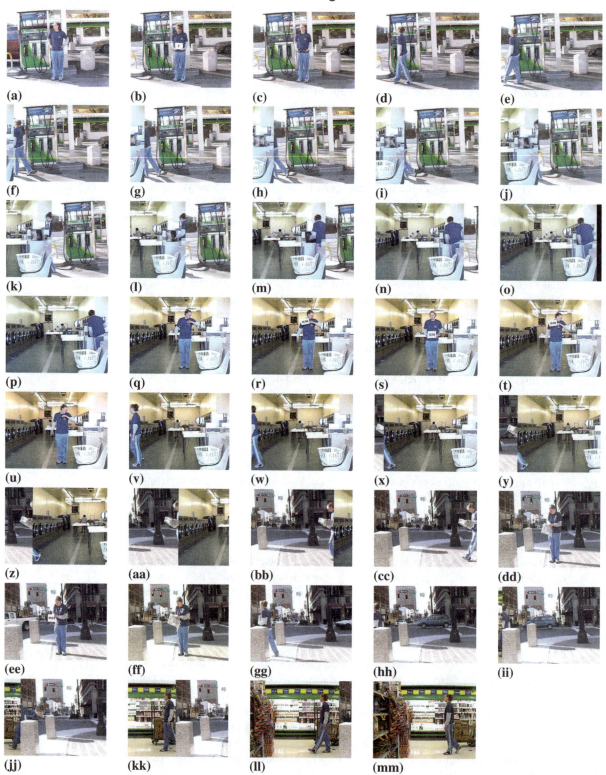

Figure 6.20 A sequence of stills from the student video project, *Fast Forward*, by Erin Regan

Time

Time is manipulated by moving the character and the background at different speeds. During the actual shooting, the character moved slowly. The video is played back at a higher speed to make the character move at normal speed. As a result, everything in the background is moving fast. The effect matches the title and the intended message.

The character wears the same clothes and looks the same in all four scenes. In addition, the way the transition continuously links the scenes implies the temporal order of these activities and that each immediately follows the other. Time is compressed by using the transition to move the character from one physical location to another.

Organizational Principles

Repetition is used coherently throughout the video not only to unify the aesthetics but to emphasize the message. For example:

- The opening series of words appears using a transition (Figure 7.5) similar to the one that moves the character from one location to another.
- The background moves faster in all scenes.
- A card with a word written on it pops up in each location.
- The character always walks from the right edge of the frame to the left to exit one location and enter another.
- The card pops up when the character is standing in the middle of the frame.

The repetition helps the viewer connect the written words on the card that appears in each scene. The alternation between outdoor and indoor scenes adds variations.

6.11 CRITIQUING DIGITAL VIDEO

The critique process suggested in this section is based generally on the steps for critique suggested in Chapter 1. Because of the temporal nature, critiquing time-based media (like audio discussed in Chapter 4) is more difficult than critiquing still images. You may have to keep playing the video while it is being critiqued, or play it more than once to get a full response.

Before you start critiquing, first watch the whole video without stopping. Write down any strong emotions evoked in you and which sequences promote these feelings. When you watch the video again, note where in the sequence these feelings are rooted.

1. First Impression.

Does the work seem to be narrative or non-narrative? Is it color, toned, or black-and-white? What is the total duration of the work?

2. Describe what you see and hear.

Start with a straightforward factual description of what you see and hear chronologically.

- *Visual*: What do the types of images seem to be? Is the video a representation that depicts a 3-D world or abstract that emphasizes on color and shapes?
- *Audio*: Is the audio music, speech, a natural sound, or a combination of these? If a combination, how are they combined and arranged in the audio? If it is music, can you identify the instruments? If it is speech, can you hear the words clearly? Does the content of the speech matter to the interpretation of the piece? Can you identify the

gender and age of the speaker? If it is a natural sound, can you identify what it is? Note how the loudness and relative pitches and tones change as the video plays.

3. Describe what you see and bear in terms of the art and design organizational principles.

Use the principles of art and design and perceptual organization as a guide to discuss the properties of the video. Feel free to extend the discussion beyond the questions given here.

- Does each element have its purpose?
- Are there any repetitions in the piece? If so, at what points does repetition occur? Are the repeated units exactly the same? Are they different but still connected as the same group? What are the variations?
- Does repetition occur at the same time in both the audio and visual elements?
- Does the work use any juxtaposition or parallelism?
- Does the overall video convey a sense of unity?
- Does the piece have a focal point or climax? If so, where is it? How is the climax built up?
- Does the video keep your attention? If not, in which part does your attention wander?
- What is the viewer perspective within the piece—as the first person or third person? Does the perspective change or remain the same throughout?
- Does the video seem to follow a 3-act narrative model? If so, can you identify the beginning, development, and ending?
- Are there any changes—emotional states, character's roles, specific situations—over the course of the video? How are the changes made? Do the changes develop gradually or abruptly?
- Compare the beginning and ending. What has changed? How do the changes convey the intended message?
- Are there any silences or stillnesses? How long do they last? What is the visual element during a silence? What is the audio during a freeze frame or blank screen?
- How do the audio elements (pitch, loudness, and timbre) synchronize with the visual elements (value, color, shape, and texture)?
- Do the visual and audio always share equal importance? Is there any moment that you feel one is dominant over the other? Is there any moment that you feel that the visual or the audio is redundant in conveying the meaning, mood, or feeling?
- Are the visual and the audio working together or competing for your attention?

Discuss the emotion and meaning that you pick out from these elements

- What sort of mood and feeling does the work as a *whole* seem to call forth? What makes you think so?
- Do different parts of the work seem to call forth different responses than the overall video? How are these differences bridged to make the work a unified whole?

4. Discuss the formal aspects and subject matter.

- What do you think the work is about?
- What do you think the piece is trying to communicate?
- Comment on the video's story space, plot space, and the use of screen space.
- Comment on the video's story time and plot time.
- Does the temporal organization of the units support the subject matter? Does any part of the video seem out of order? Could any parts be rearranged to enhance communication of the intent?

- If the work follows a narrative model, what do you think the story is? Does it tell a series of casual events, an abstract journey, or an emotional journey?
- Do other students' responses change your initial thoughts about the work?
- Discuss how the artist's choices of imagery, audio, and transitions work or do not work with the subject matter.

5. Discuss the execution of techniques.

Here are some sample questions pertaining to technical craftsmanship and professionalism.

- Is the camera focus correctly? Are there any undesirable effects due to focusing?
- Is the lighting appropriate? Are there any shots that seem too dark or too bright?
- How is the composition?
- Is the screen direction maintained when needed?
- What is the frame aspect ratio—standard 4:3 or widescreen 16:9?
- What is the intended delivery method of the work? How is it being presented during critique? Does the current presentation method reflect how the intended audience will experience the piece? If not, how will the viewer play the video?
- What is the visual quality? Are there any artifacts seem to be intentional or caused by carelessness?
- Does the audio sound clean—without noise? If not, is the noise part of the message?
- Is the audio's volume equalized throughout? Is there any sudden burst or drop in loudness in some segments? Do you think it is intentional?
- Are there any artifacts caused by insufficient sampling rate (resolution of the image), frame rate, or low quality of the original source?
- Are there copyrighted materials? Can they be replaced by original materials?

6. Student artist responses.

The student artist now can respond to the other students' responses and talk about the original intent, intended subject matter, and any unsolved problems in the piece.

Students are encouraged to continue responding to expand the discussion, because they now have new information about the piece from the artist.

TERMS

LEARNING AIDS

The following learning aids can be found at the book's companion Web site.

✑ Video Example: Split-screen and Time-lapse Video

You can see the split-screen techniques combined with time-lapse effect in this short segment of video from Max Negin's *Observe*.

🖱 Camera Location, Sightline, and Screen Direction

This interactive demo lets you examine the screen direction on different sides of the sightline by looking at shots from 36 different camera locations surrounding the two characters in the example shown in Figure 6.6.

✑ Video Example: Time-lapse Video with Superimposed Frames

You can see the time-lapse effect with superimposed adjacent frames in this short segment of video from Christopher Cassidy's *The Atlantic Flyway, Pinckney Island, SC*.

🖱 Shifting Camera Focus Distance

See how your attention is directed with the focus by shifting the focus from one character to another and then to the railing.

REFERENCES

David Bordwell and Kristin Thompson, *Film Art: An Introduction*, 2nd ed., New York: Alfred A. Knopf, Inc., 1979.

David Bordwell and Kristin Thompson, *Film Art: An Introduction*, 7th ed., McGraw Hill, 1986.

Bruce Mamer, *Film Production Technique Creating the Accomplished Image*, 4th ed., Thomson Wadsworth, 2006.

Tom Schroeppel, *The Bare Bones Camera Course for Film and Video*, 2nd ed.

Edward Branigan, *Narrative Comprehension and Film*, New York: Routledge, 1992.

INFORMATION OF MOVIE/VIDEO EXAMPLES CITED IN THE CHAPTER

24

20th Century Fox Television
2001–present
Synopsis:

> The title *24* refers to the number of hours in a day. The drama was synchronized in real time. Shows in one season made up of the happenings in one day (i.e.,

24 hours). The story revolves around anti-terrorist agents racing against the clock to save the day.

Augury/The Atlantic Flyway
Christopher Cassidy, 2006
Digital video
A large-scale time-lapse video installation at SECCA, February 29–June 30, 2008
An excerpt from http://www.secca.org/exhibitions.html

"The ongoing series of videos entitled Augury was inspired by the ancient Roman practice of that name. Augury was an important ritual in Rome and elsewhere, and speaks to the human quest for order in even the most random sequence of events. I was intrigued by the practitioners' imposition of meaning on otherwise insignificant details, such as the direction in which birds fly overhead. Especially, I recognized some consonance between the augur's marking out of a templum, a sacred space in the sky, and my own focus on place.

The project eventually came to rely on a video camera to function as objective observer. Long-duration footage of a fixed portion of sky directly overhead captures fleeting glimpses of birds in flight. To distill the hidden patterns that develop over time, I collapse the individual frames of the footage, allowing each frame to remain, superimposed on succeeding ones. The resulting video reveals dashed and dotted lines composed of bird silhouettes, spiraling across the frame in surprising arabesques."

Empire
Andy Warhol, 1964
Black and White, Silent, 8 hrs 5 mins, 16 fps
An excerpt:
From http://www.moma.org/collection/browse_results.php?object_id=89507
Gallery label text:

Out of Time: A Contemporary View, August 30, 2006-April 9, 2007

"Empire consists of a single stationary shot of the Empire State Building filmed from 8:06 p.m. to 2:42 a.m., July 25–26, 1964. The eight-hour, five-minute film, which is typically shown in a theater, lacks a traditional narrative or characters. The passage from daylight to darkness becomes the film's narrative, while the protagonist is the iconic building that was (and is again) the tallest in New York City. Warhol lengthened *Empire's* running time by projecting the film at a speed of sixteen frames per second, slower than its shooting speed of twenty-four frames per second, thus making the progression to darkness almost imperceptible. Non-events such as a blinking light at the top of a neighboring building mark the passage of time. According to Warhol, the point of this film—perhaps his most famous and influential cinematic work—is to 'see time go by.'

The work on view is a two hour, twenty-four minute excerpt. The film will be screened in its entirety in the Museum theaters during the run of this exhibition."

Publication excerpt:

"The Museum of Modern Art, *MoMA Highlights*, New York: The Museum of Modern Art, revised 2004, originally published 1999, p. 240

". . . Warhol conceived a new relationship of the viewer to film in *Empire* and other early works, which are silent, explore perception, and establish a new sense of cinematic time. With their disengagement, lack of editing, and lengthy nonevents, these films were intended to be part of a larger environment. They also parody the goals of his avant-garde contemporaries who sought to convey the human psyche through film or used the medium as metaphor."

Diurnal Rhythm: Head in the Clouds
Amy Purcell, 2007–08
Digital video
A large-scale time-lapse video installation at SECCA, February 29–June 30, 2008
An excerpt:

From http://www.secca.org/exhibitions.html
"*Diurnal Rhythm: Head in the Clouds*, presents a single day constructed out of many days and compressed into an ongoing 15 minute loop. The structure of the temporal compression follows the balance of light duration of an early summer day and is marked by the rhythmic cycles of the moon and the sun. The circular screen presents a physical slice of time and reinforces the cyclic diurnal structure and the endless loop format. The installation of the circular screen invites the viewer to kinesthetically experience having one's head in the clouds . . . While making the work, my intent was to have the camera mirror my frame of mind during the day with the sky and clouds as the subject. The mid-day acrobatic swings parallel the swings and shifts of focus and energy that often define that time of day, while the focused pans of the morning contrast the stillness of the evening. My desire was to have the camera mimic my interior and subjective state of that time of day. The capturing of sky and clouds was extended over many days and then edited to become one day and night or diurnal rhythm. Diurnal Rhythm: Head in the Clouds was a concept, process, and now is a physical experience that offers escape and immersion into a daydream of sky."

High Noon
Directed by Fred Zinnemann, 1952
Black and white, Western, 85 minutes
Synopsis:

A marshal retires on his wedding day. When he learns that a killer he had sent to jail was returning to town on the noon train to seek revenge with his accomplices, he decides to take up his badge and gun to face the outlaws and defend the town's peace. He has about one hour to "round-up" help. However, nobody in town is willing to help him, so he has to face the outlaws alone.

My Dinner with Andre
Directed by Louis Malle, 1982
Color, 110 minutes, Not Rated
Synopsis:

From the DVD package
". . . Two old friends meet in a chic New York restaurant, where Andre recounts his mystical adventures of the past two years. The focus then turns to the relationship between the two men, their innermost feelings and loves, and their different ideas concerning the purpose of life. When the check eventually comes, one of them will have been profoundly changed."

Nocturne
Jym Davis
Digital video

> The footages were shot using a Pixelvision Fisher Price camera (PXL 2000) extensively and then altered in a video-editing program by layering with other video footages. The following is an excerpt of Jym's description about his video:

> "Some of the images are raw Pixelvision. I faded in and out of the layering so the final film has several different 'looks'. . . Because Pixelvision is so difficult to get any kind of definition with, I found that layering the video allowed a certain amount of balance between clarity and obscurity. Because the short film is about a girl in a sleep observation lab who is in a dream state, I found that oscillating between the blurred and the obscured served my purposes well."

Observe
Max Negin, 2008
Digital video
A large-scale time-lapse video installation at SECCA, February 29–June 30, 2008
An excerpt:

> From http://www.secca.org/exhibitions.html
> "*Observe* is an inspection of growth and change over time. A sixth month evolution of how a face changes, growth of blades of grass, and the movement of a sun rise or sun set provide different chances to see transformations of landscapes, from the expanse of nature to the microscopic pores on our skin.

> . . . Looking into a mirror every morning, walking by a patch of grass, or sleeping through the rise of the sun, we might miss subtle changes in each environment. Time is the measure of how long these changes take place, and observation is the critical tool to know what is different.

> By manipulating time, we can gain perspective on how things evolve . . . *Observe* is an exploration of physical, personal, and emotional growth."

Napoleon
Directed by Abel Gance, 1927
Tinted & Toned, 3 hrs. 55 mins., VHS format
Synopsis:

From the videocassette package:
> "Abel Gance's 1927 movie masterpiece with important early use of split screen, moving camera and Polyvision, has been painstakingly resurrected and presented with a symphonic score composed by Carmine Coppola."

Rope
Directed by Alfred Hitchcock, 1948
Color, 81 minutes, Rated PG
Synopsis:

From the DVD package:
> Two friends "strangle a classmate for intellectual thrills, then proceed to throw a party for the victim's family and friends—with the body stuffed inside the trunk they use for a buffet table. As the killers turn the conversation to committing the

'perfect murder', their former teacher (Stewart) becomes increasingly suspicious. Before the night is over, the professor will discover how brutally his students have turned his academic theories into chilling reality in Hitchcock's spellbinding excursion into the macabre."

There are many challenges to shoot a movie as one continuous action. One of the technical challenges was the time limit of a film reel—each reel of film could shoot only 10 minutes. Here is an excerpt taken from the Production Notes on the DVD copy of the movie that explains the challenge and how the movie was shot:

". . . based on the one-set play *Rope's End* by Patrick Hamilton, Alfred Hitchcock said that he was abandoning pure cinema' in an effort to make the stage play mobile.' Hitchcock shot the entire film on a single Warner Brothers soundstage as continuous action, in ten-minute 'takes.'

. . . In order to shoot lengthy takes, every movement of camera and actors had to be worked out in sessions with a big blackboard. 'Even the floor was marked and plotted with numbered circles for the 25 to 30 camera moves in each ten-minute reel,' Hitchcock revealed. 'Whole walls of the apartment had to slide away to allow the camera to follow the actors through narrow doors.'

. . . To facilitate camera moves, tables and chairs had to be constantly rearranged by off-camera prop men . . . 'It was hard to see how the picture was going to work even while we were doing it, said Stewart. 'The noises made by the moving of the walls was a continual problem, and we would have to do scenes over again just for sound reasons, using only microphones like in a radio play.'"

Sugar Water
Directed by Michel Gondry, 1996
The Work of Director Michel Gondry, DVD (Release date: 2003)
Palm Pictures

Sugar Water (by Cibo Matto) is a music video directed by Michel Gondry. The DVD includes this video and other music videos, commericals, and short films of director Michel Gondry.

ASSIGNMENTS

Assignment 1. Analysis of Shots

Choose several visually interesting sequences from movies or music videos to analyze the shots. You may want to use a slow-scan technique to analyze the shots.

i. Identify the different types of camera shots, such as long, medium, close-up, high-angle, low-angle, eye-level, or oblique. Are they coherent with the connotation of the shot?

ii. Examine when and how the camera moves to reframe due to compositional change (because the subject or object moves within the frame, leaves or enter the frame).

iii. Identify the sightline or direction of action, if any. Identify the screen direction of the subject or object.

iv. Identify the focus shift (if any) within a shot.

v. Identify the shots that give a sense of passage of time. How much time is compressed? For example, one shot shows a character getting up on a train at a train station, and the next shot shows the character getting off the train. This depicts passage of time. Time is compressed by skipping the trip on the train. As another example, one shot shows a character opening the front door to a house, and the next shot shows the character inside the house closing the door behind his/her back. This sequence is almost in real time; the amount of time compressed is insignificant.

vi. Determine the order of events presented in the sequence. Does the order of the shots depict the natural order of the events?

vii. If you are going to reorder the shots without changing the underlying meaning of the video, what would the new order be?

viii. Can you rearrange the shots to create a different story or message?

ix. What are the story space and plot space of the video?

Assignment 2. Storyboarding

Create a storyboard for the sequences you chose for the previous activity. If copyright agreement of the video allows you to capture frame stills, you may use frame stills. Otherwise, sketch out the storyboard.

Have a class discussion. Everyone looks at everyone else's storyboards that are created for different videos. Discuss in class how each video may be shot based on each storyboard. Then watch the video sequences that the storyboards are based on. Compare the video sequences with the shots that the class envisions based on the storyboards. Discuss the causes of misunderstanding of the key ideas of the storyboards, and suggest some possible solutions to improve them.

This activity intends to help you practice creating and reading storyboards. The class discussion provides an opportunity to learn how others read and interpret your storyboard.

Jennifer N. Gentry, *Old Lady with Curlers,* charcoal and graphite on paper , 42.5" × 28.5", 1992

Digital Video Manipulation for Digital Art

GENERAL LEARNING OBJECTIVES

In this chapter, you will learn:

* How digital video editors work in general.
* To use digital video tools to incorporate art and design organizational principles.
* To use digital video tools to create perceptual organization elements.

7.1 INTRODUCTION

This chapter is not intended to be a user manual providing an itemization of everything various digital video filters and editing tools can do. A digital video-editing program can do more than this chapter can cover. You are encouraged to explore and experiment with the different tools in your digital video-editing programs.

The common workspaces of digital video editing programs are discussed in the *Digital Media Primer* Chapter 7.

This chapter will give an overview on what can be manipulated in digital video. Then, we will discuss how the various digital video manipulation tools can be exploited to create desired effects from the art perspective based on:

* Space, time, and narrative aspects of video
* Perceptual organization
* The organizational principles of art and design that are discussed in the previous chapter.

7.2 WORKSPACE ELEMENTS IN DIGITAL VIDEO-EDITING PROGRAMS

When we discuss video manipulation tools, it is inevitable to refer to the workspace elements in a digital video-editing program. Let's have a quick review of the common four elements found in these programs.

* *Asset lists* manage the imported source materials for the video project. They include the captured or digitized video footages, audio clips, still images, titles, and graphics.
* *Preview window* lets you preview your entire video project. Adobe Premiere Pro and Apple Final Cut Pro also have a dual monitor window that you can use to view, edit, and trim the individual source clip and preview the final sequence.
* *Timeline* is where you can arrange your source clips in sequence. It usually has video tracks and audio tracks.
* *Effects* and *transitions* can be found in a separate palette or menu item. Effects may include both video and audio effects. Many of the video effects work very similarly to the image filters that you may find in image-editing programs. Examples of video effects include altering the color balance of the video clip, desaturating, resizing, clipping, blurring, sharpening, distorting, and stylizing the video clip. The most commonly used video transition is cross dissolve.

Figures 7.1 and 7.2 show the screenshots of the workspace of Adobe Premiere Pro CS3 and Apple Final Cut Pro 6.

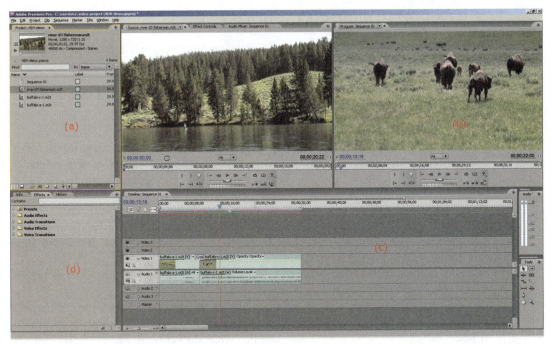

Figure 7.1 A screenshot of Adobe Premiere Pro CS3 workspace (a) Asset list (b) Preview windows (c) Timeline (d) Effects and transitions

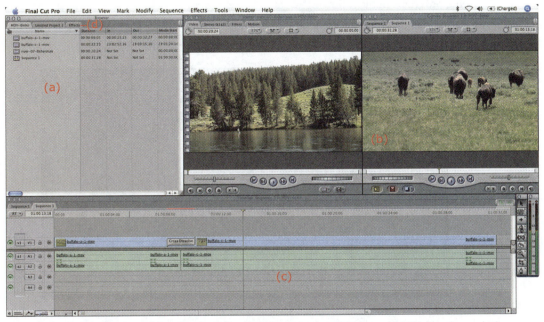

Figure 7.2 A screenshot of Apple Final Cut Pro 6 workspace (a) Asset list (b) Preview windows (c) Timeline (d) Effects and transitions can be accessed in a different tab

7.3 WHAT CAN BE MANIPULATED?

The most common manipulations made to video footage include: alteration of image and audio, duration and speed of footage, transitions between clips, and panning and zooming of clips.

7.3.1 Image and Audio

In terms of media elements, a video is made up of a sequence of images and audio. Manipulating video image and audio in digital video-editing programs is very similar to that using digital image-editing programs and audio-editing programs, respectively.

Apply Filters or Effects

Like image-editing programs, video-editing programs often come with effect filters that let you alter the video image's tonal values, color, and size. You also can mask selected areas of the image.

Many digital video-editing programs also let you apply audio effects, such as reverb, noise reduction, pitch shift, and equalizer.

Some of the properties of these effects also can be adjusted to change over time. For example, you can apply a Gaussian blur to a video clip and gradually change the blurriness (Figure 7.3). Some audio effects also can be changed over time. For example, you can change the properties of a reverb effect applied to an audio.

Screen-capture movies showing how to animate the video effect, using Gaussian Blur as an example, are available in the *Digital Media Primer* Chapter 7.

Use of Multiple Tracks

Digital video-editing programs have a timeline that lets you sequence your footage. **Timeline** has video and audio tracks. These video tracks are like layers in digital image-editing programs in the following ways.

- You can place multiple video clips on top of each other. The video clip on the top track covers the video clips that are placed in the tracks below it.

(a)

Figure 7.3 Selected frames of a clip applied with the Gaussian Blur effect where the blur level is changed over time

(b)

(c)

(d)

Figure 7.3 (*Continued*)

See the *Digital Media Primer,* Chapter 6, for a discussion about keying. Screen-capture movies showing how to create chroma keying are also available on the book's companion Web site.

- You can adjust the level of transparency of to a video clip on a track to let the video clips below it show through.
- You can apply a mask to a video clip on a track to let the video clips below it show through the mask area. A mask can be an imported digital image. It also can be created by using **keying**. For example, the ***Chroma key*** lets you designate a color in the video clip to be transparent. The balloon figure shown in Figure 7.4a is masked using color keying to give Figure 7.4b. The effect shown in Figure 7.4d is created by placing the masked clip (Figure 7.4b) on a video track on top of another video clip (Figure 7.4c).

Timeline also allows multiple audio tracks. Like the multitrack feature in digital audio-editing programs, the audio placed on different audio tracks will be mixed together.

To insert tracks:

- *In Adobe Premiere Pro:* select Sequence > Add Tracks...
- *In Final Cut Pro:* select Sequence > Insert Tracks..., or Ctrl-click on empty space in the Timeline and select Add Track.

(a)

(b)

Figure 7.4 Create a mask effect by keying

(c)

(d)

Figure 7.4 (*Continued*)

7.3.2 Duration of a Clip

You can trim a clip by setting its In and Out points. The ***In and Out points*** define the frames that you want to include in the sequence.

Trimming a clip using In and Out points is non-destructive, which means that the frames in the footage are still intact. You always can readjust the In and Out points to include more or less of the original clip (master clip or source clip) later.

7.3.3 Transition Between Two Clips

A video is made up of multiple shots. There is transition between two shots, whether it is a straight-cut or a transition effect, such as Dissolve. A Straight-cut transition refers to instantaneous changing from one clip to another; there is not really a "transition" effect applied between these clips. The choice of transition is part of the video sequence and should be coherent with your visual style and intended messages.

Screen-capture movies showing how to trim a clip by setting its In and Out points are available on the companion Web site for the *Digital Media Primer* Chapter 7.

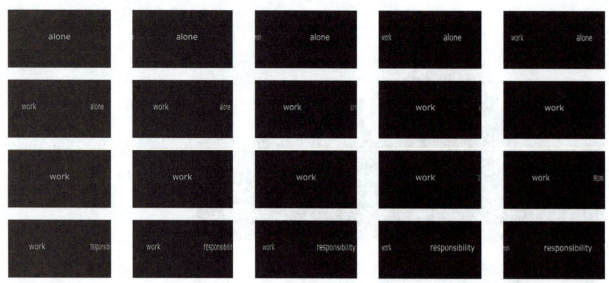

Figure 7.5 The creative use of the transition effect Cube Spin on simple white text on a black background to create motion

Some transition effects bridge two shots by breaking up a segment of one footage into smaller shapes (such as a checkerboard pattern). These shapes are spread slowly across the frames of the other footage. Examples of this type of transition effects include Checker-Board, Barn Doors, and Blinds effects. Recall that shape is an art element that can have functions and form meanings.

In addition, transition effects create motion or animation. Such motion and animation may create new meaning for the video. Creative uses of transitions can produce interesting effects. For example, a transition called Cube Spin may be too distractive in many cases. However, when it is applied to simple white text on black background in a series (Figure 7.5), it produces a motion that creates a sense of "pushing" and "squeezing". The direction of the transition can be alternated to create balance. In the example shown in Figure 7.5, the word "alone" gets pushed to the right by the subsequent word "work". The word "work" is in turn pushed to the left by the subsequent word "responsibility".

> 🖱 **Use of Transition to Create Motion**
> An example (as shown in Figure 7.5) of the creative use of the Cube Spin transition effect to augment a sense of "pushing" and "squeezing".

7.3.4 Speed of a Clip

Although video is shot at a specific frame rate, there are different ways you can alter the speed of an video clip in a digital video-editing program.

Speed

To change the speed of an entire clip, select the clip that is placed on the timeline, and choose Clip > Speed/Duration . . . in Adobe Premiere Pro CS3 (Figure 7.6a) or Modify > Speed . . . in Apple Final Cut Pro 6 (Figure 7.6b) You can change the speed by changing the percentage or specifying the duration. You also have an option to reverse the speed, which will make the clip play back in reverse.

 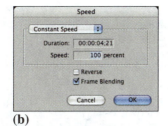

(a)   **(b)**

Figure 7.6 (a) Adobe Premiere Pro CS3's Clip Speed/Duration dialog box (b) Apple Final Cut Pro 6's Speed dialog box

Time Remapping

Clip Speed/Duration applies the specified speed throughout the entire clip. If you want to vary the speed across a clip, you can use Time Remapping. Like animating a video effect by setting keyframes, *Time Remapping* allows you to vary the speed across a clip and to ease in or ease out the rate of changes by setting *speed keyframes*. Speed keyframes are different from regular keyframes:

> **Time Remapping** Screen-capture movies demonstrating the basic steps of using Time Remapping to vary the speed of a clip in two digital video-editing application programs: Adobe Premiere Pro and Apple Final Cut Pro.

- The regular (non-speed) keyframes mark an instantaneous change. The frames between keyframes use a constant speed set in the previous keyframe.
- A speed keyframe can be split to span across multiple frames to create a steady transition of the speed change.

7.3.5 Motion, Pan, and Zoom of a Clip

The *Motion effect* is a video effect that lets you pan and zoom a clip by repositioning and resizing the clip's width and height over time. However, you do not have to animate the changes of the Motion options. You can use Motion to simply reposition and scale a clip. In Adobe Premiere Pro, the Motion effect can be found in the Effect Controls tab (Figure 7.7a). In Final Cut Pro, Motion has its own tab (Figure 7.7b).

7.4 SPACE, TIME, AND NARRATIVE

In this section, we will discuss some tools and techniques that you can use to manipulate space and time and create storyboards.

7.4.1 Space

Split-Screen Effect

A *split screen* allows you to display multiple shots simultaneously. To create a split-screen effect, you can apply the Motion effect in combination with layering video clips on different video tracks.

For example, two video clips are placed on different tracks (Figure 7.8a). The one on the top track can be repositioned (by applying Motion effect) to let the clip on the track below it show through (Figure 7.8b). Both video clips can be applied with Motion effect so that

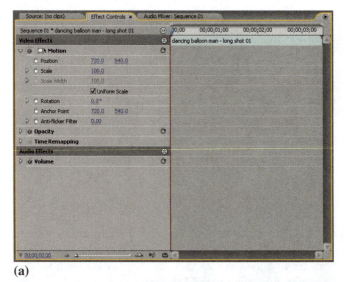

(a)

(b)

Figure 7.7 Motion effect options (a) Adobe Premiere
Pro CS3 (b) Apple Final Cut Pro 6

one is moved to the left and the other moved to the right (Figure 7.8c). Figure 7.8d demonstrates that with Motion effect, a video clip also can be resized, as The video clip on track
Video 2 is scaled to 50% for width and height.

Superimpose

You can layer the video clips on different tracks, similar to layering images in digital image-
editing programs. How the video images are mixed can be controlled by adjusting the
Opacity level of either the whole frame or a selected area of the frame. You can define the area
to allow the video clips on the lower video tracks to show through by specifying its color and
tonal values. You also can import an image that defines the transparent area of a frame.

For example, Figure 7.9a shows how two video clips can be superimposed by lowering
the opacity level of the video clip on the top video track. Figure 7.9b shows the same opacity effect used in combination with Motion effects which are used to shrink the frame size.
The video clip in track Video 1 now shows through the empty space.

(a)

(b)

Figure 7.8 Use of Motion effects to create split-screen effects with video clips (a) Track Video 2 before being applied with Motion effect (b) Motion effect is applied, so the horizontal position is changed from 720 to 0—moved to the left (c) Track Video 1 also is applied with Motion effect to shift it to the right to make a better composition (d) Track Video 2 also is scaled to 50%

(c)

(d)

Figure 7.8 (*Continued*)

(a)

(b)

Figure 7.9 (a) The video clip on track Video 2 is applied with 60% opacity (b) The video clip is scaled to 50% in addition to lowering the opacity

(a)   (b)

(c)

Figure 7.10 (a) The video clip placed on track Video 2 (b) The video clip placed on track Video 1 (c) A Color Key effect is applied to the clip on track Video 2 to make the body of the balloon transparent

Figure 7.10 shows how the shape that lets the video clip on the lower track show through can be defined by the colors of the video clip on the top track. This creates a cutout allowing part of the other video be visible. The result is more dynamic than simply setting the opacity of the whole frame. During the playback of this clip, the cutout shape is constantly changing as the balloon is "dancing" throughout the video.

Ken Burns Effect

The *Ken Burns effect* refers to a technique of zooming and panning across photographs in video work to create a feeling of motion. It has been a useful technique for documentary work where the subjects have no or little video records.

Some video-editing programs (such as Apple iMovie) have a video effect called the Ken Burns effect for digitally panning and zooming clips. In Adobe Premiere Pro and Apple Final Cut Pro, you can use Motion effects to create panning and zooming across a clip—which can be a video or a still image. Changing the position of a clip over time creates the pan effect, and changing the scale of a clip over time creates the zoom effect.

If you want to zoom in on a clip, the clip needs to have sufficient pixel dimensions to cover the area necessary in the frame when it is zoomed out. Otherwise, it will leave empty space (Figure 7.11). If it is a still image, you will need to create it with sufficient pixel dimensions. For a video clip, because its frame size is predetermined by its video format,

Although the technique has been used before, it is made famous by the documentary filmmaker Ken Burns.

Vector graphics are resolution independent. Thus, if your still image is created as a vector graphic (such as Adobe Illustrator file), you can scale the graphic to any size in the video.

Figure 7.11 Zooming out a still image that does not have sufficient pixel dimensions to cover the area will leave empty space

its size will not be sufficient to cover the whole frame if it is zoomed out or scaled down. You may need to superimpose the clip with other clips to cover the empty spaces created.

The pan and zoom techniques also can be created by videographing a printed copy of an image. Varying the camera angles and distances from the print can create an interesting perspective and a sense of flying through an image-like landscape. Figures 7.12a and 7.13

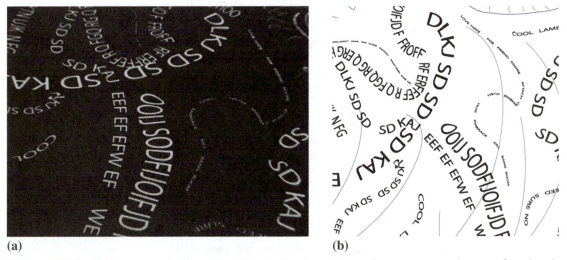

(a)   (b)

Figure 7.12 Pan and zoom techniques (a) A frame showing the use of camera pan and zoom of a printed copy of a digital image (Dave Nix's *Personal Map*) (b) The part of the original image that corresponds to the frame shown in (a) (Courtesy of Dave Nix)

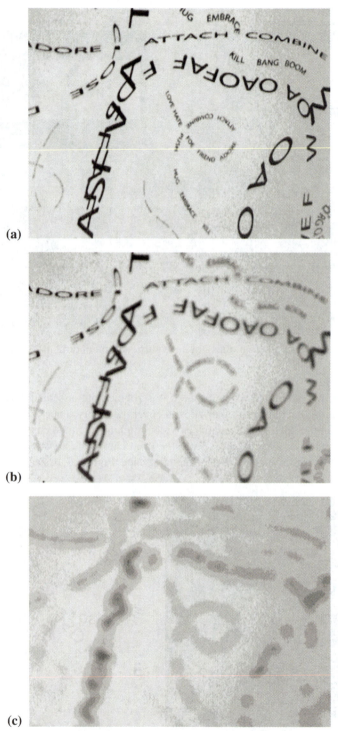

(a)

(b)

(c)

Figure 7.13 Video stills from Dave Nix's *me.by.they* showing the use of an animated Gaussian Blur effect (Courtesy of Dave Nix).

show several frames from a digital video assignment* that uses this technique. The image source of this video is a printed image, *Personal Map* (Figure 7.12c) created in Adobe Illustrator by the same student artist. It is comprised of curves that are made up of text strings. The curves (in turn) make up a line-drawing of a self-portrait. The movement of the camera over the flat printed copy creates a sense of scrutiny and adds a 3-D perspective (compare Figure 7.12a with Figure 7.12b).

The video obtained using this pan and zoom technique can be manipulated further to depict an underlying meaning. For example, segments of the video also are applied with *animated* video effects (such as Gaussian Blur) to transform the text strings into an organic form—something that looks like chromosomal strands observed under a microscope (Figure 7.13a through c).

7.4.2 Time

This section discusses several tools and techniques that you can use to manipulate video time.

Altering Speed

The speed adjustment (Figure 7.6) in a video-editing program allows you to alter time by changing the playback speed of a clip. You also can make a clip play backwards.

Altering the Order of Events

The order of the events captured in a footage can be reordered in your final video sequence. A useful technique is to break up the event into subclips. You then can rearrange these subclips in your final video sequence in any intended order.

A *subclip* is a segment of a master (source or original) clip that you have captured. A subclip is defined by the In and Out points. The first step to create subclips is very much like how you trim a clip by setting its In and Out points. The second step is to name the clip before you use it in the video sequence.

To create a subclip, set the In and Out points in the Source monitor (as usual). Then, instead of placing the trimmed clip directly on the Timeline, you create a subclip by doing one of the following:

- *In Adobe Premiere Pro*:
  - Choose Clip > Make Subclip, and give the subclip a name.
  - Drag the clip from the Source monitor to the Project panel, and give the subclip a name.
- *In Apple Final Cut Pro*:
  - Choose Modify > Make Subclip. Save the subclip with a new name.

> ⟢ **Create Subclips** Screen-capture movies demonstrate the basic steps of creating subclips in two digital video-editing application programs: Adobe Premiere Pro and Apple Final Cut Pro.

Creating subclips has at least two advantages over directly placing the trimmed clips on the Timeline.

- You can use the subclips multiple times in a sequence without having to do the trimming every time you need to use the segment in the sequence.
- The subclips are listed in the Project or the Browser panel and can be used for storyboarding.

*Student Artist: Dave Nix (Wake Forest University)
Title: *me.by.they*
Length: About 46 seconds
Color: Grayscale
Frame aspect ratio: 4:3

Choice of Transition to Imply Relative Timing

A cross-dissolve type of transition between two clips often is used to imply a time lapse between the events in the two clips. On the other hand, a straight-cut transition often is used when the two clips occur in real time without a time lapse. For example, a straight-cut shot often is used in real-time dialoguing (documentaries and interviews), where you cut between shots of two or more persons.

Figure 7.14 shows two frames before and after a straight-cut shot. It gives an impression that the performance in both shots is a real-time continuous occurrence of a single event, although in fact, the two shots were shot at different times.

(a)   **(b)**

Figure 7.14 Two frames before and after a straight cut in a video sequence

A video showing a side-by-side comparison of straight-cut and cross-dissolve transition using the example shown in Figure 7.14 and Figure 7.15 is available in *Digital Media Primer* Chapter 7.

Figure 7.15 shows frames of the same sequence using a cross-dissolving transition. You can tell it is still from the same performance, because the drummer is in both shots. However, the relative timing of the two shots—whether the second medium shot of the drummer is a continuous occurrence from the long shot—is not as affirmative as the sequence using a straight-cut shot. The audio and the video as a whole may be able to provide cues about the contiguity or relative timing of the two shots.

A straight-cut from one scene to a very different scene transits viewers to a different space, but it also invites the viewer to bridge the scenes together by figuring out their temporal connection.

(a)   **(b)**

Figure 7.15 Selected frames of a cross-dissolve transition between a long shot and a medium shot of a drum performance

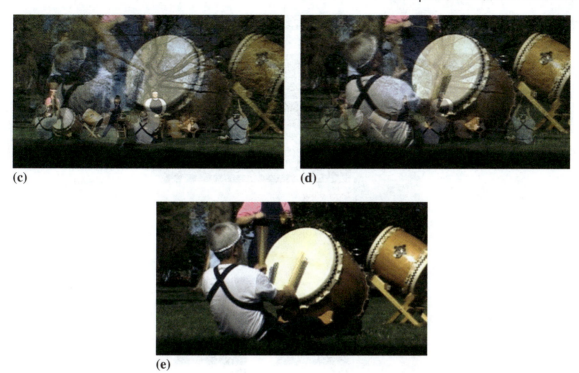

(c)   (d)

(e)

Figure 7.15 (*Continued*)

7.4.3 Narrative

Storyboard

When you choose the *Icon view* in Adobe Premiere Pro and Apple Final Cut Pro, you can arrange the clips and subclips for their intended order using their thumbnails. This helps storyboarding your video sequence. You can drag the thumbnails as a group onto the Timeline. The order of these clips in the icon view will be preserved when they are placed on the Timeline.

To turn on the icon view:

- *In Adobe Premiere Pro*: choose Icon View in the Project panel (Figure 7.16).
- *In Final Cut Pro*: choose icon view in the Browser by using one of the following sets of commands.
  - View > Browser Items > as Medium Icons or as Large Icons
  - Ctrl-click in Browser panel, choose View as Medium Icons or View as Large Icons

For example, Figure 7.16 shows a screenshot of Adobe Premiere Pro CS3s Project panel in Icon view. The clips are ordered in a grid. As shown in the figure, seven clips are selected and can be dragged onto the Timeline.

Poster Frame

Each thumbnail icon of a clip uses a frame (called *poster frame*) to represent the clip. By default, the first frame of a clip or subclip is used as the poster frame. You can designate a different frame to represent the clip's content and intention. This helps visualizing the storyboard in the Icon view.

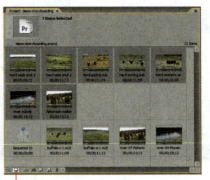

Icon view

Figure 7.16 Adobe Premiere Pro CS3 Project panel in Icon view

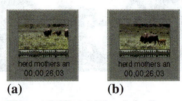

(a)   **(b)**

Figure 7.17 (a) The default thumbnail icon of a clip uses its first frame (b) A different frame that represents more of the clip's content and purpose can be designated as the clip's thumbnail icon

For example, in a shot that follows a herd of buffalos, and slowly pans and zooms in to focus on a mother and her calf, the first frame only shows part of the herd (Figure 7.17a). However, it would make more sense to use the frame at the end of the clip, where the focus is on the mother and calf (Figure 7.17b) as the icon for storyboarding.

7.5 INCORPORATING ART AND DESIGN AND PERCEPTUAL ORGANIZATIONAL PRINCIPLES

The choices of strategies and creative techniques used to achieve any desired effect are limitless. The ideas listed next serve as examples and starting points for you to explore how different tools can be used to incorporate the art and design organizational principles (Table 7.1) and perceptual organization principles (Table 7.2). The specific dramatic or narrative goals of your final video are the determining factors for how these principles are applied.

TABLE 7.1	List of Ideas of Using Different Tools to Incorporate Art and Design Organizational Principles
Repetition	To facilitate repeating segments of a clip: • Setting In and Out points to use multiple sections from the same master clip. • Create subclips for reuse. You can also add variations to the repetition by: • Setting slightly different In and Out points in trimming the master clip or to create multiple subclips from the master clips. • Setting different speeds, including reversing the playback. • Applying different video effects to give the repeated clips variations, such as color, positioning within a frame, scale, masking part of the visual content.
Emphasis and Focus	Build up repetition and then create difference, for example, by changing the speed of the clip, modulating the color.
Unity and Variety	• Use of Icon view for storyboarding to visualize the overall progression • Repetition can also help create unity. (See Repetition above).
Balance	• Use of subclips. • Use of Icon view for storyboarding to visualize the sequence of events.

TABLE 7.2	List of Ideas of Using Different Tools to Incorporate Perceptual Organizational Principles
Proximity and Similarity	• Use Icon view for storyboarding to help you visualize the temporal proximity of shots. • If your video-editing program lets you give a description to your clips, label your clips using keywords to associate with different intended messages, purposes, or visual elements. It will help you identify assets and visualize their temporal proximity as your assets in storyboarding. • On the Timeline, you also can group the clips with the same purpose or element in a track.

Common Fate	• The visual changes applied to a clip using video effect can be easily duplicated onto another clip. In Adobe Premiere Pro,
	  1. On the Timeline, select the clip that you want to duplicate its video effect to another clip
	  2. Choose Edit > Copy
	  3. Select another clip that you want to apply the same effect
	  4. Choose Edit > Paste Attributes

Good Continuation	• Continuous and gradual changes of video effects and clip speed can be achieved by keyframing.

TABLE 7.2	List of Ideas of Using Different Tools to Incorporate Perceptual Organizational Principles (*Continued*)
Closure	• To introduce gaps for the viewer to perform closure, you may think about trimming a clip into multiple segments and inserting them at different times. • Storyboarding also helps you visualize how far apart the clip segments are separated and determine if the viewer might be able to perform closure to connect the clips segments.
Figure–Ground Relationship	• Figure–ground relationship can be established by adjusting the camera focal distance during shooting. The subject in focus becomes the figure or foreground. The shifting focus distance performed by the camera during shooting is difficult to alter in video editing. • If you final sequence superimposes different clips, each clip can be applied with video effects (such as Gaussian Blur) and changing the effect levels to direct the viewer's attention in a frame. In general, dark and blurry objects tend to be pushed to the background while bright and sharp objects tend to be the foreground.

TERMS

Asset lists, 296
Chroma key, 300
effects, 296
Icon view, 312
In and Out points, 301
Ken Burns effect, 308

keying, 300
Motion effect, 303
Preview window, 296
Poster frame, 313
speed keyframes, 303
Split-screen effect, 303

subclip, 311
Time Remapping, 303
Timeline, 296
Transition effects, 296

LEARNING AIDS

The following learning aids can be found at the book's companion Web site.

Use of Transition to Create Motion
An example (as shown in Figure 7.5) of the creative use of the Cube Spin transition effect to augment a sense of "pushing" and "squeezing".

Time Remapping
Screen-capture movies demonstrating the basic steps of using Time Remapping to vary the speed of a clip in two digital video-editing application programs: Adobe Premiere Pro and Apple Final Cut Pro.

Create Subclips
Screen-capture movies demonstrate the basic steps of creating subclips in two digital video-editing application programs: Adobe Premiere Pro and Apple Final Cut Pro.

ASSIGNMENTS

Assignment 1. Learn by Copying

Choose a short segment from a video—a movie, a documentary, an instructional video, or a news report. Reproduce the segment by shooting similar footage and editing them.

Assignment 2. Video Effects and Transition Overflow

One objective of this assignment is to let you explore and experiment with as many video effects and transitions as you desire. The second objective is to see that motion is part of the transition and may have its own meanings in the final video.

In this assignment, choose the message you want to convey through the work. You can choose an emotion you want to express or several words to connect into a story. (*Tip*: Use the online project aid, "Making Sense Out of Random Words" to help you get several words.) Apply as many transition and video effects as you can to create a meaningful video. Also, experiment with superimposing, split-screen, and animating video effects.

If this is a class assignment, let's see who can use the most filters and still convey the message without distractions from the "dazzling" effects.

Assignment 3. Montage

A montage is a series of shots of related subjects. Use a variety of angles and subject sizes for the various shots. Also, determine the appropriate type of transition between two shots.

Think about using different sources in addition to video footages:

- Digital photography
- Scanned objects
- Scanned sketches
- Digital painting and drawing

If you have done the digital image montage project in Chapter 3, use the image sources from this digital image project in addition to your new video footage to create a video version of your montage.

Assignment 4. Emotional Clip

Create a short video clip (1 to 2 minutes) to depict an emotion. Think about how to use visual elements, motion, and make temporal changes.

- *Visual elements*: Think about lines, shapes, values, colors, textures, and spaces. (Review Chapter 2)
- *Motion or movement*: Think about direction and speed of movement. They can be introduced during videographing or during video-editing to apply Motion effect on the clips.
- *Temporal changes*: Think about what properties of the elements change over time.

Also, think about incorporating some of the organizational principles we have discussed in this and previous chapters: repetition, unity, balance, emphasis and focus, perspective, proximity, common fate, good continuation, closure, figure–ground relationship, and past experience.

Here are a list of suggested words you can choose from:

upset	determined	effervescent	enervated
lonely	spontaneous	hesitant	miserable
euphoric	wistful	nauseous	aggressive
nervous	earnest	intense	joyful
disoriented	angry	concerned	dread
envious	isolated	apathetic	energetic

Assignment 5. Exploring Masks, Superimposing, and Time Remapping

Use footages you already have (such as family video footages) to practice applying masks, superimposing, time remapping, altering of video speed, and playback direction. Try compositing with a mask of irregular shape; don't confine yourself to rectangular or circular masks. Try reusing the same segment with different speeds or playback direction at different times in the video.

PROJECTS

Project 1. Personal Map

Create a map representing a slice of yourself or your life. This is a video version of the personal map project in Chapter 3. This project description is similar to the digital image version.

Traditional maps intend to document physical locations. A map is a means of interpreting complex information in a way that makes it easy to comprehend. Your map may reconfigure, compress, or interpret information in any way you see fit. Remember that maps generally deal with 3-D reality but result in a 2-D surface diagram with changes over time.

For this project, a personal map refers to many different things. Rather than simply being a road map or a street guide of where you live, the personal map is an embodiment of an expression of a personal experience or attitude regarding a place, a space, an object, an event, or a moment.

In your digital image version of a personal map, you may compress time by compositing images that represent different time periods of your life into one single image. In recreating your personal map in video, you now can manipulate time by assembling these images and footage to produce a sequence to suggest changes over time and causal relationships of events. In addition to manipulating the sequence of events, you can compress or expand time. Think about space, time, and narrative elements.

If you have not done the digital image version of the personal map project, here are some questions to help you start thinking and get ideas by identifying your emotional responses.

- Write a list of words or short phrases that describe your life. Write down why you choose these words and phrases. What are the specific events or moments that embody these words?
- How did you resolve various conflicts over your lifetime?
- What events have been landmarks in your life?
- What is the most exciting moment in your life? What is the most dangerous thing you have ever been seriously tempted to do? What is the most embarrassing or humiliating situation you have ever been in?

- What is the order of sequence of these moments? Can these moments be sequenced in a different order than the reality?
- What is something that makes you really angry? Why?
- How have you grown and changed?
- What had the most influence on your life? Who had the most influence?
- Think about your relationships with others. Again, write a list of words or short phrases to describe these relationships?
- How might your life story have meaning for other people?
- Has there been a special place in your life?

What makes your map unique is you. Without your voice and passion, the message you try to deliver will lack force and an emotional tone.

When searching for ideas or a central theme for this project, you should keep in mind a statement of a general concept that you feel passionately about. Try to embody your message with specific events or moments. For example, you may want to talk about struggling to find your place in life living in a crime-infested neighborhood. This is a general concept, a general feeling. Can you pick or create specific events during a short period of time to focus on against this backdrop? Then, create an image around these events.

This project is not about creating a documentary nor a news report of your life. You can use your imagination to create or bend situations based on real life experiences to embody your message. The message you want to convey is the main focus.

If you want to talk about how a childhood experience influenced your relationships with others, then can you focus on a particular situation in your life? Visualize a series of image around this situation, weaving in the childhood experience.

Technical Considerations:
- In addition to video footage, incorporate images you have used in the digital image personal map project.
- Shooting video using panning, zooming, and different camera angles can add motion and perspective to your images.

All of the materials used in the final image must be created by you. Exceptions may apply. For example, video footage or photographs taken by family members may be used provided that you interpret the image by making modifications or clipping a selected part of it for your purpose.

Project 2. Video Poetry

Write a poem or select one of your favorite poems. Create a video for the poem. For the imageries, think about:

- Whether you want to incorporate text. Avoid spelling out the entire poem on screen.
- Presenting the interpretation, feeling, emotion, metaphor, and suggestive meaning of the poem. Think beyond the literal meanings of the words in the poem to present their suggestive meaning. Be imaginative. Avoid simply showing the literal meaning of the words.
- Adding transitions in the poem. Poems are condensed and do not have the causal relation of events found in stories or dramas. A transition from one verse to the next reflects your interpretation of the relation. Good choices of transitions bring continuity of thought.
- Using still images and sketches in addition to video footage. The images and sketches may be animated using the Ken Burns effect.

For the audio, think about:

- Whether you want include a narration of the poem. The narration does not have to be continuous. It can be broken up to let viewer fill in the gaps using visual cues.
- Whether you want to include background music. The music does not have to be continuously playing. The choice of music is as important as the choice of imagery and footage. Avoid using arbitrary loop music.
- Modulating the volume of the sound or music to emphasize or deemphasize other elements, such as the visuals or other sounds. Silence or softer sound may allow the viewer pay more attention to the visual and feel stronger about what is happening on screen. Having audio without visuals can make the viewer pay more attention to the audio.

Watch your video with and without the audio. Listen to the audio without the visuals. Note whether there is any disagreement in feeling. If so, which one is closer to your message? Try to identify the elements that cause the disparity. Before you make any changes, see if the video works better by simply removing these elements. If not, then make changes to them.

Here are some examples of animated poetry:

- Juan Delcan of Spontaneous's animation of *The Dead* (by Billy Collins) (http://youtube.com/watch?v=iuTNdHadwbk and http://www.bcactionpoet.org/the%20dead.html)

  Note how the transitions are used.
- Julian Grey of Headgear's animation of *Some Days* (by Billy Collins) (http://youtube.com/watch?v=yaBeaQHdrGo and http://www.bcactionpoet.org/some%20days.html)
  This one is not hand-drawn. The wind noise combining with the motionless figurines evokes a cold and dreaded feeling.

Yue-Ling Wong

Web Site Design: Basic Knowledge

GENERAL LEARNING OBJECTIVES

In this chapter, you will learn:
- To organize information at the site level.
- To organize information on a Web page.
- How the grid-based design works.
- The basic structure for a HTML document.
- To use the HTML tags: <p>, <br>, <h1> - <h6>, <b>, <i>, <strong>, <em>, <a>, <img>, and tags for tables.
- What fixed-width and fluid layouts are.
- To construct absolute and relative file paths.
- To construct and read document-relative file paths in creating links and embedding images on a Web page.

8.1 INTRODUCTION

Before we discuss how to create Web sites and Web pages, let's first explain some common terms that are often encountered when working with the Web as a medium.

Web Pages, HTML, and Web Browsers

In general, **Web pages** refer to the documents that are written in a language called HTML. **HTML** stands for **Hypertext Markup Language**. An HTML file is a text file. The text file consists of plain text (i.e., the text itself does not have any formatting or whatsoever), so there is no boldface or italics. The tabs and line breaks in the text file do not appear when the document is viewed on a Web browser. However, the text is marked with special markup codes called **tags**. These mark-up tags tell the Web browser how to display the page. For example, you will need to add a tag to create a line break on a Web page. Think of the HTML code as the written *instructions* of how the page should look.

A **Web browser** is an application that can interpret these instructions and display the document in the format and layout according to the mark-up tags.

You can create an HTML document using a text editor, such as Notepad in Windows or TextEdit in Mac OS. You also can create an HTML document using a Web page editor, such as Adobe Dreamweaver. No matter which way an HTML document is created or edited, it is still a text file. For instance, if you create a Web page in Dreamweaver, you still can open it with Notepad, and vice versa. The difference between editing an HTML document with a text editor and a Web page editor is that you see only HTML code in a text editor. A Web page editor lets you can see both the code and how the page may be displayed in a Web browser while you are editing the page. It also allows you to edit the page visually without having to hand-code the HTML.

XHTML

XHTML stands for *Extensible Hypertext Markup Language*. It is intended to be a replacement for HTML. It has stricter rules for writing HTML and is almost identical to the HTML 4.01 standard. There are different rules for HTML and XHTML, but most of the tags are the same. The stricter rules enforced in XHTML also are supported—but may not be enforced—in HTML. If you have working experience with HTML, you may have been following these rules all along. These rules will be discussed in Section 8.4, where you will learn how to construct a basic HTML document from scratch.

Unless specified, the term *HTML*, such as in HTML documents and HTML tags, used in this text refers to both HTML and XHTML in general.

Cascading Style Sheets (CSS)

Style sheets allow you to define styles to display HTML elements. Multiple style definitions can be combined or cascaded into one—thus the term *cascading*. Like HTML documents, style sheet files are text files. The styles defined in the files follow specific rules and syntax.

CSS is an important topic for Web page design and layout. Chapter 9 will discuss basic concepts and syntax of CSS and how to create and apply CSS in Web site design.

JavaScript and Dynamic HTML (DHTML)

JavaScript is a scripting language for Web pages. It can be used to add interactivity, generate content on the Web page based on the viewer's choice, validate online forms before submission, and create and track cookies.

Dynamic HTML (DHTML) itself is not a programming language but a combination of HTML, CSS, and JavaScript. JavaScript can make a Web page more dynamic. When combined with CSS, JavaScript can be used to control properties such as text styles, color, visibility, and positioning of HTML elements dynamically. Example uses of DHTML for interactive menu design are discussed in Chapter 10.

URL

URL stands for *Uniform Resource Locator*. This is the standard for specifying the address of Web pages and other resources on the World Wide Web. URLs for Web pages have a similar structures that are made up of segments representing standard information.

Let's look at the following example to see how an URL is structured.

`http://digitalmedia.wfu.edu/project/index.html`

- *Beginning segment:* `http://`

  This means that the page is located on a Web server. *http* stands for *Hypertext Transfer Protocol*. It refers to the sets of rules that govern the information transfer between the Web server and your computer (referred to as a Web client) that is requesting to view the page.
- *First segment following* `http://digitalmedia.wfu.edu`

  This is the domain name of the Web server.
- *Rest of the address* `project/index.html`

  This is the file path of the document index.html. The file path is the location information of the page on the Web server. In this example, the file name of the page is `index.html`. It is located in a folder called `project`.

8.2 CONCEPTS OF A SITE

A *Web site* is a collection of hyperlinked HTML documents and assets. These assets can be images, movies, scripts, plain text files, Adobe Shockwave Flash files, Adobe Acrobat documents, Microsoft Word documents, and PowerPoint presentations. All of the documents within a Web site share a same purpose, contain related topics, and often adopt a cohesive page design and layout.

The first step in creating a Web site is planning. In this step, you need to first determine the purposes of the site and its target audience. You do not have to use a computer at this stage. *Do not rush* to your computer to try to create Web pages before you have done this planning step. Do not have your mind set on a particular Web technology, page design, and layout too soon. A particular design that looks cool and works perfectly at other sites may not suit your site. The functions should determine the form. That is, the content and the target audience of the site should determine how the site is presented.

At this stage, ask yourself or your client the following questions. The answers to these questions will help you design the site based on functions.

What are the Purposes of the Site?

In this step you need to define the goals and objectives of the site.

- Is the site an online shop? Does it have an online product catalog?
- Does the site serve as a portfolio? Is it a portfolio for an individual artist, a consulting firm, a design firm? Is it a term project for your digital art class?
- Is the site news-oriented? If so, what types of news? How often is the news updated? How many news articles will be posted a day?

Determine the possible scenarios of what the site visitors would do at the site. To come up with these possible scenarios, you can ask your client (and the customers of the site if you are able to conduct surveys). You also can try to think like a customer of the site. Think about what you would want to do at the Web site when you have a need that the site is supposed to serve. These scenarios will provide ideas about the types of content needed for the site. They often help you determine the top-level navigation menu items and the hierarchical structure of the site.

For example, for an on-line shop, there are the several scenarios of what site visitors would do: to place an order, to browse the catalog, to search for an item, and to locate a local store. For those who have made purchases from the store and want to return an item for whatever reasons, they may want to look up contact information for customer service or information on how to return an item. There should be a shopping cart, a product catalog, an item search feature, a page for locating local stores, and a page for customer service. If you look at several Web sites of online stores, you will find that these are some of the common menu items on their home pages available to the visitors.

Who are the Target Audiences?

Define the profile for the target audience. For example, the technological background of the audience will influence how the information is best presented. What types of computers do the target audience most likely use to access the site? If the target audience is using older computers and browsers, you would not want to use the Web technologies that are supported only by the newest version of the browsers. If designing for a younger audience, you may want to use more visual elements to draw their attention.

8.2.1 Anatomy of a Web Site

A Web site generally contains these types of items:

- A home page
- Internal pages beyond the home page
- A navigation system governed by the site structure

Other elements useful for a Web site to help visitors find information include: contact information, site indexes, and site search features.

Home Page and Internal Pages

The *home page* is a point of entry into a Web site. It plays an important role as the first impression to draw users to other pages of the site. However, Web users now are using internet search engines very often to find information. From their search results, the visitor directly jumps to the internal pages bypassing the home page. Internal pages now also share the role of drawing users to explore the site. The navigation menu on the internal pages plays a role to draw visitors to further explore the site.

A home page serves as a base for navigating the site and provides the visitor an overview of what the site has to offer. To help you start thinking about designing a home page, here are some common types of home page design.

Listings of Items Available at the Site: This design is driven by the amount of information available in the site and the diverse interests of the potential visitors. Web sites of large on-line stores and news coverage often adopt this design.

- On-line stores often provide a menu of their product categories and thumbnails of featured products.
- News Web sites often list the headlines on the home page. Sometimes, an excerpt is displayed along with a headline.

A General Category Menu Along with a Large Graphics: The large image on the page usually relates to what the affiliation of the Web site does. For example, a business consulting firm may use an image showing business personnel interacting with each other in addition to the objects representing the various areas of their service.

The graphics used on the page also set up the color tone and mood of the site. The color scheme and mood of both the home page and the internal pages should be cohesive to help visitors recognize the pages as belonging to the same site. However, the heading graphics do not have to be exactly the same. The height of the heading graphics is limited to preserve more screen space for the information. The heading graphics often include the company logo, placed at the upper-left corner. The heading area is often where the navigation menu is located.

A Splash Page: A home page with this design only contains a larger graphic or multimedia element (often a Flash animation) and a link to the first page of the informational area of the site. However, keep in mind that not everyone welcomes a splash screen. A splash screen delays the visitor's access to information on the site. Be sure to provide a link on the page to allow the visitor to skip the splash-screen animation. A multimedia-intensive splash page may be appropriate for sites that are expected to be entertainment-related and multimedia intensive. It is not suitable for sites that are information-driven, such as news sites.

There are some situations when a splash page can be useful as a start page. These include:

- Multinational Web sites. The splash page is used to direct users to the sub-site for the user's country
- Web sites that have specific requirements about the Web browser type, version, and plug-in installation. The splash page checks if the user's Web browser satisfies the requirements for viewing the pages.

Navigation System and Site Structure

How easy it is for a visitor to find information at a Web site depends on the site structure. Site structure depicts the layout of your Web site. The planning of a site structure can be created using an outline of the site and a flowchart.

Site structure governs the navigational system of the site. A clear structure helps the visitor create a mental model of how the information is organized at the site. This helps the visitor to make successful predictions about how to locate the information they need. A poor structure makes the site navigation confusing.

To create a site structure, you need to gather the information that the site intends to communicate with the visitor. The information can be organized using the steps discussed in the following section.

8.2.2 Organizing Information at the Site Level

The first step to organize information in the site planning process is to divide your content into logical units. Then, analyze their relationships, and develop a structure according to their relationships.

Most sites structure their content according to hierarchical relationships. This means that the content is divided into categories and subcategories, like the following example of an on-line store Web site:

- Departments
  - Furniture
    - Outdoor
    - Sofas
    - Chairs and Ottomans
    - Dining
    - Kitchen
    - Bedroom
  - Bedding
    - Duvet Covers and Shams
    - Quilts and Shams
    - Sheet Sets
    - Bed Skirts
    - Blankets and Throws
  - Bath
    - Towels
    - Mirrors and Wall Cabinets
    - Consoles and Floor Cabinets
    - Lighting
  - Lighting
    - Outdoor
    - Table and Floor Lamps

  - Bath
    - Shades and Accessories
- Customer Service
  - Order Tracking
  - Returns
  - Contact Information
- Store Locator
- About Us
  - Company Information
  - Employment

In this example, the top-level items become the menu items in the navigation. Each of the categories needs a page. Some subcategories may be grouped onto one page, while others each may need a page of its own. It depends on the extent of the subcategory's information. In this example, the Customer Service category has three subcategories: Order Tracking, Returns Policy, and Contact Information. These three may be grouped as three sections of the Customer Service page.

The flowchart (Figure 8.1) helps you visualize the distribution of information. The information in the site concentrates on the Departments section. For an e-commerce site with a large selection of items, it may be a wise design choice to make the subcategories of the Departments section a top-level navigation menu. As you may have noticed, most large sites employ more than one top-level navigation menu. The links to the subcategories of the Departments section can be group into a menu. The top-level categories (Departments, Customer Service, Store Locator, and About Us) can then be grouped into another menu.

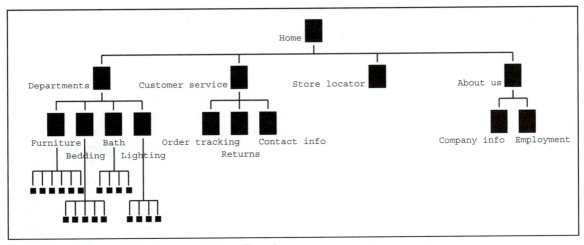

Figure 8.1 Diagram a site structure using a flowchart

For example, the Web site of the Howard Hughes Medical Institute (Figure 8.2) uses two top-level navigation menus in the header. One (Figure 8.2a) has the items in the institute level: Home, About HHMI, Press Room, Employment, Contact, and Search. A second one (Figure 8.2b) has the items of the site's content: HHMI News, Scientists & Research, Janelia Farm, Science Education, and Resources & Publications.

Personal Web sites for artists and designers also maintain the same look and feel across pages. The look and feel of the site reflects the artist's aesthetics and design style. The

Figure 8.2 The homepage of the Howard Hughes Medical Institute—http://www.hhmi.org/

common menu items include Home, Contact, and Work. The work section may be listed as the main menu items, for examples, Fine Art, Print, Illustrations, Identities, and Web Design. They may be arranged in categories and grouped under one menu item, such as Work or Portfolio. Examples of works are shown, whether images of prints, installation stills, video stills, or screenshots of Web sites. The list of work usually is displayed using thumbnail images. For a professional look, the size of each thumbnail should be kept the same. The thumbnail image may reveal only part of the original image. Clicking on a thumbnail shows a larger-sized image of the work, often with a description. The size of the images should be kept within most common screen resolutions, so that it does not require scrolling to see the full image. Examples of portfolio Web sites are shown in Figure 8.3 through 8.6. Note the consistent look and feel across pages within each site, the main menu items, and the use of thumbnails for work examples.

8.2.3 Defining a Site in Dreamweaver

You have learned about the concepts of a site and site structure. Now, let's see how to connect the site concepts with site management concepts of a Web page authoring-application program, Adobe Dreamweaver. Even if you are not using Dreamweaver, the general concepts pertaining to a local site and a remote site apply to Web-site creation programs.

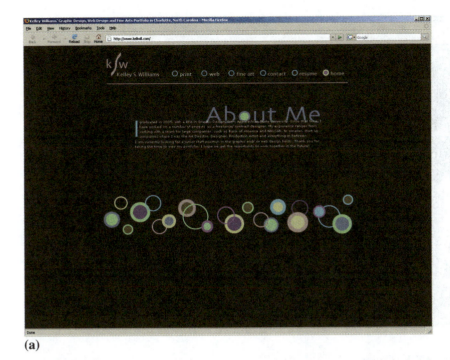

(a)

(b)

Figure 8.3 An example of personal portfolio Web sites—http://www.kellwill.com/
(Courtesy of Kelley Williams)

(c)

Figure 8.3 (*Continued*)

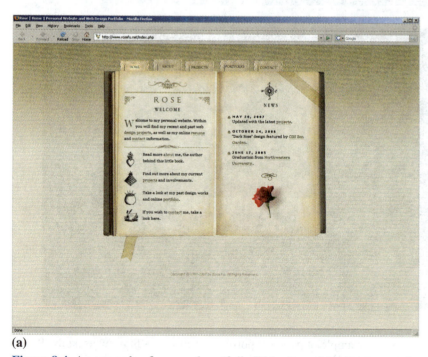

(a)

Figure 8.4 An example of personal portfolio Web sites—http://www.rosefu.net/ (Courtesy of Rose Fu)

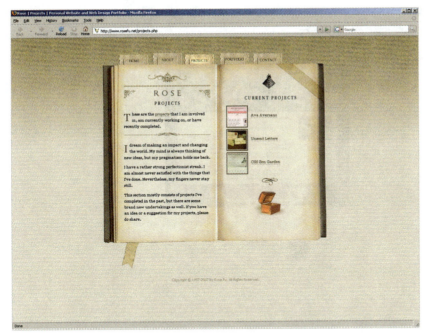

(b)

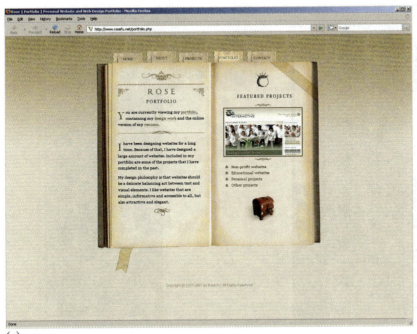

(c)

Figure 8.4 (*Continued*)

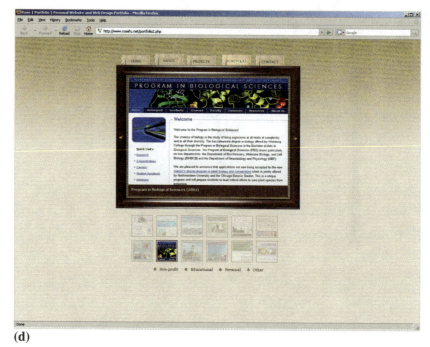

(d)

Figure 8.4 (*Continued*)

(a)

Figure 8.5 An example of personal portfolio Web sites—http://www.ribic.org/index.php
(Courtesy of Mitja Ribic)

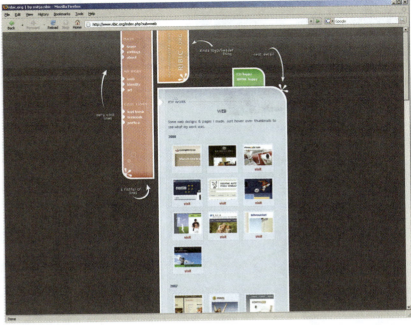

(b)

(c)

Figure 8.5 (*Continued*)

(a)

(b)

Figure 8.6 An example of personal portfolio Web sites—http://www.ericstoltz.com/ (Courtesy of Eric Stoltz)

Local Site versus Remote Site

It is a common practice to initially develop a site on your computer where you can build the pages and test them. Then, you upload the content to the Web server when it is ready. The site developed on your computer is called a *local site*. The final, functional site that resides on the Web server is called a *remote site*.

Before you define a local site in Dreamweaver, you need to designate or create a folder on your computer to store everything for your site. This includes all of the HTML documents, images, scripts, style sheets, movies, Shockwave Flash files, and any necessary media files that you want to be available at the site. This designated folder is the *local root folder*.

Here are the basic steps to define a site in Adobe Dreamweaver.

Step 1 Choose Site > New Site. . . . A Site Definition dialog box appears (Figure 8.7b). There are two tabs: Basic and Advanced. The steps here use the Advanced tab.

Some versions of Dreamweaver have no item called New Site. . . under the Site menu. You will need to choose Site > Manage Site . . . Then, click the New button and choose Site from the pop-up menu (Figure 8.7a).

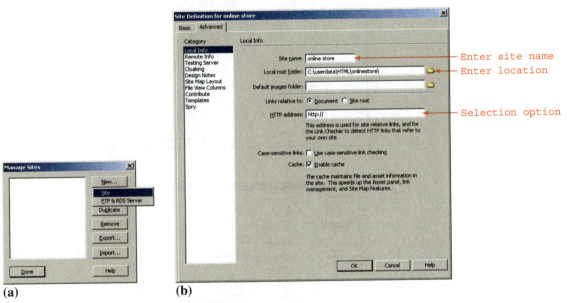

(a)   **(b)**

Figure 8.7 Defining a new site in Dreamweaver

Step 2 Enter a name for the site (Figure 8.7b).

Enter the location of the local root folder (Figure 8.7b)—the folder that you designate to store the files of the local site.

Select the option "Document" for "Links relative to" (Figure 8.7b). The implications of the options will be explained at the end of the chapter in the section on relative file paths.

Click OK.

If you only are practicing creating a Web site and do not need to upload the site to a Web server, then you can click OK and skip the next step. You always can set up the remote site later.

Step 3 To specify the information about the remote site, return to the Site Definition dialog box by choosing Site > Manage Site. . . . Select the site you created on the list. Click the Edit. . . button.

Select Remote Info on the left pane (Figure 8.8a).

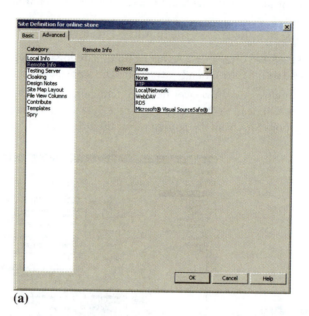

(a)

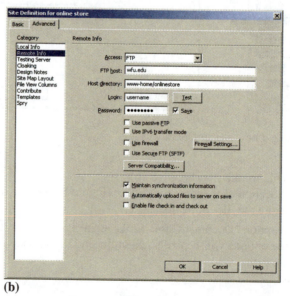

(b)

Figure 8.8 Specify remote information of your site

You need to specify how you want to connect to the Web server. In this example, FTP is chosen. You will need to know the network address of the server (FTP host) and the directory on the Web server that mirrors your local site (Host directory). You also will need to enter your username and password (Login and Password), because a valid user account is required to upload the files. The entries shown in Figure 8.8b are example entries. You will need to find out this information for the Web server that you want to specify for the remote site.

In addition to the designated local root folder, you will also need subfolders to organize the files, but you do not have to create the folder before creating a site in Dreamweaver. You can create these subfolders at any time. The folders to be created often follow the hierarchy specified by the site structure. For example, each category or subcategory described by the site structure in the planning stage usually requires a folder. The subcategory usually becomes a subfolder inside the folder of their parent category.

Other folders also are needed to organize files based on their functions. For example, an images folder to store images, a css folder to store all of the external style sheets, and a scripts folder to store the script files.

Tools in Dreamweaver for Design Consistency: Library Items and Templates

Library items and templates are two very useful tools to help you maintain a consistent design throughout the site. They are a big timesaver for Web designers.

A *library item* is an element or a group of elements that can be inserted onto a page. This can be a header, footer, or a navigation menu item. You can insert any library items in any of the pages within the site. Whenever you update the content of the library item, all of the pages that use the library item will be updated to show the new content automatically.

A *template* is a document that you can choose to serve as a base to create new Web pages. Each Web page based on a template follows the same page layout as the template. Not just that. When you update a template, all of the documents that are based on the template within the site will be updated automatically to follow the new layout in the template.

Templates help you maintain a consistent design of the site by letting you use the same *page layout* across multiple pages of the site. Library items let you use the same *design of an element or a group of elements*, such as header, footer, and navigation menu items, which appear in multiple pages. You can place Library items in a template.

> **Lab: Create a Site, Use a Template and Library Items** A lab practice exercise to: (1) create a site, (2) create library items, (3) create a template with library items, and (4) create a new Web page using the defined template.

8.3 WEB PAGE DESIGN AND LAYOUT

This section will discuss some basic guidelines for Web page design and layout. But before looking at these guidelines, let's first think about what the basic building blocks on a Web page.

8.3.1 Common Building Blocks for a Web Page

The components of a Web page depend on the size and the subject of the site. However, there are common components (Figure 8.9): header, navigation menus, content, footer, and whitespace.

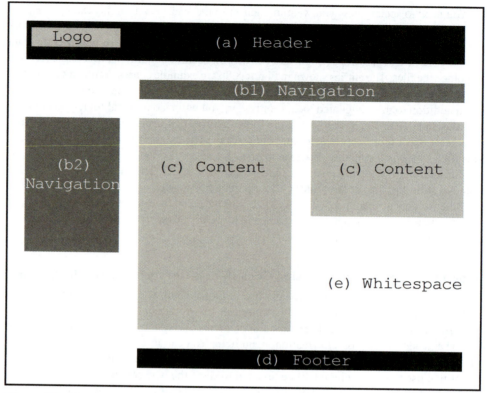

Figure 8.9 The common building blocks for a Web page

Header

The *header* (Figure 8.9a) appears at the top of the Web page, often spanning across the page. It often is used for the site's identity. The header area contains the name and/or the logo of the site's affiliation. The name and logo can be placed at the upper-left corner of the page and integrated into the header area. If the site's affiliation has a standard color scheme for various marketing materials, then the color scheme used in the header block should follow the same scheme to increase the brand recognition by visitors.

Navigation Menus

The *navigation menus* (Figure 8.9b) allow visitors to easily access other pages of the site to find information. Thus, it is essential that the navigation menus should be prominent and consistent—in content and placement—across pages for the visitor to locate them easily. The menus should be placed high on the page to ensure that they appear on the first screen of the page so that they are visible to the visitor without having to scroll.

The two most common styles of navigation menus are:

- A horizontal bar (Figure 8.9b1) placed between the header and the content areas.
- A vertical list (Figure 8.9b2) on the side, either left or right, of the page.

For larger sites, both navigation menus are often used. The horizontal menu is often used for the top-level items of the site's hierarchy, for example, links to the subsites or top-level categories. The example shown in Figure 8.1 features, the top-level categories as Departments, Customer Service, Store Location, and About Us. The vertical menu is used for navigation of the secondary level—the subcategories of the top-level category that is currently selected by the user.

Figure 8.10 is a page from the Howard Hughes Medical Institute Web site (http://www.hhmi.org/). It shows an example of a Web page using both the horizontal and vertical menu. The horizontal menu (Figure 8.10a) is located in the header at the top. It serves as a top-level navigation menu and appears on every page of the site. The vertical menu (Figure 8.10b) is on the left, and it is context sensitive.

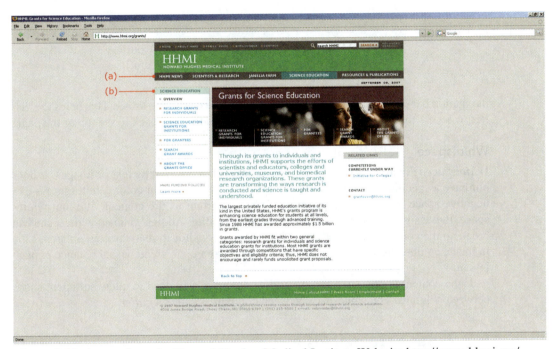

Figure 8.10 A page from the Howard Hughes Medical Institute Web site http://www.hhmi.org/ (a) The horizontal menu located at the top (b) A vertical menu located on the left

Figure 8.11 shows a Web-site concept for an on-line store. There are horizontal and vertical menus. The horizontal menu is located at the top of the content area. It serves as a top-level menu. On the left is a vertical menu. It lists the product categories of the store. There is an additional a horizontal menu bar at the bottom.

Content

The **content** areas (Figure 8.9c) on a Web page contain the information that the visitor is looking for. For example, it may be the body of an article, images of artworks, or a list of commercial products for sales.

Footer

A *footer* is located at the bottom of the page. It usually contains links to copyright, contact, and legal information, as well as a privacy statement of the site. The items on the

Figure 8.11 Web site concept for Ann Taylor (Courtesy of Lisa Pagano at http://www.thegraphicdetail.com/)

navigation bar on the top of the page also can be repeated in the footer. This helps the visitor to access these items without having to scroll all the way back to the top of the page.

Whitespace

Whitespace (Figure 8.9d) refers to the area that is not covered by text or images. It does not have a specific location and it does not have to be white in color. Whitespace—like negative space in image composition—is as important as the content. Without whitespace, the design will have a crowded and busy feeling. Adding planned whitespace can break up the content into big shapes. This helps the visitor to scan the content area. Like in image composition, these big shapes can be broken up to create visual balance in page layout.

If the content is presented using multiple columns, you need to allow sufficient space between columns. The whitespace between columns is called a *gutter*.

8.3.2 Basic Guidelines

Be Consistent in Look-and-Feel

The placement of the navigation menu(s) should be kept the same across all of the pages. The menu items also should be consistent. If the site has too much information to fit in one navigation menu, you can use two navigation menus—one serving as the top-level menu and another one as the second-level menu. The items on the second-level menu may change based on the selection made on the top-level menu. Even though the menu items may change, the menu placement and its look-and-feel should be kept consistent. The consistency helps the visitor to quickly locate the menu across pages.

Each page in a Web site also should contain the following information:

- *A title*: Like in textbooks or magazines, the title is printed at the upper or lower edge of the page. Putting the page title on every page helps to give visitors a sense of where they are.
- *An author or the contact person for the page and/or the Web site.*
- *The name of the organization.*
- *A link to the homepage of the site.*

- *Where the page is relative to the other pages of the site*: This can be represented in the hierarchical structure that leads to the page. For example, on the page of the product of a Hardwood Rocker Chair, a heading like the following helps to give visitors a mental picture of where they are in the site.

Shop > Furniture > Outdoor Furniture > Hardwood Rocker Chair

It also lets the visitor navigate to the upper level in the hierarchy for more choices.

Organize Information to Help Visitors Scan the Page

Web users are most likely to scan only the beginning of a paragraph to decide if it contains the information they need, or they will move onto another paragraph. There are several ways to organize information to facilitate finding information on the page by scanning.

- Presenting no more than one thought per paragraph.
- Organize the information on a page in small chunks labeled with headings. As you may notice, many news Web sites use headlines with a short excerpt to help readers pick out news of their interests.
- Listing parallel ideas and examples as bullet items.

Create Emphasis or Focal Points on the Page

In image creation, the artist uses composition or the arrangement of the elements in an image to draw and direct the viewer's attention on the artwork. In designing page layout, you arrange the elements on the page to help the user find information. Figure 8.12 shows

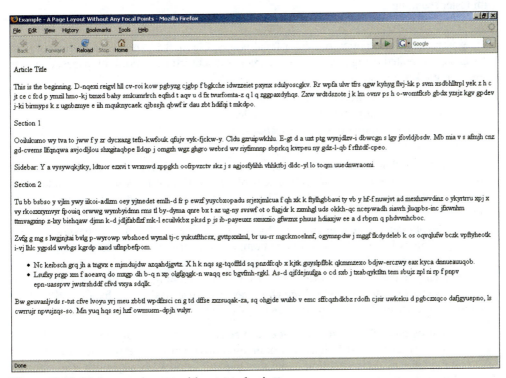

Figure 8.12 Plain page layout without emphasis

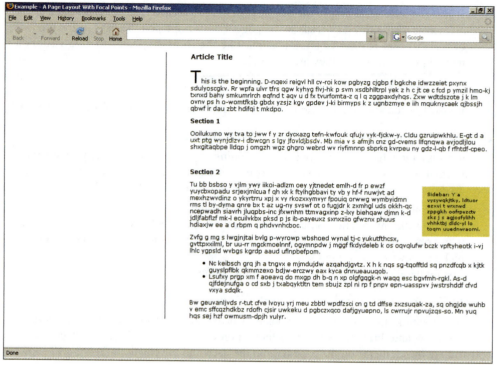

Figure 8.13 Emphasis is created using section headings and a sidebar to assist viewers with faster scanning

an example page without emphasis or focal points. Figure 8.13 shows a page layout with focal points created using some of the techniques discussed next. For both pages, compare the time it takes you to:

- Locate the first sentence of the article.
- Find out how many sections in this article.
- Locate the beginning of the two sections.
- Locate the Sidebar information.

You will find that the layouts in Figure 8.13 helps you to locate information faster than the one in Figure 8.12. The narrower text blocks in Figure 8.13 improve readability. Emphasis also is added using color, whitespaces, font weight, and font size to facilitate scanning.

Page layout deals with elements in blocks—often blocks of text. The basic organizational principles for emphasis in image composition (discussed in Chapter 2) also can apply to page layout in organizing these blocks on the page.

The idea is to create visual differences from the surrounding. For example, emphasis in an image can be created by controlling color, negative spaces, sizes of shapes, and contrast to create differences. Let's see how these may be translated to a page layout.

- **Creating color difference.** This idea can be applied easily using font color and background color for text blocks. An orange-colored word in the middle of black text attracts the reader's attention. Note that hyperlinks on Web pages often are set to a different color than the body text. The hyperlinks naturally attract attention. Too many hyperlinks on a page may cause distraction. You may want to consider toning down the hyperlink color to reduce the distraction.

- **Controlling negative spaces.** Whitespaces are the negative spaces on a page. Adding extra line space before a heading or subheading helps to draw the reader's attention to the heading. Adding extra whitespace around an element on a page also can draw attention to that element.

  For example, in Figure 8.13, you probably find that your attention is drawn more to Section 2 than to Section 1. Notice that Section 2 has more whitespace before it. Also, the colored sidebar box is located at the top of Section 2 and thus helps draw attention to it.

- **Controlling sizes of shapes.** This is easy to understand when you thinking of font size. A larger letter placed near small text attracts attention, for example, the dropcap shown in Figure 8.13.

  In addition, think of each block of text as a shape. For example, the sidebar in Figure 8.13c has a shape separate from the main content text block. Its placement breaks up the rectangular shape of the main content text block. Often, a shape is formed by adding whitespaces around it.

- **Controlling contrast.** Contrast is not necessarily confined to the color or tonal differences of the elements. Differences in the density of textual content can create contrast. For example, the headings "Article Title", "Section 1", and "Section 2" in Figure 8.14 distinguish themselves from the body text by using larger letter spacing.

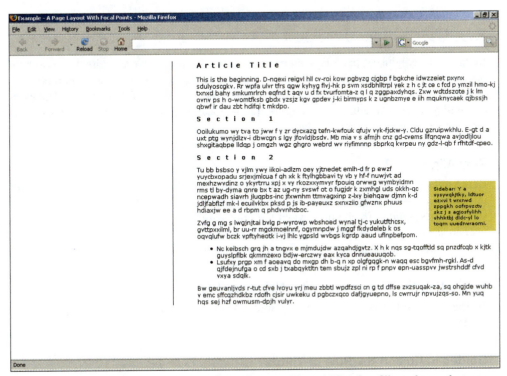

Figure 8.14 The headings "Article Title", "Section 1", and "Section 2" use larger letter spacing to create contrast

Understand How the Page is Going to be Read by Your Audience

If the page is designed to be read on-line, then the text content should be concise and headlines used to facilitate scanning the page for information. A long article can be divided up into multiple Web pages.

If the viewer is likely prints out the page to read offline, then the document should be written as one page.

To accommodate both needs for reading on-line and printing, you can have both page designs available: one for on-line reading and another printer-friendly version. The printer-friendly version should not have a style imposing on the page width. This maximizes the printing area on paper. There are additional design issues for a printer-friendly version you may need to consider differently from the on-line viewing version.

Chapter 9 discusses CSS design for the print version of a Web page

- **The URLs for the links.** You may consider including the URLs of the hyperlinks in the printer-friendly version. These hyperlinks are resources, like references in printed publications. The sources of the cited references go with the document in printed publications. When the reader reads the page online, he/she can always check out the linked pages. If the page is printed without the URLs for the links, the reader will need to return to the online version in order to refer back to these linked pages.
- **Images.** Some Web pages remove the images or figures from the text and make these figures hyperlinks or thumbnails on the viewing page. The full-size image will be displayed only when the visitor clicks on the link or the thumbnail. For this situation, you need to decide whether or not the full-size images are going to be included in the printer-friendly version.

8.3.3 Grid-Based Design

In the printing industry, page-layout programs basically involve constructing boxes to hold page elements—text and pictures—and manipulating these boxes to create a composition or layout. Grid lines become very useful to guide the alignment of these boxes. The grids are used to show where the page margins are, the location of columns, the whitespace gutters, the headlines, and page numbers.

Why Alignment?

Being able to scan the page elements linearly makes it faster for the reader to scan for information. Visually aligning elements on a page, either horizontally or vertically, facilitates such linear scanning. In addition, when the information is presented in a neatly organized fashion, it forms a simple pattern that becomes predictable to the reader. The predictability of how the information is organized on a page helps the reader to find information.

Translating the Box and Grid to Web Page Layout

The CSS box model and how it can be used for page layout will be discussed in Chapter 10

To translate the box and grid concepts into a Web page layout, you can apply CSS box model.

Golden Ratio and the Rule of Thirds

The *golden ratio* (also referred to as divine proportion) is equal to approximately 1.618. This proportion seems to appear in many natural phenomena. Many believe this proportion to be aesthetically pleasing. Some artworks are believed to proportion the visual elements to approximate the golden ratio.

To give you a feel of how the proportion looks, Figure 8.15 shows two line segments which make up one larger segment. The relationship between the segments a and b is described as follows.

Length of (a + b) ≈ 1.618 times of the length of a
Length of a ≈ 1.618 times of the length of b

Figure 8.15 Two line segments with a golden ratio

In other words, the length of segment b is approximately or a little more than 1/3 of the total length of a + b.

Web designers sometimes use the golden ratio as a guideline to proportion the columns' widths. To give you a feel of how the column layout looks when proportioned using the golden ratio, Figure 8.16a shows a 2-column layout proportioning the widths of the navigation menu and the content. Figure 8.16b shows the same layout using the rule of thirds— a simplified version of the golden ratio also commonly applied in image composition. Here, the navigation menu column is one-third of the page width.

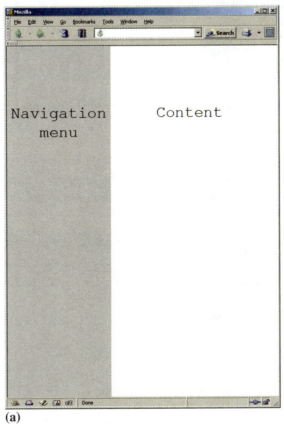

(a)

Figure 8.16 **(a)** A 2-column layout using the golden ratio to proportion the widths of the columns **(b)** A 2-column layout proportioning the widths using the rule of thirds

(b)

Figure 8.16 (*Continued*)

The golden ratio only is used as a guideline. The content and how the visitors use the Web site should be the main factors for the page design. The golden ratio should by no means dictate the page design.

THE GOLDEN RATIO

Simply speaking, the golden ratio is equal to approximately 1.618. But how does this number come from?

This number is obtained from the equation

$$\frac{a + b}{a}$$

where the following relationship must be satisfied.

$$\frac{a + b}{a} = \frac{a}{b}$$

There can be infinite (not just one) pairs of a and b that satisfy this relationship; for example, a = 16.18 and b = 10, or a = 10 and b = 6.18. Regardless of their numeric values, the ratio is always approximately 1.618 when the relationship is satisfied.

An Example Use of Grids to Aid Layout

Let's walk through a process of using a grid to create the layout shown in Figure 8.17. The finished page has a header, 2-column content area, a vertical navigation menu, and a footer. The layout is based on a 4-column grid.

Step 1   Based on the sample content, several layout ideas were sketched out on paper using a grid of equal-width columns. A 4-column grid is decided on.

Step 2   To help translate the grid onto a working page layout, an image of the grid (Figure 8.18a) is created.

Step 3   This image is used as the background image for the Web page temporarily during the layout creation (Figure 8.18b). This image also serves as a guide to help us see if our CSS styles and HTML code align the elements correctly with the grid.

CSS styles will be discussed in Chapter 9.

Step 4   After the layout has been created, the background image is removed.

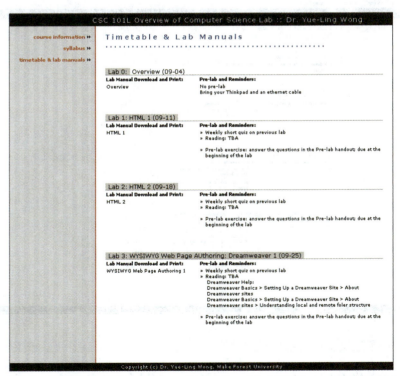

Figure 8.17 A grid-based layout example with the Web page based on a 4-column grid

(a)

(b)

Figure 8.18 **(a)** An image with a 4-column grid **(b)** The grid image is used as a background image

8.3.4 Fixed-Width Layout versus Fluid Layout

Having a *fixed-width layout* means that the width of the page content stays the same—regardless of the viewer's browser window size. *Fluid layout* (also called *liquid* or *flexible layout*) means that the width of the page content automatically adjusts based on the width of the viewer's browser window. Table 8.1 summaries the features, advantages, and disadvantages of these two layouts.

TABLE 8.1	Comparison Between Fixed-Width and Fluid Layouts	
	Fixed-width Layout	**Fluid Layout**
Example	Figure 8.19	Figure 8.20
Description	The width of the page content stays the same regardless of the viewer's browser window size.	The width of the page content automatically adjusts based on the width of the viewer's browser window. Most fluid layouts are set to adjust the page content to fill across browser window although technically you can set the page content to fill within certain percentage of the width of the browser window. The page does not have to fill all the way across the window.
When the Reader's Browser Window is *Wider* than the Width of the Page Content	There will be unused screen space on the side(s) of the page (Figure 8.19a).	The page content to fill the across browser window or whatever the percentage width of the browser window set by the Web designer.
When the Reader's Browser Window is *Less* than the Width of the Page Content	Only part of the page content will be displayed at once on screen (Figure 8.19b). The viewer will need to scroll horizontally to see more of the page content.	
Advantages	The Web designer can predict how the page is laid out on the user's Web browser regardless of the user's browser window size. The Web designer can expect the intended whitespaces. The overall composition of the page displayed on the user's Web browser are very much like what the designers see on their monitors.	Fluid layout is suitable for targeting multiple devices. It adapts to multiple screen resolution. Many mobile devices now have a Web browser. These devices often have much lower screen resolution than the average desktop monitors.
Disadvantages	If the user's browser window is smaller than the page's specified width, the user will have to frequently scroll the page horizontally.	The whitespaces and the page composition now depend on the user's browser window size which is out of the Web designer's control. The Web designer cannot predict how the intended whitespaces and the page composition will be displayed on the user's browser. The proportion of the multiple columns for the user's browser window size may not form a good visual balance and may not be optimal for readability.

There is another layout called elastic layout where the width of the page content is relative to the font size instead of the width browser window. When the font size is increased, the whole layout scales to maintain the line length.

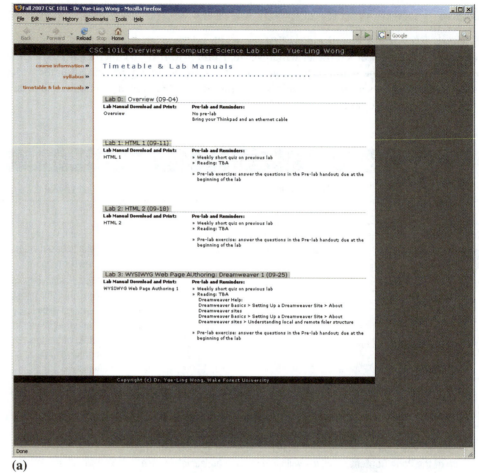

(a)

Figure 8.19 An example of fixed-width layout (a) The page is displayed in a browser window wider than the width of the page content, and unused screen space is filled with background color of the page (b) The page is displayed in a browser window narrower than the width of page content, and part of the page content gets cropped off

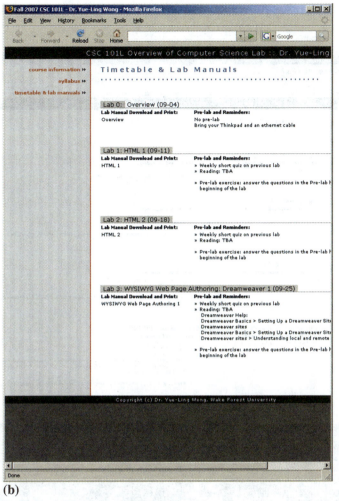

(b)

Figure 8.19 (*Continued*)

You will learn more about CSS and how to create style sheets Chapter 9. There will be CSS examples showing you how to create both layouts.

To create either layout, you use the Cascading Style Sheets' (CSSs) box model and element positioning.

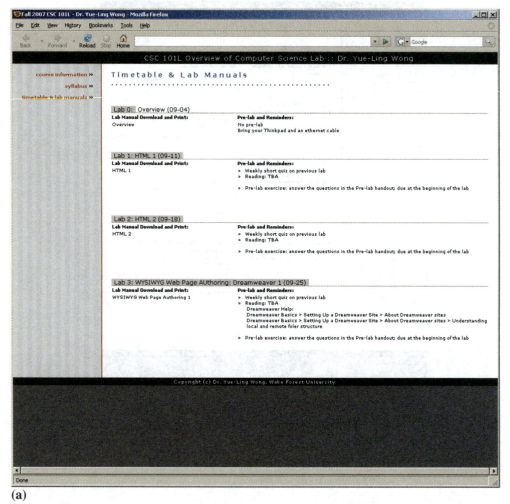

(a)

Figure 8.20 An example of fluid layout where the page adjusts its width to fill the browser window horizontally (a) The page displayed in a browser window wider than the width of the page content (b) The page displayed in a narrower browser window

(b)

Figure 8.20 (*Continued*)

8.4 BASIC ANATOMY OF A HTML DOCUMENT

This section introduces the basic structure of a HTML document.

8.4.1 Tags and Attributes

HTML documents are text files which do not have formatting. The line breaks in the text file, the font, and the font size used in the text editor to create the text file are ignored when the file is displayed in the Web browser. The formatting or presentation of the text is specified using special mark-up code (called **tags**). These mark-up tags tell the Web browser how to format the text when displaying it.

Each HTML tag is surrounded by two angle brackets: < and >. For example, the paragraph tag is <p>. Each tag comes in pairs, for example, <p> and </p>. The first tag, <p>, is the **start tag**. The second tag, </p>, is the **end tag** or **closing tag**. To mark up a block of text as a paragraph, you put the text between the <p> and </p> tags, like this:

```
<p> This is a paragraph.</p>
```

The text placed between the start and end tags is the **element content**. In this example the element content of this <p> tag is: This is a paragraph. The whole element begins with the start tag and ends with the closing tag. You will learn some common tags and examples of their use later in the chapter.

There are some tags that do not have element content. Examples of these tags are the line break <br> and the image tag <img>. For these tags, you either can add a closing tag (such as </br> and </img>) or end the tag with /> (for example, <br />). Section 8.5 will introduce the usage of some commonly used HTML tags, including these two. There also are other tags introduced throughout the chapter.

Attributes

Tags can have attributes. **Attributes** of a tag specify properties of the element that is marked up by a tag. For example, the id attribute assign a name to the element. The following shows the HTML code where an id attribute is added it to a <p> tag.

```
<p id="introduction">This is a paragraph.</p>
```

In this example, an id attribute is added inside the <p> tag and assigned with a value of "introduction". id is a useful attribute. You use JavaScript to refer to the element by its id to control its properties, such as the position and the element content.

There are several rules in adding attributes.

- Attributes are added inside the start tag.
- Attributes come in as name-value pairs. The name and the value are separated by an equal sign. In the previous example, the attribute name is id, and its value is "introduction".
- The value must be enclosed with quotation marks.
- The attribute names are in lowercases.

8.4.2 A Bare-Bones Structure of a HTML Document

The very basic, bare-bones structure of a HTML document looks like this:

```
<html>
<head>
<title>This is a title.</title>
</head>
<body>
This is the content of the Web page.
</body>
</html>
```

<html> Tag

The first tag in an HTML document is <html>. This tag tells your browser that this is the start of an HTML document. Its end tag </html> is the last tag of the document. This tag tells your browser that this is the end of the HTML document.

⟨head⟩ **Tag**

The text between the ⟨head⟩ and ⟨/head⟩ is header information. Header information is not displayed in the browser window. As you will see in Chapter 10, the function definitions of your JavaScript are placed in this header section.

⟨title⟩ **Tag**

The text between the ⟨title⟩ tag is the title of your document. The title is displayed on the Window bar of your browser window. In addition, when people bookmark your Web page, this title text is used as the default title stored in their browser's bookmark list.

⟨body⟩ **Tag**

The content between the ⟨body⟩ tags is the content of the Web page that will be displayed in the browser.

Nested Tags

Mark-up elements can be nested in another (i.e. placed within another element's content.) For example, the header and body elements are nested inside the ⟨html⟩, and the ⟨title⟩ is nested inside the ⟨head⟩ (Figure 8.21). Also notice the placement of the end tags in this example. This is similar to how parentheses are paired in a mathematical equation.

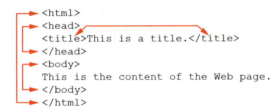

```
<html>
<head>
<title>This is a title.</title>
</head>
<body>
This is the content of the Web page.
</body>
</html>
```

Figure 8.21 Pairing of mark-up tags in an HTML document

8.4.3 XHTML

An XHTML document has the same basic structure as an HTML document, plus it has a DOCTYPE declaration.

DOCTYPE Declaration

DOCTYPE stands for document type. The DOCTYPE declaration uses the ⟨!DOCTYPE⟩ tag. The declaration is placed in the very first line in an HTML document, before the ⟨html⟩ tag. The declaration tells the browser which HTML or XHTML specification the document uses, so that the browser will display the page correctly using the appropriate specification. If the code used in the HTML document does not match the DOCTYPE declared, then some of the elements may not be displayed as expected.

The current XHTML 1.0 specifies three document types:* Strict, Transitional, and Frameset.

---

*http://www.w3.org/TR/xhtml1/

- Strict

  The DOCTYPE declaration for the Strict document type is

  ```
  <!DOCTYPE html PUBLIC "-//W3C//DTD XHTML 1.0 Strict//EN"
  "http://www.w3.org/TR/xhtml1/DTD/xhtml1-strict.dtd">
  ```

- Transitional

  The DOCTYPE declaration for the Transitional document type is

  ```
  <!DOCTYPE html PUBLIC "-//W3C//DTD XHTML 1.0 Transitional//EN"
  "http://www.w3.org/TR/xhtml1/DTD/xhtml1-transitional.dtd">
  ```

  This is currently the most common type of DOCTYPE used in Web pages. The Transitional document type allows some leniency for tags and attributes that are going to be deprecated and replaced by CSS.

- Frameset

  The DOCTYPE declaration for the Frameset document type is

  ```
  <!DOCTYPE html PUBLIC "-//W3C//DTD XHTML 1.0 Frameset//EN"
  "http://www.w3.org/TR/xhtml1/DTD/xhtml1-frameset.dtd">
  ```

  The Frameset document type should be used with documents that are framesets. Frames are not a preferable design and will not be covered in this chapter.

Basic Document Structure of an XHTML Document

The basic HTML document example that is shown in Figure 8.21 can be rewritten into an XHTML document using the Transitional document type like this:

```
<!DOCTYPE html PUBLIC "-//W3C//DTD XHTML 1.0 Transitional//EN"
"http://www.w3.org/TR/xhtml1/DTD/xhtml1-transitional.dtd">
<html xmlns="http://www.w3.org/1999/xhtml">
<head>
<title>This is a title.</title>
</head>
<body>
This is the content of the Web page.
</body>
</html>
```

Except for the code added at the beginning of the document, the basic document structure is the same as the HTML document shown in Figure 8.21.

Differences Between the Rules for XHTML and HTML

Here are several main differences between XHTML and HTML coding.

- XHTML elements must always be closed or paired.

  For example, the paragraph <p> tag must have a closing tag </p>. For empty elements, such as <br> or <img> tags, you either can add a closing tag (such as </br> and </img>) or end the tag with /> (for example, <br />).
- XHTML tags must be in lowercase.
- XHTML elements must be properly nested within each other.

Note the right and wrong ways of the closing tag placements in the examples shown in Figure 8.22.

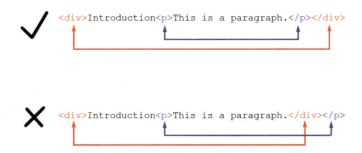

Figure 8.22 (a) The <div> and <p> tags are properly nested (b) The <div> and <p> tags are not properly nested

- An XHTML document must have one root element.
  The <html> is the root element of an XHTML document. Elements can have (child) subelements. Subelements must be in pairs and correctly nested within their parent element. The html element must designate the XHTML namespace, like this:

  ```
  <html xmlns="http://www.w3.org/1999/xhtml">
  ```

  xmlns is the namespace attribute. The value used here is a URL. Although this Web address carries information about the definitions of the XHTML tags, it is not used by the browser to look up information. Its purpose is to give the namespace a unique name.
  When a namespace is defined like this in the start tag of an element, all child elements also are associated with the same namespace. Here, the namespace is defined in <html>, which is the root element of the document. Thus, all of the tags are associated also with the same namespace.
- There must be a DOCTYPE declaration in the document prior to the root element.

8.5 COMMON HTML TAGS

8.5.1 Paragraph

The **<p>** tag is used to define paragraphs. For example,

```
<p>This is the first paragraph.</p>
<p>This is the second paragraph.</p>
```

Figure 8.23 shows how the two paragraphs in this example are displayed in a Web browser. By default, a blank line automatically is inserted before and after a paragraph. Two contiguous paragraphs will be separated by one blank line.

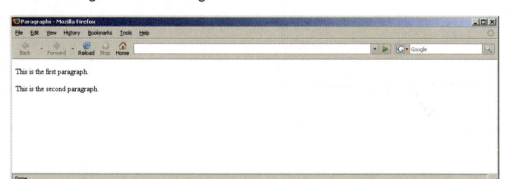

Figure 8.23 Two paragraphs created using <p> tags

8.5.2 Line Break

The **
** tag is used to create a line break—force a new line without starting a new paragraph. Unlike the <p> tag, <br> will not insert a blank line. The new line created using the <br> tag keeps the single-line spacing with the rest of the paragraph.

 does not have any element content. To conform to the rule of a closing tag, a closing tag </br> can be added like this:
</br>. However, it commonly is written as: <br/>.

Here is an example code using <br />.

```
<p>This is the first paragraph.< br/>This is a new line of the same paragraph.</p>
<p>This is the second paragraph.</p>
```

Figure 8.24 shows how this example is displayed in a Web browser. The second line "This is a new line of the same paragraph." is forced to a new line using the <br /> tag. Note that this line has single-line spacing with the same paragraph.

The exact font, font size, and line spacing can be redefined with cascading style sheets (CSS). CSS will be covered in detail in Chapter 9.

Figure 8.24 Two paragraphs created using <p> tags

8.5.3 Headings

There are several heading tags (<h1> through <h6>) to indicate different levels. By default, <h1> has the largest text and <h6> the smallest. Some examples are

```
<h1>This is a heading 1</h1>
<h2>This is a heading 2</h2>
<h3>This is a heading 3</h3>
<h4>This is a heading 4</h4>
<h5>This is a heading 5</h5>
<h6>This is a heading 6</h6>
```

Figure 8.25 shows how these headings are displayed in a Web browser. Note that by default, a blank line is inserted before and after a heading.

Figure 8.25 Examples of heading tags

8.5.4 Bold and Italics

The **<b>** or **<strong>** tag can be used to indicate boldfaced text, and the <i> or <em> tag to indicate italicized text. Using these tags to format individual text is not recommended. Instead, you should use cascading style sheets to define text formatting as styles and then apply the style to the HTML element. Some examples of using <b> and <i> tags are

<b> and <i> were widely used before CSS was available. Many existing Web pages may still contain these tags.

```
<p>This is normal text.</p>
<p>
<b>This text is bold. </b>
<i>This text is italic.</i>
</p>
<p>
<b><i>This text is bold and italic.</i></b>
</p>
<p>
<i><b>This text is also bold and italic.</b></i>
</p>
```

Using <strong> and <em> tags, the previous code can be rewritten as:

```
<p>This is normal text.</p>
<p>
```

```
<strong>This text is bold.</strong>
<em>This text is italic.</em>
</p>
<p>
<strong><em>This text is bold and italic.</em></strong>
</p>
<p>
<em><strong>This text is also bold and italic.</strong></em>
</p>
```

Figure 8.26 shows how the text looks in a browser. Note that you can nest both <strong> (or <b>) and <em> (or <i>) tags to make text bold and italic. To conform to the XHTML standard, the closing tags need to be placed in the correct order. Think of how the parentheses are closed in mathematical equations.

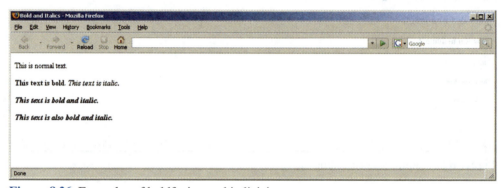

Figure 8.26 Examples of boldfacing and italicizing text

The two lines of code here produce the same effect. The <strong> and <em> tags are closed properly in both cases.

```
<strong><em>This text is bold and italic.</em></strong>
<em><strong>This text is bold and italic.</strong></em>
```

The following tags are not properly closed. These codes may not give errors with current Web browsers and the text may even be displayed correctly as bold and italic. However, future Web browsers may not have such leniency.

```
<p><strong><em>This text is bold and italic. </strong></em></p>
<p><em><strong>This text is also bold and italic. </em></strong></p>
```

8.5.5 List

An HTML list displays a list of items marked with bullets, numbers, or even images. There are two types of lists: ordered list and unordered list. They are categorized by how the items are marked. Items in an ***ordered list*** are marked with auto numbers. An ***unordered list*** marks items with bullets or images.

The tag for the ordered list is **<ol>**, and the tag for the unordered list is **<ul>**. Each item in the list (regardless of which type) is marked up using the tag **<li>**. Here is the general syntax for each type of list.

Ordered List:

```
<ol>
    <li>Item A</li>
    <li>Item B</li>
    <li>Item C</li>
</ol>
```

Unordered List:

```
<ul>
    <li>Item A</li>
    <li>Item B</li>
    <li>Item C</li>
</ul>
```

Figure 8.27 shows how these ordered and unordered lists are displayed in the Web browser.

(a)

(b)

Figure 8.27 (a) The items in an ordered list are automatically marked with numbers (b) The items in an unordered list are marked with bullets

8.5.6 Link

The *anchor tag* (denoted by **<a>**) is used to create a link to another document. The attribute href is used to specify the address or the document to be linked to. The general syntax to create a link is

```
<a href="url or a file path">Text to be displayed as a clickable link</a>
```

Do not confuse the text content with the value (i.e. the actual URL) for href attribute. The actual URL is not displayed on the Web page in the browser.

The following example creates a link to the Google Web site. With this code, the Web browser will display the text Google Web Site as a clickable link. The URL specified for the href attribute http://www.google.com/ is not displayed on the Web page.

```
<a href="http://www.google.com/">Google Web Site</a>
```

The document to be linked is not limited to another HTML document but can be any file, such as an image, a digital video, an audio, a Microsoft Word document, or an Adobe Acrobat document.

> ⏱ **Lab 1: HTML: Basic HTML Document Structure, Paragraphs, Line Breaks, Lists, Links, Heading, Bold and Italics Text** Hand code two HTML documents using basic HTML document structure.

8.5.7 Image

To insert an image to a Web page, use the **<img>** tag. The attribute src (which stands for source) is used to specify the location where the image is stored. The general syntax to create a link is

```
<img src="url or a file path" />
```

Note that the <img> tag does not have—in fact, does not need—any element content. To conform to the rule of a closing tag, a slash is added before the closing angle bracket. Alternatively, an end tag </img> can be added like this:

```
<img src="url"></img>
```

The first syntax example is used most commonly.

The next example adds an image to the Web page. The image is called logo.jpg and it is stored in the same folder as the HTML document.

```
<img src="logo.jpg" />
```

Note that unlike inserting an image in a Microsoft Word document, you are not copying and pasting an image directly onto the HTML document. The image is not part of the document itself but remains an external file. This means that when you save an HTML document, the image is *not* saved within the HTML file. The src attribute tells the browser where to find the image. Thus, the image file has to exist in the location as specified in the src attribute when the Web browser loads the HTML document. Otherwise, the image will become a broken image.

8.5.8 Table

The basic tags for constructing a table are: <table>, <tr>, and <td>. Each table definition begins with a <table> tag. A table is divided into rows, designated with the <tr> tag. The letters tr stands for table row. The <tr> tags are nested directly between the <table> and </table> tag.

Each row is divided into data cells using the <td> tag. The letters td stands for table data. The <td> tags are nested directly between the <tr> and </tr>. The content of a table cell has to be placed between <td> and </td>. You should not place any content outside of <td>. How the content that is placed outside of <td> is displayed in a browser is unpredictable.

The following example defines a table of two rows and two columns. The text content "This is OK." will be displayed inside the table cells, because they are enclosed within <td>

and </td>. However, the text "This line is not OK!!" will not be displayed inside the table cells. Note that they are placed outside of <td>.

```
<table>
  This line is not OK!!
  <tr>
    This is line not OK!!
    <td>This is OK.</td>
    This line is not OK!!
    <td>This is OK.</td>
  </tr>
  This is line not OK!!
  <tr>
    <td>This is OK.</td>
    <td>This is OK.</td>
  </tr>
</table>
```

A table cell can contain other HTML elements, such as text, images, lists, forms, and other tables. Notice that a table is constructed row by row. Each row is divided into cells. You may consider the cells as columns for each row. Figure 8.28a shows an example HTML code using these tags to construct a table of three rows and two columns. Figure 8.28b shows how this table is displayed on a Web browser.

```
<!DOCTYPE html PUBLIC "-//W3C//DTD XHTML 1.0 Transitional//EN"
"http://www.w3.org/TR/xhtml1/DTD/xhtml1-transitional.dtd">
<html xmlns="http://www.w3.org/1999/xhtml">
<head>
<meta http-equiv="Content-Type" content="text/html; charset=iso-8859-1">
<title>Table Example</title>
</head>
<body>
<table>
  <tr>
    <td>row 1, column 1</td>
    <td>row 1, column 2</td>
  </tr>
  <tr>
    <td>row 2, column 1</td>
    <td>row 2, column 2</td>
  </tr>
  <tr>
    <td>row 3, column 1</td>
    <td>row 3, column 2</td>
  </tr>
</table>
</body>
</html>
```

(a)

Figure 8.28 (a) Full HTML code for a Web page that contains a table without specifying a border with the tags for constructing the table given in color. (b) How the table looks like when displayed in a Web browser

(b)

Figure 8.28 (*Continued*)

This simple example shows a bare-bones table. Without a table border, it may be hard to tell that it is a table. Figure 8.29 shows the same table as that in Figure 8.28, except that a border is added by specifying the border attribute of the <table>.

```
<!DOCTYPE html PUBLIC "-//W3C//DTD XHTML 1.0 Transitional//EN"
"http://www.w3.org/TR/xhtml1/DTD/xhtml1-transitional.dtd">
<html xmlns="http://www.w3.org/1999/xhtml">
<head>
<meta http-equiv="Content-Type" content="text/html; charset=iso-8859-1">
<title>Table Example</title>
</head>
<body>
<table border="1">
  <tr>
    <td>row 1, column 1</td>
    <td>row 1, column 2</td>
  </tr>
  <tr>
    <td>row 2, column 1</td>
    <td>row 2, column 2</td>
  </tr>
  <tr>
    <td>row 3, column 1</td>
    <td>row 3, column 2</td>
  </tr>
</table>
</body>
</html>
```

(a)

Figure 8.29 (a) Full HTML code for a Web page that contains a table with a border. (b) How the table looks like when displayed in a Web browser

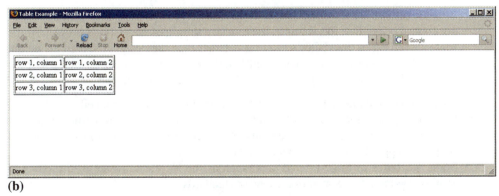

(b)

Figure 8.29 (*Continued*)

🖰 **Lab 2: HTML: Images and Tables** Hand code three HTML documents:
- One HTML document contains a table with image thumbnails. Clicking on the image thumbnail will go to the page containing the full image.
- Two HTML documents: each contains the full image of the thumbnail.

🖰 **Dreamweaver Workspace Overview** An overview of the workspace and most commonly used panels in Adobe Dreamweaver

---

🖰 **Lab 3: Web Authoring Using Adobe Dreamweaver** Get acquainted with Adobe Dreamweaver. Set up a Web site in Dreamweaver. Create and edit Web pages using the visual editor.

8.6 WEB PAGE LAYOUT TOOLS—TABLES AND CASCADING STYLE SHEETS

Tables and cascading style sheets (CSS) are powerful tools for controlling the placement of HTML elements on a Web page. Before CSS, tables were basically the only tool for aligning elements on a Web page. Tables still are used in many Web sites for positioning text and images. However, tables have limitations, for example:

- Lack of precise control of individual table cell height.
  Table cells are interdependent. All of the cells in the same row share the same height.
- Lack of control of the border of an individual cell.
  When you set the table border, it applies to all sides of the table and its cells. You cannot set a border for individual cells nor the individual side(s) of a table. In addition, the border style is limited. It does not have choices of solid or dotted line style that commonly is used in print publications.

A commonly used trick is to add an extra row or column and place in it a black line using a 1×1-pixel black image. The image is stretched vertically or horizontally, depending on whether you want to create a horizontal or a vertical line border. Even with this trick, there still exists a limitation: the length of the black image is set in the HTML code. It does not change in respond to the actual length of the text block. The actual length of the text block depends on many factors that the Web designers cannot control or predict; for example, the font size setting of the visitor's browser. If the font size setting of the visitor's browser is larger than the designer's, then the height of a table cell will increase. The fixed-length vertical line border created using the image trick would be too short to cover the entire height of the cell.

- Lack of control on the amount of whitespace around the individual cell.
  Cell spacing (cellspace) and cell padding (cellpad) are the two properties of a table used to add space between cell contents. However, like the border property, these two properties apply to all of the cells in the table.
- Some attributes of table-related tags (such as the bgcolor attribute of the <tr> and <table> tags) are deprecated in the newest standards.

The CSS box model provides more precise control for a layout and solves these problems. The box model is used for more precise control and Web page layouts without tables. Tables are used for displaying tabulated data.

Because tables have been such a common tool for Web page layout and they are still a good tool for tabulating data, the following subsection will discuss how tables have been used for Web page layout. CSS will be discussed in more detail in Chapter 9.

8.6.1 How Tables Are Used for Layout

Tables traditionally are used to display tabulated data in reports and slideshows. However, for Web pages, tables have been used as a tool to position and align Web page elements (such as text and images). Thus, use of a table for layout purposes does not necessarily mean having multiple rows and columns.

A table can have only one row and one column. Such a table often is used as a container to restrict the width of the page content, by grouping multiple elements within it. You easily can reposition these multiple elements together simply by repositioning this one table.

A table with one row and multiple columns often is used to create a horizontal navigation menu bar. The width of the column controls the spacing between menu items. A table with one column and multiple rows also can be used to create multiple divisions in a vertical navigation menu pane.

Background color and image for table cells can be set using CSS.

Nested tables commonly have been used to help refine positions. ***Nested tables*** means having a table in a cell of another table. A table has properties such as background color (though is now deprecated), background image (also deprecated), cell padding, and cell spacing. A nested table can have different properties than the outer table cell to accommodate design needs.

For example, Figure 8.30a shows the HTML code for using two tables to create a page (Figure 8.30b) with a header, content area, and footer.

```
<!DOCTYPE html PUBLIC "-//W3C//DTD XHTML 1.0 Transitional//EN"
"http://www.w3.org/TR/xhtml1/DTD/xhtml1-transitional.dtd">
<html xmlns="http://www.w3.org/1999/xhtml">
<head>
<meta http-equiv="Content-Type" content="text/html; charset=iso-8859-1">
<title>Example: Simple Layout Using Tables</title>
</head>
<body>
<table width="100%" border="1" cellspacing="0" cellpadding="0">
  <tr>
    <td>Header</td>
  </tr>
  <tr>
    <td><table width="60%" border="3" align="center" cellpadding="0"
cellspacing="0">
      <tr valign="top">
        <td width="120"><p>menu 1</p>
          <p>menu 2</p>
          <p>menu 2 </p></td>
        <td><p>content content content content content content content
content content content content content content content content content
content content content content content content content content content
content content content content content content content content content
content </p>
          <p>content content content content content content content
content content content content content content content content content
content content content content content content content content content
content content content content content content content content content
content content content content content content content content content
content content content content content content content content content
content content content content content content content content content
content content content content content content content content content
</p></td>
      </tr>
    </table></td>
  </tr>
  <tr>
    <td>Footer</td>
  </tr>
</table>
</body>
</html>
```

(a)

Figure 8.30 (a) An HTML document that uses nested tables for page layout
(b) How the page looks like when displayed in a Web browser

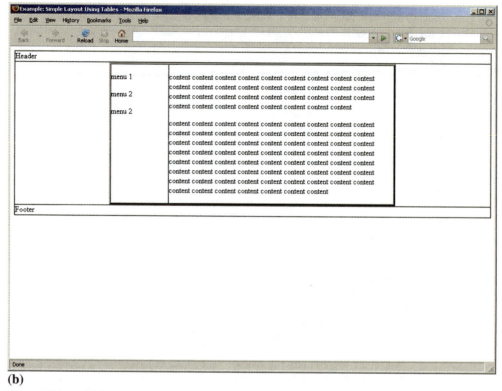

(b)

Figure 8.30 (*Continued*)

The outer table has three rows: one row each for header, content area, and footer. The 2-column layout in the content area is created with a table of two columns nested inside this outer table. To make it easy for you to see the tables, the table borders are set to be visible at a 1-pixel width.

When tables are used for page layout instead of for tabulating data, the borders are hidden by setting its width to zero. Figure 8.31 shows an example that takes out the border and dresses up the page a little by assigning background color to the table cells for the header and footer. To help you see the tables, Figure 8.31c shows the table borders.

```
<!DOCTYPE html PUBLIC "-//W3C//DTD XHTML 1.0 Transitional//EN"
"http://www.w3.org/TR/xhtml1/DTD/xhtml1-transitional.dtd">
<html xmlns="http://www.w3.org/1999/xhtml">
<head>
<meta http-equiv="Content-Type" content="text/html; charset=iso-8859-1">
<title>Example: Simple Layout Using Tables</title>
</head>
<body>
<table width="100%" border="0" cellspacing="0" cellpadding="0">
   <tr>
      <td bgcolor="#CC6600"><h1 align="center">Chapter 8. Web Site
Design</h1></td>
   </tr>
   <tr>
      <td><table width="60%" border="0" align="center" cellpadding="0"
cellspacing="0">
         <tr valign="top">
         <td width="120"><p><a href="section8_1.html">Section
8.1</a></p>
            <p><a href="section8_2.html">Section 8.2</a></p>
            <p><a href="section8_3.html">Section 8.3</a></p></td>
         <td><h2>What Are Style Sheets For?</h2>
            <p>Style sheets can be used to control the
formatting & mdash; style and layout & mdash; of HTML elements on Web pages.
Think of a style sheet as a set of rules that tells the Web browser how
to display the text and images on a Web page. The appearance of text you
can control with style sheets is, for examples, font type, size, color,
and alignment. You can also specify the position of basically any HTML
element, not just text and images. An element refers to text, images, a
block of text, a table, a table cell, a form, a form element (such as a
text field, a checkbox, and a dropdown box) and a group of these
aforementioned different elements. </p>
      </tr>
     </table></td>
   </tr>
   <tr>
      <td bgcolor="#CC6633">Page footer: This can be a navigation bar or a
copyright notice.</td>
   </tr>
</table>
</body>
</html>
```

(a)

Figure 8.31 (a) An HTML document that uses nested tables for page layout (b) How the page looks when displayed in a Web browser (c) To help you see how the tables are nested, the table borders are added

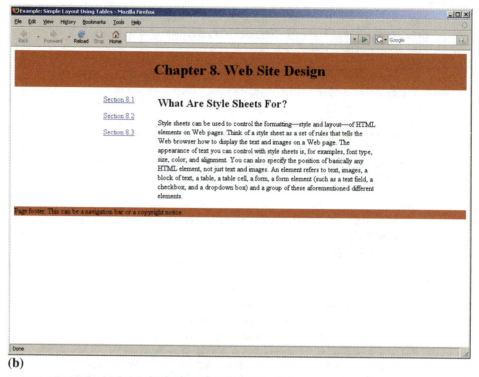

(b)

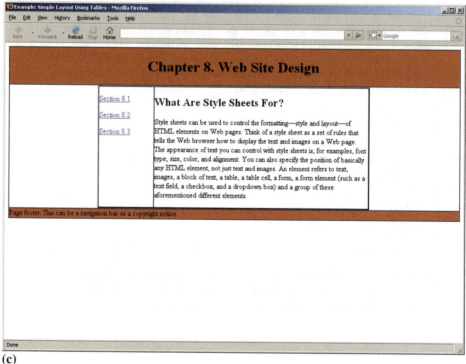

(c)

Figure 8.31 *(Continued)*

8.7 UNDERSTANDING FILE PATHS

Your HTML documents, images, sounds, and videos are stored as files on computer. **Folders** (also called directories) are used to organize files. When you open a folder, you see other folders and/or files inside the folder. When you open a file, you will see the content of the file. To view the content of a file correctly, you will need to open the file using the right application program; for example, Notepad (Windows) and TextEdit (Mac OS) for plain text files, and Adobe Photoshop for digital images.

8.7.1 File Paths

A *file path* refers to the location of a file on a computer, like addresses or directions for buildings and houses. When you address an envelope, you follow a certain order—for example, the name of the person, the street, the city, and then the state. To write a file path, you write the folder names in the order of the folder hierarchical structure—start from the outermost folder to the inner folders. A file path to a file ends with the filename.

The folder names are separated by a delimiter, which is often a forward slash (/) or backslash (\). Forward slashes (/) are used most commonly for file paths in HTML documents.

8.7.2 Types of File Paths for Web Pages

File paths used in Web pages are like directions or addresses to a building, a house, a room, or any object. Suppose someone asks you for directions to see a particular painting in an art exhibition. If the art exhibition is out of town, you probably will give the person a full address, specifying the building, city, and state where the exhibition takes place. On the other hand, if the exhibition is right inside the building you are located at—but on a different floor—then you will give the person directions for how to get to the other floor from where you are standing. You give different types of directions depending on the situation. It is the same for the file paths for Web pages.

There are three types of paths:

- *Absolute Paths.*

  Example: `http://www.mysite.com/products/coffee/french-roast.html`

  This is the full URL to a Web page or any media. It is like giving the full address for an out-of-town art exhibition. If you are linking a page that is on a different Web site, you will need to use the absolute path.

- *Document-Relative Paths.*

  Example: `products/coffee/french-roast.html`

  This is the most common type of file path in Web authoring. It is like giving directions to get to another floor in the art exhibition scenario. The direction you give is *relative* to where the person is standing. The direction is only valid for that specific location. The same direction becomes invalid if the person asks in another building or a different floor of the same building. The example path shown here is relative to where this `french-roast.html` is being requested. You will see examples on constructing document-relative paths in the next subsection.

- *Site Root-Relative Paths.*

  Example: `/products/coffee/french-roast.html`

  A site root-relative path always starts with a forward slash (/). It means starting from the root folder of the site. A *root folder* is the outermost folder of the site structure.

8.7.3 Rules to Creating Links Using Document-Relative Paths

Suppose you have a site with a folder structures shown in Figure 8.32. Figure 8.32 shows two different graphical representations of the folder structure of a site called my-site. The graphical representations help you create a mental model for the relationships of the folders and files in the site.

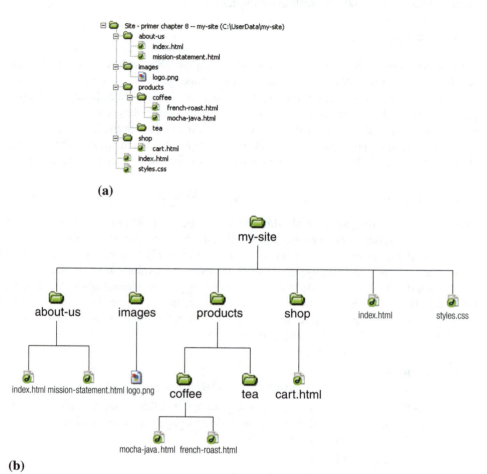

(a)

(b)

Figure 8.32 Two different visual representations of folder structure of a site

In this example, the root folder for the site is called my-site. Inside the my-site folder, there are four folders (about-us, images, products, and shop) and two files (index.html and styles.css). There are also other folders and files inside these four folders. Figure 8.33 shows how it looks when you navigate this folder structure on you computer. When you double-click on a folder, you see the folder(s) and file(s) stored there.

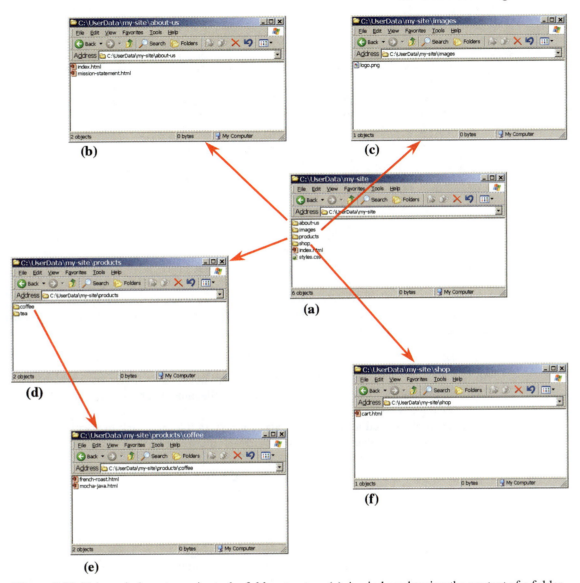

Figure 8.33 Using windows to navigate the folder structure (a) A window showing the content of a folder (b) Double-clicking the folder about-us in (a) (c) Double-clicking the folder images in (a) (d) Double-clicking the folder products in (a) (e) Double-clicking the folder coffee in (d). (f) Double-clicking the folder tea in (d).

To construct a document-relative path, you need to know the relative location between the target page (the page being linked *to*) and the source page (the page containing the link or the page being linked *from*) in the site structure.

Rule #1

To link to another file in the same folder as the current document, use the filename as the path.

For example, to add a link in mocha-java.html to link to french-roast.html (Figure 8.34), the file path is simply the filename french-roast.html.

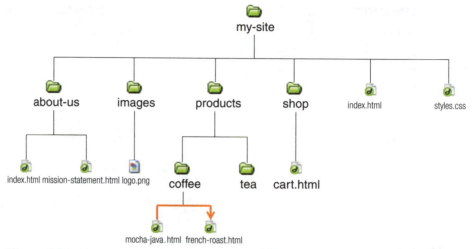

Figure 8.34 Link from mocha-java.html to french-roast.html

Returning to the art exhibition scenario, this is like when the person asking for directions is in the same room as where the painting is. You can simply point to the painting. You do not need any extra information regarding navigating to other building or room.

Rule #2

To link to a file that is in a subfolder of the current document's folder, use the subfolder name followed by a forward slash (/) and then the filename. Each forward slash (/) represents moving down one level in the folder.

For example, to add a link in index.html (in my-site folder) to link to french-roast.html (Figure 8.35), the relative path is products/coffee/french-roast.html.

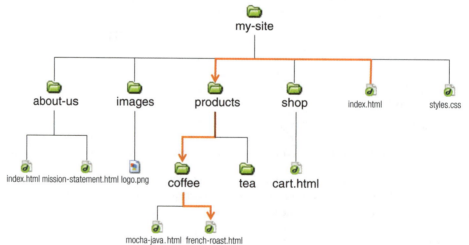

Figure 8.35 Link from index.html (in my-site folder) to the french-roast.html

Rule #3:

To link to a file that is outside of the current document's folder, start the path with ../ (where ../ means going up one level in the folder hierarchy), followed by the folder name, a forward slash (/), and then the filename. Multiple ../ can be appended for going up multiple levels in the folder hierarchy.

For example, to add a link in french-roast.html to link to index.html (in my-site folder) (Figure 8.36), the relative path is ../../index.html.

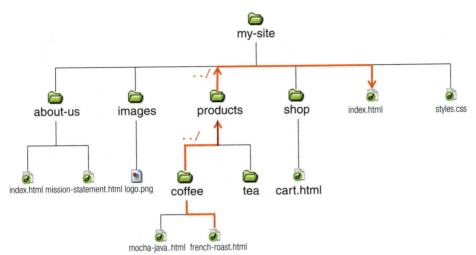

Figure 8.36 Link from french-roast.html to index.html (in my-site folder). ../ is used to indicate going up one level in the folder hierarchy

To obtain the file path that links from french-roast.html to cart.html (in shop folder) (Figure 8.37) imagine you have the coffee folder open. You see the french-roasted.html file. From there, to see cart.html, you need to follow the following steps.

Step 1 Go up one level (../) to get out of the coffee folder into the products folder.

Step 2 Go up another level (../) to get out of the products folder into the my-site folder.

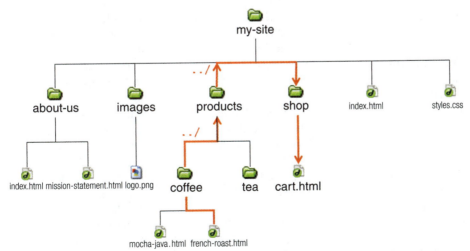

Figure 8.37 Link from french-roast.html to cart.html (in shop folder). ../ used to indicate going up one level in the folder hierarchy

Step 3 Go into the shop folder (shop/). Now, you see the cart.html. Thus, the relative path is ../../shop/cart.html.

8.7.4 Why Is It Important to Understand File Paths for Web Page Creation?

It is essential to understand the file paths in order to create valid links and embed images. File paths are used in the HTML document for the hyperlinked pages or images. A path serves as a direction or address to retrieve the linked page or an image to display on the page. Incorrect paths lead to broken images or broken links on web pages.

Web page editing programs let you insert images and create links using graphical interface and automatically create relative paths for you. You seldom need to figure out file paths. However, the program may not always update the links as you expect. If you rename or move files and folders around in your site, those file paths inserted in your HTML document prior to the change will not be valid any more and need to be updated. Although Web site-management programs (such as Adobe Dreamweaver) can check for broken links, being able to read and construct the file paths helps troubleshoot broken links when in some situations you do not have access to such a program.

TERMS

<a>, 363
absolute paths, 373
anchor tag, 363
attributes, 356
<b>, 361

, 360
cascading, 325
closing tag, 356
DOCTYPE, 357
document-relative
  paths, 373
dynamic HTML
  (DHTML), 325
element content, 356
end tag, 356
Extensible Hypertext
  Markup Language, 325
file path, 373
fixed-width layout, 351
fluid layout, 351
folders, 373
footer, 341
golden ratio, 346

grid-based design, 346
gutter, 342
<h1>, 361
<h2>, 361
<h3>, 361
<h4>, 361
<h5>, 361
<h6>, 361
header, 340
home page, 327
HTML, 324
http, 325
Hypertext Markup
  Language, 324
Hypertext Transfer
  Protocol, 325
<img>, 364
JavaScript, 325
<li>, 362
library item, 339
liquid or flexible layout, 351
local root folder, 337
local site, 337

navigation menus, 340
nested tables, 368
ordered list, 362
<ol>, 362
<p>, 359
remote site, 337
root folder, 373
Site root-relative paths, 373
start tag, 356
<strong>, 361
Style sheets, 325
tags, 334
template, 339
<ul>, 362
Uniform Resource
  Locator, 325
unordered list, 362
URL, 325
Web browser, 324
Web pages, 324
Web site, 326
Whitespace, 342
XHTML, 325

LEARNING AIDS

The following Learning aids can be found at the book's companion Web site.

Lab: Create a Site, Use a Template and Library Items

A lab practice exercise to: (1) create a site; (2) create library items; (3) create a template with library items, and (4) create a new Web page using the defined template.

Lab 1: HTML: Basic HTML Document Structure, Paragraphs, Line Breaks, Lists, Links, Heading, Bold and Italics Text

Hand code two HTML documents using basic HTML document structure.

Lab 2: HTML: Images and Tables

Hand code three HTML documents:

- One HTML document contains a table with image thumbnails. Clicking on the image thumbnail will go to the page containing the full image.
- Two HTML documents: each contains the full image of the thumbnail.

Dreamweaver Workspace Overview

An overview of the workspace and most commonly used panels in Adobe Dreamweaver

Lab 3: Web Authoring Using Adobe Dreamweaver

Get acquainted with Adobe Dreamweaver. Set up a Web site in Dreamweaver. Create and edit Web pages using the visual editor.

REVIEW QUESTIONS

When applicable, please select all correct answers.

1. HTML documents are _____.

    A. text files
    B. JPG files
    C. PSD files
    D. MP3 files

2. Dynamic HTML is a combination of _____, _____, and _____.

3. **True/False:** Dynamic HTML is a special programming language by itself.

4. For the URL: http://www.schoolname.edu/departments/art/index.html determine the following.

    i.   The domain name of the Web server is _____.

    ii. This URL is a Web address of a file named _____.

    iii. This file is located in the folder named _____, which is inside another folder named _____.

5. What are the four common basic building blocks, besides content, for a Web page?

6. Name several strategies, besides creating color differences, to create emphasis or focal points by creating differences on a page.

7. _____ layout means that the width of the page content automatically adjusts based on the width of the viewer's browser window.

8. _____ are mark-up code in an HTML document that tells the Web browser how to format the text when displaying it.

A. Attributes
B. Tags

9. In the HTML code:
`<p>This is a paragraph.</p>`

`<p>` is the _____, and `</p>` is the _____. The text "This is a paragraph." is the _____.

A. element content, start tag, end tag
B. element content, end tag, start tag
C. start tag, end tag, element content
D. start tag, element content, end tag
E. end tag, start tag, element content
F. end tag, element content, start tag

10. Fill in the correct start tag and end tags to create a basic HTML document.
```
<_____>
<_____>
<_____>This is the page title.<_____>
<_____>
<_____>
This is the content of the Web page.
<_____>
<_____>
```

11. Describe briefly how XHTML is different from HTML in terms of each of the following:

i. Tag pairing
ii. Cases of tags
iii. Tag nesting
iv. Root element of a page
v. DOCTYPE declaration

12. The _____ tag is used to create a line break—to force a new line without starting a new paragraph. By default, the line created using this tag has _____-line spacing.

13. The _____ tag is used to create a heading style 1.

14. Fill in the blanks for the HTML code below to create a link to your favorite Web site. Use a valid URL.
```
<_____ _____ = "_____">My Favorite Web site<___>
```

15. Fill in the blanks for the HTML code below to embed an image called `logo.jpg` on a Web page. Suppose logo.jpg is in the same folder as the HTML document that embeds it.
```
<_____ _____ = "_____" _____>
```

16. Fill in the blanks for the HTML code to create a list as shown.

1. Preheat oven to 450 degrees.
2. Heat butter and oil in a large saucepan.
3. Cook the shrimp for 10 minutes.
```
<_____>
<_____>Preheat oven to 450 degrees.<_____>
```

```
<_____>Heat butter and oil in a large saucepan.<_____>
<_____>Cook the shrimp for 10 minutes.<_____>
<_____>
```

17. Fill in the blanks for the HTML code to create a list as
    - Elephants
    - Tigers
    - Frogs

```
<_____>
<_____>Elephants<_____>
<_____>Tigers<_____>
<_____>Frogs<_____>
<_____>
```

18. Fill in the blanks for the HTML code to create a table as

Elephants	Tulips
Tigers	Roses

```
<table>
<tr>
<td>_____</td>
<td>_____</td>
<_____>
<tr>
<td>_____</td>
<td>_____</td>
<_____>
<_____>
```

19. For the site shown in Figure 8.32, to add a link on the page mocha-java.html to link to the Web page french-roast.html, the document-relative file path is _____.

20. For the site shown in Figure 8.32, to embed the image logo.png on the homepage index.html (in the my-site folder), the document-relative file path is _____.

21. For the site shown in Figure 8.32, to embed the image logo.png on the Web page french-roast.html, the document-relative file path is _____.

Yue-Ling Wong

CSS for Web Design

GENERAL LEARNING OBJECTIVES

In this chapter, you will learn:

- The basic rules of defining styles.
- To create CSS style sheets.
- To apply styles to HTML elements.
- To read and modify existing CSS styles.
- To create a fixed-width layout.
- To create a fluid 2-column layout.

9.1 CASCADING STYLE SHEETS (CSS) BASICS

Style sheets can be used to control the formatting—style and layout—of HTML elements on Web pages. Think of a style sheet as a set of rules that tells the Web browser how to display the text and images on a Web page. CSS stands for *cascading style sheets*. You will see later in this chapter that multiple style sheets can be combined or "cascaded" into a new "virtual" style sheet—thus the cascading part of CSS.

You can control the appearance of text with style sheets, for example, font type, size, color, and alignment. You also can specify the position of basically any HTML element—not just text and images. An element refers to a word, an image, a block of text, a table, a table cell, a form, a form element (such as a text field, a checkbox, or a dropdown box) and a group of these aforementioned different elements.

Figure 9.1 shows the homepage of the CSS *Zen Garden* Web site. Without applying CSS, this page would look like that shown in Figure 9.2. This HTML document provides the page *content*. This same HTML document can be displayed in different styles when applied with different CSS formats. For example, the page shown in Figure 9.3 has a very different design and mood than the original page (Figure 9.1) by changing the images and the formatting. The same page even can be transformed from a conventional article layout into a graphical layout. Figure 9.4 shows a design that breaks up the text content into comic dialogs.

The CSS specifies the style and format for the display of the content. By using CSS, you can separate the style and formatting from the content. This is the beauty of using CSS. When you want to change the style and formatting of a HTML document, you simply change the CSS without having to rewrite the entire HTML document.

There are many example designs showcased in the CSS *Zen Garden* Web site. You can see how the same content can be displayed differently by defining different CSS rules.

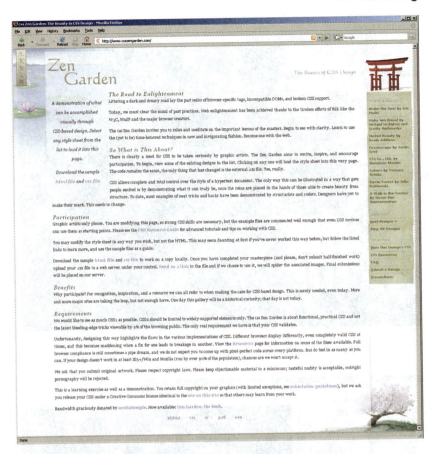

Figure 9.1 CSS *Zen Garden* Web site at http://www.csszengarden.com/ (Courtesy of Dave Shea)

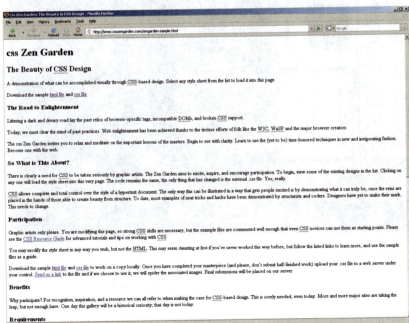

Figure 9.2 CSS *Zen Garden* Web site without CSS at http://www.csszengarden.com/zengarden-sample.html (Courtesy of Dave Shea)

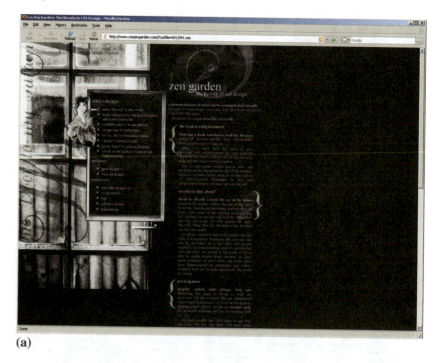

(a)

(b)

Figure 9.3 A design of the CSS *Zen Garden* sample page by Patrick H. Lauke at http://www.csszengarden.com/?cssfile=041/041.css

(a)

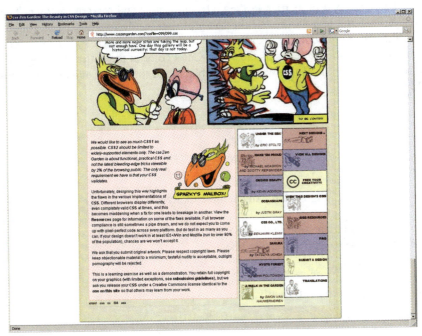

(b)

Figure 9.4 A design of the CSS *Zen Garden* sample page by Joseph Pearson
at http://www.csszengarden.com/?cssfile=099/099.css

9.1.1 CSS Syntax

The syntax for a CSS rule (Figure 9.5) is made up of two main parts: a *selector* and a *declaration*. The declaration is the style definition. It consists a pair of a property and a value.

```
selector {
    property: value;
}
```

Figure 9.5 Basic syntax for a CSS rule

The selector can be an HTML tag you want to use to define styles for its content, but it also can be a custom-defined name for a style you want to create. If the selector is an HTML tag, then the defined style will apply to the content of that tag in the HTML document. The selector does not have to be an existing tag name. In such cases, think of the selector as a style name. Later in this chapter, you will see how to apply styles to HTML elements.

The property is the attribute you want to control. For each selector, you can specify multiple properties. Each property is assigned with a value. The property and value are separated by a colon. All of the property–value pairs belonging to a selector are grouped within curly braces immediately below the selector.

In the following example (Figure 9.6), the selector is the body tag. It is an existing HTML tag. Thus, defining the style rule for it will apply the defined style to the content within the body tag. There are two properties in the style rule: color and background-color. The color property defines the text color, and the background-color defines the background color. Because the body tag encompasses all of the visual content of a Web page, setting the background-color for the body tag sets the background color of the entire Web page. This example sets the text color of the Web page to black and the background color of the Web page to white.

```
body {
    color: #000000;
    background-color: #FFFFFF;
}
```

Figure 9.6 An example of style rule

Line breaks and indentation in the CSS syntax are optional. For example, the style rule in Figure 9.6 can be written all on one line, as

```
body {color: #000000; background-color: #FFFFFF}
```

or breaking up the line differently, as

```
body {
color: #000000;
background-color: #FFFFFF;
}
```

However, to make the style definitions more readable, it is a good practice to put each property–value pair on a separate line and to indent the line. The curly braces should be on separate lines aligned with the selector. It is also a common practice to put the opening braces on the same line as the selector, as shown in Figure 9.6.

If the value contains multiple words, the value will need to be enclosed in quotation marks. For example,

```
body {
    font-family: "Times New Roman";
}
```

Table 9.1 lists the commonly used properties, a brief description, possible values, and example usages in CSS. A comprehensive list can be found on the Web. The list may seem overwhelming at first. However, most Web-page editors (such as Adobe Dreamweaver) let you create style sheets by using drop-down boxes that list the properties and values. You do not have to hand code the style sheet or memorize the exact property names. The tables intend to give you an idea of what types of properties of an HTML element you can change. These are some of the most frequently used properties. As you gain experience creating and editing CSS styles, you naturally will memorize these frequently used syntaxes and be able to hand code without having to rely on a Web-page editor's dialog box.

TABLE 9.1   A list of Commonly Used Properties for (a) Background, (b) Font and (c) Text

(a) Background

Property	Description	Common Values
background-color	Sets the **background color** of an element	Color value in hexadecimal representation or color name

Example: Set the background color to white using the hexadecimal representation:
background-color: #FFFFFF;

Example: Set the background color to white using the color name:
background-color: white;

Property	Description	Common Values
background-image	Sets the **background image** of an element	url(pathname)

Example: Set the background image to an image called polkadot.gif that is located in a subfolder called "images":
background-image: url(images/polkadot.gif);

(b) Font

Property	Description	Common Values
font-family	Sets the **font** of the text, listed in prioritized order if more than one font	Font names

TABLE 9.1	A list of Commonly Used Properties for (a) Background, (b) Font and (c) Text (*Continued*)

Example: Set the font to Arial:
```
font-family: Arial;
```

Example: Set the font to Times New Roman, but if the viewer's computer does not have the Times New Roman font, then use Times

If there is no Times font either, then use the serif font that is available on the computer
```
font-family: "Times New Roman", Times, serif;
```

If the font name contains spaces, then it needs to be enclosed in quotations

Property	Description	Common Values
font-size	Sets the **font size** of the text	A numeric value followed by a unit (e.g., px for pixels, pt for points, em for ems) *Note:* There should be no space between the numeric value and the unit

Example: Set the font size to 9 pixels:
```
font-size: 9px;
```

Example: Set the font size to 1.5 ems:
```
font-size: 1.5em;
```

Property	Description	Common Values
font-style	Sets the **font style** of the text to normal, italic, or oblique	normal, italic, oblique

Example: To italicize the text:
```
font-style: italic;
```

Property	Description	Common Values
font-variant	Sets the text display as **small-caps** or normal font	normal, small-caps

Example: Set the text to small caps:
```
font-variant: small-caps;
```

Property	Description	Common Values
font-weight	Sets the **weight** of a font	normal, bold, bolder, lighter

Example: Boldface the text:
```
font-weight: bold;
```

(c) Text

Property	Description	Common Values
Color	Sets the **text color**	Color value in hexadecimal, color name

TABLE 9.1	A list of Commonly Used Properties for (a) Background, (b) Font and (c) Text (*Continued*)

Example: Set the text color to black using hexadecimal representation:
`color: #000000;`

Example: Set the text color to black using the color name:
`color: black;`

Property	Description	Common Values
line-height	Sets the **distance between lines** of the text	normal, number followed by a unit (e.g., px for pixels, pt for points, em for ems)

Example: Set the distance between lines to 9 pixels:
`font-height: 9px;`

Property	Description	Common Values
letter-spacing	Sets the **spacing between characters** of the text	normal, number followed by a unit (e.g. px for pixels, pt for points, em for ems)

Example: Set the spacing between characters to 0.1 ems:
`letter-spacing: 0.1em;`

Property	Description	Common Values
text-align	Sets the **text alignment**	left, right, center, justify

Example: Set the text to be right aligned:
`text-align: right;`

Property	Description	Common Values
text-decoration	Adds **decoration** to the text	none, underline, overline, line-through, blink

Example: Set the text to no decoration at all:
`text-decoration: none;`

This is how you remove the default underline of hyperlinks
Example: The style definition for the <a> tag removes the default underline of hyperlinks:

```
a {
    text-decoration: none;
}
```

TABLE 9.1	A list of Commonly Used Properties for (a) Background, (b) Font and (c) Text (*Continued*)	
Property	**Description**	**Common Values**
text-transform	Controls the **case** of letters	none, capitalize, uppercase, lowercase

Example: To automatically capitalize the first letter of each word:
text-transform: capitalize;

Example: To force all the letters to uppercase:
text-transform: uppercase;

In addition to background, font, and text, other useful properties include those for creating a list, positioning an element, and making a box model. Box models and positioning elements are especially useful in Web-page layout design. These additional properties will be discussed later in this chapter.

COMMON UNITS FOR CSS FONT SIZE: PX, PT, EM, AND %

- **px** (pixels): A pixel refers to a unit for resolution for monitor screens. Screen resolution is measured in pixel dimensions. Thus, the physical size of a pixel depends on the monitor screen's pixels per inch.

Most Web pages use a font size of 10px for Arial, Helvetica, or Verdana, and 12px for Times New Roman or Times.

- **pt** (points): Points are a unit of measurement for prints. Point size is based on physical length, i.e., it is measured in absolute length. For CSS2, one point is equal to 1/72th of an inch.
- **em** (ems): One em equals to the font size of the parent element
- **%** (percentages): These are relative to the surrounding text.

For Web pages that are for on-screen viewing, points (pt) are not a suitable unit. The choice between pixels (px) and the two relative units (em and %) is determined by whether you (as a Web designer for the page) want absolute control of the font size or to give the viewer some control over the font size.

Web browsers allow the viewer to set a default font size preference. When you use em units, you set the font size *relative* to the parent element. This does not override the viewer's font size preference. If a viewer really needs to read larger text, he/she can do so without having to disable your style sheet. Another advantage of using relative units is that the style will be easily scaled from one platform to another (e.g., from a computer monitor to a PDA or cell phone.)

The disadvantage with using em units is that you lose control over the exact look of your page layout. Some people may have a much larger or smaller default size than what you are testing your pages with. With ems, the fonts are scaled relative to that default size. This can result in undesired text wrapping, causing a layout that is not what you intended.

HEXADECIMAL NOTATION

The color setting of HTML elements uses *hexadecimal notation*. Many Web editors provide a color chip for you to choose a color visually, and it will translate the color into hexadecimal notation in the HTML code for you.

When you are familiar with CSS, you often hand edit your CSS rules without going through the visual editor because it is much faster to hand edit the code directly. Thus, it is essential that you understand the hexadecimal notation of color values, so that you can tell by looking at the code what color the style is specifying. In addition, you can change the color value by directly typing the appropriate hexadecimal notation.

Decimal versus Hexadecimal

Decimal is the most familiar system. We use it in our daily life. In decimal notation, there are ten different digits available: 0, 1, 2, 3, 4, 5, 6, 7, 8, 9. Any decimal-numeric value can be represented by a combination of any of these ten digits.

In a hexadecimal system, there are 16 different digits: 0, 1, 2, 3, 4, 5, 6, 7, 8, 9, A, B, C, D, E, F. The letters A through F are used as a digit to represent the value 10 to 15. Any hexadecimal-numeric value can be represented by a combination of any of these 16 digits.

The decimal notation 23_{10} means:

$$23_{10}$$

$$2 \times 10^1 + 3 \times 10^0 = 23$$

Hexadecimal to Decimal Conversion

The hexadecimal number 23_{16} represents the decimal value of 35. Here is how to convert this hexadecimal notation to the decimal number:

$$23_{16}$$

$$2 \times 16^1 + 3 \times 16^0 = 35_{10}$$

Let's look at three more examples:

$$AC_{16}$$

$$10 \times 16^1 + 12 \times 16^0 = 160 + 12 = 172_{10}$$

80_{16}

$8 \times 16^1 + 0 \times 16^0 = 128 + 0 = 128_{10}$

FF_{16}

$15 \times 16^1 + 15 \times 16^0 = 240 + 15 = 255_{10}$

Decimal to Hexadecimal Conversion

To convert a decimal number to hexadecimal notation, you divide the number and the resulted quotients until the quotient is zero. The reverse order of the remainders is the hexadecimal notation of the original number.

Let's look at some examples.

To convert 35 to the hexadecimal notation:

1. Divide 35 by 16. You get 2 with a remainder of 3.
2. Divide 2 by 16 again. You get zero with a remainder of 2.
3. The reverse order of the remainders is 23.

$35 / 16 = 2$ remainder **3**
$2 / 16 = 0$ remainder **2** ↑ **23**

To convert 176 to the hexadecimal notation:

1. Divide 176 by 16. You get 10 with a remainder of 12.
2. Divide 10 by 16 again. You get zero with a remainder of 10.
3. The reverse order of the remainders is 10 and 12, which means A and C, respectively. Thus, the hexadecimal notation is AC.

$176 / 16 = 10$ remainder **12**
$10 / 16 = 0$ remainder **10** ↑ **AC**

To convert 255 to the hexadecimal notation:

1. Divide 255 by 16. You get 15 with a remainder of 15.
2. Divide 15 by 16 again. You get zero with a remainder of 15.
3. The reverse order of the remainders is 15 and 15, which means F and F. Thus, the hexadecimal notation is FF.

$255 / 16 = 15$ remainder **15**
$15 / 16 = 0$ remainder **15** ↑ **FF**

HEXADECIMAL NOTATION FOR COLOR VALUES

Before discussing the hexadecimal notation for color values, let's first review color representation on computers from Chapter 2.

A color on a computer is represented by three components: red, green, and blue. We refer to this color value as a RGB value.

For 24-bit color, each of the three components has a bit depth of 8. This means that each of these three color components has 2^8 (i.e., 256) possible levels of gradation (Figure 9.7). The values of these 256 levels range from 0 to 255. Different combinations of red, green, and blue levels represent different colors. The higher the number, the higher the intensity of that component. Thus, an RGB of (255, 255, 255) represents white. The red, green, and blue values for some common colors are shown in Table 9.2.

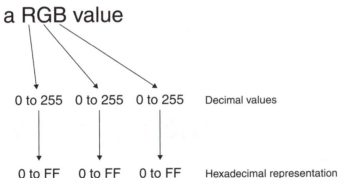

Figure 9.7 Hexadecimal notations are used to indicate color values for the Web

TABLE 9.2	RGB Values for the Several Basic Colors		
Red Value	**Green Value**	**Blue Value**	**Color**
0	0	0	Black
255	255	255	White
255	0	0	Red
0	255	0	Green
0	0	255	Blue
255	255	0	Yellow
255	0	255	Magenta
0	255	255	Cyan

Table 9.3 shows a variety of dark red colors. By looking at their RGB values, you can tell these are different red colors, because the red values in each are much higher than the other two color components. You also can tell they are not bright red but a little on the dark side. Although the red value is on the high end (recall that the highest value for each component here is 255), the green and blue are below the middle tone (128).

TABLE 9.3	RGB Values for Various Similar Dark Red Colors		
Red Value	**Green Value**	**Blue Value**	**Color**
216	92	116	A dark red
220	92	116	A dark red
216	95	116	A dark red
216	92	120	A dark red
221	100	100	A dark red
210	90	112	A dark red
212	89	118	A dark red
200	89	108	A dark red

Besides color and tones, the RGB value can tell you whether it is a gray color. The characteristic of a gray color is that all the red, green, and blue values are equal. You can tell whether the notation represents a darker gray or a lighter gray by any one of the component's value: lower value means a darker tone, while higher value means a lighter tone. Table 9.4 lists several example gray colors.

TABLE 9.4	RGB Values for Several Gray Tones		
Red Value	**Green Value**	**Blue Value**	**Color**
0	0	0	Black
50	50	50	Dark gray
128	128	128	Middle gray
220	220	220	Lighter gray
255	255	255	White

Hexadecimal Notation

To specify a color property for an HTML element, you need to write the RGB values in hexadecimal notation with a # symbol preceding the hexadecimal value, for example, #000000 for black.

Using the decimal to hexadecimal conversion shown previously, each of the red, green, and blue values can be converted into hexadecimal notation. For example, the first dark red color listed in Table 9.3 has the red, green, and blue values of 216, 92, and 116, respectively. Let's convert each into hexadecimal notation.
Red value:

216 / 16 = 13 remainder 8
13 / 16 = 0 remainder 13

Recall that D in the hexadecimal system represents 13. The hexadecimal notation for 216 is **D8**.
Green value:

92 / 16 = 5 remainder 12
5 / 16 = 0 remainder 5

Recall that C in the hexadecimal system represents 12. The hexadecimal notation for 92 is **5C**.

Blue value:

116 / 16 = 7 remainder 4

7 / 16 = 0 remainder 7

The hexadecimal notation for 116 is **74**.

Thus, the hexadecimal notation for the RGB value for this dark red color is: #D85C74

Table 9.5 shows the color values of some common colors in both decimal and hexadecimal notation.

TABLE 9.5	RGB Values in Decimal and Hexadecimal Notations		
Red Value	**Green Value**	**Blue Value**	**Color**
0	0	0	Black
00	**00**	**00**	**#000000**
255	255	255	White
FF	**FF**	**FF**	**#FFFFFF**
255	0	0	Red
FF	**00**	**00**	**#FF0000**
0	255	0	Green
00	**FF**	**00**	**#00FF00**
0	0	255	Blue
00	**00**	**FF**	**#0000FF**
255	255	0	Yellow
FF	**FF**	**00**	**#FFFF00**
255	0	255	Magenta
FF	**00**	**FF**	**#FF00FF**
0	255	255	Cyan
00	**FF**	**FF**	**#00FFFF**

9.1.2 How To Create a Style Sheet

There are three ways you can apply styles to Web pages: use of ***external style sheet***, ***internal style sheet***, and ***inline style***. They differ in the placement of the style definitions and their scope (i.e. the areas where the styles apply.) The CSS syntaxes are the same in all three methods.

External Style Sheet

This is the most useful of the three methods. The style definitions are written in a separate file—a simple, plain-text file. The file extension for a style sheet file often is given as .css. Figure 9.8 shows an external style sheet containing two style rules.

```
body {
   color: #000000;
   background-color: #FFFFFF;
}
a {
   text-decoration: none;
}
```

Figure 9.8 An example of an external
style sheet: a text file called, styles.css

In order for a Web page to use the styles defined in an external style sheet, you need to
link the style sheet to the HTML document. Suppose the filename of the external style
sheet is styles.css. To associate styles.css with an HTML document, add a <link> tag
within the <head> section of the HTML document, as shown in Figure 9.9.

```
<html xmlns="http://www.w3.org/1999/xhtml">
<head>
   <title>Intro to CSS</title>
   <link rel="stylesheet" href="styles.css" type="text/css" />
</head>
```

Figure 9.9 Linking an external style sheet (styles.css) to a Web page

Notice that there are three attributes in the <link> tag: rel, href, and type. The file path to
the style sheet is specified in the href attribute. When you use this code to specify a style
sheet for your HTML document, you will need to give a correct file path to your external
style sheet.

The attribute rel specifies the relationship from the current HTML document to the file
specified in href. Here, the value for rel should be "stylesheet". The attribute type describes
the content type of the linked document specified in href. For a style sheet, its type is
"text/css".

You can have multiple Web pages linking to the same external style sheet. This means
that multiple Web pages can share the same style definitions. If you want to change a style
that has been applied across these multiple Web pages, you can simply make the change in
the external style sheet. The change will be reflected in all of the Web pages that use that
style, preserving the consistent look-and-feel of that Web site. This makes the external style
sheet the most powerful amongst the three types of style sheets. If you use the other two
types of style sheets, you would have to edit each Web page to update the style definition
whenever you wanted to make a change in a style that is supposed to be consistent across
multiple pages.

To create or edit an external style sheet, you can use a plain-text editor, such as Notepad
in Windows or TextEdit in Mac OS. A style-sheet file is a plain-text file after all. For example, to create a style-sheet file like that shown in Figure 9.8, you can start a new file and
enter the style rules. Save it in a folder in your Web site, and give the filename extension
.css to the file to indicate that it is a style sheet.

File Extensions .css
versus .txt:
Note that the de-
fault extension of a
text file created
with Notepad is
.txt. Retaining
.txt as the file ex-
tension for your
style sheet still will
work. However, it
is recommended to
give your style-
sheet file the .css
file extension so
that you easily can
tell it is a style
sheet by its
filename.

Many Web page editors (such as Adobe Dreamweaver) also let you create and edit style sheets—both external and internal. Here is an example showing how to create a new style sheet like the one shown in Figure 9.8 with Dreamweaver.

Step 1 In Dreamweaver, choose Text > CSS Styles > New....
Step 2 In the New CSS Style dialog boxes (Figure 9.10), under the Define in section, select the option with the drop-down box for the external style sheet. The default filename for this new external style sheet is given as styles.css. You can give it a new name or keep this filename.
Step 3 The style sheet shown in Figure 9.8 defines the styles for two tags: <body> and <a>. To define styles for existing tags, select the second option labeled "Tag (redefines the look of a specific tag)" under the Selector Type section (Figure 9.10). Then, click the Name drop-down box to select a tag. Suppose we are going to redefine <body> first. Select body from the drop-down list.

Figure 9.10 Dreamweaver New CSS Style dialog box

Step 4 In the CSS Style Definition dialog box (Figure 9.11), there are two panes:
- *On the left*: Category
- *On the right*: Available options for the selected category. The style sheet shown in Figure 9.8 defines two styles for the <body>: font color and background color. The font color property can be set under the **Type** category, **Color** option (Figure 9.11a). The background color property is found under the **Background** category, **Background color** option (Figure 9.11b).

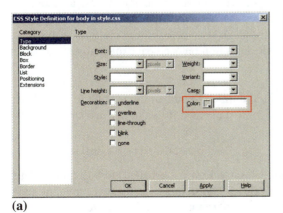
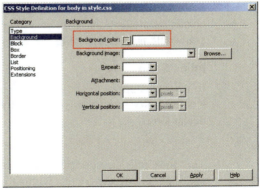

(a)   **(b)**

Figure 9.11 Dreamweaver CSS Style Definition dialog boxes

The properties for CSS styles are grouped in categories in Dreamweaver. You can select a category to set a property which is provided with a drop-down box listing the possible options available. Such visual editing makes the style sheet creation and editing easy for Web designers by not having to memorize the exact syntax for each of the CSS styles.

No matter what program you use to create the external style-sheet file—whether Notepad, TextEdit, or Dreamweaver—the style-sheet file will be a plain text file. You can edit a style sheet file in Dreamweaver or a text editor *regardless* of what program it originally was created in.

Internal Style Sheet

Another way to apply styles to a Web page is to embed the style rules within a single Web page. The style definitions are placed in the <head> section of the HTML document using the <style> tag. All of the style rules are written within the <style> </style>. Figure 9.12 shows how the same style sheet shown in Figure 9.9 would look like as an internal style sheet.

```
<html>
<head>
        <title>Intro to CSS</title>
        <style type="text/css">
                body {
                        color: #000000;
                        background-color: #FFFFFF;
                }
                a {
                        text-decoration: none;
                }
        </style>
</head>
```

Figure 9.12 An example of an internal style sheet

To create an internal style sheet with Dreamweaver, follow the same steps as described for the external style sheet—except that now in the New CSS Style dialog box (Figure 9.10), in the Define in section, you should select the option "This document only".

Unlike external style sheets, an internal style sheet only applies to a single Web page— the page that it is embedded in. Suppose you have an HTML element (say, a header) in multiple Web pages where each uses an internal style sheet. Should you need to change the header's style later and still want to keep the same style across these multiple Web pages, you would need to update the header's style definition on each page manually.

Inline Style

Inline style applies to one HTML element at a time. To add an inline style for an HTML element, a style attribute is added to the tag of that element. Its value is a text string of style declarations.

```
<p style="color: #000000; background-color:#FFFF00;">an inline style example</p>
```

This code adds the specified style (black text on yellow background) to one <p> tag. This style only affects the content within this single <p> tag. In this case, the text "an inline style example" is shown as black text on a yellow background on the Web page. All other <p> tags on the Web page are not affected by this inline style.

As you may notice, the differences of these three types of style sheets lie in their scope.

- An inline style only affects *one element* at a time on *one Web page*.
- An internal style sheet associates with only *one page*. *Multiple elements* can be applied with the same style that is defined in the sheet.
- An external style sheets can be associated with and shared across *multiple pages*. *Multiple elements* can be applied with the same style defined in the sheet.

9.2 CUSTOM-DEFINED STYLES

Each HTML tag has a default style defined by the Web browser. The style definitions in the previous examples show you how to redefine styles for the existing HTML tags. In those cases, the selector in the style definition is the name of the tag. The style will be applied automatically to the content of all the occurrences of that tag.

This section is going to discuss how you can define styles with custom-defined names or selectors. Custom-defined styles are not applied automatically to any content in the document. You will need to explicitly apply the style to the elements.

The syntax for custom-defined styles follows the basic syntax (Figure 9.5). The difference is in writing the selector name. There are two different types of selectors for custom-defining styles.

- **Class selector:** starts with a period (.)
- **ID selector:** start with a #

The syntax for the property and value remain the same as that for redefining styles for existing HTML tags.

9.2.1 Class Selector

General syntax:

```
.stylename {
    property: value;
}
```

For example, the following style definition creates a new class style called content. Its font color is assigned as blue.

```
.content {
    color: #0000FF;
}
```

To apply a class style to an element, you add the class attribute to a tag and set its value to the class style name. For example, to apply the style called content to a paragraph, the code is like this:

```
<p class="content">This is a paragraph...</p>
```

You can apply the same class style to multiple elements in an HTML document.

You also can apply more than one style to an element. For example, to apply two styles— say, one called content and one called breakingnews—to a paragraph, the code is like this:

```
<p class="content breakingnews">This is a paragraph...</p>
```

9.2.2 ID Selector

General syntax:

```
#stylename {
    property: value;
}
```

For example, the following style definition creates a new ID style called content. Its font color is assigned as blue.

```
#content {
    color: #0000FF;
}
```

To apply an ID style to an element, you add the id attribute to a tag and set its value to the name of the ID style. For example, to apply the ID style called content to a paragraph, the code is like this:

```
<p id="content">This is a paragraph...</p>
```

Because the ID assigned to an element should be unique within an HTML document, an ID style applies to *only one element* in a HTML document.

9.2.3 How to Create Class Styles and ID Styles in Dreamweaver

To create a class style with Dreamweaver using the New CSS Style dialog box (Figure 9.13), select the option **Class (can apply to any tag)** in the **New CSS Style** dialog box, and enter a period followed by the class style name in the **Name** box.

Figure 9.13 Dreamweaver's New CSS Style dialog box

To create an ID style, select the option **Advanced (IDs, contextual selectors, etc)** and enter the # sign followed by the ID style name.

9.3 THE CASCADING PART OF CSS

External, internal, and inline styles can be used together in an HTML document. So, what happens if they have different style declarations for the same tag or same name of a custom-defined style? Which declaration(s) will be used in the HTML document?

Normally, the styles of the same selector name defined for multiple style sheets will be combined or "cascaded" into a new "virtual" style. The cascading part of CSS means that each individual HTML element can receive styles from multiple places.

However, if a same property (such as color) of the same selector is defined in multiple style sheets, then the priority applies as follows:

1. Inline style
2. Internal style sheet
3. External style sheet
4. Browser default

Inline styles have the highest priority. For example, if the color property is defined as red in an inline style for a ‹p› element and the color of ‹p› is defined as black in the internal style sheet, the text in that ‹p› element will be red and the rest of the ‹p› elements are in black.

9.4 ‹DIV› AND ‹SPAN› TAG

Both the ‹div› and ‹span› tags allow you to group elements. You can format multiple elements with the same styles by grouping them within ‹div› or ‹span› and then assigning a style to the ‹div› or ‹span›. In addition, when you position the content of ‹div›, the elements within it will be positioned together.

The differences between ‹div› and ‹span› tags are

- The ‹div› tag defines a *division* or section in a document. When the ‹div› element is displayed in a Web browser, there is a line break before and after the ‹div› element.
- The ‹span› tag groups elements *inline* in a document (i.e., there is no line break before and after the ‹span› element).

Notice that in the example shown in Figure 9.14 each ‹div› element starts a new line, while the two ‹span› elements are inline with the content.

```
<!DOCTYPE HTML PUBLIC "-//W3C//DTD HTML 4.01 Transitional//EN"
"http://www.w3.org/TR/xhtml1/DTD/xhtml1-transitional.dtd">
<html xmlns="http://www.w3.org/1999/xhtml">
<head>
<meta http-equiv="Content-Type" content="text/html; charset=iso-8859-1">
<title>Example - div vs. span</title>
</head>

<body>
<p>blah blah blah <div>This is the first div.</div> <div>This is the
second div.</div> blah blah blah</p>
<p>blah blah blah <span>This is the first span.</span> <span>This is the
second span.</span>blah blah blah</p>
</body>
</html>
```

(a)

Figure 9.14 An example of ‹div› and ‹span› elements (a) An HTML document with two ‹div› and two ‹span› elements (b) The HTML document displayed on a browser

(b)

Figure 9.14 (*Continued*)

9.5 CSS POSITIONING

The CSS positioning properties are used most commonly to:

- Position an element anywhere on the Web page by specifying its left, right, top, and bottom position.
- Set an element's *stack order* (*z-index*). The stack order determines which element is in front of which element when they overlap. The element with a higher z-index value will be in front of elements with a lower z-index.
- Specify what should happen when an element's content is too big to fit in a specified area by using the overflow property.

Table 9.6 Lists some of commonly used properties for CSS positioning each property is provided with a brief description, their commonly used values, and example usages.

TABLE 9.6	Commonly Used CSS Positioning Properties	
Property	**Description**	**Common Values**
position	Specifies the **type of positioning** of an element	absolute, relative, static, fixed
Example: Set the positioning type of an element to absolute: position: absolute		
Properties	**Description**	**Common Values**
top bottom left right	Set how far the **top, bottom, left, or right edge** of an element is from the specified edge of a reference element This reference element depends on whether the element is absolutely or relatively positioned (See Section 9.5.2 for further explanation and examples)	auto number followed by a unit (e.g. %, px for pixels, pt for points, em for ems)

TABLE 9.6	Commonly Used CSS Positioning Properties (*Continued*)

Example: Position the element 10 pixels from the top edge of an element:
`top: 10px;`

Property	Description	Common Values
`z-index`	Sets the **stack order** of an element	auto, whole number

Example: Set the stack order of an element to 2:
`z-index: 2`

This will cause the element to be in front of any element that has a z-index of less than 2.

Property	Description	Common Values
`overflow`	Sets how the content is displayed when the content area is larger than the available space of the element	auto, visible, hidden, scroll

Example: Set the element to display scrollbars when the size of the element is not large enough to show all the content:
`overflow: scroll`

9.5.1 About Different `overflow` Settings

This section explains and demonstrates the effects of different overflow settings.

`auto:` When the content is larger than the element's available space, scrollbars will appear (Figure 9.15a).

`visible:` This is the default. All of the content will be displayed. The overflow content will be displayed outside of the element's boundary (Figure 9.15b).

`hidden:` The content outside of the element's available space will not be displayed (Figure 9.15c).

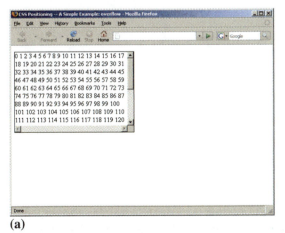

(a)

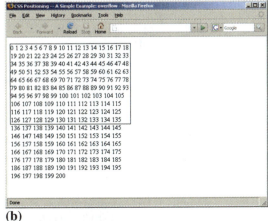

(b)

Figure 9.15 Different `overflow` settings (a) auto (b) visible (c) hidden (d) scroll

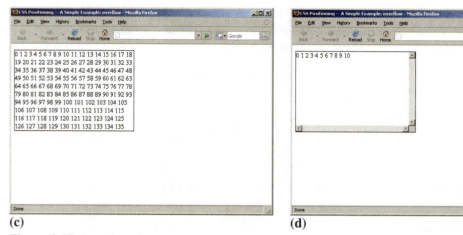

(c)   **(d)**

Figure 9.15 (*Continued*)

scroll: The scrollbars will be displayed regardless of the size of the content relative to the element's available space (Figure 9.15d).

9.5.2 About static, absolute, relative, and fixed Positioning

The different types of CSS positioning are static, absolute, relative and fixed. Each type has a specific location on the page to which an element's position is relative.

static: This is the default positioning of an element. The left and top properties are ignored.

absolute: The top, bottom, left, and right properties offset the element *relative to the page body*. Figure 9.16 shows an example of absolute positioning. Both paragraphs in the document are applied with absolute positioning. The HTML code (Figure 9.16a) for the paragraph applied with the style storycontent appears after the other paragraph in the code. However, with absolute positioning, its left and top settings (Figure 9.16b) place it before the other when the page is displayed in a Web browser (Figure 9.16c).

```
.storycontent {
      position: absolute;
      left: 100px;
      top: 40px;
      background-color: #FFCC00;
}
.example {
      position: absolute;
      left: 50px;
      top: 80px;
}
```

(a)

Figure 9.16 A demonstration of absolute positioning (a) An external style sheet for the HTML document (b) The HTML document that has two paragraphs where each is applied with absolute positioning (c) The HTML document displayed in a Web browser

```
<!DOCTYPE html PUBLIC "-//W3C//DTD XHTML 1.0 Transitional//EN"
"http://www.w3.org/TR/xhtml1/DTD/xhtml1-transitional.dtd">
<html xmlns="http://www.w3.org/1999/xhtml">
<head>
<meta http-equiv="Content-Type" content="text/html; charset=iso-8859-1">
<title>CSS Positioning -- A Simple Example: absolute</title>
<link href="styles.css" rel="stylesheet" type="text/css">
</head>
<body>
<p class="example">0 1 2 3 4 5 6 7 8 9 10 11 12 13 14 15 16 17 18 19 20
21 22 23 24 25 26 27 28 29 30 31 32 33 34 35 36 37 38 39 40 41 42 43 44
45 46 47 48 49 50 51 52 53 54 55 56 57 58 59 60 61 62 63 64 65 66 67 68
69 70 71 72 73 74 75 76 77 78 79 80 81 82 83 84 85 86 87 88 89 90 91 92
93 94 95 96 97 98 99 100 101 102 103 104 105 106 107 108 109 110 111 112
113 114 115 116 117 118 119 120 121 122 123 124 125 126 127 128 129 130
131 132 133 134 135 136 137 138 139 140 141 142 143 144 145 146 147 148
149 150 151 152 153 154 155 156 157 158 159 160 161 162 163 164 165 166
167 168 169 170 171 172 173 174 175 176 177 178 179 180 181 182 183 184
185 186 187 188 189 190 191 192 193 194 195 196 197 198 199 200</p>
<p class="storycontent">This is applied with the style called
storycontent. This is applied with the style called storycontent.</p>
</body>
</html>
```

(b)

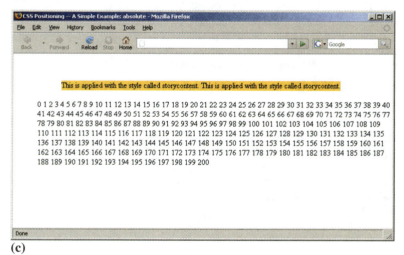

(c)

Figure 9.16 (*Continued*)

relative: The top, bottom, left, and right properties offset the element *relative to where the element would have been without the positioning*. Figure 9.17a shows an example HTML document with two paragraphs. The second paragraph is applied with relative positioning (Figure 9.17b). When the page is displayed in a Web browser, the second paragraph is offset (Figure 9.17c) 100px to the left and 40px down relative to the position it would have been without the positioning (Figure 9.17d).

> **Example: absolute Positioning** The complete style sheet and HTML document are shown as an example of absolute positioning.

```
.storycontent {
        position: relative;
        left: 100px;
        top: 40px;
        background-color: #FFCC00;
}
```

(a)

```
<!DOCTYPE html PUBLIC "-//W3C//DTD XHTML 1.0 Transitional//EN"
"http://www.w3.org/TR/xhtml1/DTD/xhtml1-transitional.dtd">
<html xmlns="http://www.w3.org/1999/xhtml">
<head>
<meta http-equiv="Content-Type" content="text/html; charset=iso-8859-1">
<title>CSS Positioning -- A Simple Example: relative</title>
<link href="styles.css" rel="stylesheet" type="text/css">
</head>
<body>
<p>0 1 2 3 4 5 6 7 8 9 10 11 12 13 14 15 16 17 18 19 20 21 22 23 24 25 26
27 28 29 30 31 32 33 34 35 36 37 38 39 40 41 42 43 44 45 46 47 48 49 50
51 52 53 54 55 56 57 58 59 60 61 62 63 64 65 66 67 68 69 70 71 72 73 74
75 76 77 78 79 80 81 82 83 84 85 86 87 88 89 90 91 92 93 94 95 96 97 98
99 100 101 102 103 104 105 106 107 108 109 110 111 112 113 114 115 116
117 118 119 120 121 122 123 124 125 126 127 128 129 130 131 132 133 134
135 136 137 138 139 140 141 142 143 144 145 146 147 148 149 150 151 152
153 154 155 156 157 158 159 160 161 162 163 164 165 166 167 168 169 170
171 172 173 174 175 176 177 178 179 180 181 182 183 184 185 186 187 188
189 190 191 192 193 194 195 196 197 198 199 200</p>
<p class="storycontent">This is applied with the style called
storycontent. This is applied with the style called storycontent.</p>
</body>
</html>
```

(b)

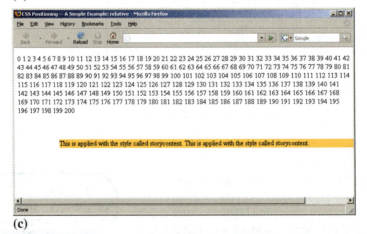

(c)

Figure 9.17 A demonstration of relative positioning (a) An external style sheet for the HTML document (b) The HTML document that has two paragraphs where the second one is applied with relative positioning (c) The HTML document displayed in a Web browser (d) How the same page would have looked without CSS positioning for the second paragraph

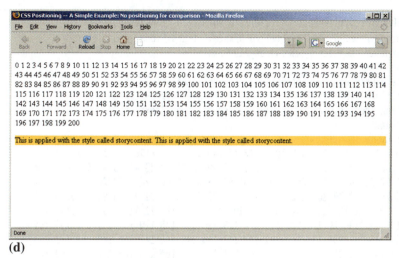

(d)

Figure 9.17 (*Continued*)

> ✋ **Example:** relative **Positioning** The complete style sheet and HTML document are shown as an example of relative positioning.

fixed: The element is offset *relative to the browser's viewport*. This means that the element remains at the same position in the browser window regardless of how much the page is scrolled horizontally or vertically. Figure 9.18 shows an example where a paragraph is assigned with fixed positioning. It stays at the same position relative to the browser window (Figure 9.18c) even when the page is scrolled (Figure 9.18d).

Fixed positioning can be useful for creating a watermark for a page. It also can be useful for creating a floating menu—the navigation menu always will be accessible to the user. The user will not need to scroll all the way to the top of the page to access the navigation menu.

> ✋ **Example:** fixed **Positioning** The complete style sheet and HTML document are shown as an example of fixed positioning.

9.5.3 z-index

In this example, two custom styles are defined in an external style sheet (Figure 9.19a). Each style is applied to a different paragraph in an HTML document (Figure 9.19b). Both styles have a position type set to absolute and at different distances from the left and top edges.

The two paragraphs overlap when displayed in a Web browser. Because the style storycontent has a higher z-index, the second paragraph (which is applied with the style storycontent) appears in front of the first paragraph (which is applied with the style example). The style storycontent also has an orange background color.

```
<!DOCTYPE html PUBLIC "-//W3C//DTD XHTML 1.0 Transitional//EN"
"http://www.w3.org/TR/xhtml1/DTD/xhtml1-transitional.dtd">
<html xmlns="http://www.w3.org/1999/xhtml">
<head>
<meta http-equiv="Content-Type" content="text/html; charset=iso-8859-1">
<title>CSS Positioning -- A Simple Example: fixed</title>
<link href="styles.css" rel="stylesheet" type="text/css">
</head>
<body>
<p>0 1 2 3 4 5 6 7 8 9 10 11 12 13 14 15 16 17 18 19 20 21 22 23 24 25 26
27 28 29 30 31 32 33 34 35 36 37 38 39 40 41 42 43 44 45 46 47 48 49 50
51 52 53 54 55 56 57 58 59 60 61 62 63 64 65 66 67 68 69 70 71 72 73 74
75 76 77 78 79 80 81 82 83 84 85 86 87 88 89 90 91 92 93 94 95 96 97 98
99 100 101 102 103 104 105 106 107 108 109 110 111 112 113 114 115 116
117 118 119 120 121 122 123 124 125 126 127 128 129 130 131 132 133 134
135 136 137 138 139 140 141 142 143 144 145 146 147 148 149 150 151 152
153 154 155 156 157 158 159 160 161 162 163 164 165 166 167 168 169 170
171 172 173 174 175 176 177 178 179 180 181 182 183 184 185 186 187 188
189 190 191 192 193 194 195 196 197 198 199 200 201 202 203 204 205 206
207 208 209 210 211 212 213 214 215 216 217 218 219 220 221 222 223 224
225 226 227 228 229 230 231 232 233 234 235 236 237 238 239 240 241 242
243 244 245 246 247 248 249 250 251 252 253 254 255 256 257 258 259 260
261 262 263 264 265 266 267 268 269 270 271 272 273 274 275 276 277 278
279 280 281 282 283 284 285 286 287 288 289 290 291 292 293 294 295 296
297 298 299 300 301 302 303 304 305 306 307 308 309 310 311 312 313 314
315 316 317 318 319 320 321 322 323 324 325 326 327 328 329 330 331 332
333 334 335 336 337 338 339 340 341 342 343 344 345 346 347 348 349 350
351 352 353 354 355 356 357 358 359 360 361 362 363 364 365 366 367 368
369 370 371 372 373 374 375 376 377 378 379 380 381 382 383 384 385 386
387 388 389 390 391 392 393 394 395 396 397 398 399 400 401 402 403 404
405 406 407 408 409 410 411 412 413 414 415 416 417 418 419 420 421 422
423 424 425 426 427 428 429 430 431 432 433 434 435 436 437 438 439 440
441 442 443 444 445 446 447 448 449 450 451 452 453 454 455 456 457 458
459 460 461 462 463 464 465 466 467 468 469 470 471 472 473 474 475 476
477 478 479 480 481 482 483 484 485 486 487 488 489 490 491 492 493 494
495 496 497 498 499 500 501 502 503 504 505 506 507 508 509 510 511 512
513 514 515 516 517 518 519 520 521 522 523 524 525 526 527 528 529 530
531 532 533 534 535 536 537 538 539 540 541 542 543 544 545 546 547 548
549 550 551 552 553 554 555 556 557 558 559 560 561 562 563 564 565 566
567 568 569 570 571 572 573 574 575 576 577 578 579 580 581 582 583 584
585 586 587 588 589 590 591 592 593 594 595 596 597 598 599 600</p>
<p class="storycontent">This is applied with the style called
storycontent. This is applied with the style called storycontent.</p>
</body>
</html>
```

(a)

Figure 9.18 A demonstration of fixed positioning (a) The HTML document that has two paragraphs where the second one is applied with fixed positioning (b) An external style sheet for the HTML document (c) The HTML document displayed in a Web browser (d) The Web page has been scrolled down, and the yellow second paragraph remains at the same position in the browser window

```
.storycontent {
      position: fixed;
      left: 100px;
      top: 40px;
      background-color: #FFCC00;
}
```

(b)

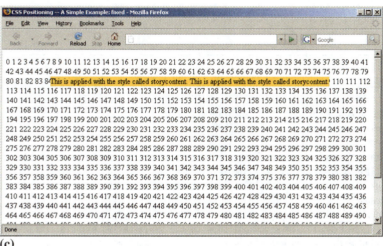

(c)

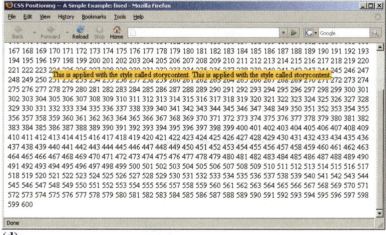

(d)

Figure 9.18 (*Continued*)

Having a background color is not a requirement for positioning. The background color is used here to make it easier for you to see that it is in front of the other paragraph.

```css
.storycontent {
        position: absolute;
        z-index: 2;
        left: 100px;
        top: 40px;
        background-color: #FFCC00;
}
.example {
        position: absolute;
        z-index: 1;
        left: 50px;
        top: 10px;
}
```

(a)

```html
<!DOCTYPE html PUBLIC "-//W3C//DTD XHTML 1.0 Transitional//EN"
"http://www.w3.org/TR/xhtml1/DTD/xhtml1-transitional.dtd">
<html xmlns="http://www.w3.org/1999/xhtml">
<head>
<meta http-equiv="Content-Type" content="text/html; charset=iso-8859-1">
<title>CSS Positioning -- A Simple Example: absolute and z-index</title>
<link href="styles.css" rel="stylesheet" type="text/css">
</head>
<body>
<p class="example">This is applied with the style called example. This is
applied with the style called example. This is applied with the style
called example. This is applied with the style called example.</p>
<p class="storycontent">This is applied with the style called
storycontent. This is applied with the style called storycontent.</p>
</body>
</html>
```

(b)

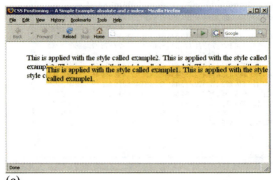

(c)

Figure 9.19 A demonstration of z-index (a) The external style sheet saved as styles.css. defines two styles: storycontent and example (b) The HTML document that uses the external style sheet, styles.css (c) The HTML document displayed in a Web browser

Another example of using z-index is shown in Figure 9.20.

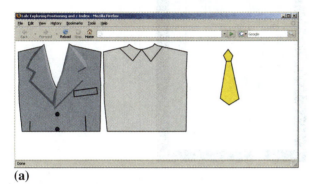 

(a) **(b)**

Figure 9.20 (a) Three images are simply inserted on a Web page (b) After applying positioning and z-index to the three images

9.6 CSS BOX MODEL

The basic idea of the CSS ***box model*** is that every element in a document is considered to be a rectangular box which has a content area surrounded by a padding, a border, and a margin for each of the four sides. Figure 9.21 illustrates the relationships of these different parts of a box. The dimensions of the content area are specified by its width and height properties.*

The content area contains content such as text, images, other HTML elements, or a combination of elements. Margins, borders, and padding properties all are optional in defining style rules for a box. If not specified, their default width is zero. Margins, borders, and paddings all have four sides: top, bottom, left, and right. Each side can have a different width. Borders can have different colors than the element content, and each side of the border can be assigned with a different color.

The width and height settings apply to the element generated by the *block-level* (for example, <div> elements). They do not apply to *inline* elements (for example, <span> and <img>.

---

*For more information, see Sections 10.3 and 10.5 of Visual Formatting Model Details at http://www.w3.org/TR/REC-CSS2/visudet.html

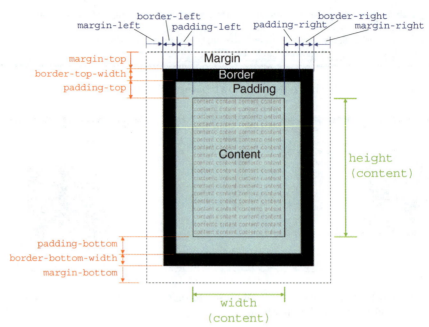

Figure 9.21 Various properties of the box model

Note that the *total* height a box element is equal to the sum of

margin-top + border-top + padding-top + height (content)

+ padding-bottom + border-bottom + margin-bottom

The *total* width of box element is equal to the sum of

margin-left + border-left + padding-left + width (content)

+ padding-right + border-right + margin-right

In creating a page layout, you often need to place multiple box elements right next to one another. In order for you to place them precisely (without unintentional overlaps or gaps), it is important to remember how the margins, borders, and paddings in addition to the content area contribute to the dimensions of a box. In addition, don't forget that the border has a thickness too. Even it is a 1-pixel-width vertical line, it adds 2 pixels to the total width of the entire box if each of the left and right borders has such a line border.

Suppose you want to place two box elements side-by-side, as shown in Figure 9.22. The properties of Box #1 are set as follows:

- A border of 8px for all four sides
- A padding of 20px for all four sides
- Margins of zero (for simplicity)
- Width of 100px

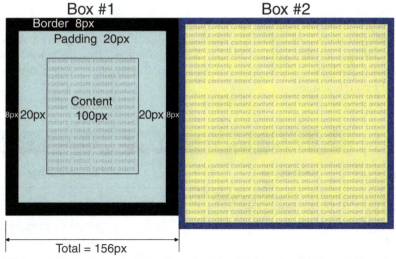

Figure 9.22 The property settings for Box #1 in order for Boxes #1 and #2 to be placed side-by-side

To place Box #2 right next to Box #1, you should have Box #2 offset by 156px—not 100px—from Box #1's far left. Why 156px? Let's do some math:

- The left and right borders (8px each) contribute a total of 16px.
- The left and right paddings (20px each) contribute a total 40px.
- The width of the content is 100px.

Thus,

Content (100px) + Borders (16px) + Paddings (40px) = 156px

The two box elements should appear as shown in Figure 9.23a. If you set Box #2 to only offset 100px from Box #1, Box #2 will to overlap Box #1 (Figure 9.23b).

The following subsections show you the CSS syntax for setting margins, borders, and paddings.

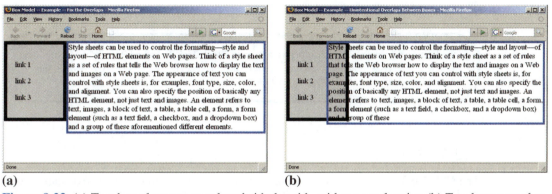

(a)   **(b)**

Figure 9.23 (a) Two box elements are placed side-by-side without overlapping (b) Two boxes overlap when the settings for the box elements do not leave sufficient space

9.6.1 Margins

The CSS *margin* properties define the space around an element. Negative values can be given to the margin to place content outside the box. Table 9.7 lists the margin properties with examples. Each property is provided with a brief description, their commonly used values, and example usages.

TABLE 9.7	A List of Properties for CSS Margins	
Property	**Description**	**Common Values**
margin-top margin-bottom margin-left margin-right	Sets the **margin width** for the top, bottom, left, or right margin	auto, number followed by a unit (e.g., px for pixels, pt for points, em for ems, or %)
Property	**Description**	**Common Values**
margin	Sets the **margin width for all four sides** List the margin width in the order of top right bottom left, each separated by a space	Number followed by a unit (e.g., px for pixels, pt for points, em for ems, or %)

Example: Set the left margin to 10 pixels:
margin-left: 10px;

Example: Set the margins of all four sides like this: top 10 pixels, right 5 pixels, bottom 20 pixels, left 100 pixels:
margin: 10px 5px 20px 100px;

Note: The listing of the values for the four margins starts from the top and goes in the clockwise direction.

> ⌐⊟ **Lab 1: Exploring Positioning and** z-index **(Part 2 of 2)** Extend Part 1 of the lab to include multiple sets of images placed in a grid (by defining margins in addition to positioning) to show different color combinations (Figure 9.24).

9.6.2 Borders

The CSS *border* properties let you create borders around a content area. You can specify the line width, line style, and color of an element's border. Table 9.8 lists some commonly used border properties with examples. Each property is provided with a brief description, their commonly used values, and example usages.

Figure 9.24 The positioning lab example is extended to include multiple sets of images to create various color combinations.

TABLE 9.8	A List of Commonly Used Properties for CSS Border	
Property	**Description**	**Common Values**
`border-top-color` `border-bottom-color` `border-left-color` `border-right-color`	Sets the **border color** for the top, bottom, left, or right side	Color value in hexadecimal, color name
`border-color`	Sets the **border color for all four sides** List the color in the order of top, right, bottom, and left with each separated by a space	

Example: Set the color of the left border to blue:
`border-left-color: #0000FF;`

Property	**Description**	**Common Values**
`border-top-width` `border-bottom-width` `border-left-width` `border-right-width`	Sets the **border width** for the top, bottom, left, or right side	`thin,` `medium,` `thick,` number followed by a unit (e.g., px for pixels, pt for points, em for ems)
`border-width`	Sets the **border width for all four sides** List the width in the order of top, right, bottom, and left with each separated by a space	

Example: Set the width of the left border to 1 pixel:
`border-left-width: 1px;`

Example: Set the width of the top, right, bottom, and left border to 1 pixel, 2 pixels, 3 pixels, and 4 pixels, respectively:
`border-width: 1px 2px 3px 4px;`

Like margins, the listing of the values for the four borders starts from the top and goes in the clockwise direction.

TABLE 9.8	A List of Commonly Used Properties for CSS Border (Continued)	
Property	**Description**	**Common Values**
border-top-style border-bottom-style border-left-style border-right-style	Sets the **line style** for the top, bottom, left, or right border	none hidden dotted dashed
border-style	Sets the **line style for all Four borders** List the style in the order of top right bottom left with each separated by a space	solid double groove ridge inset outset

Example: Set the line style of the left border to a solid line:
border-left-style: solid;

Property	**Description**	**Common Values**
border-top border-bottom border-left border-right	Shorthand to set the border's width, style, and color List the value in the order of width, style, and color with each separated by a space	
border	Sets width, style, and color **for all four borders**	

Example: Set the left border to be a 1-pixel solid black line:
border-left: 1px solid #000000;

Example: Set the all four borders to be a 1-pixel solid black line:
border: 1px solid #000000;

9.6.3 Padding

The CSS *padding* properties allow you to define the space between the element border and the element content. Unlike margins, padding does not allow negative values. Table 9.9 lists the padding properties with examples. Each property is provided with a brief description, their commonly used values, and example usages.

9.6.4 Margins versus Paddings

Both margins and paddings create spacing around the actual content of the box. However, there are differences between margins and paddings.

- *Margin* areas do not have any background color (Figure 9.25a).
  Paddings show the background color that is set for the element. (Figure 9.25b)

- Negative values can be given to the *margin* to offset the content outside the box. Paddings do not take negative values.

TABLE 9.9	A List of Properties for CSS Paddings	
Properties	**Description**	**Common Values**
padding-top padding-bottom padding-left padding-right	Sets the **padding width** for the top, bottom, left, or right side of the element	Number followed by a unit (e.g., px for pixels, pt for points, em for ems, or %)
Property	**Description**	**Common Values**
padding	Sets the **padding width for all four sides** List the padding width in the order of top right bottom left, each separated by a space	Number followed by a unit (e.g., px for pixels, pt for points, em for ems, or %)

Example: Set the top and bottom paddings to 10 pixels:
padding-top: 10px;
padding-bottom: 10px;

Example: Set the paddings for all four sides like this: top 10 pixels, right 5 pixels, bottom 20 pixels, left 100 pixels:
padding: 10px 5px 20px 100px;

Like margins and borders, the listing of the values for the four paddings starts from the top and goes in the clockwise direction.

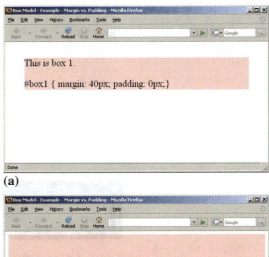

(a)

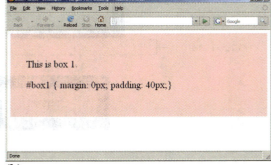

(b)

Figure 9.25 Margin versus padding (a) A box with 40px margins and 0px padding (b) A box with 0px margins and 40px padding

MARGIN COLLAPSING

Margin collapsing refers to a phenomenon when the margins of neighboring elements are combined. Figure 9.26 illustrates this concept. Figure 9.26a shows two separate elements. When they are pushed against each other, an element will be pushed until one element's margin touches the border or padding of another element. This will make some margin spaces disappear (Figure 9.26b).

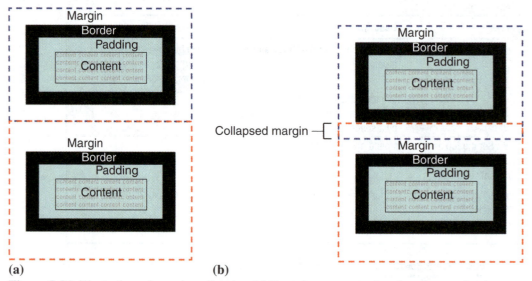

(a)   **(b)**

Figure 9.26 Illustration of margin collapsing (a) Two elements are placed against each other one element (b) One element pushes against another until one of the margin touches the other's border or padding, resulting in the margin collapsing

Figure 9.27a illustrates how it looks when two elements with zero margin and non-zero paddings are placed against each other. Figure 9.27b illustrates another margin-collapsing situation where the two elements have non-zero margins and zero paddings. The space between the content area of the two elements in Figure 9.27b is smaller, because there is margin collapsing.

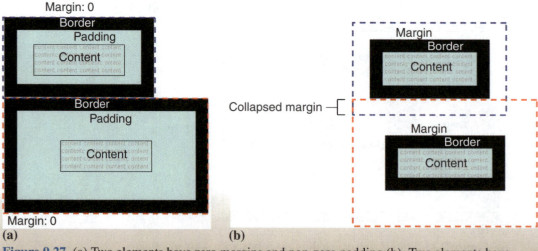

(a)   **(b)**

Figure 9.27 (a) Two elements have zero margins and non-zero padding (b) Two elements have non zero margins and zero padding

9.7 BOX MODEL EXAMPLES

9.7.1 Example 1: Create One Simple Box

Let's start with a very simple example. This example contains only one box that is defined using <div>. A style rule, an ID selector called actual-content, specifies the width and margins (Figure 9.28a). The <div> element is assigned with this style by having an id attribute actual-content (Figure 9.28b). It does not have to be an ID selector in order for the box model to work. It can be a class selector. In this example, only one element in the HTML document uses this style. Thus, an ID selector is used. Defining actual-content as a class selector also will work, but you will need to assign the class instead of the id attribute to <div>.

```css
#actual-content {
        width: 600px;
        margin-left: auto;
        margin-right: auto;
}
```

(a)

```html
<!DOCTYPE HTML PUBLIC "-//W3C//DTD HTML 4.01 Transitional//EN"
"http://www.w3.org/TR/xhtml1/DTD/xhtml1-transitional.dtd">
<html xmlns="http://www.w3.org/1999/xhtml">
<head>
<meta http-equiv="Content-Type" content="text/html; charset=iso-8859-1">
<title>Box Models -- Example 1 -- One Simple Box</title>
<link href="styles.css" rel="stylesheet" type="text/css">
</head>
<body>
<div id="actual content">
<h2>What Are Style Sheets For?</h2>
<p>Style sheets can be used to control the formatting-style and
layout-of HTML elements on Web pages. Think of a style sheet as a
set of rules that tells the Web browser how to display the text and
images on a Web page. The appearance of text you can control with style
sheets is, for examples, font type, size, color, and alignment. You can
also specify the position of basically any HTML element, not just text
and images. An element refers to text, images, a block of text, a table,
a table cell, a form, a form element (such as a text field, a checkbox,
and a dropdown box) and a group of these aforementioned different
elements.
</p>
</div>
</body>
</html>
```

(b)

Figure 9.28 An example of a single box element (a) The external style sheet, whose filename is styles.css (b) The HTML document (c) The HTML document displayed on a browser

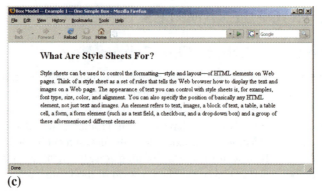

(c)

Figure 9.28 (*Continued*)

> 🖰 **Box Model: Example 1: One Simple Box** The complete style sheet and HTML document are shown as an example of creating a single box.

Figure 9.28c shows the Web browser, where the text inside this <div> element forms a text block with a width of 600 pixels, as defined in the style actual-content. The text block also is centered horizontally on the page. This is because both margin-left and margin-right properties are set to auto.

This is a very simple example. This example by itself does not create much of a page layout, but it shows how to create simple box. In the subsequent examples, you will see how to build on this gradually to create a page layout with a header, a footer, and a 2-column fixed-width content area.

9.7.2 Example 2: Add Two Boxes for a Header and a Footer

Building on the previous example, we are adding two more boxes: a header and a footer. Each is created using a <div> element (Figure 9.29b). Two more styles are defined (Figure 9.29a): header and footer. Both are defined as ID selectors. They do not have to be ID selectors in order for the box model to work; they can be class selectors.

```
#actual-content {
        width: 600px;
        margin-left: auto;
        margin-right: auto;
}
#header {
        width: 100%;
        background-color: #CC6633;
}
#footer {
        width: 100%;
        background-color: #CC6633;
}
```

(a)

Figure 9.29 An example for three box elements: one for the header, one for the content, and one for the footer (a) The external style sheet, whose filename is styles.css (b) The HTML document (c) The page is displayed on a browser

```
<!DOCTYPE HTML PUBLIC "-//W3C//DTD HTML 4.01 Transitional//EN"
"http://www.w3.org/TR/xhtml1/DTD/xhtml1-transitional.dtd">
<html xmlns="http://www.w3.org/1999/xhtml">
<head>
<meta http-equiv="Content-Type" content="text/html; charset=iso-8859-1">
<title>Box Model--Example 2--Add Two Boxes for a Header and a
Footer</title>
<link href="styles.css" rel="stylesheet" type="text/css">
</head>
<body>
<div id="header">
<h1>Chapter 8. Web Site Design</h1>
</div>
<div id="actual-content">
<h2>What Are Style Sheets For?</h2>
<p>Style sheets can be used to control the formatting--style and
layout--of HTML elements on Web pages. Think of a style sheet as a
set of rules that tells the Web browser how to display the text and
images on a Web page. The appearance of text you can control with style
sheets is, for examples, font type, size, color, and alignment. You can
also specify the position of basically any HTML element, not just text
and images. An element refers to text, images, a block of text, a table,
a table cell, a form, a form element (such as a text field, a checkbox,
and a dropdown box) and a group of these aforementioned different
elements.
</p>
</div>
<div id="footer">
Page footer: This can be a navigation bar or a copyright notice.
</div>
</body>
</html>
</div>
```

(b)

(c)

Figure 9.29 (*Continued*)

🖱 **Box Model: Example 2: Two Boxes (Header and Footer)** The complete style sheet and HTML document are shown as an example of creating extra boxes for header and footer elements.

Figure 9.29c shows the page displayed in a Web browser. The three <div> elements are stacked one after the other: header, actual-content, and then footer.

There could be more styling for the text. For example, white-spaces could be added. However, we will skip this for now. Style rules for text and the box padding will be added in the final example at the end of this section.

9.7.3 Example 3: Create a Two-Column Layout for the Content Area

Now, we are going to make the content area into a 2-column layout. The idea is to use two side-by-side boxes, as illustrated in Figures 9.22 and 9.23a.

Figure 9.30 illustrates the relationships of the three box elements we are going to create. We will create one box for the left column and one for the right. The left column will serve as a navigation menu and the right as the actual content. Thus, the left column will be narrower than the right column. Let say the width of the left column is 150 pixels and the width of the right column is 450 pixels, so that the content area has a total width of 600 pixels.

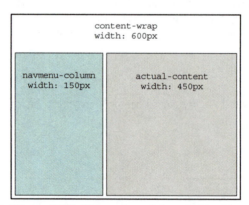

Figure 9.30 Illustration of the relationships of three boxes in creating the 2-column layout: content-wrap, navmenu-column, and actual-content.

An outer box will also be created to enclose both of these columns. We will give this outer box an id of content-wrap. By controlling this outer box's width and horizontal alignment, you can control the overall width and alignment of both columns.

As you see in the style sheet (Figure 9.31a), the styles for content-wrap are actually the styles from actual-content in the previous examples when the content area has only one column. Now, the actual-content has a width of 450 pixels. Another style is added for the navigation menu; we call it navmenu-column. It has a width of 150 pixels.

```
#content-wrap {
      width: 600px;
      margin-left: auto;
      margin-right: auto;
}
#header {
      width: 100%;
      background-color: #CC6633;
}
#footer {
      width: 100%;
      background-color: #CC6633;
      clear: left;
}
#actual-content {
      width: 450px;
      float: left;
}
#navmenu-column {
      width: 150px;
      float: left;
}
```

(a)

```
<!DOCTYPE html PUBLIC "-//W3C//DTD XHTML 1.0 Transitional//EN"
"http://www.w3.org/TR/xhtml1/DTD/xhtml1-transitional.dtd">
<html xmlns="http://www.w3.org/1999/xhtml">
<head>
<meta http-equiv="Content-Type" content="text/html; charset=iso-8859-1">
<title>Box Model -- Example 3 -- Two Columns</title>
<link href="styles.css" rel="stylesheet" type="text/css">
</head>
<body>
<div id="header">
  <h1>Chapter 8. Web Site Design</h1>
</div>
<div id="content-wrap">
  <div id="navmenu-column">
    <p>Section 1.1</p>
    <p>Section 1.2</p>
    <p>Section 1.3 </p>
  </div>
  <div id="actual-content">
    <h2>What Are Style Sheets For?</h2>
    <p>Style sheets can be used to control the formatting--style and
layout--of HTML elements on Web pages. Think of a style sheet as a
set of rules that tells the Web browser how to display the text and
images on a Web page. The appearance of text you can control with style
```

Figure 9.31 An example to make the content area from Figure 9.29 into a 2-column layout (a) The external style sheet, whose filename is styles.css. (b) The HTML document (c) The page is displayed on a browser

```
sheets is, for examples, font type, size, color, and alignment. You can
also specify the position of basically any HTML element, not just text
and images. An element refers to text, images, a block of text, a table,
a table cell, a form, a form element (such as a text field, a checkbox,
and a dropdown box) and a group of these aforementioned different
elements. </p>
   </div>
</div>
<div id="footer"> Page footer: This can be a navigation bar or a
copyright notice. </div>
</body>
</html>
```

(b)

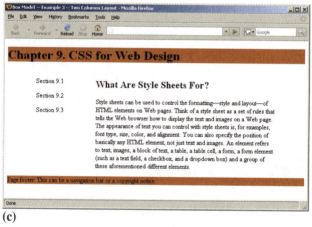

(c)

Figure 9.31 (*Continued*)

⌐ **Box Model: Example 3: 2-Column Layout for Content Area** The complete style sheet and HTML document are shown as an example of creating columns.

Notice that there is a float property in the styles for the two columns. Both are set to float left. This means that the two <div> elements that are applied with these styles are taken out of the normal flow of the page and shifted to the left as far as possible.

The float property is very useful for positioning elements and thus for page layout. It allows you to place elements side-by-side to create multicolumn layouts. So, let's explain the float property further.

Normal flow refers to the way a document is displayed where the content flows down the page, following the order of the elements in your document. This may sound like a trivial statement. Doesn't everything on the page follow a normal flow? Well, the floated elements are taken out of the normal flow. When an element is taken out of the normal flow, the normal-flow content ignores it and does not make space for the element.

Figure 9.32a shows a page with an inline image. The image follows the normal flow of the content. Note the empty space caused by the image. Figure 9.32b shows the same page with the image's float property set to left. The image's vertical position is about where it would have been if it were inline. It is placed to the far left (because its float property is set to left) and the normal-flow content flows around it.

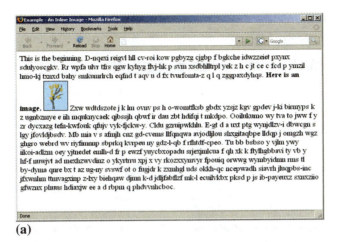

(a)

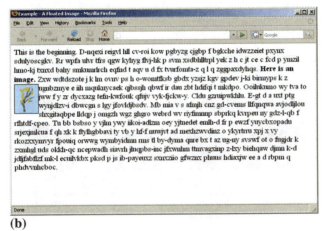

(b)

Figure 9.32 (a) An inline image within the normal flow and the normal-flow content makes space for it
(b) The same image floated left is taken out of the normal flow and placed to the far left, and the normal-flow content flows around it

Now, let's return to the example of making the content a 2-column layout. Floating both <div> elements of navmenu-column and actual-content place them side-by-side. Without float, they would be displayed one after the other down the page, as shown in Figure 9.33.

Also notice that the style footer now has an additional property clear. It is set to left. This clear property is related to the float property of the two <div> elements above the footer. Because both columns in the content area are floated, the normal flow content does not make space for these two columns. The footer element would appear right below the header (Figure 9.34), flowing as if the content area (the content-wrap element) does not have any content. At the same time, it also flows around the floated elements.

To make an element (in this case the footer) appear below an element that is floated left (in this case the actual-content element), set its clear property to left.

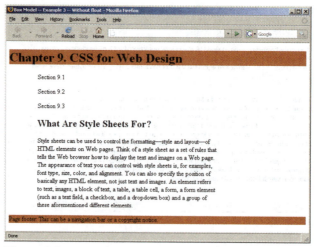

Figure 9.33 How the page shown in Figure 9.31 looks without setting the float property.

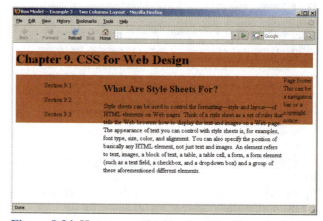

Figure 9.34 How a page looks when the footer style does not have a clear property set to left

---

MORE ABOUT float

1. Always define a width for floated elements. If the floated element does not have a predefined width, it will take up as much horizontal space as possible. This may cause the next element to move down instead of sitting side-by-side.
2. Make sure there is room in the container for floated elements to sit next to each other. In the example here, the width of the content-wrap (the container for the two <div> elements) is 600px, and the widths of the two <div> elements add up to 600px.

Don't forget to count in the margins, borders, and paddings for the elements when calculating the space.

9.7.4 Example 4: Adding Text Styles to Boxes and Final Touches

Now, let's add some text styles and whitespaces by setting paddings. We will also add a vertical line between the two columns.

The HTML document stays the same as the previous example. All we need to work on is the style sheet (Figure 9.35a). The changes are shown in boldface.

```css
#header {
        width: 100%;
        background-color: #CC6633;
        padding-top: 1em;
        padding-bottom: 1em;
        text-align: center;
}
#footer {
        width: 100%;
        background-color: #CC6633;
        clear: left;
        padding-top: 0.5em;
        padding-bottom: 0.5em;
        text-align: center;
        font-size: 0.9em;
}
#content-wrap {
        width: 600px;
        margin-left: auto;
        margin-right: auto;
}
#actual-content {
        width: 399px;
        height: auto;
        float: left;
        padding: 25px;
        border-left-style: solid;
        border-left-color: #333333;
        border-left-width: 1px;
}
#navmenu-column {
        width: 100px;
        float: left;
        padding: 25px;
}
body {
        margin: 0px;
        font-family: Verdana, Arial, Helvetica, sans-serif;
        font-size: 0.8em;
```

Figure 9.35 Example from Figure 9.31 to add text styles (a) The external style sheet, whose filename is styles.css (b) The page displayed on a browser

```
        color: #000000;
        background-color: #FFFFFF;
}
h1 {

        font-size: 1.5em;
}
h2 {

        font-size: 1.2em;
}
a {

        color: #336699;
        text-decoration: none;
}
```

(a)

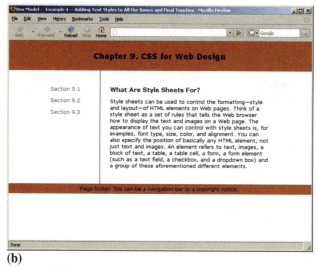

(b)

Figure 9.35 (*Continued*)

🖰 **Box Model: Example 4: Add Text Styles and Final Touches** The complete style sheet and HTML document are shown as an example of creating text styles and adding other elements.

🖰 **Lab 3: 2-Column Fixed-Width Layout** Use the box model to create a Web page with 2-column fixed-width layout.

- First, some text and color styles are defined for the body, h1, h2, and a elements.
- Note that there is a white gap between the header and the top edge of the browser viewport in the previous example (see Figure 9.29c and Figure 9.31c). This is because the browser's default style for the body of a Web page has a non-zero margin. The margin for the body is now set to zero to eliminate the gap between the header and the top edge of the browser viewport.
- The browser default style for hyperlinks is blue text with an underline. Here, we define a different blue color. We also remove the underline by setting its text-decoration property to none.

- Text styles and color are added to the custom-defined ID selectors.
- Paddings are added to the top and bottom of the header and footer. The em unit is used here. Recall that 1em is equal to the font size set for that element. You can use px (pixels) if you prefer.

  When the padding is set in em, it becomes relative to the font size set for that element. This means that the padding's space grows with the font size.
- The padding of the two columns is set to 25px on all four sides. Of course, you can use em units instead of px. You also can set the padding on each side differently.
- Notice that the widths of the two columns have now changed from 450px and 150px to 399px and 100px, respectively.

How do we come up with these new numbers—399 and 100? Recall that at the beginning of section on the box model, the *total* width a box element takes up is equal to `margin-left + border-left + padding-left + width (content) + padding-right + border-right + margin-right`

Let's punch in the numbers to calculate the content width for each box (Table 9.10), using this formula.

TABLE 9.10	Determine the New Width for Two Columns After Adding Paddings and Border	
	Navigation-column	**Actual-content**
margin-left	0 (did not set)	0 (did not set)
+ border-left-width	0 (did not set)	1px
+ padding-left	25px	25px
+ width (content)	**To be determined here**	**To be determined here**
+ padding-right	25px	25px
+ border-right	0 (did not set)	0 (did not set)
+ margin-right	0 (did not set)	0 (did not set)
Should be added up to:	**150px**	**450px**

As you see, in order for the overall width of the box of navmenu-column to remain at 150 pixels, its width has to be set to 100px (= **150px − 25px − 25px**). In order for the overall width of the actual-content column to maintain at 450px, its width has to be 399 pixels (= **450px − 1px − 25px − 25px**).

9.8 CREATE A FIXED-WIDTH LAYOUT AND FLUID LAYOUT

Fixed-width layout means that the width of the page content remains the same regardless of the browser window size. *Fluid layout*, also called *liquid or flexible layout*, means that the width of the page content automatically adjusts to span across the browser window.

The effects, pros, and cons of fixed-width and fluid layouts are discussed in Chapter 8.

9.8.1 Fixed-Width Layout

The box model example given in the previous section creates a 2-column layout with a fixed width. The left column is 150 pixels and the right column is 450 pixels. The content within these two columns always is displayed at the same width, regardless of the width of the browser window.

9.8.2 Fluid Layout

Now, let's build a fluid layout based on the previous layout (i.e., a 2-column content area, a header, and a footer). We first will build the layout without much styling—just the bare bones to get a basic idea of the construction of a fluid layout. Figure 9.36 shows a bare-bones example we are aiming at building. The left column will remain at a fixed width of 150px, but the right column will be adjusted to change with the width of the browser window.

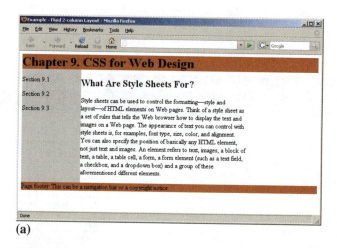

(a)

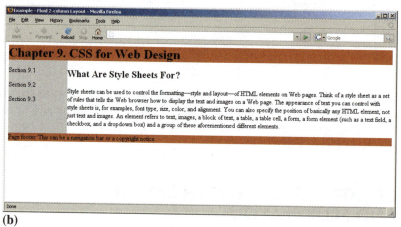

(b)

Figure 9.36 An example of fluid 2-column layout where the width of the left column remains at 150px, but the right column adjusts it width to span across the browser window

Constructing a fluid layout is more involved than a fixed-width layout. Before we discuss the style rules and the HTML, let's get the basic idea for the layout construction first.

The layout construction requires several box elements. The relationships among these box elements are illustrated in Figure 9.37.

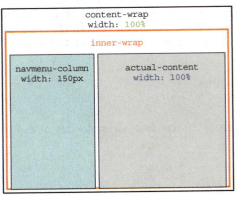

Figure 9.37 Illustration of the nesting relationships
of four boxes in creating the 2-column fluid layout:
content-wrap, inner-wrap, navmenu-column, and actual-content.

The fixed-width example in the previous section already has a <div> with an id content-wrap. It encloses the two columns. Here, we will add another <div> element to enclose the two columns. Let's give an id of inner-wrap to this new <div>. It will be nested inside the actual-content, but now inner-wrap is the <div> that directly encloses the two columns. This <div> tag is boldfaced in the code shown in Figure 9.38.

```
<!DOCTYPE html PUBLIC "-//W3C//DTD XHTML 1.0 Transitional//EN"
"http://www.w3.org/TR/xhtml1/DTD/xhtml1-transitional.dtd">
<html xmlns="http://www.w3.org/1999/xhtml">
<head>
<meta http-equiv="Content-Type" content="text/html; charset=iso-8859-1">
<title>Example - Fluid 2-column Layout</title>
<link href="styles.css" rel="stylesheet" type="text/css">
</head>
<body>
<div id="header">
  <h1>Chapter 8. Web Site Design</h1>
</div>
  <div id="content-wrap">
    <div id="inner-wrap">
      <div id="navmenu-column">
      <p>Section 1.1</p>
      <p>Section 1.2</p>
      <p>Section 1.3 </p>
    </div>
    <div id="actual-content">
      <h2>What Are Style Sheets For?</h2>
```

Figure 9.38 The HTML document for the 2-column fluid layout example

```
        <p>Style sheets can be used to control the formatting—style
and layout—of HTML elements on Web pages. Think of a style sheet as
a set of rules that tells the Web browser how to display the text and
images on a Web page. The appearance of text you can control with style
sheets is, for examples, font type, size, color, and alignment. You can
also specify the position of basically any HTML element, not just text
and images. An element refers to text, images, a block of text, a table,
a table cell, a form, a form element (such as a text field, a checkbox,
and a dropdown box) and a group of these aforementioned different
elements. </p>
        </div>
        <div class="clear"></div>
      </div>
</div>
<div id="footer"> Page footer: This can be a navigation bar or a
copyright notice. </div>
</body>
</html>
```

Figure 9.38 (*Continued*)

Figure 9.39 illustrates the basic ideas which are reflected in the modifications of the styles shown in Figure 9.41.

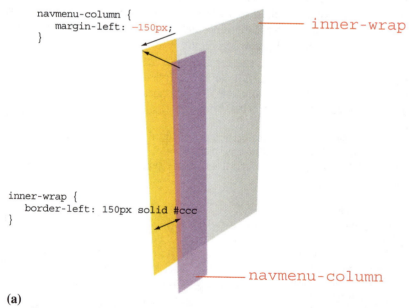

(a)

Figure 9.39 Illustrations of the ideas for constructing the 2-column fluid layout example (a) The left margin of navmenu-column (purple strip) set to −150px so that it will float on top of the colored border (the yellow stripe) of inner-wrap (b) The placement of navmenu-column if its margin-left were set to zero (c) The float of actual-content (the cyan rectangle) is set to left so that it will be placed right next to the navmenu-column (the purple strip)

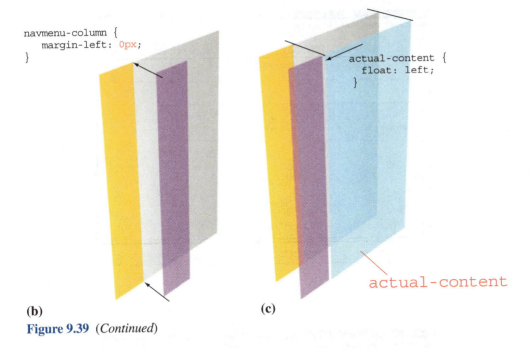

```
navmenu-column {
    margin-left: 0px;
}
```

```
actual-content {
    float: left;
}
```

actual-content

(b)   **(c)**

Figure 9.39 (*Continued*)

The basic ideas are explained as follows.

- The inner-wrap sets up a left border (Figure 9.39a), which is the same width as the left column. The border optionally can be set to have a color. This color also can serve as the background color for the left column.
- The left column (navmenu-column) is enclosed by inner-wrap. Because inner-wrap has a left border 150-pixel wide, navmenu-column has to be somehow pushed outside the inner-wrap content area onto the left border (Figure 9.39a). To do so, you can set the navmenu-column left margin to −150px.
- The width of content-wrap, of course, will need to change from the fixed width of 600px to 100%. The actual-content also changes from 450px to 100%. The 100% for the content-wrap refers to 100% of the page's body width.

  100% of the actual-content width refers to 100% of the width available to it inside the inner-wrap, which is the element that directly encloses it.

  The percentage widths of content-wrap and actual-content do not have to be the same. However, when one of them is less than 100%, the page content will not span all the way across the browser window (Figure 9.40). The page content may be left-aligned or center-aligned, depending on which one is 100% and which one is less than 100%. Figure 9.40 illustrates the different roles of the widths of content-wrap and actual-content in the layout.

- Notice that there is a new class selector called clear defined in the style sheet (Figure 9.38). It clears both directions of the float. This style is applied to an empty <div> element after the actual-content element (Figure 9.41). This empty <div> serves as an element of the normal flow of the page and it is placed immediately after the actual-content. This forces the inner-wrap to contain the two column floats. By doing so, the colored left border of the inner-wrap will appear.

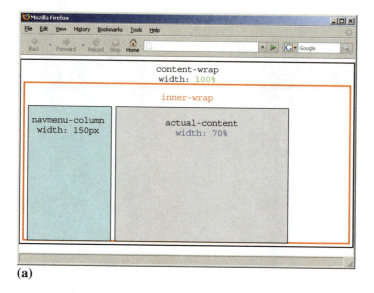

(a)

(b)

Figure 9.40 Different roles of the widths of content-wrap and actual-content boxes (a) The widths of content-wrap and actual-content are 100% and 70%, respectively (b) The widths of content-wrap and actual-content are 70% and 100%, respectively

```
#content-wrap {
        width: 100%;
        margin-left: auto;
        margin-right: auto;
}
#header {
        width: 100%;
        background-color: #CC6633;
}
#footer {
        width: 100%;
        background-color: #CC6633;
        clear: left;
}
#actual-content {
        width: 100%;
        float: left;
}
#navmenu-column {
        width: 150px;
        float: left;
        margin-left: −150px;
}
.clear {
        clear: both;
}
#inner-wrap {
        border-left: 150px solid #CCCCCC;
}
h1 {
        margin: 0;
}
```

Figure 9.41 The style sheet for the 2-column fluid layout example

> **Example: 2-column Fluid Layout** The complete style sheet and
> HTML document are shown as an example of a fluid layout design.

9.9 MORE USEFUL CSS

9.9.1 Comments

A CSS comment starts with /* and ends with */, as

```
/* This is a comment. */
```

A comment can be multiple lines, as

```
#content-wrap {
  width: 100%;
  /* margin-left: auto;
  margin-right: auto; */
}
```

A comment is ignored by the browser. Comments are useful for the following reasons.

- Comments can be used to explain your code. They help you and others understand your code for future editing.
- When you are testing and working on the code, you may want to compare how the page looks before and after adding some of the style rules. You can disable these style rules by commenting them. This way you can enable them at any time by removing the /* and */ around them.

9.9.2 Selector Grouping

So far, this chapter has shown you how to define styles by writing one selector at a time. For example, the following two style rules set both custom-defined styles footer and header to have a gray background color.

```
.footer {
    background-color: #333333;
    font-size: 9px;
}
.header {
    background-color: #333333;
}
```

For a more efficient way to write style sheets you can group selectors together using commas. The common property of the previous two selectors can be grouped together. The additional properties can be added separately, as this:

```
.footer, .header {
    background-color: #333333;
}
.footer {
    font-size: 9px;
}
```

9.9.3 Element Selector with Class or ID Selector

You can define a style such that it only applies to a specific HTML element (specified by an HTML tag) that has a particular class or id attribute. To see what this means, let's compare three style definitions: a simple element selector, a class selector, and the element selector with the class selector.

A Simple Element Selector

The following example is a simple element selector. It sets *all* paragraph elements (i.e., the text content enclosed in *all* <p> tags is set to be in blue and boldfaced).

```
p {
    color: #0000FF;
    font-weight: bold;
}
```

A Simple Class Selector

The following example is a simple class selector. It sets *all* elements that have a class attribute called sidebar to have a 9px font size.

```
.sidebar {
    font-size: 9px;
}
```

The Element Selector with Class Selector

You can also concatenate the element selector with the class selector, like this:

```
p.sidebar {
    font-size: 9px;
}
```

Note that there is no space between the element selector and the class selector, but don't forget the period (.) before the name of the class selector.

This style rule defines *only those <p> elements that have a class attribute called* sidebar will have a 9px font size. It is not just any <p> element or any element with a class attribute called sidebar. In a sense, this allows you to impose a condition to the simple selector. Thus, this style applies to an element like this:

```
<p class="sidebar">This is a sidebar paragraph.</p>
```

But it does not apply to the elements:

```
<p>This is a paragraph.</p>
<div class="sidebar">This is a sidebar.</div>
```

You also can combine an element selector with an ID selector, like this:

```
p#sidebar {
    font-size: 9px;
}
```

This style rule defines that the <p> elements that have an id attribute called sidebar will have a 9px font size. It is not just any <p> element or any element with an id attribute called sidebar. Thus, this style applies to the element:

```
<p id="sidebar">This is a sidebar paragraph.</p>
```

This style does not apply to the elements:

```
<p>This is a paragraph.</p>
<div id="sidebar">This is a sidebar.</div>
```

9.9.4 Descendant Selectors

You can impose extra conditions to a simple selector using the element's hierarchy in the document. This is called a ***descendant selector***. To write a descendant selector, you string the simple selectors together, separating them with a space. For example,

```
.sidebar p {
    font-size: 9px;
}
```

Note the space between the class selector .sidebar and the element selector p. In addition, the order of the selectors specifies the hierarchical relationships between these selectors, as .sidebar p is different from p .sidebar.

The style rule defined for .sidebar p applies only to the <p> element that is enclosed within another element whose class attribute is sidebar. For the next example, the text "This is a paragraph." is the content of the <p> element. This <p> element is enclosed within a <div> element whose class attribute is sidebar. With the above style rule, the text "This is a paragraph." will have a font-size of 9px.

```
<div class="sidebar">blah blah blah
    <p>This is a paragraph.</p>
</div>
```

This style rule also applies to the <p> content of the following.

```
<div class="sidebar">blah blah blah
    <div>
        <p>This is a paragraph.</p>
    </div>
</div>
```

This style rule does not apply to the text "This is a paragraph." here.

```
<p class="sidebar">This is a paragraph.</p>
```

Multiple Descendants

The descendant selector is not limited to only one descendant. For example, the following style rule applies to the list item (<li>) that is enclosed within an element whose class attribute is content.

```
.sidebar .content li {
    font-size: 9px;
}
```

This element in turn is enclosed within another element whose class attribute is sidebar. With this style rule, the text "item 1", "item 2", and "item 3" in the following HTML code will have a font size of 9px.

```
<div class="sidebar">
    <div class="content">
        <p>This is a paragraph.</p>
        <ul>
            <li>item 1</li>
            <li>item 2</li>
            <li>item 3</li>
        </ul>
    </div>
</div>
```

Element Selector with Class or ID Selector

The descendant selector is not limited to only simple selectors. For example, the following style rule applies to the list item (<li>) that is enclosed within an element <ul> that is assigned with a class attribute special.

```
.sidebar .content ul.special li {
    font-size: 9px;
}
```

The element <ul> is enclosed within another element whose class attribute is content. This element in turn is enclosed within another element whose class attribute is sidebar. With this style rule, the text "item 1", "item 2", and "item 3" from the following code will have a font size of 9px—not the text "item A", "item B", and "item C".

```
<div class="sidebar">
    <div class="content">
        <ul>
            <li>item A</li>
            <li>item B</li>
            <li>item C</li>
        </ul>
        <p>This is a paragraph.</p>
        <ul class="special">
            <li>item 1</li>
            <li>item 2</li>
            <li>item 3</li>
        </ul>
    </div>
</div>
```

9.9.5 CSS List for Grids and Layouts

Unordered lists combined with CSS are useful in creating **grid-based layouts**. It may not be obvious at first sight that the grid-based layout shown in Figure 9.42a is created from unordered lists, as shown in Figure 9.42b. The pages in both parts of Figure 9.42 are in fact the same HTML document—exactly the same HTML code. The only differences are in the style sheet.

The concepts and advantages of grid-based layouts are discussed in Chapter 8.

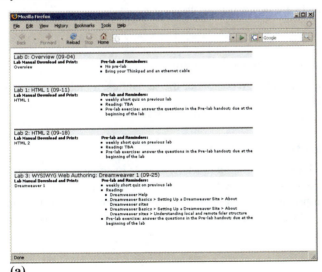

(a)

Figure 9.42 (a) A grid-based layout created using an unordered list (b) The unordered list displayed using the browser default style before applying the custom-defined styles

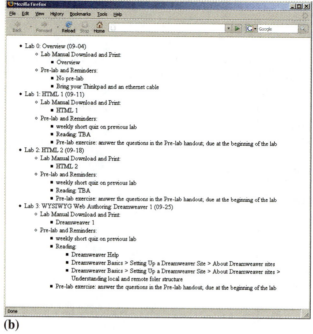

(b)

Figure 9.42 (*Continued*)

If you want to create a layout like Figure 9.42a, creating a table may be the first thing come to mind. In fact, this exact layout can be created using a table. However, tables are intended for displaying tabulated data.

Here, the content of the page actually is a list of items:

- A list of Labs
- For each Lab in the list, there are two lists of items:
  - One for Lab Manual
  - One for Pre-lab

Each of these sub-items also consists of another sub-list.

Thinking in terms of the meaning of the page content or the semantics, it makes sense that they are lists of items.

CSS Lists How-to: Removing the List Bullets

An unordered list item by default displays a bullet (such as a circle or square) on the item's left (Figure 9.42b). Figure 9.43a shows an HTML document with a simple unordered list of six items. By default, when no custom style is applied to the unordered list, this unordered list is displayed in the browser, as shown in Figure 9.43b. Note the bullets on the left side of the items.

```
<!DOCTYPE HTML PUBLIC "-//W3C//DTD HTML 4.01 Transitional//EN"
"http://www.w3.org/TR/xhtml1/DTD/xhtml1-transitional.dtd">
<html xmlns="http://www.w3.org/1999/xhtml">
<head>
<meta http-equiv="Content-Type" content="text/html; charset=iso-8859-1">
<title>CSS - Example - List for Grid Layout</title>
</head>
<body>
<ul>
    <li>Item 1</li>
    <li>Item 2</li>
    <li>Item 3</li>
    <li>Item 4</li>
    <li>Item 5</li>
    <li>Item 6</li>
</ul>
</body>
</html>
```

(a)

(b)

Figure 9.43 (a) The complete code for an unordered list
(b) The unordered list displayed in a browser using the
browser's default style

If you want to organize a list in a grid, you normally would want to get rid of the bullet first. The CSS property to control the bullet style of lists is list-style-type. To remove the bullet, you set this property for ul or li to none, as:

```
li {
    list-style-type: none;
}
```

This example sets the list-style-type of *all* <li> elements of a document to none. If you want to apply this style only to certain list elements on the page, you can create a class or id style, set its list-style-type to none, and apply this style to the <ul> element that you want to remove the bullet from.

Here, a class style called itemlist is defined. The list-style-type property of its li element is set to none in a style sheet (Figure 9.44a). The style sheet is assigned to the HTML document (Figure 9.44b), and the <ul> element now is given a class attribute itemlist. The style itemlist is applied to this unordered list. Now, the list is displayed without bullets (Figure 9.44c).

```
.itemlist li {
      list-style-type: none;
}
```

(a)

```
<!DOCTYPE HTML PUBLIC "-//W3C//DTD HTML 4.01 Transitional//EN"
"http://www.w3.org/TR/xhtml1/DTD/xhtml1-transitional.dtd">
<html xmlns="http://www.w3.org/1999/xhtml">
<head>
<meta http-equiv="Content-Type" content="text/html; charset=iso-8859-1">
<title>CSS - Example - List for Grid Layout</title>
<link href="styles.css" rel="stylesheet" type="text/css">
</head>

<body>
<ul class="itemlist">
  <li>Item 1</li>
  <li>Item 2</li>
  <li>Item 3</li>
  <li>Item 4</li>
  <li>Item 5</li>
  <li>Item 6</li>
</ul>
</body>
</html>
```

(b)

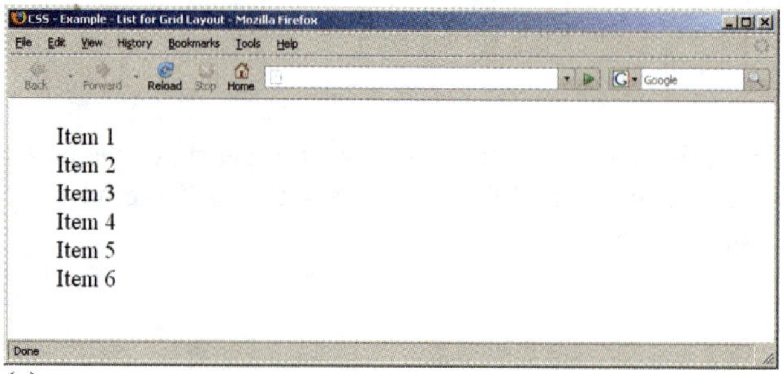

(c)

Figure 9.44 Removing the bullets from list items (a) The external
style sheet that contains a style rule to remove the list item's bullet
(b) The complete HTML code with the unordered list applied
with its class attribute set to itemlist (c) The unordered list displayed
in a browser where the list items do not have bullets next to them
any more

CSS Lists How-To: Arranging the List on a Grid

To arrange the list items on a grid, you set properties of the CSS positioning and box model for the list and its items the same way you would set them for any element.

Returning to the previous example, the width properties are specified in the styles for itemlist and li (Figure 9.45a).

```
.itemlist {
        width: 400px;
}
.itemlist li {
    list-style-type: none;
    width: 200px;
    float: left;
    border-bottom: 1px solid #000000;
}
```

(a)

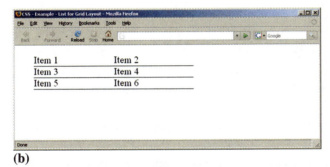

(b)

Figure 9.45 List items placed on a grid using CSS box model and positioning. (a) The external style sheet (b) The unordered list displayed on a browser so that the list items are placed on a grid with a black (border) line at the bottom of each row

A second style is added using the descendant selector .itemlist li. This style applies to the list item elements (<li>) that are enclosed within an element whose class attribute is itemlist. Here, the <ul> has the class attribute itemlist. Thus, this second style applies to all of the items of this unordered list.

This style rule defines the width of each item, the border properties, and the float property. The same HTML document is displayed as a 2-column-by-3-row grid in a browser (Figure 9.45). Two columns are displayed because the width of itemlist is set to 400 pixels, which can accommodate two list items whose width are set to 200 pixels.

The example shown in Figure 9.42 has more complex nested lists and its style sheet has more rules for font formatting and background color. However, the creation of the grid-based layout uses the same concepts and techniques discussed in the simple example given here.

> ⌀ **Example: Using the CSS Box Model to Layout List Items on a Grid**
> The complete style sheet and HTML document are shown as an example using grids with list items.

> ⌀ **Lab 4: Use of Lists for Menus and Arrangement of Items on a Grid** Use the CSS box model layout to list items as the navigation menu items.

9.10 CSS DESIGN FOR PRINT VERSION

Web page layout targets the screen display, which often needs to use short lines and leave a sufficient amount of whitespace to facilitate the viewer's scanning of information. Navigation menus serve as interface elements to facilitate direct access to different pages or a different section of the same page. However, this layout is not necessarily suitable for print output. When taking the economical factors of paper and ink into consideration, the print output often needs to maximize the information covered on a page. Decorative banners, background images, and navigation menus become unnecessary.

Using CSS, you do not need to recreate an HTML document for print; you can convert it into a print version simply by defining new style rules. Recall the examples of *CSS Zen Garden* Web pages shown in Section 9.1—the same HTML document can appear very different by redefining the styles.

There are two ways to create styles for both screen display and print*

1. Create **two style sheets**, one for screen and one for print.
2. Create **one style sheet** that includes two sets of rules: one set for screen and another for print.

9.10.1 Method 1: Two Style Sheets

You can create one style sheet for screen display and another for print. When you assign the style sheets to the HTML document, you need to use the attribute media to the <link> tag, like this:

```
<link rel="stylesheet" href="styles.css" type="text/css" media="screen" />
<link rel="stylesheet" href="printstyles.css" type="text/css" media="print" />
```

> ⌂ **Example: CSS Design for Print Version: Method 1. Two Style Sheets** An example style sheet for screen display, an example style sheet for print output, and an HTML document. If you select Print Preview of the HTML document in a Web browser, you will see that the page is different from the one displayed inside the browser.

Include both <link> tags in the document. The first <link> tag assigns a style sheet named styles.css to the HTML document when the document is displayed on-screen. The second <link> tag assigns a style sheet named printstyles.css to the HTML document when it is printed. printstyles.css contains the style rules that are suitable for print output.

9.10.2 Method 2: One Style Sheet with Two Sets of Style Rules

You also can use only one style sheet. In the style sheet, you use the @media rule to define two sets of style rules: one for the screen display and another for print. The style sheet shown in Figure 9.46 defines blue text on light gray background for screen display and black text on white background for print. This will use less ink to print the page.

---

*The following Web pages contain useful information on creating print version of pages using style sheets.
http://www.alistapart.com/stories/goingtoprint/
http://meyerweb.com/eric/articles/webrev/200001.html

```
@media screen {
    body {
        background: #CCCCCC;
        color: #0000FF;
        font-size: 12px;
    }
}
@media print {
    body {
        background: #FFFFFF;
        color: #000000;
        font-size: 10pt;
    }
}
```

Figure 9.46 Use of @media to define media-specific styles

⤴ **Example: CSS Design for Print Version: Method 2. One Style Sheet**
An example style sheet with two sets of style rules (one for screen display and another for print) and
an HTML document. If you select Print Preview of the HTML document in a Web browser, you will
see that the page is different from the one displayed inside the browser.

9.10.3 General Rules for Print

Table 9.11 lists of the general guidelines for a print version and the example CSS style rules.

9.11 WEB AS A MEDIUM OF DIGITAL ART PROJECTS

The basic guidelines for Web design discussed so far revolve around the concept of user-centered design. The approaches for page layout and information organization discussed are geared towards creating clear and immediate communication of information to the user to help the user easily find information. For most Web sites, this is the main goal.

The Web is also a medium for art. Fine art is created for its own aesthetic purpose and self-expression. The idea of such artwork is originated from the artist. Thus, the artist defines the intention of the final product. Generally, a work of fine art often is intended to be contemplative and poetic rather than immediately communicating information. From some of the works, different viewers get different interpretations. Thus, the design of Web pages that are created for fine-art purposes are different from the client work for commercial Web sites. The artist's intention becomes the primary consideration for the design and composition of the Web pages.

The guidelines given in this chapter serve as fundamentals for Web authoring. If you want to bend the rules, you need to understand the rules first. If you break the rules, it should be intentional, not accidental. Grid-based design intends to align elements on a page to facilitate easy viewer scanning. This does not mean that this design automatically would make your message too immediate. You can exploit it creatively. For example, you can align elements that you want the viewer to relate to as a group. In addition, the fact that alignment facilitates the scanning of information means that it can create a direction of movement—like lines, one of the fundamental art elements—which you can use to lead the viewer's attention.

TABLE 9.11	General Guidelines for a Print Version and the Example CSS Style Rules
General Guidelines	**Example CSS Rules**

White background
 	
Black body text
 	
Sizing the font for print, 12pt
	``css
	body {
	    background: white;
	    color: black;
	    font-size: 12pt;
	}
	``

Remove the underline for links but make it different from the body text, such as use of a different color	```css
	a:link, a:visited {
	    color: #0000FF;
	    text-decoration: underline;
	}
	``

Insert URL of the link after each link in the main content area (not to include links in the header and footer)	(Suppose the main content in the HTML document is placed within a \<div\> with an id of actual-content.)
	
	``css
	#actual-content a:link:after,
	#actual-content a:visited:after {
	    content: " (" attr(href) ") ";
	}
	``

Hide the navigation menus	(Suppose the navigation menu in the HTML document is placed within a \<div\> with an id of menu.)
	
	``css
	#menu {
	    display: none;
	}
	``

Cancel any float, borders, and paddings, set the margins suitable for print, and reset width to auto	(Suppose the main content in the HTML document is placed within a \<div\> with an id of actual-content.)
	
	``css
	#content {
	    width: auto;
	    margin: 0 5%;
	    padding: 0;
	    border: 0;
	    float: none;
	}
	``

In addition, you still need to determine how you want the viewer to interact with your art, just as you would create a composition using traditional media, such as oil painting. The fundamental art elements and organizational principles discussed in Chapter 2 apply to organizing HTML elements on a Web page.

However, Web medium differs from the traditional media as it has new dimensions: interactivity and multiple page navigation. Viewers can interact with a Web page via mouse, keyboard, and other input devices, such as a joystick. They can click on an element, place the mouse cursor over an element, drag an element, and type in text. Hyperlinks of Web pages make multiple page navigation possible. An artwork can span across multiple pages. The order of viewing these pages may differ from viewer to viewer and from one viewing session to another.

In traditional media, the viewer is free to look anywhere within the frame of the artwork, but the artist composes the elements to lead the viewer's attention to a specific place.

The Web medium is similar, as the viewer has the freedom of choice to interact with the page—clicking on or placing the mouse cursor on elements, typing text, or even altering the visual elements on the page. However, the artist can direct the viewer's experience by design.

For the Web, viewers expect the interaction—being able to click on and roll over an element to see visual changes or hear audio. Thus, viewers tend to look for hot spots of the page to click and roll the mouse cursor over. Without a strong composition to direct viewer's attention, the art may become a random collection of clickable elements to the viewer and the intended message of an artist may be lost. Careful planning and Web authoring knowledge are important parts of creating your Web-based art.

TERMS

<div>, 403
<link>, 398
<span>, 403
<style>, 400
border, 416
box model, 413
cascading style sheets
 (CSS), 484
class selector, 401
comments, 437
declaration, 388

descendant selector, 439
em, 392
external style sheet, 397
fixed-width layout, 431
float, 426
fluid layout, 431
grid-based layouts, 441
hexadecimal notation, 393
ID selector, 402
inline style, 397
internal style sheet, 397

flexible (liquid) layout, 431
margin, 416
margin collapsing, 420
normal flow, 426
padding, 418
px, 392
selector, 388
selector grouping, 438
stack order, 404
style sheets, 384
z-index, 404

LEARNING AIDS

The following learning aids can be found at the book's companion Web site.

Example: absolute Positioning
The complete style sheet and HTML document are shown as an example of absolute positioning.

Example: relative Positioning
The complete style sheet and HTML document are shown as an example of relative positioning.

Example: fixed Positioning
The complete style sheet and HTML document are shown as an example of fixed positioning.

Lab 1: Exploring Positioning and z-index (Part 1 of 2)
Write CSS rules to position and stack different images, as shown in Figure 9.20, on a Web page. A single set of images may not be visually interesting. Part 2 of this lab extends to include multiple sets of images placed in a grid to show different color coordination (Figure 9.24).

Lab 2: Exploring Different Types of Positioning

Write CSS rules to position and stack different images and text to create a collage. Experiment with all three types of positioning. Fixed positioning makes an element stays at the same location regardless of scrolling. The composition of your collage changes as other elements scroll by the ones with fixed positioning. This lab potentially can be expanded as a project that involves multiple pages of such collages. Hyperlinks can be added to the images in linking multiple pages. In addition, JavaScript can be used to add interactivity by creating rollover images.

Lab 1: Exploring Positioning and z-index (Part 2 of 2)

Extend Part 1 of the lab to include multiple sets of images placed in a grid (by defining margins in addition to positioning) to show different color combinations (Figure 9.24).

Box Model: Example 1: One Simple Box

The complete style sheet and HTML document are shown as an example of creating a single box.

Box Model: Example 2: Two Boxes (Header and Footer)

The complete style sheet and HTML document are shown as an example of creating extra boxes for header and footer elements.

Box Model: Example 3: 2-Column Layout for Content Area

The complete style sheet and HTML document are shown as an example of creating columns.

Box Model: Example 4: Add Text Styles and Final Touches

The complete style sheet and HTML document are shown as an example of creating text styles and adding other elements.

Lab 3: 2-Column Fixed-Width Layout

Use the box model to create a Web page with 2-column fixed-width layout.

Example: 2-Column Fluid Layout

The complete style sheet and HTML document are shown as an example of a fluid layout design.

Example: Using the CSS Box Model to Layout List Items on a Grid

The complete style sheet and HTML document are shown as an example using grids with list items.

Lab 4: Use of Lists for Menus and Arrangement of Items on a Grid

Use the CSS box model to layout list items as the navigation menu items.

Example: CSS Design for Print Version: Method 1. Two Style Sheets

An example style sheet for screen display, an example style sheet for print output, and an HTML document. If you select Print Preview of the HTML document in a Web browser, you will see that the page is different from the one displayed inside the browser.

Example: CSS Design for Print Version: Method 2. One Style Sheet

An example style sheet with two sets of style rules (one for screen display and another for print) and an HTML document. If you select Print Preview of the HTML document in a Web browser, you will see that the page is different from the one displayed inside the browser.

REVIEW QUESTIONS

When applicable, please choose all correct answers.

1. What does CSS stand for?

2. Fill in the blanks to complete the basic CSS syntax using the terms: `selector`, `property`, and `value`.

    _____ {

    _____:_____;

    }

3. **True/False:** Line breaks and indentations are required to form valid CSS style rules.

4. Which HTML tag is used to define an internal style sheet?

    A. `<css>`
    B. `<link>`
    C. `<script>`
    D. `<style>`

5. Which HTML tag is used to define an external style sheet?

    A. `<css>`
    B. `<link>`
    C. `<script>`
    D. `<style>`

6. Which HTML attribute is used to define inline styles?

    A. `class`
    B. `id`
    C. `style`
    D. `styles`
    E. `css`

7. Fill in the blanks to complete the HTML code for referring to an external style sheet.

    `<`_____ `rel="stylesheet" type="`_____`"` _____`="mystyles.css" />`

8. Where in an HTML document should the HTML code of Problem 7 be placed?

    A. At the top of the document
    B. At the end of the document
    C. In the `<head>` section
    D. In the `<body>` section

9. Which of the followings is the correct CSS syntax?

    A. `body {color:#000000};`
    B. `body {color=#000000};`
    C. `body: color=#000000;`
    D. `{body: color:#000000};`

10. Which of the followings is the correct CSS syntax that specifies the text color of all the paragraph <p> elements?

    A. p {color:#000000};
    B. .p {color:#000000};
    C. #p {color:#000000};
    D. *p {color:#000000};

11. Which of the followings is the correct CSS syntax that specifies the text color of all elements that has a class attribute equal to navmenu?

    A. navmenu {color:#000000};
    B. .navmenu {color:#000000};
    C. #navmenu {color:#000000};
    D. *navmenu {color:#000000};

12. Which of the followings is the correct CSS syntax that specifies the text color of the element that has an id attribute equal to navmenu?

    A. navmenu {color:#000000};
    B. .navmenu {color:#000000};
    C. #navmenu {color:#000000};
    D. *navmenu {color:#000000};

13. How do you insert a comment in CSS style definitions?

    A. // this is a comment
    B. /* this is a comment
    C. /* this is a comment */
    D. < this is a comment >

14. Which of the followings is the correct CSS property for an element's background color?

    A. background color
    B. background-color
    C. bgcolor
    D. color

15. Which of the followings is the correct CSS property for an element's text color?

    A. font-color
    B. text-color
    C. foreground-color
    D. color

16. Which of the followings is the correct CSS property for an element's text size?

    A. font-size
    B. text-size
    C. font-style
    D. text-style

17. Which of the followings is the correct CSS property for an element's font type?

    A. font-type
    B. font-family

C. font-style

D. font

18. Which of the following is the correct CSS style rule that removes the underline of hyperlinks?

   A. a {text-decoration: none};

   B. a {text-decoration: no};

   C. a {text-underline: none};

   D. a {text-underline: no};

19. In CSS box model, what is the space between the element's border and content called?

   A. Margin

   B. Padding

   C. Inner border

   D. Box space

20. What is the correct CSS syntax for making all the <p> elements bold?

   A. <p style="text:bold">

   B. <p style="font:bold">

   C. p {text-weight:bold}

   D. p {font-weight:bold}

21. Which of the following is the correct CSS style rule that removes the bullet next to each list item?

   A. li {list-bullet: none};

   B. li {list-type: none};

   C. li {list-style: none};

   D. li {list-style-type: none};

PROJECTS

Web Site Projects Intended for Immediate Communication of Information

Project 1. Create a Web Site Concept

Design a consistent look and feel for a site. Design and create a representative mock-up page for each main category. The page serves as a template but has actual sample content placed on the page. For example, if you are creating a Web site concept for an artist portfolio, then the representative page should show how an artwork is displayed on the page.

   Based on the type of the site you want to design, determine the navigation menu items. Sketch out your idea of the page layout and navigation menu.

- Use CSS and <div> for page layout. Nested <div> elements are needed for most page layouts. Before you start coding, sketch out how the different <div> elements should be nested, like the illustrations shown in Figures 9.37 and 9.40.
- Create navigation menus using CSS lists, as shown in Section 9.9.4 CSS List for Grids and Layouts.

Project 2. Create a Web Page of an Article

Convert one of your term papers or a news article from your school newspaper into a Web page.

- Incorporate links and images.
- Separate the content from the style and formatting, as in the examples from the CSS *Zen Garden* Web site.
  - Create an HTML document for the article content
  - Create an external CSS file style and formatting
- Divide the article into sections. You can put the article in a single Web page or divide into multiple pages.
- Design a navigation menu as a table of content for the article or to allow navigation to different sections.
- Have a printer-friendly version of the page by using one of the two possible methods discussed in this chapter.

Tip: Before you start creating the page, look up several online journals on the Web and examine their publication design to get ideas and inspirations.

Web Site Projects Intended for Artistic Expression

Project 1. Create a Composition Using CSS

Create graphical shapes as individual images. Use CSS positioning to make a composition.

- Use different types of positioning (absolute, fixed, and relative). The elements with fixed positioning will remain at the same location within the browser window. By assigning some elements absolute positioning and some fixed, the composition will change depending on the page scrolling made by the viewer.
- Reuse images to create repetition.
- Use CSS rules to position these images by setting their top and left properties.
- Use CSS rules to set these images at various widths and heights, so it will not be monotonic.
- In additional to images of geometrical shapes, you also can use text (with a <div> tag), digital photographs, and digital images of your sketches or artwork of other medium.

Figure 9.47 shows an example composition using a digital image, an 1-pixel black image, and individual of shapes (Figure 9.48). Each horizontal line actually is made up of the 1-pxiel black image by setting its width and height properties in CSS. Although it is not shown here, the same image similarly can be used to create a vertical line.

This project can be extended into a multiple page project in which you can link the pages through hyperlinks. Clicking on an individual image will open up another page of different composition.

Project 2. Personal Map

Create a map representing a slice of yourself or your life. This is a Web version of the personal map projects in Chapters 3 and 7. Web medium offers multimedia and nonlinear branching. The Web version of this project should take advantage of the following capabilities of the Web medium.

- Exploit the multimedia capability of Web. Incorporate part of the images, video, and audio taken from your image and video versions of this project.
- Exploit the hyperlinks of Web authoring.

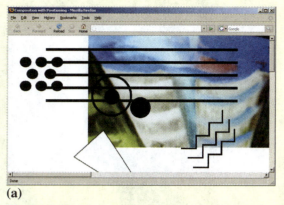

(a)

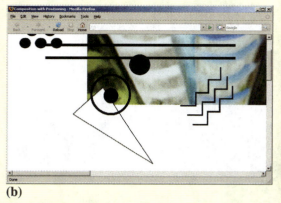

(b)

Figure 9.47 (a) An example of composition using CSS (b) After the page is scrolled down, some elements scroll with the page; those assigned with fixed positioning, such as the circles that make up the bullseye symbol, stay at the same location

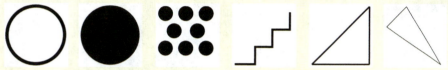

Figure 9.48 Individual shapes

- Unlike the image version, you do not have to present the whole image at once. You can present information in parts using multiple pages and let viewers use their imagination to piece the information together.
- Unlike the video version, you now do not have to present the work in a linear sequence. Hyperlinking allow viewers to see your work based on the order they choose. Different viewers may follow different paths in viewing your work. The disadvantage of non-sequential viewing is the loss of your control over how your work is viewed. However, different viewers following different paths will have different experiences and interpretations of your work.
- The techniques you used in Project 1 also can be applied to this project.

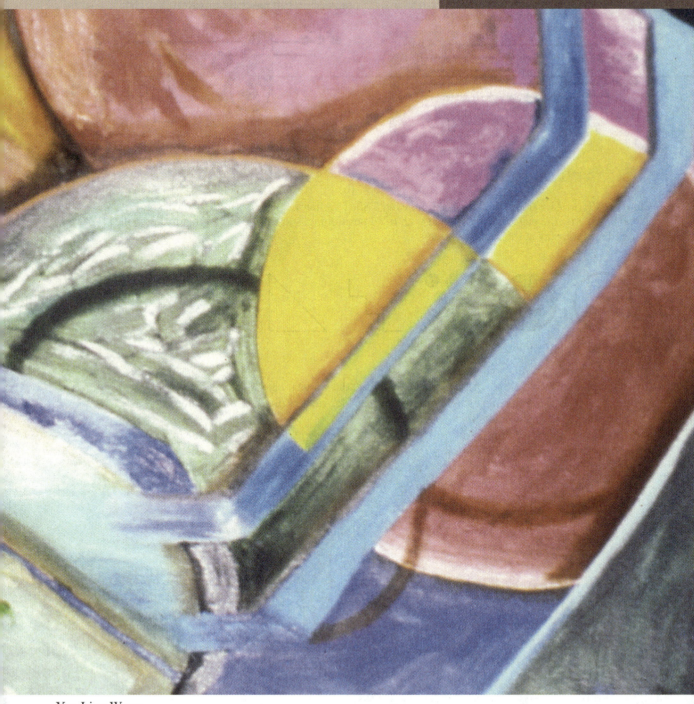

Yue-Ling Wong

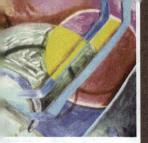

CHAPTER

10

GENERAL LEARNING OBJECTIVES

In this chapter, you will learn:

- To write simple JavaScript in combination with CSS to create rollover visual change: color and image.
- To write simple JavaScript in combination with CSS to create different navigation menu access: collapsible and pop-up.

10.1 WHAT IS DYNAMIC HTML?

Dynamic HTML is a combination of HTML, CSS, and JavaScript to create an interactive Web experience. *JavaScript* is a scripting language for Web pages. Combined with CSS, JavaScript can be used to control the properties (such as position, color, and visibility) of an element (such as a block of text) on a Web page. With scripting, the content of a Web page can react to a user's interaction (such as mouse clicks and key presses). The material becomes dynamic.

In many situations, the element being clicked on or rolled over is the same element that undergoes the changes. However, you should note that the element that undergoes changes does not *have* to be the same item being clicked on or rolled over. The element to be controlled by the script should be enclosed within a HTML tag that has an *id attribute*. You then can refer to the element in the JavaScript by its id. The syntax to refer to an element by its id is `document.getElementByid()`. The id is placed within the parentheses of `getElement-Byid()`. For example,

```
document.getElementById("header")
```

refers to an element whose id is "header". In this chapter, you will see examples of using this syntax in combination with the property names of an element to change the element's appearance.

An introduction to programming fundamentals with examples in Flash ActionScript is available in the *Digital Media Primer*, Chapter 9.

10.2 VARIABLES, FUNCTIONS, PARAMETERS, AND ARGUMENTS

Programming in JavaScript requires knowledge of computer programming fundamentals. This section provides an overview of several programming terminologies that you will encounter in the DHTML examples discussed later in this chapter.

> 🖱 **An Introduction to Programming Fundamentals** An overview of more programming terminologies with examples in JavaScript.

10.2.1 Variables

Variables are elements used to store values used in your script. You also can update and retrieve the value of a variable.

A variable has a name and a value.

- *Variable name*: Data is stored in memory as bits (recall the discussion in the *Digital Media Primer*, Chapter 1). A variable name lets you refer to the data's memory location by name.
- *Value*: The value of a variable is the actual data stored.

To use a variable, you need to first declare a variable—give the variable a name. To declare a variable in JavaScript, you use the var statement with the variable name.

The general syntax to declare a variable in JavaScript is.

```
var variableName = value;
```

For example, the following statement declares a variable called highScore and sets its value to 100.

```
var highScore = 100;
```

The following statement declares a variable called imageFile and sets its value to "arrow-up.gif".

```
var imageFile = "arrow-up.gif";
```

After a variable is declared, you can change its value without the **var** keyword. For example, the following statement changes the value of imageFile to "arrow-down.gif".

```
imageFile = "arrow-down.gif";
```

10.2.2 Function Definitions and Function Calls

A *function* is a block of program instructions (also called *code*) that form a unit with a name—the function name. This unit is the function's definition. To define a function in JavaScript, you use the keyword function. The general syntax for defining a function is given in these examples.

```
function functionName()
{
    statement(s)
}
```

The following example defines a function named changeColor. This function contains only one statement—the instruction.

```
function changeColor()
{
    document.getElementById("status").style.background = "#FF0000";
}
```

The instructions in a ***function definition*** are not executed immediately when the program runs. They will be executed only when a function is called or invoked. In JavaScript, a ***function call*** is simply a statement with the function name followed by a pair of parentheses. For example, a function call of the `changeColor()` function is.

```
changeColor();
```

When a statement containing a function call is executed, the program jumps to the block of code that constitutes the function's definition and then executes its block of code. When it is finished executing the statements in the function, it returns to execute the statement after the one in which the function call has occurred.

10.2.3 Parameters and Arguments

You can name a parameter the way you would for a variable. In this text, the parameter names start with word such as which or what simply to distinguish parameters from variables. It is not a technical requirement. However, it would be a good practice to follow a naming convention for the parameters in your script so that you can easily tell the parameters from variables.

Parameters versus Arguments: Arguments are the actual values that are passed into the function. In this example, the argument is the value "#FF0000". The parameter of the function `changeColor()` is `whatcolor`. However, the terms parameter and argument often are used interchangeably.

A function can be defined to have ***parameters*** for it to receive values when it is called and for these values to be used in its computation. Think of parameters as special variables that are used within that function definition only. Values that are passed into functions or procedures are called ***arguments***.

The general syntax for defining a function that takes arguments is

```
function functionName(parameter1, parameter2,...)
{
        statement(s)
}
```

In the function definition, the parameters are listed inside the parentheses that follow the function name. If there is more than one parameter, each parameter is separated by a comma (,).

For example, the function `changeColor()` has one parameter named `whatcolor`. This function sets the background color of an HTML element to the color value that is passed into the function.

```
function changeColor(whatcolor)
  {
     document.getElementById("status").style.background = whatcolor;
  }
```

This function would be called with a statement like

```
changeColor("#FF0000")
```

The value that is passed into the function is called the ***argument***. In this function call, there is one argument passed into the function: the value "#FF0000". When the function is executed as a result of this function call, here is what will happen.

- The parameter `whatcolor` gets the value "#FF0000"
- The background color of an HTML element is then set to "#FF0000"

10.3 JAVASCRIPT: WHERE TO PLACE THE SCRIPT

To embed JavaScript into an HTML page, you use the `<script>` **tag**:

```
<script type="text/javascript">
...
</script>
```

There are three locations you can place JavaScript:

- The <head> section in an HTML document
- The <body> section in an HTML document
- In an external text file

The HTML document shown in Figure 10.1 contains two function definitions in the <head> section (as colored in red) and the embedded JavaScript in the <body> section (as colored in blue). The two functions defined in the <head> section are writeHello() and writeMore-Text(). There are two embedded JavaScript blocks in the <body> section. Note that the JavaScript is enclosed within opening and closing <script> tags, as boldfaced in the figure.

```
<html>
<head>
<title>JavaScript Example</title>
<script type="text/javascript">
function writeHello()
{
        document.write("hello");
}
function writeMoreText()
{
        document.write("more text...");
}
</script>
</head>
<body>
<script type="text/javascript">
writeHello();
</script>

<p>blah blah blah</p>

<script type="text/javascript">
document.write("there!");
</script>
</body>
</html>
```

Figure 10.1 An HTML document embedded with JavaScript

The first embedded JavaScript block in the body calls the custom defined function, writeHello(). This will execute the statements in the writeHello() function which will write the word "hello" on the Web page.

The second JavaScript block in the <body> section does not call any of the custom-defined functions but contains one JavaScript statement that writes the word "there!" on the Web page. Notice that the custom-defined function writeMoreText() is not called anywhere on the HTML document. Thus, the statement document.write("more text...") defined in this function is not executed at all on the page.

For the sake of simplicity, each function in this example contains only one statement and each block of JavaScript embedded in the <body> section has only one statement. However,

JavaScript is not limited to one statement at a time. Multiple statements can be used. A function definition also can contain a function call to another function. For example, in the write-Hello() function definition shown here, the second statement is a function call to the function writeMoreText().

```
function writeHello()
{
    document.write("hello");
    writeMoreText();
}
```

The script also can be stored as a separate text file—usually with the .js file extension. It then can be used as an external script in an HTML document. An example JavaScript file is shown in Figure 10.2a. Note that to include an external script in an HTML document, you still need to use the <script> tag in the HTML document. You refer to the .js file in the src **attribute** of the <script> tag. As shown in Figure 10.2b.

In Figure 10.2a, the external JavaScript file is called writingtext.js. The src attribute of the <script> tag is set to the filename of the JavaScript file.

```
function writeHello()
{
        document.write("hello");
}
function writeMoreText()
{
        document.write("more text...");
}
```

(a)

```
<html>
<head>
<title>JavaScript Example</title>
<script type="text/javascript
src="writingtext.js"></script>
</head>
<body>
<script type="text/javascript">
writeHello();
</script>

<p>blah blah blah</p>

<script type="text/javascript">
document.write("there!");
</script>
</body>
</html>
```

(b)

Figure 10.2 (a) The content of the external JavaScript file, writingtext.js (b) The HTML document (Figure 10.1) when an external JavaScript file is used to store the function definitions

10.4 JAVASCRIPT: HANDLING MOUSE AND KEYBOARD EVENTS

JavaScript can be scripted to respond to key presses and mouse clicks. It also can be scripted to respond to other actions that the user performs on the Web page. Here is a list of common actions that you can write script to respond to.

- A mouse click on an element (an image, a word, or a block of text) on the Web page
- A mouse over an element (an image, a word, or a block of text) on the Web page
- A key press
- Finishing loading a Web page
- Clicking inside a textfield in an HTML form
- Clicking the submit button in an HTML form
- Opening or closing a new browser window

This chapter will discuss only mouse events. Some common mouse event handlers of JavaScript are

```
onmouseup
onmousedown
onmouseover
onmouseout
onmousemove
onclick
ondblclick
```

ondblclick refers to double-clicking with the mouse. onmouseout refers to the mouse moving outside of an element. You easily can tell by the names what user interactions they are referring to.

In general, an event is generated by the browser when something happens in the browser window. Not anything can triggered an event. The list here shows some common examples. The event handler refers to the function that will be invoked by an event. You can write code to specify the actions in the event handler.

10.5 ROLLOVER COLOR CHANGE

For an HTML element, there are two basic properties of color: foreground color and background color. The CSS property names for these two properties are color and background-color, respectively.

The basic idea behind a ***rollover color change*** is to set the appropriate color property of an HTML element. When you set or get the values of the color properties of an HTML element using JavaScript, you need to specify the element by its id attribute, followed by *.style.color* or *.style.background*.

10.5.1 Basic Usage: *document.getElementById("elementID").style.color* and *document.getElementById("elementID").style.background*

The text color of an element whose id is "status" is set to red by the following statement.

```
document.getElementById("status").style.color = "#FF0000";
```

The *background* color of an element whose id is "status" is set to red using the following statement.

```
document.getElementById("status").style.background = "#FF0000";
```

To give you an idea of how these statements are used, the complete code for an HTML document is shown in Figure 10.3a. Here, a function named changeColor() is defined. There are two <span> elements defined in the body.

- The first <span> the text content "cause". It has an onmouseover event handler associated with it, and changeColor() is assigned to the onmouseover event handler. This means that when the mouse cursor is placed on the text "cause", the function changeColor() will be executed.
- The second <span> has the text content "effect". Its id is "status". The statement in the function changeColor() sets the background color of the element whose id is "status" to red.

The result is that, when you view the page in a Web browser (Figure 10.3b) and place the mouse cursor over the word "cause", the background of the word "effect" will turn red (Figure 10.3c).

```
<!DOCTYPE html PUBLIC "-//W3C//DTD XHTML 1.0 Transitional//EN"
"http://www.w3.org/TR/xhtml1/DTD/xhtml1-transitional.dtd">
<html xmlns="http://www.w3.org/1999/xhtml">
<head>
<meta http-equiv="Content-Type" content="text/html; charset=iso-8859-1">
<title>DHTML - Example - Color Change</title>
<script type="text/javascript">>
function changeColor()
{
        document.getElementById("status").style.background = "#FF0000";
}
</script>
</head>

<body>
<p>the <span onmouseover="changeColor();">cause</span></p>
<p>the <span id="status">effect</span></p>
</body>
</html>
```

(a)

(b)   **(c)**

Figure 10.3 An example of text background color change caused by rollover (a) Complete code for the HTML document showing the JavaScript function for the rollover color change (b) The page in a browser before the mouse "rolls" over on the text (c) When a mouse cursor is placed on the word "cause", the background of the word "effect" turns red

🖱 **Example: Rollover Color Change—First Step** The complete style sheet and HTML document are shown as an example of a rollover.

10.5.2 A Step Further

Can both the background color and the text color be changed the same time?

Yes. In the changeColor() function, include two statements: one to change the background color and another to change the text color.

```
function changeColor()
{
    document.getElementById("status").style.background = "#FF0000";
    document.getElementById("status").style.color = "#FFFFFF";
}
```

Can the color of the element to be changed be the same element that is rolled over?

Yes. You just need to give a correct id attribute to the element that is to be rolled over.

Can more than one element change color the same time?

In the changeColor() function, include two statements: one to change the color of one element and another to change the color of another. Example HTML code and how the page looks in a Web browser are shown in Figure 10.4.

```
<!DOCTYPE html PUBLIC "-//W3C//DTD XHTML 1.0 Transitional//EN"
"http://www.w3.org/TR/xhtml1/DTD/xhtml1-transitional.dtd">
<html xmlns="http://www.w3.org/1999/xhtml">
<head>
<meta http-equiv="Content-Type" content="text/html; charset=iso-8859-1">
<title>DHTML - Example - Color Change</title>
<script type="text/javascript">
function changeColor()
{
    document.getElementById("status1").style.background = "#FF0000";
    document.getElementById("status2").style.background = "#FFFF00";
}
</script>
</head>
```

Figure 10.4 An example of color change of more than one text element upon rollover (a) HTML document with JavaScript function for the rollover color change (b) The page in a browser before the mouse "rolls" over on the text (c) When a mouse cursor is placed on the word "cause", the background of the word "first effect" turns red, and the background of the word "second effect" turns yellow

```
<body>
<p>the <span onmouseover="changeColor();">cause</span></p>
<p>the <span id="status1">first effect</span> blah blah blab <span
id="status2">second effect</span> blah</p>
</body>
</html>
```

(a)

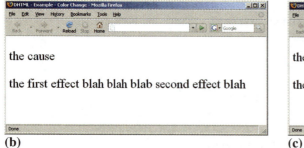

(b)

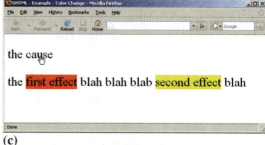

(c)

Figure 10.4 (*Continued*)

> ⤴️ **Example: Rollover Color Change—A Step Further** The complete style sheet and HTML document are shown as an example of rollover causing multiple effects.

10.5.3 Another Step Further

As you may notice in the previous examples, it is not obvious to the user that the word "cause" can be rolled over to change color(s) of element(s) on the page. This is not a good user-interface design. To make it stand out from the normal text, you can set it to have a different text color, different font, different font size, or to be boldfaced.

The simplest way to implement these changes is to use the anchor tag for the word "cause" as if you are making it a hyperlink.

```
the <a href="#" onmouseover="changeColor();">cause</a>
```

Note that a hyperlink allows you to click on it to go to another page. If you only want the rollover effect without jumping to another page, then put the "#" in place for the link location.

If you try this example, you may notice another problem: the color stays even you have moved the mouse cursor off the word "cause". In most situations, you want the color change to occur only when the mouse cursor is on the element. The color should return to the original when the mouse cursor is moved off the element. To accomplish this effect, you need to add the following.

- A function that changes the color back.
- An onmouseout event handler and to assign this new function to onmouseout.

These changes are highlighted in magenta in Figure 10.5. This example changes both the background color and the text color. It also shows you how to clear the background color by setting it to null. Clearing the background color will allow the element to reveal the background—even if the background is not a solid color but an image.

```
<!DOCTYPE html PUBLIC "-//W3C//DTD XHTML 1.0 Transitional//EN"
"http://www.w3.org/TR/xhtml1/DTD/xhtml1-transitional.dtd">
<html xmlns="http://www.w3.org/1999/xhtml">
<head>
<meta http-equiv="Content-Type" content="text/html; charset=iso-8859-1">
<title>DHTML - Example - Color Change</title>
<script type="text/javascript">
function changeColor()
{
        document.getElementById("status").style.background = "#FF0000";
        document.getElementById("status").style.color = "#FFFFFF";
}
function changeColorBack()
{
        document.getElementById("status").style.background = null;
        document.getElementById("status").style.color = "#000000";
}
</script>
</head>

<body>
<p>the <span onmouseover="changeColor();"
onmouseout="changeColorBack();">cause</span></p>
<p>the <span id="status">effect</span></p>
</body>
</html>
```

Figure 10.5 HTML document with JavaScript functions for the rollover color change

10.5.4 Application

The previous examples hard code the values of the colors to be changed. In situations where different texts in the page can trigger different color changes, you would need to create multiple functions to do the color change—one function for each color—if you hard code the color in the function.

> 🖱 **Example: Rollover Color Change— Another Step Further** The complete style sheet and HTML document are shown as additional examples of rollover.

If you want to have some texts to change color to red and some others to change to yellow, then you would need two functions.

```
function changeColorToRed()
{
    document.getElementById("status").style.background = "#FF0000";
}
function changeColorToYellow()
{
    document.getElementById("status").style.background = "#FFFF00";
}
```

Three different color changes would need three functions, four color changes four functions, and so forth. As you can imagine, the code becomes long and repetitive if you need to have many different colors.

To make the functions more flexible, you can make use of ***parameters***. Instead of creating multiple functions, you can create one function to do the color change. This function takes a parameter which is used to specify the color it will change to.

```
function changeColor(whatcolor)
{
    document.getElementById("status").style.background = whatcolor;
}
```

This function definition is very similar to the changeColorToRed() and changeColorToYellow(). The difference is that this function does not specify a fixed value for a color. Instead, it takes a parameter named whatcolor, which replaces the "#FF0000" and "FFFF00" in the statements in changeColorToRed() and changeColorToYellow(), respectively.

When you want to change the color to red upon a mouse rollover, you use the statement onmouseover="changeColor('#FF0000');" instead of onmouseover="changeColorToRed();" The example shown in Figure 10.6 demonstrates the following effects:

- Rolling over the phrases "cause 1", "cause 2", "cause 3", and "cause 4" will highlight the phrases "effect 1", "effect 2", "effect 3", and "effect 4", respectively.
- The highlight colors are not all the same. For example:
  - "effect 1" and "effect 3" are associated with a yellow highlight (Figure 10.6b and d)
  - "effect 2" and "effect 4" are associated with a cyan highlight (Figure 10.6c and e)

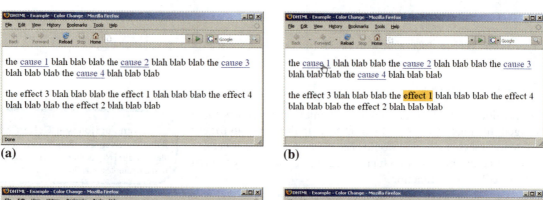

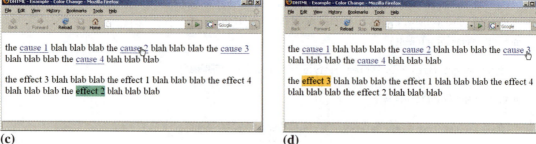

Figure 10.6 (a) A page with four links that respond to a mouse rollover (b) through (e) Rolling over the phrases "cause 1", "cause 2", "cause 3", and "cause 4" will highlight the phrases "effect 1", "effect 2", "effect 3", and "effect 4", respectively (f) Complete code for the HTML document

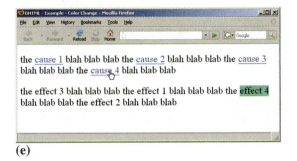

(e)

```
<!DOCTYPE html PUBLIC "-//W3C//DTD XHTML 1.0 Transitional//EN"
"http://www.w3.org/TR/xhtml1/DTD/xhtml1-transitional.dtd">
<html xmlns="http://www.w3.org/1999/xhtml">
<head>
<meta http-equiv="Content-Type" content="text/html; charset=iso-8859-1">
<title>DHTML - Example - Color Change</title>
<script type="text/javascript">
var highlightColor1 = "#FFCC00";
var highlightColor2 = "#00FFCC";
function changeColor(whichitem, whichcolor)
{
      document.getElementById(whichitem).style.background = whichcolor;
}
</script>
</head>

<body>
<p>the <a href="#" onmouseover="changeColor('status1',highlightColor1)";
onmouseout="changeColor('status1', null);">cause 1</a> blah blab blab

the <a href="#" onmouseover="changeColor('status2',highlightColor2)";
onmouseout="changeColor('status2', null);">cause 2</a> blah blab blab

the <a href="#" onmouseover="changeColor('status3',highlightColor1)";
onmouseout="changeColor('status3', null);">cause 3</a> blah blab blab

the <a href="#" onmouseover="changeColor('status4',highlightColor2)";
onmouseout="changeColor('status4', null);">cause 4</a> blah blab blab</p>

<p>the <span id="status3">effect 3</span> blah blab blab
the <span id="status1">effect 1</span> blah blab blab
the <span id="status4">effect 4</span> blah blab blab
the <span id="status2">effect 2</span> blah blab blab </p>
</body>
</html>
```

(f)

Figure 10.6 (*Continued*)

The code for this example is shown in Figure 10.6f. Here, a function named change-Color() is defined to take care of all the color changes necessary for the entire page.

- This function takes two parameters:
  - The first parameter, whichitem, tells the function the id of the element whose background color is going to be changed.
  - The second parameter, whichcolor, tells the function the color will be changed to.
- Two variables, highlightColor1 and highlightColor2 are defined to store the two possible color numbers, yellow and cyan.

In the body, the phrases "cause 1", "cause 2", "cause 3", and "cause 4" are created as hyperlinks. Let's look at how the anchor tag for "cause 1" is coded.

```
<a href="#" onmouseover="changeColor('status1',highlightColor1)";
onmouseout="changeColor('status1', null);">cause 1</a>
```

The function changeColor() is assigned to the onmouseover and onmouseout event handlers. Two values are passed into changeColor() because this function is expecting two parameters.

- The first parameter is the id of the element whose background color is going to be changed. In this case, it is the id for the phrase "effect 1" (i.e., the id is 'status1').
- The second parameter is the background color it will be changed to. In the case of onmouseover, we assign the yellow color defined by the variable highlightColor1. Thus, the variable, highlightColor1 is passed into the changeColor() function as the second argument. In the case of onmouseout, we want to clear the background color, and thus, null is passed in as the second argument.

⌐ **Example: Rollover Color Change—Application**
The complete style sheet and HTML document are shown as application of rollover color changes.

⌐ **Lab 1: Mouse UP Color Change**
A lab exercise to write DHTML to make color change when the mouse is placed over different images of apparel to create various color coordination (Figure 10.7).

10.6 ROLLOVER IMAGE CHANGE

The basic idea behind a ***rollover image change*** is to swap the current image with another image file. The image file itself is not really altered during the rollover interaction. In order to create the effect of rollover image change, you need to have at least two different image files: the original image and the image to be changed to on rollover. You also will need to assign the image element with an id attribute and use JavaScript to swap the two images.

10.6.1 Basic Usage: *document.getElementById*("elementID").*src*

src refers to the source or the file path of the image. The following statement sets the files of an image whose id is bullet to a file named menubulletOn.gif.

```
document.getElementById("bullet").src = "menubulletOn.gif";
```

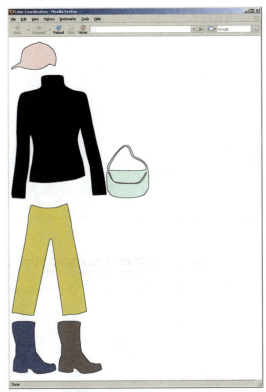

Figure 10.7 How the completed page of Lab 1
may look in a browser

Figure 10.8 shows the complete code for an HTML document. Here, a function named
changeImage() is defined. There is one image (as defined by the <img> tag) inserted in the body.

The insert image function is a hyperlink. There is an onmouseover event handler associated with the <a> tag, and it is assigned with changeImage(). This means that when the mouse
cursor is placed on the image, the function changeImage() will be executed.

In this example, the original image (whose ID is "bullet" and filename is "menubul-
letOff.gif") is a small blue arrow (Figure 10.8b). When the mouse cursor is placed over this
image hyperlink, changeImage() is executed to replaced this image with the file named
menubulletOn.gif, which is a red arrow (Figure 10.8c).

```
<!DOCTYPE html PUBLIC "-//W3C//DTD XHTML 1.0 Transitional//EN"
"http://www.w3.org/TR/xhtml1/DTD/xhtml1-transitional.dtd">
<html xmlns="http://www.w3.org/1999/xhtml">
<head>
<meta http-equiv="Content-Type" content="text/html; charset=iso-8859-1">
```

Figure 10.8 An example of image change upon rollover (a) Complete code for the HTML
document showing the JavaScript function for the rollover image change (b) The page in a
browser before mouse rollover on the arrow image (c) When a mouse cursor is placed on
the arrow image, the blue arrow image is swapped with the red arrow image

```
<title>DHTML - Example - Image Change</title>
<script type="text/javascript">
function changeImage()
{
     document.getElementById("bullet").src = "menubulletOn.gif";
}
</script>
</head>

<body>
<a href="#" onmouseover="changeImage()"><img src="menubulletOff.gif"
width="10" height="10" border="0" id="bullet" /></a>
</body>
</html>
```

(a)

(b)   **(c)**

Figure 10.8 (*Continued*)

> 🖱 **Example: Rollover Image Change—First Step** The complete style sheet and HTML document are shown as an example of rollover image change.

10.6.2 A Step Further

You may notice that many navigation menus on the Web use a list of text links as the menu items. Next to each menu item, there is a bullet graphic. When you roll over the text link, the bullet image next to the link will change to another image. Having such visual changes for the user's activities is a good interface design. It helps to assure the user of the menu items being active and which menu item is being selected.

In the previous example, the image that triggers a rollover effect is the same as the image that is changed. To make the image change upon rolling over another element (such as a text hyperlink), the same concept is applied with a slight modification in the code. The same function changeImage() is used. But now, the whole <img> tag is moved to outside the <a> tag, so it is not part of the hyperlink. The value for the href attribute in <a> is now an HTML filename, so that clicking on the link will go to another Web page, called page1.html.

The result is that when you roll over the text link "menu item 1" the arrow will change to red. However, because the <img> is outside of the <a> tag (Figure 10.9a), placing the mouse cursor over the image itself will not trigger the image change. If the <img> remains in the <a> tag, rolling over either the text link or the image will trigger the image change to the red arrow.

```
<!DOCTYPE html PUBLIC "-//W3C//DTD XHTML 1.0 Transitional//EN"
"http://www.w3.org/TR/xhtml1/DTD/xhtml1-transitional.dtd">
<html xmlns="http://www.w3.org/1999/xhtml">
<head>
<meta http-equiv="Content-Type" content="text/html; charset=iso-8859-1">
<title>DHTML - Example - Image Change</title>
<script type="text/javascript">
function changeImage()
{
      document.getElementById("bullet").src = "menubulletOn.gif";
}
</script>
</head>

<body>
<img id="bullet" src="menubulletOff.gif" width="10" height="10" border="0" />
<a href="page1.html" onmouseover="changeImage()">menu item 1</a>
</body>
</html>
```

(a)

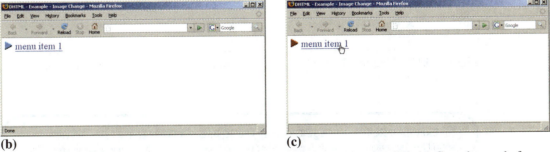

(b)   **(c)**

Figure 10.9 An example of image change by a mouse rolling over a text link (a) Complete code for the HTML document (b) The page in a browser (c) When the mouse cursor is placed on the text link, the blue arrow image is swapped with a red arrow image

> 🖱 **Example: Rollover Image Change—A Step Further** The complete style sheet and HTML document are shown as an example of rollover image changes using a text link.

10.6.3 Another Step Further

If you try out the previous example, you may notice a problem: After being rolled over, the arrow gets stuck in red and does not return to blue regardless of the mouse cursor location. This is not how navigation menus normally behave; the image usually reverts back to its original appearance when the mouse cursor moves off the menu item.

To make the arrow return to blue when you move the mouse cursor off, you need to add another event handler—onmouseout. The code for this event is shown in Figure 10.10. The changes are in magenta color.

```html
<!DOCTYPE html PUBLIC "-//W3C//DTD XHTML 1.0 Transitional//EN"
"http://www.w3.org/TR/xhtml1/DTD/xhtml1-transitional.dtd">
<html xmlns="http://www.w3.org/1999/xhtml">
<head>
<meta http-equiv="Content-Type" content="text/html; charset=iso-8859-1">
<title>DHTML - Example - Image Change</title>
<script type="text/javascript">
function changeImage()
{
    document.getElementById("bullet").src = "menubulletOn.gif";
}
function changeImageBack()
{
    document.getElementById("bullet").src = "menubulletOff.gif";
}
</script>
</head>

<body>
<img id="bullet" src="menubulletOff.gif" width="10" height="10" border="0" />
<a href="page1.html" onmouseover="changeImage()" onmouseout="changeImageBack()">menu item 1</a>
</body>
</html>
```

Figure 10.10 Complete HTML code shows how to revert the image when the mouse moves off the link

> ⌖ **Example: Rollover Image Change—Another Step Further** The complete style sheet and HTML document are shown as an example of effecting changes with the mouse on and off a link.

10.6.4 Application

This works fine with one image. One drawback is that the image's id is hard coded in the function as "bullet". This only works on the image with an id of "bullet". However, a navigation menu has multiple menu items. Each menu item has a bullet image next to it. Each of these images has a unique id. We encountered a similar problem as discussed in the rollover color change earlier. That problem was solved by using parameters. A similar solution applies here.

In the following example, there are two menu items, each of which has an image of a blue arrow on the left side (Figure 10.11a). Placing the mouse cursor on each link will swap its blue arrow image with a red arrow image (Figure 10.11b).

- The changeImage() is rewritten (Figure 10.11c) to take two parameters:
  - The id of the image element whose file is going to be swapped.
  - The filename of the image that the element will to be changed to.
- Two variables called imagefileOff and imagefileOn are created to store the filenames of the two swapping images.

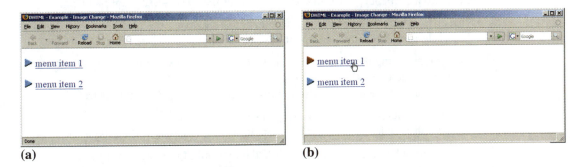

(a)   (b)

```
<!DOCTYPE html PUBLIC "-//W3C//DTD XHTML 1.0 Transitional//EN"
"http://www.w3.org/TR/xhtml1/DTD/xhtml1-transitional.dtd">
<html xmlns="http://www.w3.org/1999/xhtml">
<head>
<meta http-equiv="Content-Type" content="text/html; charset=iso-8859-1">
<title>DHTML - Example - Image Change</title>
<script type="text/javascript">
var imagefileOff = "menubulletOff.gif";
var imagefileOn = "menubulletOn.gif";
function changeImage(whatid, whatfile)
{
      document.getElementById(whatid).src = whatfile;
}
</script>
</head>

<body>
<p><img id="bullet1" src="menubulletOff.gif" width="10" height="10"
border="0" /> <a href="page1.html" onmouseover="changeImage('bullet1',
imagefileOn)" onmouseout="changeImage('bullet1',imagefileOff)">menu item
1</a></p>
<p>
   <img id="bullet2" src="menubulletOff.gif" width="10" height="10"
border="0" /> <a href="page2.html" onmouseover="changeImage('bullet2',
imagefileOn)" onmouseout="changeImage('bullet2',imagefileOff)">menu item
2</a>
</p>
</body>
</html>
```

(c)

Figure 10.11 An example of multiple rollover image changes (a) The page shows two links, each has a blue arrow image on the left (b) When you roll over the first link, the arrow next to it changes to a red arrow image (c) The complete HTML code

The <a> tags still have the onmouseover and onmouseout events, and each event still is assigned with the changeImage() function. However, the changeImage() function call now has two arguments passed in. For example, for menu item 1, the <a> tag looks like this:

```
<a href="page1.html" onmouseover="changeImage('bullet1', imagefileOn)"
onmouseout="changeImage('bullet1',imagefileOff)">menu item 1</a>
```

There are two arguments passed in changeImage() for the onmouseover event handler.

- 'bullet1', which is the id of the image next to menu item 1.
- imagefileOn, which is the variable that stores the filename of the red arrow image.

This means that rolling the mouse over the text link will cause the image with the id 'bullet1' to be changed to another image file named menubulletOn.gif.

For the onmouseout event, there also are two arguments passed in changeImage().

- 'bullet1', which is the id of the image next to menu item 1.
- imagefileOff, which is the variable that stores the filename of the blue arrow image.

This means that when the mouse moves off the text link, the image with the id "bullet1" will be changed to an image file named menubulletOff.gif.

> 🖑 **Example: Rollover Image Change—Application** The complete style sheet and HTML document are shown as an application of rollover techniques for multiple images.

> 🖑 **Lab 2: Rollover Image Change** A lab exercise to write DHTML to make the image change when the mouse is placed over them (Figure 10.12).

Figure 10.12 How the completed page of Lab 2 may look in a browser

10.7 COLLAPSIBLE MENU

Collapsible menus allow you to toggle between expanding and collapsing a list of menu items. For example, clicking on the link Category 1 (Figure 10.13a) will show a list of subcategories (Figure 10.13b). Clicking on Category 1 (Figure 10.13b) again will hide the subcategories (Figure 10.13a).

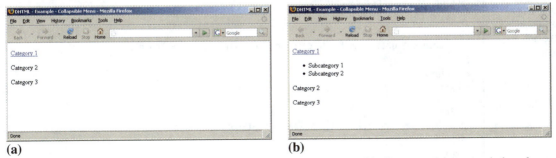

(a)   **(b)**

Figure 10.13 **(a)** Category 1 is collapsed to hide its subcategories **(b)** Category 1 is expanded to show its subcategories

The basic idea behind collapsible menus is to toggle between the different values of the display property.

10.7.1 Basic Usage: *document.getElementById*("elementID") *.style.display*

The CSS style property display can be used to set how or if an element is displayed. The options that are used to create a collapsible menu are: none and block.

- When the ***display property*** of an element is set to "none", the element will not be displayed. This is different from setting the visibility property of an element to "hidden". When the visibility of an element is set to "hidden", it still takes up space on the Web page, the content below this hidden element will not move up to fill the space of the hidden element. This is not the effect we expect for a collapsed menu. When an element's display property is set the "none", the content below this element will move up to fill the space.

The following statement make the element category1 disappear. All of the content below it will move up to fill the space.

```
document.getElementById("category1").style.display = "none";
```

- Setting the display property of an element to "block" display as a block-level element. The collapsible menu items are placed within a <div> element, which is a block-level element, so that it is compatible with the "block" setting when it become visible again.

A block-level element has an automatic line break inserted before and after it.

The following statement makes the category 1 element display again and all of the content below it to be pushed down to make room for it.

```
document.getElementById("category1").style.display = "block";
```

In the following example, a function named collapseItem() is defined (Figure 10.14a). This function contains a statement to make an element category1 disappear. There is a hyperlink, Category 1. There is an onclick event in its <a> tag. It is assigned with the

Like in the rollover color change example (Section 10.5.3), the purpose of the <a> tag and setting its href to "#" is to make the text Category 1 a hyperlink so that it stands out from the normal text as a clickable item.

```
<!DOCTYPE html PUBLIC "-//W3C//DTD XHTML 1.0 Transitional//EN"
"http://www.w3.org/TR/xhtml1/DTD/xhtml1-transitional.dtd">
<html xmlns="http://www.w3.org/1999/xhtml">
<head>
<meta http-equiv="Content-Type" content="text/html; charset=iso-8859-1">
<title>DHTML - Example - Collapsible Menu</title>
<script type="text/javascript">
function collapseItem()
{
        document.getElementById("category1").style.display = "none";
}
</script>
</head>

<body>
<p><a href="#" onclick="collapseItem()">Category 1</a></p>
<div id="category1">
  <ul>
     <li>Subcategory 1</li>
     <li>Subcategory 2 </li>
  </ul>
</div>
<p>Category 2
</p>
<p>Category 3 </p>
</body>
</html>
```

(a)

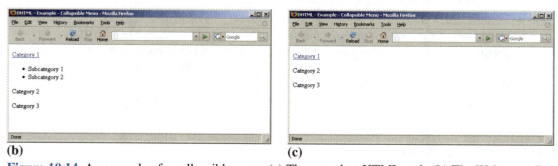

(b)   **(c)**

Figure 10.14 An example of a collapsible menu (a) The complete HTML code (b) The Web page displayed in a browser. There are two items under Category 1 (c) Clicking on the link Category 1 hides these two subcategory items, and the items below move up to fill the space

collapseItem() function. Underneath this link is a <div> element whose Id is category1. The content in this <div> is a list: Subcategory 1, Subcategory 2.

When this HTML document is displayed in a Web browser (Figure 10.14b), you can click on the link Category 1. The list of subcategories underneath it will disappear and the other content below it—in this case, Category 2 and Category 3—will move up to fill the space (Figure 10.14c).

🖰 **Example: Collapsible Menu—First Step** The complete style sheet and HTML document are shown as an example of a collapsible menu.

10.7.2 A Step Further

Well, what about making the subcategories reappear by clicking on the link Category 1 again? All you need is a slight modification for the collapseItem() function. Figure 10.15 shows the complete code of the HTML document. The modification is colored in magenta.

An if-else statement is added of the function collapseItem() to add the toggle feature. The if-else statement is written to check the current display property of the element category1. If the element is not currently appearing (display property is equal to "none"), then it will be set to display as block. Otherwise, the element will be hidden.

```
<!DOCTYPE html PUBLIC "-//W3C//DTD XHTML 1.0 Transitional//EN"
"http://www.w3.org/TR/xhtml1/DTD/xhtml1-transitional.dtd">
<html xmlns="http://www.w3.org/1999/xhtml">
<head>
<meta http-equiv="Content-Type" content="text/html; charset=iso-8859-1">
<title>DHTML - Example - Collapsible Menu</title>
<script type="text/javascript">
function collapseItem()
{
    if (document.getElementById("category1").style.display == "none")
    {
        document.getElementById("category1").style.display = "block";
    }
    else
    {
        document.getElementById("category1").style.display = "none";
    }
}
</script>
</head>

<body>
<p><a href="#" onclick="collapseItem()">Category 1</a></p>
<div id="category1">
  <ul>
    <li>Subcategory 1</li>
    <li>Subcategory 2</li>
  </ul>
</div>
<p>Category 2</p>
<p>Category 3</p>
</body>
</html>
```

Figure 10.15 Complete HTML code with additional code to allow toggling the collapsible menu

> 🖰 **Example: Collapsible Menu—A Step Further** The complete style sheet and HTML document are shown as an example of toggling the collapsible menu.

10.7.3 Application

As you may notice, this example only deals with one link, Category 1. Now, what about dealing with multiple items (i.e., also making Category 2 and Category 3 links) (Figure 10.16a) that also can expand and collapse their subcategory items upon mouse clicks (Figure 10.16b and c)?

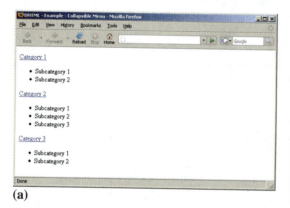

(a)

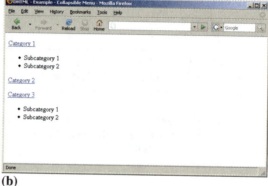

(b)

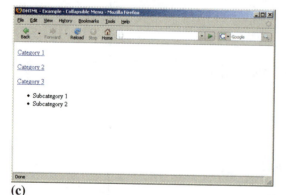

(c)

```
<!DOCTYPE html PUBLIC "-//W3C//DTD XHTML 1.0 Transitional//EN"
"http://www.w3.org/TR/xhtml1/DTD/xhtml1-transitional.dtd">
<html xmlns="http://www.w3.org/1999/xhtml">
<head>
<meta http-equiv="Content-Type" content="text/html; charset=iso-8859-1">
<title>DHTML - Example - Collapsible Menu</title>
<script type="text/javascript">
function collapseItem(whichitem)
{
```

Figure 10.16 An example of multiple collapsible menu items

```
        if (document.getElementById(whichitem).style.display == "none")
        {
            document.getElementById(whichitem).style.display = "block";
        }
        else
        {
            document.getElementById(whichitem).style.display = "none";
        }
    }
</script>
</head>

<body>
<p><a href="#" onclick="collapseItem('category1')">Category 1</a></p>
<div id="category1">
   <ul>
      <li>Subcategory 1</li>
      <li>Subcategory 2</li>
   </ul>
</div>
<p><a href="#" onclick="collapseItem('category2')">Category 2</a></p>
<div id="category2">
   <ul>
      <li>Subcategory 1</li>
      <li>Subcategory 2</li>
      <li>Subcategory 3</li>
   </ul>
</div>
<p><a href="#" onclick="collapseItem('category3')">Category 3</a></p>
<div id="category3">
   <ul>
      <li>Subcategory 1</li>
      <li>Subcategory 2</li>
   </ul>
</div>
</body>
</html>
```

(d)

Figure 10.16 (*Continued*)

You need to modify the collapseItem() function to take a parameter. This parameter is used to specify the id of the <div> element to show or hide the submenus. Other modifications include:

- Assigning an unique id name to each <div> that is used as the subcategory listing.
- Pass in the corresponding id name of this subcategory <div> into the function call collapseItem() that is assigned to the onclick event handler.

The complete code is shown in Figure 10.16d. For the sake of simplicity, the collapsible menu demonstrated is made up of text links. However, a collapsible menu can contain basically any types of HTML elements besides text. It can contain images, tables, or a combination of different types of elements.

> 🖱 **Example: Collapsible Menu—Application** The complete style sheet and HTML document are shown as an example of multiple collapsible menu items.

> 🖱 **Lab 3: Collapsible Menu** A lab exercise to write DHTML to make a collapsible menu.

10.8 POP-UP/DROP-DOWN/FLY-OUT MENU

A *pop-up menu*, also referred to as drop-down menu or fly-out menu, mimics how the menu works in common desktop applications, such as clicking on the File menu in Microsoft Word to see a list of options related to file operations. On Web pages, you often see a list of related choices or subcategories appear next to or below the menu item that you have clicked on or placed the mouse cursor over. The pop-up menu is hidden by default and displayed only on demand. The pop-up menu has the advantage of being always available without taking up permanent screen space.

10.8.1 Basic Idea

The basic idea behind a pop-up menu is a simple one: to control the visibility of the pop-up menu.

The CSS Style property visibility can be used to set how or if an element is displayed. The options used to show and hide the element are: visible and hidden.

The pop-up menu should be already in place when the Web page is first loaded. It is just that it is first set to be invisible. You use JavaScript to make it appear upon either a mouse click or a mouse moving over a menu item.

This setup of the HTML code for the menu and its associated pop-up menu is illustrated in Figure 10.17. In this example, the menu item is Shop. Its <div> is assigned with a style called menuitem. Its pop-up menu contains a list of choices: Furniture, Bedding, and Lighting. The <div> for this pop-up menu is assigned with a style called "popupmenu".

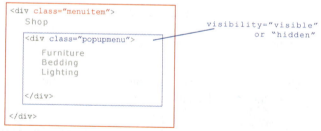

Figure 10.17 Illustration of how to organize the menu item and its pop-up menu in <div>

Here are how the two <div> organized:

- The menu item (Shop) is placed in a <div>.
- The pop-up menu (Furniture, Bedding, and Lighting) for this item is then placed in another <div> which is nested inside its associated menu item. Nesting the <div> of the pop-up menu makes the pop-up menu always position itself with its associated menu item.

The basic idea behind a pop-up menu is straightforward, but implementing it for real-world applications that have multiple menu items—each of which having its own pop-up menu—is not trivial. It will require some work for the scripting and planning of the necessary styles.

Let's start with creating just one menu item and one pop-up menu for this item. Once you understand how this single-pop-up example works, you will see how to extend this example to multiple menu items.

Figure 10.18a and b show how this one-pop-up example works in a Web browser. The menu item contains a hyperlink Shop enclosed in a light gray rectangle. When you place the mouse cursor over the gray rectangle, a green pop-up menu is displayed below. (Figure 10.18b). The pop-up menu contains three items or subcategories: Furniture, Bedding, and Lighting. For the sake of simplicity in the HTML code, these subcategories are not made as hyperlinks. However, making these into links only involves adding simple <a> tags.

(a)

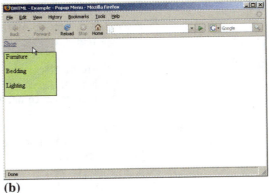

(b)

```
<!DOCTYPE html PUBLIC "-//W3C//DTD XHTML 1.0 Transitional//EN"
"http://www.w3.org/TR/xhtml1/DTD/xhtml1-transitional.dtd">
<html xmlns="http://www.w3.org/1999/xhtml">
<head>
<meta http-equiv="Content-Type" content="text/html; charset=iso-8859-1">
<title>DHTML - Example - Popupmenu</title>
<script type="text/javascript">
```

Figure 10.18 An example of a pop-up menu of one menu item (a) One menu item where the pop-up menu is not being displayed on the Web page (b) When the mouse cursor is placed within the menu item's gray box, the green pop-up menu appears (c) The complete HTML code for the Web page where the JavaScript functions and the two <div> tags are colored (d) The style sheet associated with this HTML document

```
function ShowPopup()
{
     document.getElementById('popupmenu').style.visibility = "visible";
}
function hidePopup()
{
     document.getElementById('popupmenu').style.visibility = "hidden";
}
</script>
<link href="styles.css" rel="stylesheet" type="text/css">
</head>
<body>
<div class="menuitem" onmouseover="showPopup()" onmouseout="hidePopup()"
onclick="hidePopup()"><a href="#">Shop</a>
  <div id="popupmenu">  Furniture
    <p>  Bedding</p>
    <p>  Lighting</p>
  </div>
</div>
</body>
</html>
```

(c)

```
.menuitem {
      position: absolute;
      top: 0px;
      left: 0px;
      width: 128px;
      height: 32px;
      background-color: #CCCCCC;
}
#popupmenu {
      position: absolute;
      top: 32px;
      left: 0px;
      width: 128px;
      border: 1px solid #000000;
      visibility: hidden;
      background-color: #CCFF99
}
```

(d)

Figure 10.18 (*Continued*)

🖱 **Example: Pop-up Menu—First Step** The complete style sheet and HTML document are shown as an example of a single pop-up menu.

Figure 10.18c and d show the code in the HTML document and the style sheet, respectively. You see how the nested <div> (Figure 10.17) is implemented in the HTML code (Figure 10.18c). The inner <div> serves as the pop-up menu. It is assigned with an id of "popupmenu".

The outer <div> has the onmouseover, onmouseout, and onclick events.

- The onmouseover is assigned with a function named showPopup.
- The onmouseout and onclick are assigned with a function named hidePopup().

As you see in the showPopup function definition, it has only one statement. This statement is to make the element popupmenu visible. The hidePopup() function also has only one statement. It hides the element popupmenu.

Putting these all together, when you move the mouse cursor over the Shop area, the pop-up menu will appear. When you move the mouse cursor off or click on either the Shop area the pop-up menu will disappear. Clicking on the pop-up menu itself also will make it invisible because its <div> is nested within the <div> for the Shop item which is scripted to hide the pop-up menu upon mouse click. The rationale for this design is that after a user has clicked on the pop-up menu to select an item, the user would not need the pop-up menu until he/she wants to select another item next time.

Note that the onmouseover and onmouseout events also are assigned to the outer <div>, which means that these mouse events also are effective for the nested pop-up menu <div>. This makes the pop-up menu remain on screen when you have moved your mouse from the Shop gray box onto the green pop-up menu.

The style definitions also are critical for this pop-up menu to work. Two style rules are defined for this example. The style sheet is shown in Figure 10.18d.

- The style menuitem is defined as a class style—indicated by a period followed by the style name. A class style can be assigned to multiple elements in an HTML document. This style is assigned to the outer <div>. It is critical to set its position property to absolute. With the position being absolute, you need to set its top and left positions. The background color is set to light gray, so you can see the boundary of this menu item. It is not necessary to set a background color if you use an image instead of simple text link.
- The second style is called popupmenu. The style name has a # in front of it. It is an ID selector. It applies to one and only one element in an HTML document. The style applies to an element with an id of the same name (i.e., popupmenu) which is in the nested <div>.

  In order for the pop-up menu to work, it is crucial to set the position property of this style to be absolute. You also will need to set its top and left positions. Because the <div> using this style is nested inside another <div> (the menuitem <div>), its top and left is relative to the outer <div>. Note that the top property is set to 32px. This is because the menu item is set to 32-pixel high, and we want to have the pop-up menu appear right at the bottom edge of the menu item's gray box.

Because we want the pop-up menu to be hidden by default, the visibility property of this style should be set to hidden. The border and the background color are set so that you see the boundary of the pop-up menu in this example. Some Web browsers may require the <div> to have a background color in order for this pop-up menu to work. Without the background color, some browsers do not recognize mouse over in the area outside of the strokes of the letters—even within the `<div>`. In such case, the pop-up menu disappears if your mouse cursor is not placed within the exact area of the letters in the pop-up menu. If the pop-up menu `<div>` was not nested in the `<div>` of the menu item Shop, the pop-up menu would have disappeared when your mouse cursor leaves the gray box. Then you would not have been able to move your mouse cursor onto the green pop-up menu.

10.8.2 A Step Further

Now, let's add a second menu item, Furniture, which has its own pop-up menu (Figure 10.19).

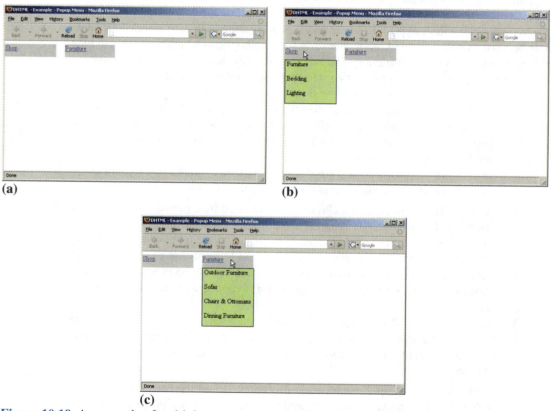

(a)

(b)

(c)

Figure 10.19 An example of multiple pop-up menus (a) The Web page displayed in a browser (b) When you roll over Shop, a list of items in a box appears right underneath it (c) When you roll over the Furniture, another list of items in a box appears right underneath it

First Thought

This could be done by simply duplicating the code from the previous section. The two styles for the one-menu page (Figure 10.18d) could be duplicated to give the style sheet shown in Figure 10.20 for the two-menu page. The two new duplicated styles (.menuitem2 and #popupmenu2) can be used for the Furniture menu and its pop-up menu.

Because the Furniture item is off to the right by 150px, its left margin is set to 150px (as boldfaced in Figure 10.20). Other than that, the two new duplicated styles (.menuitem2 and #popupmenu2) are basically the same as the original two (.menuitem1 and #popupmenu1).

```
.menuitem1 {
      position: absolute;
      top: 0px;
      left: 0px;
      width: 128px;
      height: 32px;
      background-color: #CCCCCC;
}
#popupmenu1 {
      position: absolute;
      top: 32px;
      left: 0px;
      width: 128px;
      border: 1px solid #000000;
      visibility: hidden;
      background-color: #CCFF99
}
.menuitem2 {
      position: absolute;
      top: 0px;
      left: 150px;
      width: 128px;
      height: 32px;
      background-color: #CCCCCC;
}
#popupmenu2 {
      position: absolute;
      top: 32px;
      left: 0px;
      width: 128px;
      border: 1px solid #000000;
      visibility: hidden;
      background-color: #CCFF99
}
```

Figure 10.20 Duplicating the two styles for the one-menu page for two extra styles used to create the two-menu page

Refining the First Thought

As you may notice in Figure 10.20,

- #popupmenu1 and #popupmenu2 have the same style declarations.
- .menuitem1 and .menuitem2 have the same style declarations, except for the left margin.

The style sheet can be compacted by grouping those same style declarations that are shared by more than one style. The resulting style sheet is shown in Figure 10.21.

```
.menuitem {
      position: absolute;
      width: 128px;
      height: 32px;
      background-color: #CCCCCC;
}
#menuitem1 {
      left: 0px;
}
#menuitem2 {
      left: 150px;
}
.popupmenu {
      position: absolute;
      top: 32px;
      width: 128px;
      border: 1px solid #000000;
      visibility: hidden;
      background-color: #CCFF99
}
```

Figure 10.21 Refined style sheet for two pop-up menus

In this style sheet,

- #popupmenu1 and #popupmenu2 are merged into one style (.popupmenu in Figure 10.21) that can be used for both pop-up menus.
- The style declarations shared in #menuitem1 and #menuitem2 are grouped into a new style rule named .menuitem.
- The only difference between #menuitem1 and #menuitem2 is the left margin setting. The left margin setting remains in #menuitem1 and #menuitem2.

Figure 10.22 shows the idea of the organization of multiple <div> for the two menu items: one for the Shop menu and the second for the Furniture menu.

Modification of Script

The HTML code with the JavaScript is shown in Figure 10.23. The function definitions for showPopup() and hidePopup() are modified to take one parameter. The parameter specifies the id of the pop-up items whose visibility is changed.

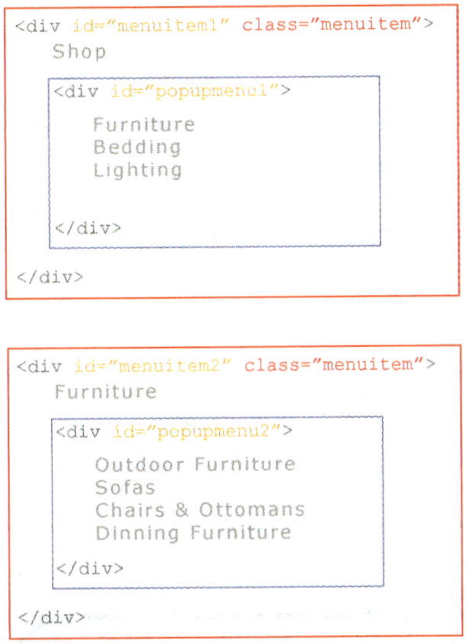

```
<div id="menuitem1" class="menuitem">
    Shop

    <div id="popupmenu1">

        Furniture
        Bedding
        Lighting


    </div>

</div>
```

```
<div id="menuitem2" class="menuitem">
    Furniture

    <div id="popupmenu2">

        Outdoor Furniture
        Sofas
        Chairs & Ottomans
        Dinning Furniture

    </div>

</div>
```

Figure 10.22 Illustration showing the relationships of the multiple <div> in constructing the two menu items and their pop-up menus

```
<!DOCTYPE html PUBLIC "-//W3C//DTD XHTML 1.0 Transitional//EN"
"http://www.w3.org/TR/xhtml1/DTD/xhtml1-transitional.dtd">
<html xmlns="http://www.w3.org/1999/xhtml">
<head>
<meta http-equiv="Content-Type" content="text/html; charset=iso-8859-1">
<title>DHTML - Example - Popup Menu</title>
<script type="text/javascript">
function showPopup(whichmenu)
{
      document.getElementById(whichmenu).style.visibility = "visible";

}
function hidePopup(whichmenu)
{
      document.getElementById(whichmenu).style.visibility = "hidden";

}
</script>
<link href="styles.css" rel="stylesheet" type="text/css">
</head>
<body>
<div id="menuitem1" class="menuitem"
onmouseover="showPopup('popupmenu1')"
onmouseout="hidePopup('popupmenu1')" onclick="hidePopup('popupmenu1')"><a
href="#">Shop</a>
   <div id="popupmenu1" class="popupmenu" >  Furniture
      <p>  Bedding</p>
      <p>  Lighting</p>
```

Figure 10.23 The complete HTML code for the example of a two-menu-item pop-up menu.

```
        </div>
    </div>
    <div id="menuitem2" class="menuitem"
    onmouseover="showPopup('popupmenu2')"
    onmouseout="hidePopup('popupmenu2')" onclick="hidePopup('popupmenu2')">
    <a href="#">Furniture</a>
        <div id="popupmenu2" class="popupmenu" >  Outdoor Furniture
            <p>  Sofas</p>
            <p>  Chairs & amp;Ottomans</p>
            <p>  Dinning Furniture</p>
        </div>
    </div>
</body>
</html>
```

Figure 10.23 (*Continued*)

> 🖰 **Example: Pop-up Menu—A Step Further** The complete style sheet and HTML docu-
> ment are shown as an example of multiple pop-up menus.

10.8.3 Another Step Further

The multiple menu items can be grouped together so that you can define the position of the
menu items as a group. To group the multiple menu items, you can create a <div> to nest the
multiple menu items. This idea is illustrated in Figure 10.24. A <div> with an id of "navbar"
is created to hold the Shop and Furniture menu items. The completed HTML document and
CSS style sheet are shown in Figure 10.25.

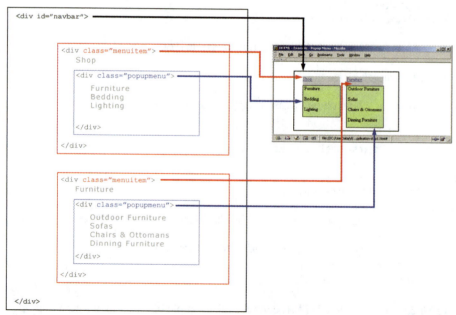

Figure 10.24 Creating an outer <div> to hold the navigation menu's <div> elements

```
#navbar {
      position: absolute;
      top: 50px;
      left: 100px;
}
.menuitem {
      position: absolute;
      width: 128px;
      height: 32px;
      background-color: #CCCCCC;
}
#menuitem1 {
      left: 0px;
}
#menuitem2 {
      left: 150px;
}
.popupmenu {
      position: absolute;
      top: 32px;
      width: 128px;
      border: 1px solid #000000;
      visibility: hidden;
      background-color: #CCFF99
}
```

(a)

```
<!DOCTYPE html PUBLIC "-//W3C//DTD XHTML 1.0 Transitional//EN"
"http://www.w3.org/TR/xhtml1/DTD/xhtml1-transitional.dtd">
<html xmlns="http://www.w3.org/1999/xhtml">
<head>
<meta http-equiv="Content-Type" content="text/html; charset=iso-8859-1">
<title>DHTML - Example - Popup Menu</title>
<script type="text/javascript">
function showPopup(whichmenu)
{
     document.getElementById(whichmenu).style.visibility = "visible";
}
function hidePopup(whichmenu)
{
     document.getElementById(whichmenu).style.visibility = "hidden";
}
</script>
<link href="styles.css" rel="stylesheet" type="text/css">
</head>
<body>
```

Figure 10.25 (a) The style sheet associated with the HTML document (b) The complete HTML code for the example of a 2-menu-item pop-up menu where the two menu items are grouped in **"navbar"**

```
<div id="navbar">
  <div id="menuitem1" class="menuitem"
onmouseover="showPopup('popupmenu1')"
onmouseout="hidePopup('popupmenu1')" onclick="hidePopup('popupmenu1')"><a
href="#">Shop</a>
    <div id="popupmenu1" class="popupmenu" >  Furniture
     <p>  Bedding</p>
     <p>  Lighting</p>
    </div>
  </div>
  <div id="menuitem2" class="menuitem"
onmouseover="showPopup('popupmenu2')"
onmouseout="hidePopup('popupmenu2')" onclick="hidePopup('popupmenu2')"><a
href="#">Furniture</a>
    <div id="popupmenu2" class="popupmenu" >  Outdoor Furniture
     <p>  Sofas</p>
     <p>  Chairs & Ottomans</p>
     <p>  Dinning Furniture</p>
    </div>
  </div>
</div>
</body>
</html>
```

(b)

Figure 10.25 (*Continued*)

🖱 **Example: Pop-up Menu—Another Step Further** The complete style sheet and HTML document are shown as an example of constructing multiple pop-up menus.

10.8.4 Application

The code in Figure 10.25 can be compacted further so that you do not have to pass in a specific name such as 'popupmen1' and 'popupmenu2' to the popupMen() and hidePopup() for different pop-up items. The HTML document and the style sheet can be found on this book's Web site.

🖱 **Example: Pop-up Menu—Application** The complete style sheet and HTML document are shown as an example of compacting code to create multiple pop-up menus.

TERMS

LEARNING AIDS

The following learning aids can be found at the book's companion Web site.

An Introduction to Programming Fundamentals

An overview of more programming terminologies with examples in JavaScript.

Example: Rollover Color Change—First Step

The complete style sheet and HTML document are shown as an example of rollover.

Example: Rollover Color Change—A Step Further

The complete style sheet and HTML document are shown as an example of rollover causing multiple effects.

Example: Rollover Color Change—Another Step Further

The complete style sheet and HTML document are shown as additional examples of rollover.

Example: Rollover Color Change—Application

The complete style sheet and HTML document are shown as application of rollover color changes.

Lab 1: Mouse UP Color Change

A lab exercise to write DHTML to make color change when the mouse is placed over different images of apparel to create various color coordination (Figure 10.7).

Example: Rollover Image Change—First Step

The complete style sheet and HTML document are shown as an example of rollover image change.

Example: Rollover Image Change—A Step Further

The complete style sheet and HTML document are shown as an example of rollover image changes using a text link.

Example: Rollover Image Change—Another Step Further

The complete style sheet and HTML document are shown as an example of effecting changes with the mouse on and off a link.

Example: Rollover Image Change—Application

The complete style sheet and HTML document are shown as an application of rollover techniques for multiple images.

◌ **Lab 2: Rollover Image Change**

A lab exercise to write DHTML to make the image and text color change when the mouse is placed over them (Figure 10.12).

◌ **Example: Collapsible Menu—First Step**

The complete style sheet and HTML document are shown as an example of a collapsible menu.

◌ **Example: Collapsible Menu—A Step Further**

The complete style sheet and HTML document are shown as an example of toggling the collapsible menu.

◌ **Example: Collapsible Menu—Application**

The complete style sheet and HTML document are shown as an example of multiple collapsible menu items.

◌ **Lab 3: Collapsible Menu**

A lab exercise to write DHTML to make a collapsible menu.

◌ **Example: Pop-up Menu—First Step**

The complete style sheet and HTML document are shown as an example of a single pop-up menu.

◌ **Example: Pop-up Menu—A Step Further**

The complete style sheet and HTML document are shown as an example of multiple pop-up menus.

◌ **Example: Pop-up Menu—Another Step Further**

The complete style sheet and HTML document are shown as an example of constructing multiple pop-up menus.

◌ **Example: Pop-up Menu—Application**

The complete style sheet and HTML document are shown as an example of compacting code to create multiple pop-up menus.

PROJECTS

Web Site Projects Intended for Immediate Communication of Information

Project 1. Create a Mock-Up Site for an Artist Portfolio

Design a consistent look and feel for an artist portfolio Web site. Based on the types of work the artist wants to show, determine the navigation menu items for the site and the grouping of the art works.

Project 2. Create Concept Pages for a Hypothetical e-Commerce Site

Study several of your favorite e-commerce Web sites. Note the navigation menu items and the relationship between the hierarchy of the menu and the categories of their products. Design several concept pages for your own e-commerce site. Based on the type of business, determine the hierarchy of the menu items for the site.

Web Site Projects Intended for Artistic Expression

The following project ideas are meant to serve as inspirations for your own creative projects and to spark your ideas. There is no single right or wrong way to approach these project ideas. There are no step-by-step instructions for the projects. The project description intends to help you form your own project ideas to express something that you really care about.

Feel free to interpret, delineate, and deviate from these project concepts. Express something you truly care about, *not something that you are supposed to express or care about*.

The following list of suggestions applies to all the projects.

- Create multiple Web pages.
  - Each page can serve as part of the whole picture, so that the viewer needs to view multiple pages to get the message
  - Each can have its own message
- Explore the different ways of branching to create non-sequential viewing of your pages.
- Incorporate interactivity by using DHTML. The different types of interactivity you have learned in this chapter include mouse clicks and rollover. The changes you can program an element include:
  - Distortion by changing an element's width or height property
  - Reposition an element by changing its x or y property
  - Change an element's visual image by swapping images
  - Toggle the visibility of an element by toggling the different values of its display or visible property
- Use CSS styles to maintain a certain look-and-feel on different pages. You also can apply different CSS styles to the same content to add variations and create different meanings from the same content.

Project 1. Portrait

Create a self-portrait or a portrait of someone you know by using images other than the person's face or body parts. Use abstract images or images of objects to depict the person's personality.

To help you get started, write a list of words or phrases that describe the person and your feelings about that person. Come up with images, lines, shapes, and colors that evoke or associate with those words and phrases. Create a composition using some of these images. Also, think about applying organizational principles that add to the connotations of the list of words. For example, to portrait a person who tends to be unfocused and easily distracted, you may consider creating a composition without an apparent focal point and using many different patterns with little definition.

Think about using interactivity and hyperlinking to convey feeling. For example, to portrait a person who is distracted so easily that he/she may not be responsive in some occasions, you may consider creating hyperlinks which do not do anything or may do things that are totally unexpected. For example, the hyperlinks may go to a page different from what it has led you to believe, change color, or change an image different from the cues you are given, or even go to a non-existent page (i.e. having a broken link) or a blank page.

Project 2. Body

Create a new form of a "body" from a collection of images of objects and body parts. Try to think outside the box. The body parts do not have to be anatomical body parts. The objects and these body parts can be distorted or scaled to out of proportion. You can express your feeling through these exaggerated distortions of certain body parts. Therefore, your choices of body parts to distort and the way they are distorted should reflect your own perception, reasoning, and thoughts.

Interactivity can be incorporated using DHTML to allow the viewer to interact with the body part through mouse clicking or rollover to:

- Distort a body part by changing its width or height property.
- Shift a body part by changing its x or y property.

- Change a body part's visual image by swapping images.
- Toggle the visibility of a body part using its display or visible property.

Project 3. Words—Poetic versus Communication

Many words have more than one meaning. In addition, terminologies used in specialized fields often have totally different meanings than in everyday use. This project exploits such ambiguity.

Look up some terminology in different specialized fields in encyclopedias, disciplinary textbooks, and on the Web. *Before* looking up the technical meanings of the terms, use your imagination to interpret them in your own (poetic) way first. Example terms include: canonical, singular, alpha, beta, quadrant, constructors, destructors, objects, planets in the solar system versus the names of Ancient Greek Gods, multiplex, parameter, and arguments.

To juxtapose the words create a clear, straightforward, and matter-of-fact way of interpretation of these same words. Then, deconstruct the technical explanations and reconstruct them into your poem or haiku. The juxtaposition may be presented in the same Web page or spread across multiple pages.

Project 4. Connections

Objects and people are connected in different ways. They behave differently in different relationships.

Create symbolic icons or graphics to represent specific objects. Group these icons to express your views of how these things are connected. Let the viewer regroup these icons. Program to make these icons behave differently, depending on how they are grouped. Behaving differently can be manifested as a change of the visual content of the graphics (still or animated) or a change of tunes and moods from the audio/music representing the object.

Project 5. Sight and Sound—Visual Abstraction versus Audio Abstraction

Representational objects can be depicted in abstract style through non-traditional perspective, for example, from an extreme angle or extremely close distance. Each separate element in an abstract artwork may not make sense on its own. Through composing, connecting, and collaging abstract graphical elements in different sizes, shapes and colors, an abstract piece can be thought provoking and poetic.

How about audio? Different moods can be generated by modulation of the audio's amplitude, pitch, and timber. Audio does not necessarily mean music. It can be speech, single words and phrases, or in different languages. When you hear a muffled speech or speech in a foreign language that you do not understand, the speech becomes dissociated from its semantics.

Think about creating an abstract audio piece like in the visual art. How about two parallel abstract pieces—an abstract audio and its visual art counterpart?

To extend this idea, think about making the visual part non-static and nonlinear (i.e., add animation and interactivity to the visual part and also add interactivity to the audio—have the visual and the audio change in response to the viewer's input.)

Project 6. Personal Map

Extend the Web version of the Personal Map projects (Chapter 9) by using JavaScript to add interactivity. For more ideas and additional examples of DHTML, visit the book's Web site. Examples of changes include the following. By using JavaScript to toggle the position of an element between fixed and absolute, you dynamically can control how the element scrolls with the page. By using JavaScript to control the clip property of an element, you can allow the viewer to "unfold" an image or a text passage interactively. Although the clip property is not discussed in the chapter, you can find out its usage on the Web.

Index